MODERN HISTORY OF JAMMU AND KASHMIR

CONCEPTS IN COMMUNICATION
INFORMATICS & LIBRARIANSHIP
(CICIL)

For a list of titles in this series,
see pp. 808 at the end of the book

About the Authors

J.C. Aggarwal (*b.* 1928), fromer Deputy Director of Education/Executive Director of Delhi Bureau of Textbooks, Delhi Administration has had a varied experience in the field of education. He had singly/jointly authored about 150 books on Education, Social Sciences and Current Problems. In collaboration with S.P. Agrawal, he had written *Modern History of Punjab, Documentation Encyclopaedia of UNESCO and Education* (in two Parts); *Women's Education in India; National Policy on Education: Agenda for India 2001; Indian Writings on Education, 1979 to 1986,* and *Vocational Education in India.* His other recent publications include: *Yearbook of Indian Education, 1991: World Overview; Ramamurti Report 1990 on National Policy on Education in India;* and *Survey of Educational Documents in the World since 1983,* etc.

S.P. Agrawal (*b.* 1929) was Director, National Social Science Documentation Centre, ICSSR, Government of India and thereafter Member Secretary, Indian Association of Social Science Institutions. He was also the Vice-Chairman of the Asia and Pacific Information Network in Social Sciences (APINESS). In 1988 he was awarded the degree of Doctor of Philosophy in Education (*Honoris Causa)* by International University Foundation. Presently, he is Member, Round Table on Research in Reading, IFLA, and Member, International Committee for Social Science Information and Documentation. He is also Member of Board of Studies of National Archives of India and Hindi Advisory Committee, Ministry of Coal, Government of India. Born and brought up in the cradle of freedom movement which he joined at the tender age of twelve, he gained an insight into political problems and developed a sense of responsibility which bore fruit as an information scientist committed to Gandhiji's philosophy and action-plan in the field and its social concept. He has written extensively on various aspects of education, Indian polity and library and information science.

Concepts in Communication
Informatics & Librarianship—64

General Editor : **S.P. Agrawal**

MODERN HISTORY OF JAMMU AND KASHMIR

A look back into ancient glorious Kashmir
focusing confrontation and failures leading to present
turbulent Kashmir and a peep ahead.

(Including Select Documents and Comprehensive Reference Bibliography covering all aspects of Jammu and Kashmir, 1844-1994)

Volume I
Ancient Times to Shimla Agreement

J.C. AGGARWAL
former Executive Director
Delhi Bureau of Textbooks, Delhi Administration

S.P. AGRAWAL
former Member Secretary
Indian Association of Social Science Institutions, New Delhi

Specific contribution on 'Sources of the History of Kashmir',
by **Dr (Mrs) Madhvi Yasin**

CONCEPT PUBLISHING COMPANY, NEW DELHI - 110059

ISBN 81-7022-556-6 (Set)
ISBN 81-7022-557-4 (Volume I)

First Published 1995

J.C. **Aggarwal** (*b.* 1928)
S.P. **Agrawal** (*b.* 1929)

Published and Printed by
Ashok Kumar Mittal
Concept Publishing Company
A/15-16, Commercial Block, Mohan Garden
NEW DELHI-110059 (India)

GENERAL EDITOR'S INTRODUCTION

Kashmir with its shining lakes and sparkling rivers, majestic mountains and trees and lovely gardens and meadows is indeed a paradise on earth. Its claim as world number one in regard to its scenic beauty and health-giving climate cannot be disputed. During the 16th century the great Persian poet 'Urfi' was so much charmed with this enchanting land that he wrote a beautiful poem in praise of it. Its first verse reads: 'If any sickly and half-dead creature, nay even if a bird which is roasted, is brought here, it will regain its life with all its vigour and vitality'. During 18th century the English poet Thomas Moore too was enthralled with the grandeur and beauty of this place that he wrote a poem of exquisite beauty known as 'Lalla Rukh':

> Who has not heard of the Vale of Cashmere
> With its roses the brightest that earth ever gave
> Its temples, and grottos, and mountains as clear
> As the love-lighted eyes that hang over their wave

Kashmir had also one special feature. It has the recorded history from ancient times down to the present day. Kalhana and his early successors tell us about the life and culture of this land of Rishi Kashyap during the Hindu and Buddhist times. During the mediaeval period we have had a galaxy of Persian historians and chroniclers who have made detailed study about every aspect of this country. A study into the people of this land will reveal that for centuries Muslims and Hindu Pandits lived in peace and harmony. Unlike the Hindus and Muslims of the plains these two communities of this valley had common language and almost common cultural heritage. 'Temperamentally, culturally and ethnically a Kashmiri Pandit is closer to his Muslim counterpart than to the Hindu countrymen outside the Valley and the same is true of the Kashmiri Muslims *vis-a-vis* Muslims of India and Pakistan.'

Today things have changed. This tourist paradise is in turmoil. It has become hostile even to the tourists who are source of the livelihood of thousands of its inhabitants. Several of misguided the militant Kashmiri youth have taken up arms against their Government and have turned into terrorists spreading death and destruction everywhere. Pakistan, always perhaps on the look-out for fermenting trouble in Kashmir, abetted and aided these misguided youth. It not only trained them for military operations but provided arms and ammunitions in abundance. As a result of this, the militants terrorised the State forcing mass exodus of Pandits from their ancestral land to the plains in India. The militants not only attacked Pandits but also a large number of Muslims who were the votary of secularism and humanism. It is said that Pakistan is not only helping the terrorists to fight Indian security forces, but makes all out efforts to internationalise the Kashmir problem and that it does not miss any opportunity to raise the issue at every global forum accusing Indian security forces of grave human rights violations closing its eges to what it is doing and what it is getting done through these terrorists. But it has not succeeded so far in its designs. The recent Geneva fiasco is an abject lesson to it.

Of late there has been some improvement in the situation in Kashmir which kindles hope for the resumption of the political process in the State. The security forces have succeeded to some extent in containing the militancy. Moreover, certain recent development have also great bearing on the situation there. One is the amicable settlement in respect of *Hazratbal Shrine* which was quite explosive and ominous. The other is the *Amarnath Yatra* which the security forces managed successfully to the satisfaction of all. One should appreciate the gesture of all the sections of militants save the Harkat-ul-Ansar that they allowed the *Yatris* to make a peaceful trip to the shrine. But one should not read too much in these events. It is still not opportune time to start political process as it will take time to restore normalcy in the State. What is needed is that the Government at the Centre which is mainly responsible for bringing the problem to this stage should make every effort to assure the alienated Kashmiris that their legitimate grievances would be looked into sympathetically and their urges and aspirations would receive due consideration. To this end it is very much necessary to strengthen the administrative machinery which may be able to take effective steps in this direction and to increase the pace of development activities for the benefit of the people. The Government should also endeavour to alley the fear-ful conception of the Kashmiris in regard to the status granted to them by the Constitution under Article 370.

The books on Kashmir dealing with its diverse aspects are legion. However, the present publication is of different category. It is a comprehensive reference book and a guide about the modern history of the Jammu and Kashmir. In it, every effort has been made to bring all important documents about the Kashmir problem at one place. These documents include the treaties and agreements between the British Government and Maharaja Gulab Singh of Jammu, between the Governments of India and of Pakistan.

It also includes the correspondence between Government of India and UN bodies and Government of Pakistan, speeches made in the Security Council by Council members and representatives of India and Pakistan, resolutions adopted in UN bodies, specially the Security Council. Besides these, the book also contains relevant documents and papers pertaining to 1965 conflict between India and Pakistan, Tashkent Summit, etc. Couple of other documents, though having a bearing, have not been included because authentic copies were not readily available. The publication will certainly prove a boon to the researchers, historions, political activists and journalists.

Special mention may be made about the bibliography on the subject which this reference book contains. It is most comprehensive and has very wide coverage. Not an aspect of the Kashmir problem is there which it has not touched upon.

S.P.AGRAWAL

PREFACE

The book is primarily designed to serve as a compact and comprehensive source of reference on the Kashmir Issue. An attempt is made here to bring together at one place the different perceptions on the subject.

Absolute objectivity in the selection of documents and happenings is rather a myth.

The documents may be convenient or inconvenient to the concerned parties.

An overview of Kashmir in its facets—Cultural, Economic, Educational, Geographical, Historical, Political and Religious is provided in the introductory part of the book.

Volume I covers the documents relating to period 1846 to 1964 and Volume II thereafter. More than 130 documents including Agreements, Letters, Reports, Speeches and Telegrams etc. are included.

Bibliography covering more than three thousand entries is likely to prove very useful to the readers who intend to go deeper in the matter.

We extend our gratitude to all authors and publishers whose books have been consulted and quoted.

It is very unfortunate that the 'Paradise on Earth' tends to become a 'Hell on Earth', and the land of saints and seers become the land of sinners. We pray for the reversal of this trend !

J.C. AGGARWAL
S.P. AGRAWAL

CONTENTS

VOLUME I

VOLUME II

Appendices

1

Jammu and Kashmir at a Glance

1.1. A Paradise on Earth : Crown of India and a Great Centre of Hindu and Buddhist Culture in Ancient India

Kalhan, a great poet-historian describes the glory and sublimity of Kashmir in his famous work entitled *Rajtarangini* (AD 1147-1149) in these words :

> "Kashmira is studded with high cliffs, and cannot be conquered even by the strength of a good army, and the people are afraid of nothing but of the future world. In winter there are hot baths by the river, in summer the cool river-banks, and the rivers are calm, and not infested with water animals. It is a country where the sun shines mildly, being the place created by Kashayapa as if for this glory. . . the saffron iced water, and grapes, which are rare even in heaven, are common here. Kailasa is the best place in the three worlds, Himalaya the best part of Kailasa, and Kashmira the best place in Himalaya. . ."

It is full of shrines; *Rajatarangini* mentions several gods :

> A wooden image of Shiva, the destroyer of vice, to touch which is to gain salvation.

> Brahma in the shape of fire, the goddess Saraswati in the form of a Swan in a lake on the top of the Devibheng Rock whence the Ganges takes it rise.

Emperor Jahangir (1605-1627) in his memoirs, has paid glowing tribute to Valley of Kashmir in these words :

> "Kashmir is a garden of eternal spring, a delightful flowerbed and heart-expanding heritage for 'dervishes'. Its pleasant meads and enchanting cascades are beyond all description. There are running streams and fountains beyond count."

1.2. Brief History of Kashmir

1.2.1. Origin of the Valley

Legend in the *Rajaturangini* and *Nilmat Puran* has it that the Valley of Kashmir was once a large lake. 'Rishi' Kashyap drained off the water of the lake and made it a place of abode. The Geologists state that geological changes made way for the outflow of water by subsidence of the mount at Khadinayar, Baramula. Thus emerged the Valley of Kashmir – 'The Paradise on Earth' (now tending towards 'Hell on Earth').

1.2.2. Vedic Period

Anil Maheshwari in his book *A Brief History of Kashmir from the Vedic Period to the Modern Period* (1993) observes, that Kashmir has been an inseparable part of the Indian sub-continent from the time of *Vedas,* perhaps even before it. The Rig Vedic Indians were fully acquainted with the valley as a geographical entity and sang hymns to its rivers in the famous *Nadi Sukta* of the *Rig Veda*.

1.2.3. Mahabharata Period

Kalhana begins the history of Kashmir with the reign of King Gonanda I (2448 BC) and records the reigns of over 100 kings (excluding the missing records of 35 kings) during the period 2448 BC to AD 1101.

Gonanda, the first known King of Kashmir was a relation and friend of Jarasandha, King of Magadha who was father-in-law of Krishna, King of Mathura. Gonanda went to the help of Jarasandha but was defeated and killed by Krishna who also killed Jarasandha. Jarasandha's son, Damodra, thereafter became the King of Kashmir but he was also killed in his fight with Krishna.

1.2.4. Buddhist Period

It is claimed that Mahatma Buddha himself deputed his celebrated disciple Majjhantika to spread the doctrine in Kashmir along with 500 other monks. According to a legend Buddha himself visited Kashmir.

King Ashoka is said to have founded the old city of Srinagar (Shrinagari as he called it). He built about 500 Buddhist monasteries and probably gave away entire Kashmir as a gift to the Buddhist Sangha. Hundreds of monks went to distant lands from this place to preach the new religion. In return several scholars came from Tibet, China and Central Asia and settled in the Valley permanently.

Ashok's son, Jaluka was a devotee of Shiva.

There was a revival of Buddhism during the period of Kushan kings.

1.2.5. First and Second century AD

During the rule of Kanishka (First century AD), a historical Buddhist Council was held at Srinagar

1.2.6. Rule of the Ujjain Empire (6th century AD)

In the early sixth century AD, control of the Valley came into the hands of the Huns. The Valley regained freedom in AD 530, but soon came under the rule of the Ujjain empire.

1.2.7. Valley under Lalitaditya (AD 724-761)

On the decline of the Vikramaditya dynasty of Ujjain, the valley had its own rulers. There was a synthesis of Hindu and Buddhist cultures. Lalitaditya was one of the most important Hindu rulers of Kashmir. He extended his rule up to Bengal in the east, Konkan in the south, Turkistan in the north-west and Tibet in the north-east. Kalhana records that during Lalitaditya's rule, his victories were annually celebrated. Al Beruni, a great historian remarks, "The second of Chaitra is a great festival day in Kashmir in honour of victory of its King over the Turks.

Lalitaditya constructed temples dedicated to Shiva, Vishnu and other Hindu gods. He also gave liberal grants to Buddhists. He patronised men of letters.

1.2.8. Avantivarman (AD 855-883)

It is said that never before were the Kashmiris so happy and prosperous as during the reign of King Avantivarman. Kashmir became a land of piety, peace and plenty. He executed a number of improvement schemes – drainage, irrigation and agriculture. He prohibited killing of any living creature. The King built several temples and 'Maths'. He also founded the city of Avantipur. Avantivarman patronised men of letters and scholars.

1.2.9. Jaya Simha (AD 1128-1155) : Period of Aryan Renaissance in Kashmir

The King himself set high standard of conduct and undertook various measures to improve the moral tone of the society. The poor were helped in a number of ways. Liberal grants were given to scholars. He built a number of temples and 'Maths' including the famous 'Simhapura Maths'.

1.2.10. Invasion Dulacha (AD 1320)

In 1320, the Hindu Kingdom of Kashmir received its first blow by the invasion by Dulacha, a Mongol warrior and adventurer who hailed from Turkistan.

1.2.11. First Muslim Ruler of Kashmir (14th century AD)

Rinchana, son of a chief during the reign of King Suhadeva, who was defeated by Dulacha, seized the throne after the flight of Suhadeva. Rinchana was a Ladakhi Buddhist. He restored law and order. He embraced Islam and assumed the title of Sultan Sadr-ud-Din Kashmir. Thus Kashmir got its first Muslim ruler. Rinchana's rule was shortlived as he died in AD 1323.

1.2.12. Coming of Islam to Kashmir (14th century AD)

Islam came to Kashmir in the 14th and 15th century AD. Zain-ul-Abedin (1420-70) was the most famous of the Muslim rulers.

who came to Kashmir when the Hindu King Sinha Dev fled before the Tatar invasion. Later, Chaks overran Haider Shah, son of Zain-ul-Abedin; they continued to rule till 1586 when Akbar conquered Kashmir.

1.2.13. Kashmir under the Mughals (AD 1589)

Akbar himself visited Kashmir several times; his army had little difficulty in entering Srinagar in AD 1586. In AD 1589, Kashmir became a province of the Mughal empire. Life in Kashmir, during the reigns of Jahangir and Shah Jahan, has been described by Thomas Moore in *Lalla Rukh* as, "All love and light/visions by day and feast by night."

During the reign of Aurangzeb (AD 1658-1707), Kashmir saw as many as 14 Governors. One of his Governors namely Iftikhar Khan (1671-75), persecuted Kashmiri Pandits who approached the ninth Sikh Guru, Teg Bahadur. Guru Teg Bahadur had to lay down his life to defend the people's right of choice of religion. On the spot, where he was beheaded under the orders of Mughal Emperor Aurangzeb, stands Gurudwara Sisganj in Delhi

1.2.14. Kashmir under Sikh Rulers (AD 1819-1846) and Dogra Rulers (1846-1947)

Jammu has also been mentioned in *Mahabharata* and two recent finds of Harappan remains and artifacts of Mauryan, Kushan and Gupta periods of Akhnoor have added new dimensions to its ancient character. The land of Jammu was divided into 22 hill principalities. Raja Maldev, one of the Dogra rulers, conquered many territories to consolidate his kingdom. Raja Ranjit Dev ruled over Jammu from 1733 to 1782. His successors were weak and, thus, Maharaja Ranjit Singh annexed the territory to Punjab. He later handed over the Jammu Raj to Gulab Singh, an ascion of the old Dogra ruling family, who had grown powerful among Ranjit Singh's Governors and had annexed almost the whole Jammu region. The State was governed by the Dogra rulers until 1948 with the paramountancy resting upto 1947 in the British Crown's representative in India.

The period saw four rulers: Maharajas Gulab Singh (1846-57), Ranbir Singh (1857-85), Partap Singh (1885-1925) and Hari Singh (1925-1952).

1.3. Location

Jammu and Kashmir State is situated between 32°17′ and 36°58′ north latitude and 73°26′ and 83°30′ east longitude. Its boundaries extend to Russian Turkistan in north, Tibet in east, Punjab in south and Pakistan in west. Geographically the state can be divided into four zones. First, the submontane and semi-montane plain commonly known as *Kandi belt*; the second, hills including Siwalik Ranges; the third, mountains of Kashmir Valley and Sir Punjab range; and the fourth, Tibetan tract of Ladakh, Kargil, Gilgit and Skardu.

Basic Data

Area	222,236 sq km
Population	77,18,700 (1991 Census)
Percentage of total Population of India	0.91
Density of Population	76
Capital	Srinagar (Summer) Jammu (Winter)
Principal Languages	Urdu, Kashmiri, Dogri, Pahari, Balti, Ladakhi, Punjabi, Gujri and Dadri

Notes

1. Includes 78,114 sq km under illegal occupation of Pakistan, 5,180 sq km illegally handedover by Pakistan to China and 37,555 sq km under illegal occupation of China.
2. The population figure excludes population of areas under illegal occupation of Pakistan and China where census could not be taken.

Districts: Area, Population and Headquarters

	District	Area (sq km)	Population	Headquarters
1.	Anantnag	3,984	6,56,351	Anantnag
2.	Badgam	1,371	3,67,262	Badgam
3.	Baramula	4,588	6,70,142	Baramula
4.	Doda	11,691	9,13,395	Doda
5.	Jammu	3,097	9,43,395	Jammu
6.	Kargil	14,036	65,952	Kargil
7.	Kathua	2,651	3,69,123	Kathua
8.	Kupwara	2,379	3,28,743	Kupwara

(Contd.)

9.	Ladakh	8,26,665	68,380	Leh
10.	Pulwama	1,398	4,04,978	Pulwama
11.	Punch	1,674	2,24,197	Punch
12.	Rajauri	2,630	3,02,500	Rajauri
13.	Srinagar	2,228	7,08,328	Srinagar
14.	Udhampur	4,550	4,53,636	Udhampur

1.4. Agriculture

About 80 per cent of the population of the State depends on agriculture. Paddy, wheat and maize are the major crops. Barley, bajra and jowar are cultivated in some parts. Gram is grown in Ladakh.

1.5. Industry

Handicrafts is the traditional industry of the State. Handicrafts production includes mainly papier-mache, wood carving, carpets, shawl-making, embroidery. This sector provides employment to more than 2 lakh persons. Woollen items like tweed, blazer, blankets, dhussas, kani shawal, etc., are exported in large quantities. The small sector generates employment for more than one lakh persons.

1.6. Education

A. Institutions

S.No.	Institutions	Number	
		J&K	All India
1.	Universities	3	164
2.	Research Institutions	8	55
3.	Arts, Science and Commerce Colleges	32	5,334
4.	Engineering and Technology Colleges	1	299
5.	Medical College (M.B.B.S only)	2	133
6.	Teacher Training Colleges	4	557
7.	(10+2) Hr. Sec. Schools	239	18,880
8.	High/Post Basic School	995	62,984
9.	Middle/Senior Basic School	2,669	1,53,921
10.	Primary/Junior Basic School	9,338	5,72,541
11.	Pre-Primary/Pre Basic Schools		13,662
12.	Teacher Training Schools	14	13,000
13.	Polytechnic Institutes	4	1,040
14.	Technical Industrial Arts and Craft Schools	33	3,039

B. Enrolment

	Category	Enrolment J&K	Enrolment All India
1.	Ph.D/D.Sc/D.Phil	242	38,675
2.	M.A.	1,518	2,01,617
3.	M.Sc.	1,126	74,095
4.	M.Com.	193	75,147
5.	B.A./B.A. (Hons)	12,638	18,22,711
6.	B.Sc./B.Sc. (Hons)	18,452	7,63,948
7.	B.Com/B.Com (Hons)	3,117	10,07,189
8.	B.E./B.Sc (Engg)/B. Arch	522	2,63,082
9.	B.Ed/B.T.	1,182	1,00,028
10.	M.B.B.S.	859	79,551
11.	Hr. Sec. (10+2 Pattern) Classes XI-XII	49,613	47,93,891
12.	High/Post Basic (IX-X)	1,19,119	1,57,53,586
13.	Middle/Sr. Basic (VI-VIII)	3,27,526	3,87,88,581
14.	Primary/Jr. Basic (I-V)	7,89,254	10,53,70,216
15.	Pre-Primary/Pre-Basic Stage	16,800	14,63,486
16.	Teacher Training Schools	399	1,32,402
17.	Polytechnic Institutes	537	3,87,628
18.	Technical Industrial, Arts and Crafts Schools	3,288	5,19,278

C. Enrolment Ratios

		J&K	All India
(a)	Classes I-V	88.7	105.7
(b)	Classes VI-VIII	65.1	67.5

Note: Data for the year 1992-93

1.7. Festivals

Janmashtami, the birthday of Lord Krishna is celebrated on the eighth dark fortnight of *Bhadon* (August-September). *Dussehra* or *Vijay Dashmi* on the tenth of bright fortnight of *Assuj* is celebrated as the day of victory of Rama over Ravana. *Shivratri* festival is also celebrated in Jammu and Kashmir. Four Muslim festivals celebrated in the state are *Id-ul-Fitr, Id-uz-Zuha, Id-i-Milad-ul-Nabi* and *Miraj Alam. Muharam* is also observed.

The *Hemis Gumps Festival* of Ladakh is internationally known. A special feature of the *Hemis Festival* is its mask dance. In Spituk Monastery in Leh, enormous statues of goddess *Kali* are exhibited once in the year on the occasion of the annual festival which falls in January.

Other festivals celebrated are *Lohri* marking the climate of the winter; *Singh Sankranti* observed in Rambon and adjoining villages: *Mela Pat* observed in Bhaderwah and Kishtwar in the month of *Chaitra*, etc.

1.8. Tourist Centres and Places of Cultural Importance

Amar Nath : Shrine situated at a height of about 4000 metres and built by nature and not man. It is blessed by Shiva. A fifteen feet high *Shivalinga* of ice is formed annually. It starts its formation on the first day of *Shukla Paksha* every month and starts dissolving gradually in *Krishna Paksha*. Thousands of devotees from all parts of the country come here on the full moon day of the month of *Shravan* (*Raksha Bandhan* day).

Anantnag : Known for sulphur spring. It has temple of Shiva and Radha-Krishna.

Avantisvamin Temple Avantipur: King Avantivarman (AD 855-883) built two magnificent temples, namely, Avantisvamin and Avantisvara at Avantipur, a town founded by him. Percy Brown remarked, "where as Martand temple was an expression of the sudden glory when Kashmir re-established the consciousness of its own might, Avantisvamin temple is a sophisticated and more elegant structure produced by a maturity of experience acquired during the passage of time."

Baramula (Varahmool): Located North-west of Srinagar. It is said to be related to Varah incarnation of God. When Hiranyaksha took away the earth to *Pataal*, Lord Vishnu is said to have appeared as an incarnation in the form of a boar and liberated the earth. Several ancient temples still exist at this place.

Burzahom : A site of excavation where objects discovered date back to about 2,500 BC.

Charari Sharif : There is a shrine of the celebrated saint Sheikh Noor-ud-Din, popularly known as Nundu Rishi.

Gulmarg : Meadow of flowers. It is known as Gaurimarg—the way of Gauri, the consort of Lord Shiva. It is an ideal place for tracks. It has the highest natural golf course in the world.

Jammu : Gateway to the Kashmir Valley. It is the winter capital of the State of Jammu and Kashmir. The city was founded three thousand years ago by King Jambulochan. Relics belonging to the Maurya and Gupta period have been found here. The town is studded with temples. The famous Raghunath Temple is also at Jammu. Other places of importance are: Ranbireswar Temple, Ranbir canal and Bahu Fort. Jammu has been the centre of activities of the Dogra rulers.

Leh : It is the headquarter of the largest district with the smallest population. It is the land of Buddhist Lamas. It was an important commercial centre in ancient times.

Martanda Temple, Matan : The temple was constructed by King Lalitaditya (AD 724-761) in honour of the sun god. It is observed by Younghusband :

> "The temple is built on the most sublime site occupied by any building in the world—finer than the site of Parthenon, or the Taj, or of St. Peters. It is second only to the Egyptians in massiveness and strength and to the Greeks in elegance and grace. No one without an eye for natural beauty would have chosen that special site for the construction of temple and no one with an inclination to the ephemeral and transient would have built it on so massive and enduring a scale."

Pahalgaon : Encircled by a full dozen snow-capped peaks and pine and fir woods, it is a famous hill resort. It is the base for the journey to the sacred Amarnath cave.

Pari Mahal : Now in ruins, it was built as a library and abode of learning by Prince Dara Shukoh who stayed in Kashmir in AD 1640, 1645 and 1654.

Srinagar : Summer capital of the State of Jammu and Kashmir Adi Shankaracharya visited this place and established a *Shivalinga* on a hill. The hill is known Shankaracharya Parwat. A temple on it is also known by the same name. Shiva temple is said to have been built between 2629 to 2564 BC.

Dal Lake, Chashma Shahi, Nighat Bagh, Shalimar Bagh, Harwan Hari Parvat Fort, Hazratbal Shrine, Jami Masjid are the other important places.

Vaishno Devi, Vaishno Mata or Vaishnavi Devi : Sacred place containing three idols of Maha Saraswati, Maha Lakshmi and Maha Kali—all images of Vaishno Devi. It is about 70 km from Jammu. The pilgrims proceed to Katra from Jammu and from there they climb up the mountain and cover a distance of 13 km (usually on foot) for the *darshan* of the Mata. The feet of these idols are washed by perennial flow of water. This flow is called *Vanganga*. Vaishno Devi is considered to be one of the *Siddha Peethas*. The place draws lakhs of devotees every year.

2

Documents Relating to the British Government, The State of Lahore and Maharaja Gulab Singh of Jammu, 1846

2.1. Treaty between the British Government and the State of Lahore, March 9, 1846

Whereas the treaty of amity and concord, which was concluded between the British Government and the late Maharaja Ranjit Singh, the ruler of Lahore in 1809, was broken by the unprovoked aggression on the British provinces by the Sikh Army, in December last : And whereas, on that occasion, by the proclamation dated the 13th of December, the territories then in the occupation of Maharaja of Lahore, on the left or British bank of the river Sutlej, were confiscated and annexed to the British provinces; and since that time, hostile operations have been prosecuted by the two Governments, the one against the other, which have resulted in the occupation of Lahore by the British troops: And whereas it has been determined that upon certain conditions, peace shall be re-established between the two Governments, the following treaty of peace between the Honourable English East India Company, and Maharaja Dalip Singh Bahadur, and his children, heirs, and successors, has been concluded, on the part of the Honourable Company, by Frederick Currie, Esq; and Brevet-Major Henry Montgomery Lawrence, by virtue of full powers to that effect vested in them by the Right Honourable Sir Henry Hardinge, G.C.B., one of Her Brittanic Majesty's most Honourable Privy Council, Governor-General appointed by the Honourable Company to direct and control all their affairs in the East-Indies, and on the part of His

Highness the Maharaja Dalip Singh, by Bhai Ram Singh, Raja Lal Singh, Sardar Tej Singh, Sardar Chattar Singh Attariwala, Sardar Ranjor Singh Majithia, Diwan Dina Nath, and Fakir Nur-ud-din vested with full powers and authority on the part of his Highness.

Article 1. There shall be perpetual peace and friendship between the British Government, on the one part, and Maharaja Dalip Singh, his heirs and successors on the other.

Article 2. The Maharaja of Lahore renounces for himself, his heirs and successors all claim to or connection with the territories lying to the South of the river Sutlej, and engages never to have any concern with those territories or the inhabitants thereof.

Article 3. The Maharaja cedes to the Honourable Company in perpetual sovereignty, all his forts, territories, and rights in the Doab and country, hill and plain, situated between the rivers Beas and Sutlej.

Article 4. The British Government having demanded from the Lahore State, an indemnification for the expenses of the war, in addition to the cession of territory described in Article 3, payment of a one and a half crores of rupees; and the Lahore Government being unable to pay the whole of this sum at this time, or to give security satisfactory to the British Government for its eventual payment; the Maharaja cedes to the Honourable Company, in perpetual sovereignty, as equivalent for one crore of rupees all his forts, territories, rights, and interests in the hill countries which are situated between the rivers Beas and Indus, including the Provinces of Kashmir and Hazara.

Article 5. The Maharaja will pay to the British Government the sum of fifty lacs of rupees, on or before the ratification of this treaty.

Article 6. The Maharaja engages to disband the mutinous troops of the Lahore army, taking from them their arms; and his Highness agrees to reorganize the regular, or Ain, regiments of infantry, upon the system, and according to the regulations as to pay and allowances, observed in the time of the late Maharaja Ranjit Singh. The Maharaja further engages to pay up all arrears to the soldiers that are discharged under the provisions of this article.

Article 7. The regular army of Lahore State shall hence-forth be limited to 25 battalions is infantry, consisting of 800 bayonets each with 12,000 cavalry : this number at no time to be exceeded without the concurrence of the British Government. Should it be necessary at any time for any special cause, that this force should be increased, the cause shall be fully explained to the British Government; and when the special necessity shall have passed, the regular troops shall be again reduced to the standard specified in the former clause of this article.

Article 8. The Maharaja will surrender to the British Government all the guns, thirty-six in number, which have been pointed against the British troops, and which having been placed on right bank of the river Sutlej, were not captured at the Battle of Sobraon.

Article 9. The control of the rivers Beas and Sutlej, with the continuation of the latter river, commonly called the Ghara and Panjnad, to the confluence of the Indus from Mithankot, and the control of the Indus from Mithankot to the borders of Baluchistan, shall, in respect to tolls and ferries, rest with the British Government. The provisions of this Article shall not interfere with the passage of boats belonging to the Lahore Government on the said rivers, for the purpose of traffic or the conveyance of passengers up and down their course. Regarding the ferries between the countries respectively, at the several ghats of the said rivers, it is agreed that the British Government after defraying all the expenses of management and establishments, shall account to the Lahore Government for one half of the net profits of the ferry collections. The provisions of this Article have no reference to the ferries on that part of the river Sutlej which forms the boundary of Bahawalpur and Lahore respectively.

Article 10. If the British Government should, at any time, desire to pass troops through the territories of his Highness the Maharaja, for the protection of the British territories, or those of their allies, the British troops shall, on such special occasions, due notice being given, be allowed to pass through the Lahore territories. In such case the officers of the Lahore State will afford facilities in providing supplies and boats for the passage of rivers; and the British Government will pay the full price of all such provisions and boats, and will make fair compensation for all private property that may be endamaged. The British Government will, moreover, observe all due consideration to the religious feelings of the inhabitants of those tracts through which the army may pass.

Article 11. The Maharaja engages never to take, or retain in his service, any British subject, nor the subject of any European or American State, without the consent of the British Government.

Article 12. In consideration of the services rendered by Raja

Gulab Singh of Jammu to the Lahore State, towards procuring the restoration of relations of amity between the Lahore and British Governments, the Maharaja hereby agrees to recognize the independent sovereignty of Raja Gulab Singh, in such territories and districts in the hills as may be made over to the said Raja Gulab Singh by separate agreement between himself and the British Government, with the dependencies thereof, which may have been in the Raja's possession since the time of the late Maharaja Kharak Singh and the British Government in consideration of the good conduct of Raja Gulab Singh, also agrees to recognize his independence in such territories, and to admit him to the privileges of a separate treaty with the British Government.

Article 13. In the event of any dispute or differences arising between the Lahore State and Raja Gulab Singh, the same shall be referred to the arbitration of the British Government; and by its decision the Maharaja engages to abide.

Article 14. The limits of the Lahore territories shall not be, at any time, changed without the concurrence of the British Government.

Article 15. The British Government will not exercise any interference in the internal administration of the Lahore State; but in all cases or questions which may be referred to the British Government, the Governor-General will give the aid of his advice and good offices for the furtherance of the interests of the Lahore Government.

Article 16. The subjects of either State shall, on visiting the territories of the other, be on the footing of the subjects of the most favoured nation.

This treaty consisting of sixteen articles has been this day settled by Frederick Currie, Esq; and Brevet-Major Henry Montgomery Lawrence, acting under the directions of the Right Honourable Sir Henry Hardinge, G.C.B. Governor-General, on the part of the British Government, and by Bhai Ram Singh, Raja Lal Singh, Sardar Tej Singh, Sardar Chattar Singh Attariwala, Sardar Ranjor Singh Majithia, Diwan Dina Nath and Fakir Nur-ud-din, on the part of Maharaja Dalip Singh; and the said treaty has been this day ratified by the seal of the Right Honourable Sir Henry Hardinge, G.C.B. Governor-General, and by that of His Highness Maharaja Dalip Singh.

Done at Lahore this 9th day of March in the year of our Lord 1846 corresponding with the 10th day of Rabi-ul-awal 1262 Hijri and ratified the same day.

2.2. Articles 5,6 and 7 (Supplementary Article to the Treaty of Lahore, March 9, 1846) March 11, 1846

Article 5. The British Government agrees to respect the bonafide rights of those jagirdars within the territories ceded by Articles 3 and 4 of the Treaty of Lahore dated 9th instant, who were attached to the families of the late Maharaja Ranjit Singh, Kharak Singh and Sher Singh; and the British Government will maintain those jagirdars in their bonafide possession during their lives.

Article 6. The Lahore Government shall receive the assistance of the British local authorities in recovering the arrears of revenue justly due to the Lahore Government from their Kardars and managers in the territories ceded by the provisions of Articles 3 and 4 of the treaty of Lahore, to the close of the Kharif harvest of the current year, viz., 1902 of the Sambat Bikramajit.

Article 7. The Lahore Government shall be at liberty to remove from the forts in the territories specified in the foregoing article, all treasure and state property with the exception of guns: Should, however, the British Government desire to retain any part of the same property, they shall be at liberty to do so; paying for the same at a fair valuation; and the British officers shall give their assistance to the Lahore Government, in disposing on the spot of such part of the aforesaid property as the Lahore Government may not desire to retain.

2.3. Treaty concluded at Amritsar between the British Government and Maharaja Gulab Singh of Jammu, March 16, 1846.

Treaty between the British Government on the one part, and Maharaja Gulab Singh of Jammu on the other, concluded on the part of the British Government by Frederick Currie, Esq; and Brevet-Major Henry Montgomery Lawrence, acting under the orders of the Right Honourable Sir Henry Hardinge, G.C.B., one of Her Brittanic Majesty's most Honourable Privy Council, Governor-General, appointed by the Honourable Company to direct and control all their affairs in East-Indies, and by Maharaja Gulab Singh in person.

Article 1. The British Government transfers and makes over for ever, in independent possession, to Maharaja Gulab Singh and the heirs male of his body, all the hilly or mountainous country, with its dependencies, situated to the eastward of the river Indus, and westward of the river Ravi, including Chamba and excluding Lahul, being part of the territories ceded to the British Government by the Lahore State, according to the provisions of Article 4 of the Treaty of Lahore, dated 9th March 1846.

Article 2. The eastern boundary of the tract transferred by the foregoing Article to Maharaja Gulab Singh shall be laid down by commissioners appointed by the British Government and Maharaja Gulab Singh respectively for the purpose, and shall be defined in a separate engagement after survey.

Article 3. In consideration of the transfer made to him and his heirs by the provisions of the foregoing Articles, Maharaja Gulab Singh will pay to the British Government the sum of seventy-five lacs of rupees (Nanak Shahi), fifty lacs to be paid on the ratification of this treaty and twenty-five lacs on or before the Ist of October of the current year AD 1846.

Article 4. The limits of the territories of Maharaja Gulab Singh shall not be, at any time, changed without the concurrence of the British Government.

Article 5. Maharaja Gulab Singh will refer to the arbitration of the British Government any disputes or questions that may arise between himself and the Government of Lahore or any other neighbouring State, and will abide by decision of British Government.

Article 6. Maharaja Gulab Singh engages for himself and heirs to join, with the whole of his military force, the British troops, when employed within the hills or in the territories adjoining his possessions.

Article 7. Maharaja Gulab Singh engages never to take or retain, in his service any British subject, nor the subject of any European or American State, without the consent of the British Government.

Article 8. Maharaja Gulab Singh engages to respect, in regard to the territory transferred to him, the provisions of Articles 5,6 and 7 of the separate engagement between the British Government and the Lahore Durbar dated 11th March 1846.

Article 9. The British Government will give its aid to Maharaja Gulab Singh in protecting his territories from external enemies.

Article 10. Maharaja Gulab Singh acknowledges the supremacy of the British Government and will, in token of such supremacy, present annually to the British Government one horse, twelve perfect shawl goats of approved breed (six male and six female) and three pairs of Kashmir shawls.

This treaty consisting of ten Articles has been this day settled by Frederick Currie, Esq; and Brevet-Major Henry Montgomery Lawrence, acting under the directions of the Right Honourable Sir Henry Hardinge, G.C.B., Governor-General, on the part of the British Government, and by Maharaja Gulab Singh in person and the said treaty has been this day ratified by the seal of the Right Honourable Sir Henry Hardinge, G.C.B. Governor-General.

Done at Amritsar, this 16th day of March in the year of our Lord 1846 corresponding with 17th day of Rabi-ul-awal 1262 Hijri.

3

Documents Leading to the Independence of India and Merger of States, 1946-47

3.1. Statement of British Cabinet Mission, May 16, 1946

Consequences of the setting up of the New Dominion – (1) As from the appointed day (August 15, 1947)

(b) the suzerainty of His Majesty over the Indian States lapses, and with it, all treaties and agreements in force at the date of the passing of this Act between His Majesty and the Rulers of Indian States, all functions exercisable by His Majesty at that date with respect to Indian States, all obligations of His Majesty existing at that date towards Indian States or the rulers thereof, and all powers, rights, authority or jurisdiction exercisable by His Majesty at that date in or in relation to Indian States by treaty, grant, usage, sufferance or otherwise;

(c) . . .

. . . Provided that, notwithstanding anything in paragraph (b) or paragraph (c) of this sub-section, effect shall, as nearly as may be, continue to be given to the provisions of any such agreement as is therein referred to which relate to customs, transit and communications, posts and telegraphs, or other like matters, until the provisions in question are denounced by the Ruler of the Indian State or person having authority in the tribal areas on the one hand, or by the Dominion or Province or other part thereof concerned on the other hand, or are superseded by subsequent agreements.

Section 14. Before putting forward our recommendation we turn to deal with the relationship of the Indian States to British India. It is quite clear that with the attainment of Independence by British India, whether inside or outside the British Commonwealth, the relationship which has hitherto existed between the Rules of the States and the British Crown will no longer be possible. Paramountcy can neither be retained by the British Crown nor transferred to the new Government. This fact has been fully recognised by those whom we interviewed from the States. They have at the same time assured us that the States are ready and willing to co-operate in the new development of India. The precise form, which their co-operation will take, must be a matter for negotiation during the building up of the new Constitutional structure, and it by no means follows that it will be identical for all the States. We have not therefore dealt with the States in the same detail as the Provinces of British India . . .

3.2. Memorandum* on States' Treaties and Paramountcy Presented by Cabinet Delegation to His Highness the Chancellor of the Chamber of Princes, May 22, 1946

1. Prior to the recent statement of the British Prime Minister in the House of Commons an assurance was given to the Princes that there was no intention on the part of the Crown to initiate any change in their relationship with the Crown or the rights guaranteed by their treaties and engagements without their consent. It was at the same time stated that the Princes' consent to any changes which might emerge as a result of negotiations would not unreasonable be withheld. The Chamber of Princes has since confirmed that the Indian States fully share the general desire in the country for the immediate attainment by India of her full stature. His Majesty's Government have now declared that if the Succession Government or Governments in British India desire independence, no obstacle would be placed in their way. The effect of these announcements is that all those concerned with the future of India wish her to attain a position of independence within or without the British Commonwealth. The Delegation have come here to assist in

*This is in amplification of paragraph 14 of the Statement issued on May 16th by the Cabinet Delegation and His Excellency the Viceroy.

resolving the difficulties which stand in the way of India fulfilling this wish.

2. During the interim period, which must elapse before the coming into operation of a new Constitutional structure under which British India will be independent or fully self-governing, paramountcy will remain in operation. But the British Government could not and will not in any circumstances transfer paramountcy to an Indian Government.

3. In the meanwhile, the Indian States are in a position to play an important part in the formulation of the new Constitutional structure for India, and His Majesty's Government have been informed by the Indian States that they desire, in their own interests and in the interests of India as a whole, both to make their contribution to the framing of the structure, and to take their due place in it when it is completed. In order to facilitate this they will doubtless strengthen their position by doing everything possible to ensure that their administrations conform to the highest standard. Where adequate standards cannot be achieved within the existing resources of the State they will no doubt arrange in suitable cases to form or join administrative units large enough to enable them to be fitted into the Constitutional structure. It will also strengthen the position of States during this formulative period if the various Governments which have not already done so take active steps to place themselves in close and constant touch with public opinion in their State by means of representative institutions.

4. During the Interim period it will be necessary for the States to conduct negotiations with British India in regard to future regulation of matters of common concern, especially in the economic and financial field. Such negotiations, which will be necessary whether the States desire to participate in the new Indian Constitutional structure or not, will occupy a considerable period of time, and since some of these negotiations may well be incomplete when the new structure comes into being, it will, in order to avoid administrative difficulties, be necessary to arrive at an understanding between the States and those likely to control the Succession Government or Governments that for a period of time the then existing arrangements as to these matters of common concern should continue until the new agreements are completed. In this matter, the British Government and the Crown Representative will lend such assistance as they can, should it be so desired.

5. When a new fully self-governing or independent Government or Governments come into being in British India, His Majesty's Government's influence with these Governments will not be such as to enable them to carry out the obligations of paramountcy. Moreover, they cannot contemplate that British troops would be retained in India for this purpose. Thus, as logical sequence and in view of the desires expressed to them on behalf of the Indian States, His Majesty's Government will cease to exercise the powers of paramountcy. This means that the rights of the States which flow from their relationship to the Crown will no longer exist and that all the rights surrendered by the States to the paramount power will return to the States. Political arrangements between the States on the one side and the British Crown and British India on the other will thus be brought to an end. The void will have to be filled either by the States entering into a federal relationship with the Successon Government or Governments in British India, or failing this, entering into particular political arrangements with it or them.

INSTRUMENT OF ACCESSION OF ....

WHEREAS the India Independence Act, 1947, provides that as from the fifteenth day of August, 1947, there shall be set up an Independent Dominion known as INDIA and that the Government of India Act, 1935 shall, with such omissions, additions, adaptations and modification as the Governor-General may by order specify be applicable to the Dominion of India;

AND WHEREAS the Government of India Act, 1935, as so adapted by the Governor-General provides that an Indian State may accede to the Dominion of India by an Instrument of Accession executed by the Ruler thereof:

NOW, THEREFORE,

I..

Ruler of .... in the exercise of my sovereignty in and over my said State, do hereby execute this my Instrument of Accession, and

1. I hereby declare that I accede to the Dominion of India with the intent that the Governor-General of India, the Dominion Legislature, the Federal Court and any other Dominion authority established for the purposes of the Dominion shall, by virtue of this my Instrument of Accession, but subject always to the terms thereof, and for the purposes only of the Dominion, exercise in relation to the

State of .... (hereinafter referred to as "this State") such functions as may be vested in them by or under the Government of India Act, 1935, as in force in the Dominion of India on the 15th day of August 1947 (which Act as so in force is hereinafter referred to as "the Act").

2. I hereby assume the obligation of ensuring that due effect is given to the provisions of the Act within this State so far as they are applicable therein by virtue of this my Instrument of Accession.

3. I accept the matters specified in the Schedule hereto as the matters with respect to which the Dominion Legislature may make laws for this State.

4. I hereby declare that I accede to the Dominion of India on the assurance that if an agreement is made between the Governor-General and the Ruler of this State whereby any functions in relation to the administration in this State of any law of the Dominion Legislature shall be exercised by the Ruler of this State, then any such agreement shall be deemed to form part of this Instrument and shall be construed and have effect accordingly.

5. The terms of this my Instrument of Accession shall not be varied by any amendment of the Act or of the Indian Independence Act, 1947, unless such amendment is accepted by me by an Instrument supplementary to this Instrument.

6. Nothing in this Instrument shall empower the Dominion Legislature to make any law for this State authorising the compulsory acquisition of land for any purpose, but I hereby undertake that should the Dominion for the purpose of a Dominion law which applies in this State deem it necessary to acquire any land, I will at their request acquire the land at their expense or if the land belongs to me transfer it to them on such terms as may be agreed, or, in default of agreement, determined by an arbitrator to be appointed by the Chief Justice of India.

7. Nothing in this Instrument shall be deemed to commit me in any way to acceptance of any future Constitution of India or to fetter my discretion to enter into arrangements with the Government of India under any such future Constitution.

8. Nothing in this Instrument affects the continuance of my sovereignty in and over this State, or save as provided by or under this Instrument, the exercise of any powers, authority and rights now enjoyed by me as Ruler of this State or the validity of any law at present in force in this State.

9. I hereby declare that I execute this Instrument on behalf of this State and that any reference in this Instrument to me or to the Ruler of the State is to be construed as including a reference to my heirs and successors.

Given under my hand this .... day of August, Nineteen hundred and forty-seven.

....

I do hereby accept this Instrument of Accession.

Dated this .... day of August, Nineteen hundred and forty-seven.

....

(*Governor-General of India*)

SCHEDULE

THE MATTERS WITH RESPECT TO WHICH THE DOMINION LEGISLATURE MAY MAKE LAWS FOR THIS STATE

A. Defence

1. The naval, military and air forces of the Dominion and any other armed force raised or maintained by the Dominion; any armed forces, including forces raised or maintained by an Acceding State, which are attached to or operating with, any of the armed forces of the Dominion.

2. Naval, military and air force works, administration of cantonment areas.

3. Arms; firearms; ammunition.

4. Explosive.

B. External Affairs

1. External affairs; the implementing of treaties and agreements with other countries; extradition including the surrender of criminals and accused persons to parts of His Majesty's dominions outside India.

2. Admission into, and emigration and expulsion from, India, including in relation thereto the regulation of the movements in India of persons who are not British subjects domiciled in India or subjects of any acceding State; pilgrimages to places beyond India.

3. Naturalisation.

C. Communications

1. Posts and telegraphs, including telephones, wireless, broadcasting, and other like forms of communication.

2. Federal railways; the regulation of all railways other than minor railways in respect of safety, maximum and minimum rates and fares, station and service terminal charges, inter-change of traffic and the responsibility of railway administrations as carriers of goods and passengers; the regulation of minor railways in respect of safety and the responsibility of the administrations of such railways as carriers of goods and passengers.

3. Maritime shipping and navigation, including shipping and navigation on tidal waters; Admiralty jurisdiction.

4. Port quarantine.

5. Major ports, that is to say, the declaration and delimitation of such ports, and the constitution and powers of Port Authorities therein.

6. Aircraft and air navigation; the provision of aerodromes; regulation and organisation of air traffic and of aerodromes.

7. Lighthouses, including lightships, beacons and other provisions for the safety of shipping and aircraft.

8. Carriage of passengers and goods by sea or by air.

9. Extension of the powers and jurisdiction of members of the police force belonging to any unit to railway area outside that unit.

D. Ancillary

1. Election to the Dominion Legislature, subject to the provisions of the Act and of any Order made thereunder.

2. Offences against laws with respect to any of the aforesaid matters.

3. Inquiries and statistics for the purposes of any of the aforesaid matters.

4. Jurisdiction and powers of all courts with respect to any of the aforesaid matters but, except with the consent of the Ruler of the Acceding State, not so as to confer any jurisdiction or powers upon any courts other than courts ordinarily exercising jurisdiction in or in relation to that State.

STANDSTILL AGREEMENT BETWEEN DOMINION AND STATES

Agreement between the State of .... And the Dominion of India.

Whereas it is to the benefit and advantage of the Dominion of India as well as of the Indian States that existing agreements and administrative arrangements in the matters of common concern, should continue for the time being between the Dominion of India or any part thereof and the Indian State –

Now therefore it is agreed between the....................State and the Dominion of India that:

1\. (1) Until new agreements in this behalf are made, all agreements and administrative arrangements as to matters of common concern now existing between the Crown and any Indian State shall, in so far as may be appropriate, continue as between the Dominion of India or, as the case may be the part thereof, and the State.

(2) In particular, and without derogation from the generality of sub-clause (1) of this clause the matters referred to above shall include the matter specified in the Schedule to this Agreement.

2\. Any dispute arising out of this Agreements or out of the agreements hereby continued, shell, unless any provision is made therein for arbitration by an authority other than the Governor-General or Governor, be settled by arbitration according, as far as may be, to the procedure of the Indian Arbitration Act, 1899.

3\. Nothing in this Agreement includes the exercise of any paramountcy functions.

.....................................State,

....

Secretary to the Government of India

SCHEDULE

1. Air Communications.
2. Arms and equipment.
3. Control of commodities.

4. Currency and coinage.
5. Customs.
6. Indian States Forces.
7. External Affairs
8. Extradition.
9. Import and Export Control.
10. Irrigation and Electric Power.
11. Motor vehicles.
12. National Highways.
13. Opium.
14. Posts, Telegraph and Telephones.
15. Railways (including police and other arrangements in Railway lands)
16. Salt.
17. Central Excises, relief from double income-tax and other arrangements relating to taxation.
18. Wireless.

4

Correspondence between Concerned Parties Prior to India's Reference of Kashmir Issue to the Security Council, 1947-1948

(Including Instrument of Accession and Its Acceptance)

4.1. Telegram from Prime Minister of Jammu and Kashmir, Srinagar to Sardar Abdur Rab Nishtar, States Relations Department, Karachi, August 8, 1947

Jammu and Kashmir Government would welcome Standstill Agreement with Pakistan on all matters on which these exist at present moment with outgoing British India Government. It is suggested that existing arrangements should continue pending settlement of details and formal execution of fresh agreement.

4.2. Telegram from Foreign Secretary to the Government of Pakistan, Karachi, to Prime Minister of Jammu and Kashmir, Srinagar, August 15, 1947

Your telegram of the 12th. The Government of Pakistan agree to have a Standstill Agreement with the Government of Jammu and Kashmir for the continuance of existing arrangements pending settlement of details for formal execution of fresh agreements.

4.3. Telegrams Exchanged between Government of Jammu and Kashmir and Government of India

Government of Jammu and Kashmir

Jammu and Kashmir Government would welcome Standstill Agreement with Union of India on all matters on which these exist at the present moment with outgoing British Indian Government. It is suggested that existing arrangements should continue pending settlement of details and formal execution of fresh agreement.

Reply from Government of India

Government of India would be glad if you or some other Minister duly authorised in this behalf could fly to Delhi for negotiation of Standstill Agreement between Kashmir Government and Indian Dominion. Early action desirable to maintain intact existing agreements and administrative arrangements.

4.4. Letter from Sheikh Mohammed Abdullah to Maharaja of Jammu and Kashmir, September 26, 1947

May it please Your Highness,
It is after about one and half year's incarceration that—as long wished—I had an opportunity of having detailed talks with Thakur Nachint Chand Ji. What unfortunate things happened during this period in the State, I need not mention. But this is now realised by every well-wisher of the State that many of the regrettable happenings of the past have mainly been due to the misunderstandings which appear now to have deliberately been created by interested people in order to achieve their own ends. R.B. Ramchandra Kak, the ex-Prime Minister, through his mischievous methods and masterly manoeuvrings brought these misunderstandings to a climax and succeeded in his attempt, though temporarily, to a certain extent. He painted me and my organisation in the darkest colours and in everything that we did or attempted to do to bring Your Highness and your prople closer, base and selfish motives were attributed to me. But God be thanked that all these enemies of Your Highness and the State stand exposed today.

In spite of what has happened in the past, I assure Your

Highness that myself and my party have never harboured any sentiment of disloyalty towards Your Highness' person, throne or dynasty. The development of this beautiful country and the betterment of its people is our common aim and interest and I assure Your Highness the fullest and loyal support of myself and my organisation. Not only this, but I assure Your Highness that any party, within or without the State, which may attempt to create any impediments in our efforts to gain our goal, will be treated as our enemy and will be treated as such.

In order to achieve the common aim set forth above, mutual trust and confidence must be the mainstay. Without this it would not be possible to face successfully the great difficulties that beset our State on all sides at present.

Before I close this letter I beg to assure Your Highness once again of my steadfast loyalty and pray that God under Your Highness' aegis bring such an era of Peace, Prosperity and Good Government that it may be second to none and be an ideal for others to copy.

Yours Highness' Most Obedient Subject,
S.M. Abdullah

4.5. Telegram from Foreign Secretary to the Government of Pakistan to the Prime Minister of Jammu and Kashmir, October 12, 1947

Men of Pakistan Army who have recently returned from leave at their homes in Poonch report that armed bands, which include troops, are attacking Muslim villages in the State. Their stories are confirmed by the large number of villages that can be seen burning from Murree hills. The Pakistan Government are vitally interested in the maintenance of peace on their borders, and the welfare of Muslims in the adjoining territories, and on those grounds alone would be justified in asking for an assurance that steps be taken to restore order in Poonch. One feature of the present situation in Poonch which, however, makes it peculiarly dangerous to the friendly relations which the Pakistan Government wishes to retain with Kashmir, is that the Pakistan Army obtains a large number of recruits from Poonch. Feeling in the battalions to which these men belong is rapidly rising and the situation is fraught with danger. The Pakistan Government wishes to avoid such a situation as they are sure do the Government of Kashmir, but if it is to be avoided, immediate and effective steps must be taken to end the present state of affairs, and in particular, if it is true that State troops are taking part in the attack of Muslims, to ensure the restoration of their discipline. The Government of Pakistan would like to be informed of the action taken.

4.6. Reply from the Prime Minister of Jammu and Kashmir to Government of Pakistan, October 15, 1947

This Government has ample proof of infiltration. As is the result in every Government, including Pakistan Dominion, Military has to take action when disturbances caused cannot adequately be dealt with by Civil Administraion. If this action hurts anyone's feelings, Government hopes you will agree that it is for them to help in the task of restoration of peace. Government is prepared to have an impartial inquiry made into the whole affair with a view to remove misunderstanding and to restore cordial relations which this Government has strictly kept in view so far even in spite of provocations by the people across the border and has maintained it in its true spirits. If, unfortunately this request is not heeded, Government, much against its wishes, will have no option but to ask for assistance to withstand aggressive and unfriendly action of the Pakistan people along our border.

4.7. Telegram* from Prime Minister of Jammu and Kashmir to Governor-General of Pakistan, October 18, 1947

Ever since August fifteenth in spite of agreement to observe Standstill Agreement on matters on which agreement existed on August 14 with British India, increasing difficulties have been felt not only with regard to supplies from West Punjab of petrol, oils, food, salt, sugar and cloth but also in the working of the postal system which has been most detrimental to the people as well as the administration. Saving Bank accounts refused to be operated. Postal certificates not cashed. Cheques by branches here of West Punjab Banks not honoured. Even Imperial Bank branches put hard to meet obligations owing failure of remittances form Lahore Currency

---

* Copy telegraphed to Prime Minister of Pakistan also.

Officer. Motor vehicles registered in the State have been held at Rawalpindi. Railway traffic from Sialkot to Jammu has been discontinued. While the State has offered safe passage to about one lakh Muslim refugees from Pathankot to Sialkot, the Rawalpindi people have murdered and wounded in cold blood over 180 out of a party of 220 Kashmir nationals being conveyed to Kohala at State request. People armed with modern long-range fire arms have infiltrated in thousands in Poonch and committed horrors on non-Muslims, murdering, maiming and looting them and burning their houses as well as kidnapping women. Instead of cooperation asked for through every possible local as well as provincial authorities and Central authority, paper promises have been made actually followed by more rigorous action than before. Press and Radio of Pakistan appear actually to have been licensed to pour volumes of fallacious, libellous and false propaganda. Smaller feudatory States have been prompted to threat even armed interference into the State. Even private people in Pakistan are allowed to wire unbearable threats without any checks by the Pakistan Dominion post offices. To crown all, the State is being blamed for acts which actually are being committed by Pakistan people. Villages are being raided from Sialkot, in addition to actual infiltration in Poonch. The Government cannot but conclude that all is being done with the knowledge and connivance of local authorities. The Government also trusts that it would be admitted that these acts are extremely unfriendly if not actually bordering on inimical. Finally the Government wish to make it plain that it is not possible to tolerate this attitude any longer without grave consequences to the life, property of people which it is sacredly bound to defend at all costs. The Government even now hopes that you would personally look into the matter and put a stop to all the iniquities which are being perpetrated. If, unfortunately, this request is not heeded the Government fully hope that you would agree that it would be justified in asking for friendly assistance and oppose trespass on its fundamental rights.

4.8. Telegram from Governor-General of Pakistan to Maharaja of Jammu and Kashmir, October 20, 1947

I have received telegram of the 18th October from your Prime Minister regarding the situation in Kashmir which, I regret, was released to the Press before it reached me and before I could deal with it. My Government have already been in communication with your Government and I deplore that your Prime Minister should have restored to the tone and language adopted in his telegram to me which embodies a threat to seek outside assistance and is almost in the nature of an ultimatum. This is hardly the way for any responsible and friendly Government to handle the situation that has arisen.

2. On 15th October your Prime Minister sent a telegram to my Government making similar allegations in the same offensive manner as have been repeated in his telegram of 18th October now addressed to me without waiting for the reply for his earlier telegram from my Government. My Government have already replied to that telegram on the 18th October and this reply shows clearly that your Government's wholly one-sided and exparte allegations cannot be supported. Since your Government have released to the Press the telegram addressed to me under reply, my Government have no other course left open and have, therefore, decided to release to the Press their reply referred to above refuting your allegations.

3. The allegation in the telegram under reply that the Standstill Agreement has not been observed is entirely wrong. The difficulties that have been felt by your administration have arisen as a result of the widespread disturbances in East Punjab and the disruption of communications caused thereby particularly by the shortage of coal. These difficulties have been felt actually by the West Punjab Government themselves. The difficulties with regard to banking facilities were caused by the lack of staff in the various banks and cannot be laid at the door of the West Punjab Government, who have in fact tried their best to ensure protection to the banks. The failure of remittances from Lahore Currency Officer has nothing to do with the Pakistan Government since the Lahore Currency Officer is under the Reserve Bank of India. Your Government's complaints regarding Press reports and telegrams by private persons are also wide off the mark. Your Government do not realize that there is no censorship in West Punjab. The complaint about local and provincial authorities is thus wholly unfounded. It is a travesty of the truth to call the promises of the Central Government paper promises, as your Government alleges. My Government adhere to those assurances and have every intention of carrying out the Standstill Agreement.

4. In order to remove various difficulties relating to communications and supply of goods my Government suggested long

ago that representatives of the Governments of Pakistan and Kashmir should meet. That request was ignored. In the circumstances I am, reluctantly, forced to the conclusion that the unfounded allegations and accusations are only a smoke-screen to cover the real aim of your Government's policy. A recent instance of this policy is the differential treatment accorded to leaders of the Kashmir National Conference and the Muslim Conference. On the one hand, your Government has released Sheikh Abdullah who was tried and convicted of high treason, removed the ban on his colleagues and allowed the National Conference a free field in which to carry on their propaganda. On the other hand, Mr. Ghulam Abbas and his colleagues whose alleged offence was only that they disobeyed the order banning the meeting of the Muslim Conference are still rotting in jail and the Muslim Conference organization is not allowed its elementary right of civil liberties. The course which your Government is pursuing in suppressing the Mussalmans in every way, the atrocites which are being committed by your troops and which are driving Muslims out of the State, various indications given in the Press, particularly the release to the Press of your Prime Minister's telegram addressed to me containing unfounded allegations and the threat to enlist outside assistance, show clearly that the real aim of your Government's policy is to seek an opportunity to join the Indian Dominion through a *coup d'etat* by securing the intervention and assistance of that Dominion. This policy is naturally creating deep resentment and grave apprehension among your subjects, 85 per cent of whom are Muslims.

5. The proposal made by my Government for a meeting with your accredited representatives is now an urgent necessity. I suggest that the way to smooth out difficulties and adjust matters in a friendly way is for your Prime Minister to come to Karachi and discuss the developments that have taken place instead of carrying on acrimonious and bitter controversy by telegrams and correspondence. I would also repeat that I endorse the suggestion made in your Prime Minister's telegram of 15th October and accepted by my Government in their reply of 18th October to have an impartial inquiry made into the whole affair."

4.9. Telegram* from Prime Minister of India to Prime Minister of Great Britain, October 25, 1947

1. A grave situation has developed in the State of Kashmir. Large numbers of Afridis and other tribesmen from the Frontier have invaded State territory, occupied several towns and massacred large numbers of non-Muslims. According to our information, tribesmen have been equipped with motor transport and also with automatic weapons and have passed through Pakistan territory. Latest news is that the invaders are proceeding up the Jhelum valley road towards the valley of Kashmir.

2. We have received urgent appeal for assistance from the Kashmir Government. We would be disposed to give favourable consideration to such request from any friendly State. Kashmir's northern frontiers, as you are aware, run in common with those of three countries, Afghanistan, the U.S.S.R. and China. Security of Kashmir, which depends upon its internal tranquillity and existence of stable Government is vital to security of India, especially since part of southern boundary of Kashmir and India are common. Helping Kashmir, therefore, is an obligation of national interest to India. We are giving urgent consideration to the question as to what assistance we can give to the State to defend itself.

3. I should like to make it clear that question of aiding Kashmir in this emergency is not designed in any way to influence the State to accede to India. Our view which we have repeatedly made public is that the question of accession in any disputed territory or State must be decided in accordance with wishes of the people and we adhere to this view. It is quite clear, however, that no free expression of the will of the people of Kashmir is possible if external aggression succeeds in imperilling the integrity of its territory.

4. I have thought it desirable to inform you of the situation because of its threat of international complications.

4.10. Letter from His Highness Hari Singh, Maharaja of Jammu and Kashmir to Lord Mountbatten, Governor-General of India, October 26, 1947

My dear Lord Mountbatten,
I have to inform your Excellency that a grave emergency has arisen in

*Repeated to Prime Minister of Pakistan, October 26, 1947

my State and request immediate assistance of your Government.

As your Excellency is aware the State of Jammu and Kashmir has not acceded to the Dominion of India or to Pakistan. Geographically my State is contiguous to both the Dominions. It has vital economical and cultural links with both of them. Besides my State has a common boundary with the Soviet Republic and China. In their external relations the Dominions of India and Pakistan cannot ignore this fact.

I wanted to take time to decide to which Dominion I should accede, or whether it is not in the best interests of both the Dominions and my State to stand independent, of course with friendly and cordial relations with both.

I accordingly approached the Dominions of India and Pakistan to enter into Standstill Agreement with my State. The Pakistan Government accepted this Agreement. The Dominion of India desired further discussions with representatives of my Government. I could not arrange this in view of the developments indicated below. In fact the Pakistan Government are operating Post and Telegraph system inside the State.

Though we have got a Standstill Agreement with the Pakistan Government that Government permitted steady and increasing strangulation of supplies like food, salt and petrol to my State.

Afridis, soldiers in plain clothes, and desperadoes with modern weapons have been allowed to infilter into the State at first in Poonch and then in Sialkot and finallly in mass area adjoining Hazara District on the Ramkot side. The result has been that the limited number of troops at the disposal of the State had to be dispersed and thus had to face the enemy at the several points simultaneously, and that it has become difficult to stop the wanton destruction of life and property and looting. The Mahora power-house which supplies the electric current to the whole of Srinagar has been burnt. The number of women who have been kidnapped and raped makes my heart bleed. The wild forces thus let losse on the State are marching on with the aim of capturing Srinagar, the summer Capital of my Government, as first step to over-running the whole State.

The mass infiltration of tribesmen drawn from the distant areas of the North-West Frontier coming regularly in motor trucks using Mansehra-Muzaffarabad Rood and fully armed with up-to-date weapons cannot possibly be done without the knowledge of the Provincial Government of the North-West Frontier Province and the

Government of Pakistan. In spite of repeated requests made by my Government no attempt has been made to check these raiders or stop them from coming to my State. The Pakistan Radio even put out a story that a Provisional Government has been set up in Kashmir. The people of my State, both the Muslims and non-Muslims, generally have taken no part at all.

With the conditions obtaining at present in my State and the great emergency of the situation as it exists, I have no option but to ask for help from the Indian Dominion. Naturally they cannot send the help asked for by me without my State acceding to the Dominion of India. I have accordingly decided to do so and I attach the Instrument of Accession for acceptance by your Government. The other alternative is to leave my State and my people to free-booters. On this basis no civilized Government can exist or be maintained. This alternative I will never allow to happen as long as I am Ruler of the State and I have life to defend my country.

I am also to inform your Excellency's Government that it is my intention at once to set up an interim Government and ask Sheikh Abdullah to carry the responsibilities in this emergency with my Prime Minister.

If my State has to be saved immediate assistance must be available at Srinagar. Mr. Menon is fully aware of the situation and he will explain to you, if further explanation is needed.

In haste and with kindest regards,

Your sincerely,
Hari Singh

4.11. Instrument of Accession of Jammu and Kashmir State, October 26, 1947

Whereas the Indian Independence Act, 1947, provides that as from the fifteenth day of August, 1947, there shall be set up an independent Dominion known as India, and that the Government of India Act, 1935, shall, with such omissions, additions, adaptations and modifications as the Governer-General may by order specify, be applicable to the Dominion of India.

And whereas the Government of India Act, 1935, as so adapted by the Governor-General provides that an India State may accede to the Dominion of India by an Instrument of Accession executed by the Ruler thereof:

Now, therefore, I Shriman Inder Mahandar Rajrajeshwar Maharajadhiraj Shri Hari Singhji Jammu Kashmir Naresh Tatha Tibbet adi Deshadhipathi Ruler of Jammu and Kashmir State in the exercise of my sovereignty in and over my said State do hereby execute this my Instrument of Accession, and

1. I hereby declare that I accede to the Dominion of India with the intent that the Governor-General of India, the Dominion Legislature, the Federal Court and any other Dominion authority established for the purposes of the Dominion shall, by virtue of this my Instrument of Accession, but subject always to the terms thereof, and for the purposes only of the Dominion, exercise in relation to the State of Jammu and Kashmir (hereinafter referred to as "this State") such functions as may be vested in them by or under the Government of India Act, 1935, as in force in the Dominion of India, on the 15th day of August 1947, (which Act as so in force is hereafter referred to as "the Act")

2. I hereby assume the obligation of ensuring that due effect is given to the provisions of the Act within this State so far as they are applicable therein by virtue of this my Instrument of Accession.

3. I accept the matters specified in the Schedule hereto as the matters with respect to which the Dominion Legislature may make laws for this State.

4. I hereby declare that I accede to the Dominion of India on the assurance that if an agreement is made between the Governor-General and the Ruler of this State whereby any functions in relation to the administration in this State of any law of the Dominion Legislature shall be exercised by the Ruler of this State, then any such agreement shall be deemed to form part of this Instrument and shall be construed and have effect accordingly.

5. The terms of this my Instrument of Accession shall not be varied by any amendment of the Act or of the India Independence Act, 1947, unless such amendment is accepted by me by an Instrument supplementary to this Instrument.

6. Nothing in this Instrument shall empower the Dominion Legislature to make any law for this State authorising the compulsory acquisition of land for any purpose, but I hareby undertake that should the Dominion for the purpose of a Dominion law which applies in this State deem it necessary to acquire any land, I will at their request acquire the land at their expense or, if the land belongs to me, transfer it to them on such terms as may be agreed or, in

default of agreement, determined by an arbitrator to be appointed by the Chief Justice of India.

7. Nothing in this Instrument shall be deemed to commit me in any way to acceptance of any future Constitution of India or to fetter my discretion to enter into arrangements with the Government of India under any such future Constitution.

8. Nothing in this Instrument effects the continuance of my sovereignty in and over this State, or, save as provided by or under this Instrument, the exercise of any powers, authority and rights now enjoyed by me as Ruler of this State or the validity of any law at present in force in this State.

9. I hereby declare that I execute this Instrument on behalf of this State and that any reference in this Instrument to me or to the Ruler of the State is to be construed as including a reference to my heirs and successors.

Given under my hand this twenty-sixth day of October, Nineteen hundred and forty-seven.

Hari Singh,
Maharajadhiraj of Jammu and Kashmir State.

4.12. Acceptance of Instrument of Accession of Jammu and Kashmir State by the Governor-General of India, October 27, 1947

I do hereby accept this Instrument of Accession.

Dated this twenty-seventh day of October, Nineteen hundred and forty-seven.

Mountbatten of Burma
Governor-General of India

4.13. Reply of Governor-General Lord Mountbatten to Maharaja of Jammu and Kashmir signifying his Acceptance of the Instrument of Accession, October 27, 1947

My dear Maharaja Sahib,
Your Highness' letter dated 26th October has been delivered to me by Mr. V.P. Menon. In the special circumstances mentioned by your Highness my Government have decided to accept the accession of Kashmir State to the Dominion of India. In consistence with their Policy that in the case of any State where the issue of accession has been the subject of dispute, the question of accession should be

decided in accordance with the wishes of the people of State, it is my Government's wish that as soon as law and order have been restored in Kashmir and her soil cleared of the invader the question of the State's accession should be settled by a reference to the people.

Meanwhile in response to your Highness' appeal for military aid, action has been taken today to send troops of the Indian Army to Kashmir to help your own forces to defend your territory and to protect the lives, property and honour of your people.

My Government and I note with satisfaction that your Highness has decided to invite Sheikh Abdullah to form an interim Government to work with your Prime Minister.

With kind regards,

I remain,
Your sincerely,
Mountbattten of Bürma

4.14. Memorandum Communicating Message of British Prime Minister to Prime Minister of Pakistan, Communicated by High Commissioner for the United Kingdom in Karachi, October 27, 1947

I have received message from Prime Minister of India stating that grave situation has developed in Kashmir. That tribesmen equipped with motor transport and automatic weapons entered Kashmir territory through Pakistan. That they have occupied several towns and have killed large numbers of non-Muslims, and that they are advancing on Srinagar. Mr. Nehru says that Government of India have received urgent appeal for assistance from Kashmir Government and that they are considering this appeal. He adds that he would like to make it clear that the question of aiding Kashmir in this emergency is not designed in any way to influence the State to accede to India.

I have sent Mr. Nehru a reply saying that we have received no confirmed reports of the scale and importance of any incursions there may have been, and begging him not to let his answer to this appeal take the form of armed intervention by the forces of India. I would also appeal to you to do everything possible to prevent armed intervention in Kashmir by Muslims from Pakistan, or by tribesmen seeking to pass through Pakistan-administered territory on their way to Kashmir. I hope that it will be possible for you to use your influence with any such who have already entered Kashmir to return home. I am informing Mr. Nehru that I am making this appeal to you.

I also suggest for your consideration, as I am suggesting to Mr. Nehru, that it might be most useful step towards settlement of difficult question of Kashmir's future if it could be discussed by you, Mr. Nehru, and Maharaja of Kashmir at a meeting to be held as soon as possible at some suitable place. Ends.

4.15. Telegram from Indian Prime Minister Jawaharlal Nehru to Liaquat Ali Khan, Prime Minister of Pakistan, October 28, 1947

For Mr. Liaquat Ali Khan from Jawaharlal Nehru.

I have communicated to you text of telegram I sent to Prime Minister, United Kingdom, regarding Kashmir situation. I have also sent you text of correspondence between Governor-General of India, and Maharaja of Kashmir regarding accession of Kashmir State to Indian Union. I have sent a further message to Prime Minister, U.K., informing him of imminent peril of Srinagar and Kashmir from raiders and of action we have taken to give protection to people there. I want to invite your Government's cooperation in stopping the raiders entering Kashmir territory from Pakistan. These raids have already resulted in large-scale death and destruction and if they are not stopped immediately will lead to ruin of Kashmir. The consequences of success of such irresponsible raiders anywhere will be far-reaching all over India. Therefore, in interest of both Pakistan and India, such raids must be stopped. As raiders come across Pakistan territory it should be possible to stop them there. I wish to assure you that action Government of India has taken has been forced upon them by circumstances and imminent and grave danger to Srinagar. They have no desire to intervene in affairs of Kashmir State after raiders have been driven away and law and order established. In regard to accession also it has been made clear that this is subject to reference to people of State and their decision. Government of India have no desire to impose any decision and will abide by people's wishes, but those cannot be ascertained till peace and law and order prevail. Protection of Kashmir from armed raids thus becomes first objective and in this we trust we shall have your cooperation.

4.16. Telegram from Prime Minister of India, to Prime Minister of Pakistan, October 28, 1947 (Extract)

I would welcome an early opportunity of meeting you and discussing various problems that have arisen, more specially development in Kashmir about which I have informed you. I earnestly hope that there will be co-operation between Pakistan and India in stopping raids and putting down disorder and then leaving choice about future to people of Kashmir. I am glad to learn that you are likely to visit Delhi for Joint Defence Council meeting soon.

4.17. Telegram* from Prime Minister of Pakistan to Prime Minister of India, October 30, 1947

For Pandit Nehru from Liaquat Ali Khan,
I have received your telegrams including that of 28th October to which I reply. The position is that Sikh attacks on Muslims in East Punjab in August greatly inflamed feeling throughout Pakistan and it was only with greatest difficulty the Pathan tribes were prevented from entering West Punjab to take revenge on Hindus and Sikhs. Muslims in Poonch were attacked and those in Jammu massacred by mobs led by Kashmir State Forces and when it was evident that there was to be a repetition in Kashmir of that in East Punjab it became impossible wholly to prevent tribes from entering that State without using troops which would have created a situation on frontier that might well have got out of control.

Your recent action of sending troops to Kashmir on pretext of accession has made things infinitely worse. The whole of the frontier is stirring and feeling of resentment among tribes is intense. The responsibility for what is happening is entirely yours. There was no trouble in Poonch or Jammu till State troops started killing Muslims. All along Kashmir Government has been in close touch with you. At the same time they ignored or refused our offers of friendly discussion. On 2nd October I suggested that both Pakistan and Kashmir should appoint representatives to discuss supplies to Kashmir and mutual allegations of border raids. The Prime Minister, Kashmir, replied that he was too busy. When in spite of this we sent Shah, Joint Secretary, Ministry of Foreign Affairs and States to

*PUNSG, Lahore to FOREIGN, New Delhi.

Kashmir the Prime Minister refused to discuss with him. On 15th October Prime Minister, Kashmir, threatened that unless we agreed to an impartial enquiry into what was happening he would ask for assistance to withstand aggression on his borders. We immediately agreed to an impartial enquiry since when no more has been heard from Kashmir of this proposal.

The Pathan raid on Kashmir did not start till 22nd October. It is quite clear therefore that Kashmiri's plan of asking for Indian troops—and it could hardly have been unilateral—was formed quite independently of this raid and all evidence and action taken shows it was pre-arranged. It would seem rather to have been made after failure of their troops to suppress people of Poonch and in anticipation of reaction which they expected to their massacre of Moselems in Jammu.

I in my turn appeal to you to stop the Jammu killings which still continue. Yesterday West Punjab was again invaded by a well armed mob who after a fight with villagers retreated leaving two Gurkha soldiers in uniform dead behind them. As long as this sort of thing continues passions are bound to become further inflamed.

4.18. Telegram from Prime Minister of India to Prime Minister of Pakistan, October 31, 1947

From Jawaharlal Nehru for Mr. Laiquat Ali Khan.
Your Telegram dated 30th October. I have repeatedly expressed to you my sentiments regarding the cycle of retaliation which has plunged West and East Punjab in tragedy. Both in public and private I have condemned atrocities irrespective of community of the perpetrators—Sikh, Hindu or Muslim. If Hindus and Sikhs have killed or driven out Muslims in any part of Kashmir I condemn their action without reserve. I find it impossible, however, to accept either your version of the causes and course of attack on Kashmir or the baseless suggestion that we have sent troops to Kashmir on pretext of "accession." We are perfectly willing to have all events investigated during last 15 months to find out what have been basic causes and on whom blame rests. What has happened in Kashmir stands apart and must be judged as such more specially in view of imminent danger of widespread disaster which Kashmir valley has had to face which would have the most far-reaching consequences in regard to relations between India and Pakistan.

2. The Government of India entirely agree that no raids from one territory to another should take place and they must be stopped by all means at our disposal. It is patent that they have had nothing to do even remotely with occurrences in or near Kashmir State till they sent their troops to Srinagar on 27th October. Before accession Kashmir was not our responsibility even though we were greatly interested in its future . . .

7. Our assurance that we shall withdraw our troops from Kashmir as soon as peace and order are restored and leave the decision about the future of the State to the people of Kashmir and to the world. You lay on us the responsibility for what is happening. I should have thought that this could more appropriately and fairly be placed on those who have been attacking and invading Kashmir. To accuse us of provocation and aggression when all that we have done is to go to the rescue of a people threatened with loss of life, property and honour, is a singular perversion of truth and reason. It gives me no pleasure to write to you in this strain. I am convinced that if Pakistan and India are to live in peace, leaders on both sides must have trust in one another and act with understanding and restraint. Mutual mistrust and recrimination can only lead to consequences which would be to the advantage of neither India nor Pakistan. I have done everything possible to think and act in this spirit. It was not possible for us to refuse the request of the Kashmir Government to help them prevent raiding bands from committing massacre, arson and loot and ruining Kashmir. I should have thought that it was equally to your advantage to prevent this and hence my appeal to you to stop these raiders at the source.

9. I have no knowledge of the raid you refer to in Jammu in your last paragraph. I am inquiring about it. We shall certainly do our utmost to stop all raids and I appeal to you to do the same. I understand, however, that there is concentration of Pakistan troops on the Jammu border.

4.19. Broadcast to the Nation by Prime Minister of India, November 2, 1947

I want to speak to you tonight about Kashmir, not about the beauty of that famous valley, but about the horror which it has had to face recently. We have passed through very critical days and the burden of taking vital and far-reaching decisions has fallen upon us. We have taken those decisions and I want to tell you about them.

The neighbouring Government, using language which is not the language of Governments or even of responsible people, has accused the Government of India of fraud in regard to the accession of Kashmir to the Indian Union. I cannot emulate that language nor have I any desire to do so, for, I speak for a responsible Government and a responsible people. I agree that there has been fraud and violence in Kashmir but the question is: "who is responsible for it?" Already considerable parts of the Jammu and Kashmir State have been overrun by raiders from outside, well-armed and well-equipped, and they have sacked and looted the towns and villages and put many of the inhabitants to the sword. Fightfulness suddenly descended upon this lovely and peaceful country and the beautiful city of Srinagar was on the verge of destruction.

I want to say at once that every step that we have taken in regard to Kashmir has been taken after the fullest thought and consideration of the consequences and I am convinced that what we have done was the right thing. Not to have taken those steps would have been a betrayal of a trust and cowardly submission to the sword with its accompaniment of arson, raping and slaughter.

For some weeks past we had received reports of infiltration of raiding bands into the State territory of Jammu Province. Also of a concentration of armed men near the border of Kashmir with the North-West Frontier Province. We were naturally concerned about this not only because of our close ties with Kashmir and her people but also because Kashmir is a frontier territory adjoining great nations and therefore we were bound to take interest in the developments there. But we were anxious not to interfere and we took no step whatever to intervene even though a part of Jammu Province was overrun by these raiders.

It has been stated that there were raids from the Jammu side across the Pakistan border and that there was communal trouble in Jammu and Muslims were killed and driven away. In the past we have not hesitated to condemn evil, however might have committed it, whether Hindu or Sikh or Muslim, and so if Hindus or Sikhs or any functionaries of the State misbehaved in Jammu Province, certainly we condemn them and regret their deeds.

But I have before me a detailed list of 95 villages in the Jammu Province which have been destroyed by the raiders from Pakistan. Bhimbar, a considerable town, had also been sacked and destroyed.

Other towns are besieged and a considerable part of Poonch and Mirpur areas is in possession of the raiders. Does this indicate that aggression took place from the Kashmir side on to West Punjab or does it not show that there has been continuous organised aggression from West Punjab into Kashmir State? There raiders possess the latest type of modern arms. It is reported that they have used flame-throwers and a disabled tank has been discovered with them.

About this time we were asked by the Kashmir State to provide them with arms. We took no urgent steps about it, and although sanction was given by our States and Defence Ministries, actually no arms were sent.

On the night of the 24th October I learnt of another raid, this time from the Abbottabad-Mansara Road which enters Kashmir near Muzaffarabad. We were told that armed and well-equipped persons in over one hundred lorries had broken in, had sacked Muzaffarabad and killed many persons there, including the District Magistrate and were proceeding along the Jhelum Valley road towards Srinagar. The State forces were spread out in small numbers all over the State and they could not stop this armed and well-organised raid. The civil population, Hindu and Muslim, fled before the raiders.

It was on the 24th night that for the first time a request was made to us on behalf of the Kashmir State for accession and military help. On the 25th morning we considered this in the Defence Committee but no decision was taken about sending troops in view of the obvious difficulties of the undertaking. On the 26th morning we again considered this matter. The situation was even more critical then. The raiders had sacked several towns and had destroyed the great Power House at Mahoora which supplies electricity to the whole of Kashmir. They were on the point of entering the valley. The fate of Srinagar and the whole of Kashmir hung in the balance.

We received urgent messages for aid not only from the Maharaja's Government but from representatives of the people, notably that great leader of Kashmir, Sheikh Mohammed Abdullah, the President of the National Conference. Both the Kashmir Government and the National Conference pressed us to accept the accession of Kashmir to the Indian Union. We decided to accept this accession and to send troops by air, but we made a condition that the accession would have to be considered by the people of Kashmir later when peace and order were established. We were anxious not to finalise anything in a moment of crisis, and without the fullest opportunity to the people of Kashmir to have their say. It was for them ultimately to decide.

And here let me make clear that it has been our policy all along that where there is a dispute about the accession of a State to either Dominion, the decision must be made by the people of that State. It was in accordance with this policy that we added a proviso to the Instrument of Accession of Kashmir.

We decided to send troops on the afternoon of 26th October. Srinagar was in peril and the situation was urgent and critical. Our staff worked hard that day and night, and at day-break on the 27th our troops went by air. They were small in numbers to begin with, but immediately on arrival they rushed into action to stop the invader. Their gallent Commander, a brave officer of our Army, was killed the next day.

Since then, troops and equipment have been flown over daily, and I should like to express my high appreciation and the appreciation of my Government for the fine work which our staff have done, as well as the pilots and the air crews who have thrown themselves into this adventure with heart and soul. The air lines have co-operated with us fully and to them also I am grateful. Our youngmen have shown how they can rise to the occasion in a moment of crisis to serve their country.

Srinager was in peril and the invader was almost on its door step. There was no administration left there, no troops, no police. Light and power had failed and there were a vast number of refugees there and yet Srinagar functioned without obvious panic and the shops were opened and people went about the streets. To what was this miracle due? Sheikh Abdullah and his colleagues of the National Conference and their unarmed volunteers, Muslim and Hindu and Sikh, took charge of the situation, kept order and prevented panic. It was a wonderful piece of work that they did at a moment when the nerves of most people might have failed them. They did so because they were determined to protect their country from to ruthless invader who was destroying their country and trying to compel them by terrorism to join Pakistan. Whatever the future may hold, the people of the Valley of Kashmir have exhibited during these past few days remarkable courage, capacity for organisation and unity.

It would be well if this lesson was understood by the whole of India which has been poisoned by communal strife. Under the inspiration of a great leader, Sheikh Abdullah, the people of the Valley, Muslim and Hindu and Sikh, were together for the defence of their common country against the invader. Our troops could have done little without this popular support and co-operation.

The Maharaja of Kashmir deserves to the congratulated on his decision to make Sheikh Abdullah the head of the Administration at this critical juncture. That was a wise step which other rulers might well follow, making their people trustees and defenders of freedom.

It must be remembered, therefore, that the struggle in Kashmir is a struggle of the people of Kashmir under popular leadership against the invader. Our troops are there to help in this struggle, and as soon as Kashmir is free from invader, our troops will have no further necessity to remain there and the fate of Kashmir will be left in the hands of the people of Kashmir.

We have passed through days of peril not only for Kashmir but for the whole of India. That peril is less now, but it is by no means over and many dangers confront us. We have to be very vigilant and well prepared for whatever may happen. The first step in this preparation is to put an end completely to every manner of communal strife in India, and to stand up as a United Nation to face every danger which might threaten our freedom. External danger can only by faced effectively when there is internal peace and order, and an organised nation.

We talk about the invaders and raiders in Kashmir, and yet these men are fully-armed and well-trained and have competent leadership. All of these have come across and from Pakistan territory. We have a right to ask the Pakistan Government how and why these people could come across the Frontier Province or West Punjab, and how they have been armed so effectively. Is this not a violation of International Law and an unfriendly act towards a neighbour country? Is the Pakistan Government too weak to prevent armies marching across its territory to invade another country, or is it willing that this should happen? There is no third alternative.

We have asked the Pakistan Government repeatedly to stop these raiders from coming, and to withdraw those who have come. It should be easy for them to stop them for the roads into Kashmir are very few and have to pass over bridges. We on our part have no intention of using our troops in Kashmir when danger of invasion is passed.

We have declared that the fate of Kashmir is ultimately to be decided by the people. That pledge we have given, and the Maharaja has supported it, not only to the people of Kashmir but to the world. We will not, and cannot back out of it. We are prepared when peace and law and order have been established to have a referendum held under international auspices like the United Nations. We want it to be a fair and just reference to the people, and we shall accept their verdict. I can imagine no fairer and juster offer.

Meanwhile we have given our word to the people of Kashmir to protect them against the invader and we shall keep our pledge.

4.20. Broadcast to the Nation by Prime Minister of Pakistan, November 4, 1947

I am speaking to you tonight from my sick-bed. I wish to talk to you about Kashmir, because the affairs of Kashmir have reached a critical phase and have now assumed international importance, and because I know that Kashmir is uppermost in your mind as it is in mine.

In the exhilaration of self-styled gallantry and valour, some erstwhile sympathisers of the oppressed people of Kashmir seem to have forgotten the history of this beautiful land. Let us, therefore, briefly recall it for their benefit.

This piece of God's earth along with the human beings inhabiting its hills and valleys was, under the infamous Amritsar Treaty, sold by the British to a Dogra chieftain for the paltry sum of Rs. 75 lakhs.

The present Maharaja inherits the people of Kashmir from his forefathers as though they were so many cattle. It is this immoral and illegal ownership that the gallantry and valour of Indian troops is defending today by spilling the blood of the suppressed slaves who had been bartered away by the British.

During the past 100 years of Dogra rule, this highly gifted and most attractive race of Kashmiris has been dragged down to the lowest depths of misery. In recent years they have made many attempts to fight for their freedom. Time and again they had been thwarted but time and again they have risen to defy tyranny.

The fight is not yet at an end. But I would like my listners to know that today the people of Kashmir are fighting not only for their freedom, but also for their very existence. For their misfortunes have, in recent months, taken on a darker side. They have been caught in the meshes of a widespread plan for the extermination of Muslims. This plan has succeeded in Alwar, in Bharatpur, in Patiala, in Faridkot, and in Kapurthala. And all these you will note are States that have acceded to the Indian Union.

Only yesterday Muslims formed the majority of the population in Kapurthala. There are hardly any left there now. When we asked the Indian Government to protect the Muslims in these States, we were told that these events were the States' internal affairs and the Indian Government could not interfere. After the massacre of Muslims in East Punjab and the East Punjab States, the forces of annihilation turned to Jammu and Kashmir.

Towards the end of September, the I.N.A. and the Rashtriya Sewak Sangh shifted their headquartes from Amritsar to Jammu, and thousands of Sikh refugees, so called, began to infiltrate into Kashmir. These socalled Sikh refugees came from East and not West Punjab. They came armed with modern weapons and were provided with more weapons by the State authorities. They set about their foul business in Jammu and Poonch repeating the horrible drama that they had enacted in East Punjab and with the same type of characters playing the leading roles.

In the beginning of October, news of the bestial deeds perpetrated on the innocent people of Kashmir began to trickle through. In a short time the trickle became a torrent. Burning villages could be seen from the Murree Hills. Thousands of terror-stricken refugees poured into Pakistan.

It was at this stage that the people of Kashmir, in sheer desperation, turned on their oppressors. Kashmiris, and specially the inhabitants of Poonch, have many relatives in Hazara and in West Punjab. Consequently feeling in certain parts of Pakistan rose very high and some people from the North-West Frontier Province and the tribal area, stirred by the atrocities in Kashmir, rushed to the aid of their brethren. It is the oppressed, enslaved and entrapped people of Kashmir struggling for their freedom and now for their lives and their sympathisers, whom the Indian Government is helping to wipe out. The declared object of the Indian Government is to strengthen the Maharaja's hands. How bloodstained these hands are is quite well-known to the leaders of India, even though they may choose to forget this fact now.

The stress has deliberately been shifted to the so-called raiders, as if the people of Kashmir themselves had suddenly slipped off their minds the memory of the century-old oppression, and had overnight become enamoured of their tyrannical oppressors. To present the rebellion of an enslaved people to the world as an invasion from outside simply because some outsiders have shown active sympathy with it, is a dishonest rewriting of history.

Much has been made of modern arms that are alleged to have been used against the Army and a tall structure of insinuation and innuendo has been built on this detail. It is, however, forgotten that many of those who are fighting the invading troops of India come from the 60,000 *ex*-Army men of Poonch who are not incapable of capturing the arms of their enemy.

Let us, therefore, not be misled by the laboured picture, so elaborately drawn, of the 'gallant' Indian Army saving the beautiful land of Kashmir and its people from invading hordes. It is not invading hordes but the patriots of Kashmir that the Indian Army is shooting and bombing. It is not Kashmir but a tottering despot that the Indian Government and their camp-followers are trying to save.

In his broadcast, the Prime Minister of India has been tilting at windmills. The armies of Pakistan have not marched into Kashmir as the armies of India, in one guise or another, marched into Junagadh and Manavadar when these States acceded to Pakistan. The Indian Government regarded the accession of Junagadh to Pakistan as a threat to their security.

The accession of Kashmir to India is a much greater threat to the security of Pakistan. We do not recognise this accession. The accession of Kashmir to India is a fraud, perpetrated on the people of Kashmir by its cowardly Ruler with the aggressive help of the Indian Government.

The release of Sheikh Abdualla who had been convicted of his treason, and the continued imprisonment of Muslim Conference leaders who had been convicted of mere technical offences, is only a part of the conspiracy. When the history of this tragic episode comes to be written, it will reveal the treachery of many self-styled patriots and lovers of justice. But the patriots of Kashmir will sooner or later prick this bubble, no matter how strong the forces arrayed against them. Our heart goes out to them—our brethren in this mortal struggle, for the choice before them now is freedom or death. If the plans of their enemies succeed, they will be exterminated as Muslims in various other parts of India have been exterminated. It is presumably after such extermination that the India Government propose that a referendum should be held. What use is a referendum after the voters have been driven away from their homes, or silenced in death?

The world knows how we have consistently and repeatedly tried to reach a better under..anding with the Kashmir Government. The Kashmir Government have ignored or rejeced all these approaches. On October 2nd I suggested to the Prime Minister of Kashmir that all question outstanding between the two States including that of supplies under the Standstill Agreement and mutual accusations of border raids, should be discussed by representatives of the two Governments. The Prime Minister of Kashmir replied that at the moment he was too busy to discuss these matters. Nevertheless we sent a representative to Srinagar to discuss these matters with the State. The Prime Minister, however refused to hold discussions with him and he had to return.

On October 14th the Prime Minister of Kashmir in a telegram to me threatened that unless Pakistan agreed to an impartial inquiry he would be compelled to ask for outside assistance to withstand the unfriendly acts of Pakistan people on his border. I at once accepted the proposal for an impartial inquiry, and asked the Prime Minister of Kashmir to nominate a representative for this purpose.

The Government of Kashmir have since made no further reference to this matter. On October 20th Mr. Jinnah in reply to a telegram from the Kashmir Government, called attention to the repeated attempts of Pakistan to improve its relations with Kashmir and asked the Prime Minister of Kashmir to come to Karachi and talk things over. No reply was sent to this request.

Mr. Jinnah also pointed out that the threat to call in outside help amounted almost to an ultimatum, and showed that the real aim of the Kashmir Government's policy was to seek an opportunity to join the Indian Union by means of a *coup d' etal*.

The refusal of the Kashmir Government to send a representative to discuss things and to nominate a representative for an impartial inquiry and their failure to reply to Mr. Jinnah's invitation to the Prime Minister to come to Karachi, their deliberate causing of disturbances in their State by employing their troops to attack Muslims, the fact that by 9 a.m. on the morning of the day on which Kashmir's accession was accepted Indian airborne troops had landed in Srinagar clearly show the existence of a plan for accession against the will of the people, possible only by occupation of the country by

Indian troops.

Even though all sorts of accusations were made against Pakistan by the Kashmir Government (and it was to redress these alleged wrongs that the Indian Government claims to have sent military aid to the Kashmir Government) yet at no stage did the Indian Dominion ask the Pakistan Government about these accusations and allegations or try to find a solution of this problem by joint consultation. It was only after India had accepted Kashmir's accession and sent forces into Kashmir that the Pakistan Government was informed of the action.

After the unwarranted occupation of Kashmir by the India Government, Mr. Jinnah proposed that an immediate conference should be held in Lahore. It was to be attended by the Governors-General and the Prime Ministers of the two Dominions and the Maharaja and his Prime Minister. This invitation was accepted and the conference was to be held on October 29th. At the last minute the conference was postponed as Pandit Nehru fell ill. It was arranged then that the Conference should be held on November 1st and attended by the Governors-General and the two Prime Ministers. This Conference also did not take place because on the morning of November 1st again at the last minute we were informed that Pandit Nehru was not well enough to come to Lahore.

In this way the idea of the conference receded into the background, so far as the Indian Dominion is concerned. If the India Government really wanted to discuss this most vital and urgent matter, surely the Deputy Prime Minister could have come in place of Pandit Nehru.

On November 1st, Lord Mountbatten came to Lahore alone to attend the meeting of the Joint Defence Council and took the opportunity to see Mr. Jinnah. At this meeting certain suggestions were made to Lord Mountbatten, but no further communication has been received by me or Mr. Jinnah from the India Government. Instead, Pandit Nehru has chosen to hurl across the world reckless accusations against the Pakistan Government, regardless of true facts. His broadcast was arranged after Lord Mountbatten's return to Delhi, and what the validity of his accusations is I have already told you. That is where the matter stands today. The issues are for you and the world to judge.

4.21. Telegram from Prime Minister of India to Prime Minister of Pakistan, December 12, 1947

Ever since my return from Lahore I have given most earnest thought to settlement of all outstanding matters in dispute between India and Pakistan. My colleagues share my desire for such a settlement which is essential for well-being of both India and Pakistan. It is our good fortune that agreements have already been arrived at in regard to many matters in controversy. But you will appreciate that it is difficult to make any progress if conflict and indifference continue between the two countries. Such a conflict is likely to affect all our other relations and may lead to a deterioration of situation.

2. The major cause of this conflict at present is Kashmir. We have discussed this matter with you at great length without resolving our differences or finding a way out of the impasse. I reiterate the arguments which have been repeatedly advanced in support of our position. You are fully seized of them.

3. We have given further thought, in the light of our discussion in Lahore, to the question of inviting United Nations to advise us in this matter. While we are prepared to invite U.N.O. observers to come here and advise us as to proposed plebiscite, it is not clear in what other capacity the United Nations help can be sought. According to your own declaration to us you are not party to present struggle in Kashmir. We cannot treat with irregular invaders as a State. No Government can deal with such raids which have brought death and destruction to Kashmir except through military means. We owe an obligation to the people of Kashmir to restore peaceful and normal conditions. We have pledged ourselves to this end. We would be glad to cooperate in an attempt to restore peace by settlement.

4. I trust that you will appreciate the logic and reasonableness of our position and our earnest desire to find a solution which is honourable to all concerned. I hope to meet you when you visit Delhi on December 22nd to attend the next meeting of the Joint Defence Council and to discuss this matter further with you. I confess, however, that I find myself unable to suggest anything beyond what I have offered already, namely, to ask U.N.O. to send impartial observers to advise us regarding the plebiscite.

I hope that your health continues to improve.

4.22. Telegram from Prime Minister of Pakistan to Prime Minister of India, December 16, 1947

Your Telegram No. Primin 448 dated 12th December.

As you know, I am most desirous for a settlement of all matters in dispute between India and Pakistan. So are my colleagues. And I agree with you that the major issue outstanding between the two Dominions is Kashmir and, as I pointed out before also, Junagadh. During our discussions in Delhi and Lahore I explained to you how vital a place Kashmir occupies in relation to Pakistan. The security of Pakistan is bound up with that of Kashmir, and the ties of religion, cultural affinity and economic inter-dependence bind the two together still closer. The security and well-being of the people of Kashmir is of the highest importance to the people of Pakistan. We are, therefore, vitally interested in peaceful and honourable conditions for the people of Kashmir so that freed from all pressure, external or internal, they might of their own free will decide to which Dominion they wish to accede. The test of any course of action should therefore be whether it leads to the creation of conditions in which a really free plebiscite can be held. To my mind, the problem can only be solved by an act of statesmanship in the light of the basic realities of the situation and not by any legal disputations as how Pakistan is a party to the dispute or how U.N.O. can be brought in. I hope when we meet on the 22nd December we shall be able to discuss the matter in this spirit.

Many thanks for your enquiry about my health. I am feeling better now.

4.23. Letter from Prime Minister of India to Prime Minister of Pakistan, handedover in Person in New Delhi, December 22, 1947

On various occasions, I have drawn your attention to the aid which the invaders of the Jammu and Kashmir State are deriving from Pakistan. Those who come from tribal areas have free transit through Pakistan territory, and many of these invaders are nationals of Pakistan. They are operating against Kashmir from bases in Pakistan. Much of their modern military equipment has been obtained from Pakistan sources; mortars, artillery and Mark V-mines are not normally the kind of armament which tribesmen or civilians possess.

Motor transport, which the invaders have been using, and the petrol required for it, could also be obtained in Pakistan only. Food and other supplies are also secured from Pakistan; indeed, we have reliable reports that the invaders get their rations from military messes in Pakistan. According to our information large numbers of these invaders are receiving militry training in Pakistan under officers of the Pakistan Army and other Pakistan nationals.

2. The forms of aid, enumerated in the preceding paragraph, which the invaders are receiving constitute an act of hostility and aggression against India because they are being used against a State which has acceded to the Indian Dominion and is a part thereof.

3. The Government of India, while protesting against the action of the Pakistan Government in furnishing, or allowing such assistance to be furnished, and urging that the Pakistan Government should stop such help and call upon the invaders to withdraw, have so far taken no action which might involve entry by Indian forces into Pakistan territory. They have been hoping all these weeks, though with diminishing hope, that the Pakistan Government themselves whould put a stop to aid to the invaders which is help to India's enemies. Since protests have failed to bear fruit, the Government of India now formally ask the Government of Pakistan to call upon Pakistan nationals to cease participation in the attack on Jammu and Kashmir State, and to deny to the invaders:

1. all access to, and use of Pakistan territory for operations against Kashmir State;
2. all military and other supplies;
3. all other kinds of aid that might tend to prolong the present struggle.

4. The Government of India have always desired and still earnestly desire to live on terms of friendship with Pakistan. They sincerely hope that the request which they have now fromally made will be acceded to promptly and without reserve. Failing such response they will be compelled to take such action, with due regard to their rights and obligations as a member of the United Nations, as they may consider necessary to protect their own interests, and those of the Government and people of Jammu and Kashmir State.

4.24. Letter from Prime Minister of Pakistan to Prime Minister of India, December 31, 1947

Please refer to your demi-official letter dated the 22nd December in which you have brought formal charges against the Pakistan Government for aiding and abetting the so-calleds 'invaders' of Kashmir in their fight against the forces of the Maharaja and of the Indian Dominion.

2. Despite the ominous hint containted in paragraph three, I trust I am right in assuming that your letter is not an "ultimatum" but a fore-runner of a formal reference of the matter to the U.N.O. If so, nothing could be more welcome, for, you will recollect, this is exactly what the Pakistan Government has been suggesting throughout as the most effective method of ironing out our mutual differences. I am, therefore, sincerely glad to find that you propose at last to adopt this particular line of approach to our problems.

3. I must, however, confess my disappointment that your proposal apparently restricts the reference to the single issue of Kashmir. The episode of Kashmir considered by itself would look like a sentence torn out of its context. It is but an act in the unparalleled tragedy which is being enacted before our eyes ever since the announcement of the scheme of partition. A reference to the U.N.O., therefore, in my opinion, must cover much larger ground and embrace all the fundamentals of the differences between the two Dominions. As I see it, it is neither Kashmir alone nor Junagadh and Manavadar, nor even the terrible tragedy of wholesale massacres of Muslim men, women and children in extensive areas of the Indian Dominion, but a totality of these horrors and iniquities, indicating but one consistent sinister pattern, which should rightly form the subject matter of international investigation. If the root causes of the evil, which is vitiating our relations, are not determined and removed, it is much to be feared that fresh incidents will continue to threaten the peace not only between the two Dominions, but in a much wider field.

4. The case of Kashmir is simple and our attitude has been explained frankly and repeatedly both in our communications to you and our official statements to the Press. The Pakistan Government has not accepted and cannot accept the so-called 'accession' of the Jammu and Kashmir State to India. We have said it before and repeat that the 'accession' was fraudulent inasmuch as it was

achieved by deliberatety creating conditions with the object of finding an excuse to stage the 'accession'. It was based on violence because it furthered the plan of the Kashmir Government to liquidate the Muslim population of the State. The accession was against the well-known will of an overwhelming majority of the population and could not be justified on any grounds whether moral or constitutional; geographical or economic; cultural or religious.

5. The sole responsibility for the disturbances which occurred in the State must squarely lie on the Maharaja and his Government who, despite the advice tendered by the Pakistan Government, persisted in their policy of repression of Muslims. Repression was followed by resistance particularly in the area of Poonch which is inhabited by a large number of ex-soldiers. The resistance in its turn was met with more repression till the Dogra savagery, supported by the brutality of Sikh and Rashtriya Sewak Sangh bands, created a reign of terror in the State. This State of affairs naturally aroused strong feelings of sympathy throughout Pakistan, particularly among the Muslims living in the contiguous areas who had numerous ties of relationship with the persecuted people of the State. Some of these people went across to assist their kinsmen in their struggle for freedom and indeed for existence itself. The stage was thus set for the pre-planncd intervention by the forces of the Indian Dominion to quell this spontaneous popular rising against the culmination of the age-long tyranny of the Dogra rule. The repeated warnings of the Pakistan Government went unheeded. The hasty and ill-advised action completely changed the picture and the Frontier tribesmen, a ferociously freedom-loving people, naturally took up the challenge in support of their Kashmir co-religionists fighting for their survival and liberation. If the Government of India had extended to the Pakistan Government the courtesy of consulting it before embarking on its enterprise and suddenly landing troops in Kashmir, or even notifying Pakistan of its proposed action thus providing an opportunity for discussion and consultation, it might have been possible to avert the tragedy of Kashmir. The action of the Government of India served to swell the torrent of popular resentment until it became impossible for the Pakistan Government to stem it without embarking on large-scale military operations.

6. As regards the charges of aid and assistance to the 'invaders' by the Pakistan Government we emphatically repudiate them. On the contrary, and solely with the object of maintaining friendly relations

between the two Dominion, the Pakistan Government have continued to do all in their power to discourage the tribal movement by all means short of war. This caused bitter resentment throughout the country but, despite a very serious risk of large-scale internal disturbances, the Pakistan Government has not deviated from the policy.

In view of this background it would not be surprising if some nationals of Pakistan were taking part in the struggle for the liberation of Kashmir along with the forces of the Azad Kashmir Government. You must have already heard of an international Brigade composed of representatives of many nations in the world who are likewise fighting on the side of the Azad Kashmir Government. In regard to the modern military equipment that you allege to be in the possession of the Azad Kashmir forces, our information is that these force are poorly equipped and such few modern weapons as they might possess, have either been captured from the Dogra and Indian troops or have been in the possession of the ex-soldiers of Poonch since the days of the British. As you know, there are large numbers of Poonchis in the Pakistan Army and if some of them, while on leave in their homes, rendered assistance to their kith and kin in defence of their hearths and homes, it is scarcely to be wondered at.

7. On the contrary, it is the Indian Government which must answer the charge of conspiracy with the Maharaja of Kashmir in repudiation of the very principles on which it had only one month before opposed Junagadh's accession to Pakistan. The plea that the accession is only temporary pending restoration of peaceful conditions is too flimsy to stand examination, particularly in the light of recent negotiations in the course of which a perfectly fair and workable plan of withdrawal of opposing forces followed by a referendum under impartial aegis suggested by us, was turned down by your Government. But all this fits in with the general 'pattern of the Indian Government's political attitude towards Pakistan ever since it became evident that partition was the only possible solution of our constitutional problems.

8. The story begins as early as the middle of 1946 following the demonstration of Muslims throughout the country after the last provincial elections. It became clear that Pakistan was the unalterable goal of the Muslims. The inevitability of the partition of the country, which now became evident to all, gave rise to a wave of

deep resentment among the Hindu and Sikh population of the sub-continent. As a direct result of this severe communal rioting occurred in several towns and Provinces of India such as Calcutta, Noakhali, Bihar, Bombay, Garhmukteshwar, Rawalpindi, Lahore and Amritsar. Such communal strife had not been unknown previously, but what was astonishing was the unprecedented scale of killings that took place in Bihar and Garhmukteshwar proving beyond doubt the existence of a well-settled plan of extermination of the Muslims. It was during these disturbances that the Rashtriya Sewak Sangh came to be known as the author of some of the most brutal massacres. The orgy of blood, however, died down in due course, but, as latter events proved, only temporarily.

9. The political activity which took place in the early part of 1947 produced a lull, but soon after the partition plan was announced on the 3rd June 1947, clear indications began to be received that the country was going to be plunged into a blood bath by the fanatical Sikhs and the militant Hindu groups headed by the Rashtriya Sewak Sangh who had made no secret of their opposition to the partition scheme, in spite of its being accepted by the representatives of all the three major communities.

10. The process of partition itself was marked by all manner of obstructions aimed at depriving Pakistan of its rightful share of financial and other assets. Even in cases is which agreement was reached, the implementation was delayed or sabotaged.

11. At this stage the main chain of events which eventually brought untold suffering to millions of people of East Punjab, Rajputana and the United Provinces was set in motion with carefully prepared attack on a special train carrying Pakistan Government employees and their families from Delhi to Karachi on the 9th August 1947. As the plan unfolded itself, it became clear that the Sikhs, encouraged and actively assisted by the Hindus, had determined to liquidate by violent and bloody means the entire Muslim population of East Punjab. The object of the plan was to kill or drive out Mussalmans in order to settle the Sikh population which was being pulled out of West Punjab under a planned scheme. The *modus operandi* was to disarm the Muslim population and then to leave it at the mercy of armed bands who were actively assisted by the Army and the police. There is abundant evidence that this plan had the full support and active assistance not only of the officers of the Provincial Government, but also of the Sikh States such as

Patiala, Kapurthala and Faridkot. Alwar and Bharatpur had already set the example in elimination their entire Muslim population, but they were soon outdone. Kapurthala, which, like Kashmir, was a Muslim-majority State, has today not a single Muslim left. Similarly large tracts of Muslim majority areas which under the Boundary Award had been most unjustly included in East Punjab were depopulated. The whole country was ravaged by fire and sword; vast numbers were butchered and countless women were abducted. Indeed decency forbids mention of some crimes committed against women. Millions were forcibly and ruthlessly driven out of their homes. The process went on, sector by sector, and culminated in the tragedy that was enacted in Delhi, the Capital of India. According to the Government of India itself there was a complete breakdown of administration for a number of days. The destruction and descreation of mosques, tombs and holy places, and forcible conversions on a mass scale, were special features of these happenings.

12. This plan of liquidation of the Muslim population is still proceeding despite the pious professions of the Government of India. The latest example of this is provided by the happenings in the holy city of Ajmer. The Government of Pakistan find difficult to believe that under the circumstances the Government of India are innocent of all complicity in this vast scheme of 'genocide' started by the Sikhs and Hindus and encouraged and supported by persons in authority as means of destroying the newly created State of Pakistan. The Mussalmans of India are being subjected to calculated insults and humilations. All sorts of tests of loyalty are being demanded from them. The one on which particular emphasis is laid is that they should denounce Pakistan and try to undo the partition and express their readiness to fight Pakistan on the side of India in the event of war between the two Dominions. It is a matter for deep regret that even to-day responsible members of the Government of India, including yourself, openly declare their intention or hope of bringing Pakistan back into the Indian Union, well knowing that this can be done only through conquest by arms. Such an attitude can only mean that the Hindu and Sikh leaders while giving their agreement to the partition plan did so without any intention of permitting its implementation and, further, that India is determined to undo the settlement by all means available at its disposal. In other words Pakistan's very existence is the chief 'causes belli' so far as India is

concerned. It is this impossible position which manifests itself, time and again, in all of India's dealings with Pakistan whether political, economic or financial and unless an effective remedy is found, it is difficult to see how a direct clash can be avoided with the best will in the world.

13. The events which took place following the announcement of the accession of Junagadh and Manavadar States to Pakistan lend further support to the contention of the Pakistan Government that the Government of India intend by all possible means at their disposal to destroy Pakistan.

In accordance with the agreed scheme of partition and the Indian Independence Act, 1947, Indian States were under no compulsion to join either of the two Dominions. Notwithstanding this clear provision, the Government of India by a combination of threats and cajolery forced a number of States into acceding to the Indian Union. The Rulers of Junagadh and Manavadar were similarly threatened with dire consequences but they stood firm and exercised their right of joining Pakistan in preference to India. This was the signal for India to launch with full force her attack, using every possible weapon in order to force the States against their will to change their affiliation. Protests were made to the Pakistan Government, pointing out that a State which had a Hindu-majority population could not accede to Pakistan as the country had been divided on a communal basis. Another reason given was that Junagadh was not physically contiguous to Pakistan and that its accession to Pakistan was calculated to cause disruption in the integrity of India. Simultaneously with these protests, the Government of India put large bodies of Indian troops on the borders of Junagadh and encouraged the neighbouring Hindu States, which had acceded to India, to do likewise. In clear violation of the Standstill Agreement, the Junagadh State was subjected to an economic blockade involving stoppage of all vital supplies, including food, cloth and coal into the State territory. Lines of communication, including railway and telegraph, were operated in such a manner that it became impossible for the State or the Muslim population of Junagadh to communicate with the outside world. A strong Press campaign calculated to destroy the State administration and to create panic among the population was launched both inside and outside the State.

Another line of attack was adopted by setting up the so-called

'Provisional Government' with headquarters first at Bombay and later at Rajkot, which claimed the right to liberate the non-Muslim population of the Junagadh State. The so-called 'Azad Fauj' of the 'Provisional Government' was created and armed by the officers of the Indian Dominion. The 'Provisional Government' not only proceeded to seize by force State property in Rajkot, but by methods of sheer 'gangsterism' created conditions in which it became impossible for the State Administration to function. At this point the Government of India sent its troops and occupied the State under the plea of an alleged 'invitation' by the Dewan. Since then an orgy of murder arson, rape and loot has been let loose in Kathiawar by the military forces of India in exactly the same manner as in Northern India, and hundreds of thousands of Muslims have had to flee from the State. According to newspaper reports, Mr. Samaldas Gandhi, the head of the so-called Provisional Government, has openly thanked a member of your Government for all the assistance received. All this was done in sheer disregard of the international conduct and ordinary neighbourly decency. In the interest of peace between the two Dominions Pakistan refrained from sending a single soldier to Junagadh. Occupation by force of Junagadh, which is Pakistan territory, is a clear act of aggression against Pakistan.

14. In case of Manavadar even the thin camouflage of a semblance of justification was not considered necessary and the State was taken under military occupation without the slightest explanation being given. A similar fate befelt the Talukdari States of Sardargarh, Bantva, Sultanabad and Mangrol. The unfortunate rulers of some of these States have been kept in detentian and have been subjected to considerable pressure to wean them from their affliction to Pakistan.

15. This brief account of India's dealings with a friendly State can leave no doubt in the mind of any impartial person that the new India does not feel herself bound by any moral or international code of rules. The military *coup d'etat* by which the occupation of Junagadh and Manavadar and other State's was achieved, is of one piece with the general scheme of destroying the integrity and the very existence of Pakistan to which reference has been made. We have formally drawn your attention to the various acts of hostility culminating in actual seizure of Pakistan territory by the India Government in Junagadh, but have not received even the courtesy of a reply. Perhaps now that you propose to take the case of Kashmir to the U.N.O., you would be good enough to let us know why, in spite of

our clear request, you have not withdrawn from the territories of Junagadh, Manavadar and Mangrol, etc.?

In this connection it is of interest to note that the arguments advanced by India for refusing to accept the accession of Junagadh to Pakistan have been conveniently and completely ignored in connection with the accession of Kashmir to the Indian Dominion. This again is fully in keeping with the general political attitude of India towards Pakistan.

16. These are not the only examples of aggression against Pakistan territory. Numerous raids by armed bands, assisted by the police and military, have taken place across the border into Pakistan. The Royal Indian Air Force have made repeated attacks on Pakistan territory causing damage to life and property.

17. Another illustration of the same attitude is provided by the refusal of the Indian Government to implement the recent financial agreement of all outstanding cases which had been referred to the Arbitral Tribunal. The India Government is deliberately withholding the payment of Rupees fifty-five crores of the cash balances which is the legal due of the Pakistan Government according to this agreement. This is the latest manifestation of their desire to strangle Pakistan financially and economically which characterised the partition proceedings. In the case of military stores there has been a similar refusal to implement the agreement. The Supreme Commander, who was appointed as a neutral authority under the Joint Defence to carry into effect the partition of the armed forces and military stores, was forced despite the protestations of the Pakistan Government, to leave by your Government long before he could complete his task. At the time this was done the Indian representatives on the Joint Defence Council pledged the word of the India Cabinet that Pakistan would receive her due share of military stores. This pledge, like other similar pledges of the India Government, has not been honoured and the slight trickle of military stores to Pakistan shows signs of stopping altogether.

18. To sum up, our counter-charges against the Dominion of India are as follows:

1. that India has never wholeheartedly accepted the partition scheme, but her leaders paid lip-service to it merely in order to get the British troops out of the country;
2. that India is out to destroy the State of Pakistan which her

leaders persistently continue to regard as part of India itself;

3. that the systematic sabotage against the implementation of partition, the stoppage of such essential requirements as coal and rail transport, the deliberate withholding of Pakistan's share of funds and arms and equipment, and the wholesale massacres of Muslim population are all designed toward one aim, namely, the destruction of Pakistan; and
4. that India's forcible occupation of Junagadh, Manavadar and other States in Kathiawar which had acceded to Pakistan, as well as the fraudulent procurement of the accession of Jammu and Kashmir State, are acts of hostility against Pakistan whose destruction is India's immediate objective.

19. I, however, note with pleasure your assurance that the Government of India have always desired and still earnestly desire to live on terms of friendship with Pakistan. On behalf of the Pakistan Government I fully and sincerely reciprocate this desire. I am constrained, however to observe that the Government of India have at no stage afforded any practical proof of their desire to live on terms of friendship with Pakistan, more particularly in the case of Junagadh and Kashmir. On my side, I can assure you that the earnest desire of the Government of Pakistan to live on terms of friendship with India has, in many instances, restrained the Government of Pakistan from taking action which would not only have been legally justifiable but was in several instances urgently called for and yet was not adopted in the hope that the attitude of the Government of India might, even during these later stages, be more favourably affected towards Pakistan. I find it more and more difficult to persuade myself to continue to entertain that hope. The course of events, very briefly set out above, would normally have been treated as a chain of aggression justifying extreme action on the part of the aggrieved Government. Now that your letter of the 22nd December 1947 has indicated an intention on the part of the Government of India to invite the intervention of the United Nations, a course which the Pakistan Government has so far ineffectively suggested to the Government of India, for the resolving of their differences, I have taken this opportunity to invite your attention to the main heads of the differences between the two Governments that stand in the way of an amicable adjustment of our relations. It is my most earnest

hope that these differences may be speedily composed and that our relations will thereafter ever continue to be on the most cordial, co-operative and friendly basis. I trust you will agree that intervention of the United Nations, whatever from it is to take, should be invited in respect of all these matters, so that all pending differences may be speedily resolved.

5

Matter Goes to the Security Council, 1948 (Correspondence, Discussions and Resolutions)

5.1. Letter* from Representative of India, Concerning the Situation in Jammu and Kashmir, to President of Secutiry Council, January 1, 1948

1. Under Article 35 of the Charter of the United Nations, any member may bring any situation, whose continuance is likely to endanger the maintenance of international peace and security, to the attention of the Security Council. Such a situation now exists between India and Pakistan owing to the aid which invaders, consisting of nationals of Pakistan and of tribesmen from the territory immediately adjoining Pakistan on the North-West, are drawing from Pakistan for operations against Jammu and Kashmir, a State which has acceded to the Dominion of India and is part of India. The circumstances of the accession, the activities of the invaders which led the Government of India to take military action against them, and the assistance which the attackers have received and are still receiving from Pakistan are explained later in this memorandum. The Government of India request the Security Council to call upon Pakistan to put an end immediately to giving of such assistance which is an act of aggression against India. If Pakistan does not do so, the Government of India may be compelled in self-defence, to enter Pakistan territory, in order to take military action against the

* Document No. S/628 in SCOR, 3rd Year Supplement for November 1948, p. 139-144

invaders. The matter is therefore one of extreme urgency and calls for immediate action by the Security Council for avoiding a breach of international peace.

2. From the middle of September, 1947, the Government of India had received reports of infiltration of armed raiders into the western parts of the Jammu Province of the Jammu and Kashmir State; Jammu adjoins West Punjab which is a part of the Dominion of Pakistan. These raiders had done a great deal of damage in that area and taken possession of part of the territory of the State. On the 24th of October, the Government of India heard of a major raid from the Frontier Province of the Dominion of Pakistan into the Valley of Kashmir. Some 2,000 or more fully armed and equipped men came in motor transport, crossed over to the territory of the State of Jammu and Kashmir, sacked the town of Muzaffarabad, killing many people, and proceeded along the Jhelum Valley Road towards Srinagar, the summer capital of the Jammu and Kashmir State. Intermediate towns and villages were sacked and burnt, and many people killed. These raiders were stopped by Kashmir State troops near Uri, a town some 50 miles from Srinagar, for sometime, but the invaders got round them and burnt the power-house at Mahura, which supplies electricity to the whole of Kashmir.

3. The position, on the morning of the 26th of October, was that these raiders had been held by Kashmir State troops and part of the civil population, who had been armed, at a town called Baramula. Beyond Baramula there was no major obstruction up to Srinagar. There was immediate danger of these raiders reaching Srinagar, destroying and sacking the capital and massacring large numbers of people, both Hindus and Muslims. The State troops were spread out all over the State and most of them were deployed along the western border of Jammu Province. They had been split up into small isolated groups and were incapable of offering effective resistance to the raiders. Most of the State officials had left the threatened area and civil administration had ceased to function. All that stood between Srinagar and the fate which had overtaken places on the route followed by the raiders was the determination of the inhabitants of Srinagar, of all communities, practically without arms, to defend themselves. At this time, Srinagar had also a large population of Hindu and Sikh refugees who had fled there from West Punjab, owing to communal disturbances in that area. There was little doubt that the refugees would be massacred if the raiders

reached Srinagar.

4. Immediately after the raids into Jammu and Kashmir State commenced, approaches were informally made to the Government of India for the acceptance of the accession of the State to the Indian Dominion. (It might be explained, in parenthesis, that Jammu and Kashmir form a State whose Ruler, prior to the transfer of power by Britain to the Dominions of India and Pakistan, had been in treaty relations with the British Crown which controlled its foreign relations and was responsible for its defence. The treaty relations ceased with transfer of power on August 15th last, and Jammu and Kashmir, like other States, acquired the right to accede to either Dominon).

5. Events moved with great rapidity and the threat to the Valley of Kashmir became grave. On the 26th of October, the Ruler of the State, His Highness Maharaja Sir Hari Singh, appealed urgently to the Government of India for military help. He also requested that the Jammu and Kashmir State should be allowed to accede to the Indian Dominion. An appeal for help was also simultaneously received by the Government of India from the largest popular organization in Kashmir, the National Conference, headed by Sheikh Abdullah. The Conference further strongly supported the request for the State's accession to the Indian Dominion. The Government of India were, thus, approached not only officially by the State authorities, but also on behalf of the people of Kashmir, both for military aid and for the accession of the State of India.

6. The grave threat to the life and property of innocent people in the Kashmir Valley and the security of the State of Jammu and Kashmir, that had developed as a result of the invasion of the Valley, demanded immediate decisions by the Government of India on both requests. It was imperative, on account of the emergency, that the responsibility for the defence of Jammu and Kashmir State should be taken over by a government capable of discharging it. But, in order to avoid any possible suggestion that India had taken advantage of the State's immediate peril for her own political advantage, the Dominion Government made it clear that, once the soil of the State had been cleared of the invader and normal conditions restored, its people would be free to decide their future by the recognized democratic method of a plebiscite or referendum which, in order to ensure complete impartiality, might be held under internationl auspices.

7. The Government of India felt it their duty to respond to the

appeal for armed resistance because:

(i) They could not allow a neigbouring and friendly State to be compelled by force to determine either its internal affairs or its external relations; and

(ii) The accession of Jammu and Kashmir State to the Dominion of India made India legally responsible for the defence of the State.

8. The intervention of the Government of India resulted in saving Srinagar. The raiders, were driven back from Baramula to Uri and are held there by Indian troops. Nearly 19,000 raiders face the Dominion Forces in this area. Since the operations in the Valley of Kashmir started, pressure by the raiders against the Western and South-western border of the Jammu and Kashmir State has been intensified. Exact figures are not available. It is understood, however, that nearly 15,000 raiders are operating against this part of the State. State troops are beseiged in certain areas. Incursions by the raiders into the State territory involving murder, arson, loot and the abduction of women continues. The booty is meant to further the recruitment of tribesmen to the ranks of the raiders. In additions to those actively participating in the raids, a large number of tribesmen and others, estimated at 100,000 have been collected in different places in the districts of West Punjab bordering the Jammu and Kashmir State and many of them are receiving military training under Pakistan nationals, including officers of the Pakistan Army. They are looked after in Pakistan territory, fed, clothed, armed and otherwise equipped, and transported to the territory of the Jammu and Kashmir State with the help, direct and indirect of Pakistan officials, both military and civil.

9. As already stated, raiders who entered the Kashmir Valley in October came mainly from the tribal areas to the North-west of Pakistan, and, in order to reach Kashmir, passed through Pakistan territory. The raids along the South-west of the State, which had preceded the invasion of the Valley proper, had actually been conducted from Pakistan territory and Pakistan nationals had taken part in them. This process of transit across Pakistan territory and the utilization of that territory as a base of operations against Jammu and Kashmir State continue. Recently, military operations against the Western and South-western borders of the State have been

intensified and the attackers consist of the nationals of Pakistan as well as tribesmen. These invaders are armed with modern weapons, including mortars and medium machineguns, wear the battledress of regular soldiers and, the recent engagements have fought in regular battle-formation and are using the tactics of modern warfare. Man-pack wireless sets are in regular use and even Mark V-mines have been employed. For their transport the invaders have all along used motor vehicles. They are undoubtedly being trained and, to some extent, led by regular officers of the Pakistan Army. Their rations and other supplies are obtained from Pakistan territory.

10. These facts point indisputably to the conclusions:

(a) that the invaders are allowed transit across Pakistan territory;
(b) that they are allowed to use Pakistan territory as a base of operations;
(c) that they include Pakistan nationals;
(d) that they draw much of their military equipment, transport and supplies (including petrol) from Pakistan; and
(e) that Pakistan officers are training, guiding and otherwise actively helping them.

There is no source other than Pakistan from which they could get such quantities of modern military equipment, training and guidance. More than once, the Government of India had asked the Pakistan Government to deny to the invaders facilities which constitute an act of aggression and hostility against India, but without any response. The last occasion on which this request was made was on the 22nd December, when the Prime Minister of India handed-over personally to the Prime Minister of Pakistan a letter in which various forms of aid given by Pakistan to the invaders were briefly recounted and the Government of Pakistan were asked to put an end to such aid promptly and without reserve. No reply to this letter as yet been received, in spite of a telegraphic reminder sent on the 26th.

11. It should be clear from the foregoing recital that the Government of Pakistan are unwilling to stop the assistance in material and men which the invaders are receiving from their territory and from their nationals including Pakistan Government personnel, both military and civil. This attitude is not only unneutral but constitutes active aggression against India, of which the State of

Jammu and Kashmir forms a part.

12. The Government of India have exerted persuasion and exercised patience to bring about a change in the attitude of Pakistan. But they have failed, and are, in consequence, confronted with a situation in which their defence of the Jammu and Kashmir State is hampered and their measures to drive the invaders from the territory of the State are gravely impeded by the support which the raiders derive from Pakistan. The invaders are still on the soil of Jammu and Kashmir, and the inhabitants of the State are exposed to all the atrocities of which a barbarous foe is capable. The presence, in large numbers, of the invaders in those portions of Pakistan territory which adjoin parts of Indian territory other than the Jammu and Kashmiir State is a menance to the rest of India. The Government of India have no option, therefore, but to take more effective military action in order to rid Jammu and Kashmir State of the invader. Indefinite continuance of the present operations prolongs the agony of the people of Jammu and Kashmir, is a drain of India's resources and a constant threat to the maintenance of peace between India and Pakistan.

13. In order that the objective of expelling the invader from Indian territory and preventing him from launching fresh attacks should be quickly achieved, Indian troops would have to enter Pakistan territory; only thus could the invaders be denied the use of bases and cut off from their sources of supplies and reinforcements in Pakistan. Since the aid which the invaders are receiving from Pakistan is an act of aggression against India, the Government of India are entitled, in international law, to send their armed forces across Pakitan territory for dealing effectively with the invaders. However, as such action might involve armed conflict with Pakistan, the Government of India, ever anxious to proceed according to the spirit of the Charter of the United Nations, desire to report the situation to the Security Council in accordance with the Provisions of Article 35 of the Charter. They, therefore, fell justified in requesting the Council to ask the Government of Pakistan:

(i) to prevent Pakistan Government personnel, military and civil, participating in or assisting the invasion of Jammu and Kashmir State;

(ii) to call upon other Pakistan nationals to desist from taking any part in the fighting in Jammu and Kashmir State;

(iii) to deny to the invaders:
   (a) access to and use of its territory for operations against Kashmir;
   (b) military and other supplies; and
   (c) all other kinds of aid that might tend to prolong the present struggle.

14. The Government of India would stress the special urgency of the Security Council taking immediate action on their request. They desire to add that the military operations in the invaded area have, in the past few days, been developing so rapidly that they must, in self-defence, reserve to themselves the freedom to take, at any time when it may become necessary, such military action as, they may consider, the situation requires.

15. The Government of India deeply regret that a serious crisis should have been reached in their relations with Pakistan. Not only is Pakistan a neighbour but, in spite of the recent separation, India and Pakistan have many common ties and common interests. India desires nothing more earnestly than to live with her neighbour State on terms of close and lasting friendship. Peace is to the interest of both States; indeed to the interests of the world. The Government of India's approach to the Security Council is inspired by the sincere hope that; through the prompt action of the Council, peace may be preserved.

P.P. Pillai
Representative of India to the UN

5.2. Cable* from Prime Minister of Pakistan to UN Secretary General, January 3, 1948

The Pakistan Ambassador to the United States of America has informed us that India's case against Pakistan regarding Kashmir has been fixed for the first hearing on January 6th and you have asked him for cabled credentials of our representatives. We have not yet seen India's reference to the Security Council as it was telegraphed on January lst in a cypher which we could not decipher and we had to ask for repetition twice. The text has not yet been deciphered and India has promised to send us a copy by air tomorrow afternoon. In

---

* Document S/629.

the circumstances it is impossible for us to prepare our case and place it before the Security Council by the 6th. We are also proposing to send our Foreign Minister as our chief delegate to present our case before the Security Council. The Foreign Minister has gone to Burma to represent Pakistan in Burma Independence celebrations and returns to Karachi on the 7th of January. We request stay of proceedings to give us reasonable time to prepare our case and to dispatch our delegation. This is clearly necessary for a proper consideration of the case. Meanwhile, we are directing Mr. Hasan Ispahani, our Ambassador in U.S.A., to proceed to New York and to remain in touch with you.

5.3. Reply from UN Secretary-General Trygve LIE to Prime Minister of Pakistan, January 3, 1948

In reply to your Excellency's cable of 3 January, I have the honour to inform you that in accordance with the rules of procedure and a specific request by the Indian Government, the Security Council is meeting on 6th January. Your communication will be put before the Council and your representative, Ambassador Ispahani, may request the necessary delay for preparing your case. Only the Security Council may grant this request.

5.4. Speech of Security Council President F. Van Langenhove (Belgium), January 6, 1948

The agenda includes the examination of the letter, dated Ist January 1948, on the situation in the State of Jammu and Kashmir, addressed by the Indian representative to the President of the Security Council.

The Security Council was convened following the receipt of the communication referred to in our agenda as document S/628. Since the notices were sent out, the Secretary-General has received a telegram from the Government of Pakistan, dated 3rd January, asking for the consideration of this question to be adjourned; this telegram and also the Secretary-General's reply, referring the request to the Security Council, are given in document S/629.

Before embarking on consideration of these several communications I shall read, for the information of the Security Council, the two telegrams which I requested the Secretary-General to send to the Minister of Foreign Affairs of India and to the

Minister for Foreign Affairs of Pakistan on my behalf, (document S/636). These telegrams are identically worded; they read as follows:

"The Security Council is on the point of undertaking the examination of the request submitted to it by India, which invokes Article 35 of the Charter of the United Nations. Prior to such examination, and without prejudice to any decision on the part of the Council, I venture, as President of the Security Council, to address an urgent appeal to each of the two States which appear to be most closely concerned in the matter to refrain from any step incompatible with the Charter and liable to result in an aggravation of the situation, thereby rendering more difficult any action by the Security Council.

"I am addressing the same communication to the Minister of Foreign Affairs of Pakistan [India].

"I have the honour to be, etc."

The two documents (S/628 and S/629) seem to me to require decisions by the Security Council on the following points:

1. Should India and Pakistan be allowed to participate, in accordance with Article 31 of the Charter, in the discussion of the case submitted to the Security Council by the Government of India?
2. Should the Council grant the Pakistan Government's request to stay proceedings to enable it to prepare its case and give its delegation time to arrive?

I propose that the Council take a decision on each of the two points I have mentioned.

In the first place, are there any objections to India and Pakistan being allowed, under Article 31 of the Charter, to take part without voting in the discussion of the question brought before the Council by the Government of India?

If there is no objection I shall assume that the Council agrees to invite these two States to participate in the discussion.

I now come to the second point: should the Council approve the postponment requested by the Pakistan Governmant?

This raises a preliminary question: does the Council consider it necessary to invite the Indian and Pakistani representatives to participate in the consideration of this request for a postponement?

I think I am justified in saying that the presence of these two representatives would enable us to ask the Pakistan representative to specify the extent of the postponement requested by his Government and would, moreover, give the Indian representative an opportunity to state the views of his Government on this subject.

Are there any objections to the representatives of India and Pakistan being asked to take their places at the Council table at once?

As there is no objection, I assume the Council agrees.

The Secretary-General has prepared a report concerning the credentials of Mr. M.C. Setalvad, Representative of the Government of India, and, in event of his being absent, of Mr. P.P. Pillai.

The Secretary-General has also prepared a report on the credentials of Sir Mohammed Zafrullah Khan, the Minister for Foreign Affairs of Pakistan, and, in the event of his being absent of Mr. M.A. Hasan Ispahani.

These two reports (documents S/631 and S/633 have been circulated. I presume that they evoke no objections.

I shall now ask the representatives of India and Pakistan to take their places at the Council table.

5.5. First Resolution Adopted* at 229th Meeting of Security Council, January 17, 1948

The Security Council

Having heard statements on the situation in Kashmir from representatives of the Governments of India and Pakistan.

Recognizing the urgency of the situation,

Taking note of the telegram addressed on 6th January 1948 by its President to each of the parties and of their replies thereto, in which they affirmed their intention to conform to the Charter of the United Nations.

1. *Calls upon* both the Government of India and the Government of Pakistan to take immediately all measures within their power (including public appeals to their people) calculated to improve the situation, and to refrain from making any statements and from doing or causing to be done or permitting any acts which might aggravate the situation;

---

*Adopted by 9 votes to none, with 2 abstentions (Ukrainian Soviet Socialist Republic, Union of Soviet Socialist Republics) Res. 38 (1948); UN Document No. S/651.

2. *Further requests* each of those Governments to inform the ouncil immediately of any material change in the situation which curs or appears to either of them to be about to occur while the atter is under consideration by the Council, and consult with the ouncil thereon.

ecision

t its 229th meeting, on 17th January 1948, the Council decided that e President should invite the representatives of India and Pakistan take part in direct talks under his guidance in an effort to find me common ground on which the structure of a settlement might built.

5.6. Draft Resolution* Submitted by the Representative of Belgium in the Security Council for its 230th Meeting, January 20, 1948

he Security Council,

onsidering that it may investigate any dispute or any situation which ight, by its continuance, endanger the maintenance of international eace and security: that, in the existing state of affairs between India nd Pakistan, such an investigation is a matter of urgency.

dopts the following Resolution:

(A) A Commission of the Security Council is hereby established, omposed of representatives of three Members of the United ations, one to be selected by India, one to be selected by Pakistan, nd the third to be designated by the two so selected.

"Each representative on the Commission shall be entitled to elect his alternates and assistants.

(B) The Commission shall proceed to the spot as quickly as ossible. It shall act under the authority of the Security Council and accordance with the directions it may receive from it. It shall keep e Security Council currently informed of its activities and of the evelopment of the situation. It shall report to the Security Council egularly, submitting its conclusions and proposals.

UN Document No. S/654

(C) The Commission is invested with a dual function:

1. To investigate the facts pursuant to Article 34 of the Chart of the United Nations;
2. To exercise, without interrupting the work of the Securi Council, any mediatory influence likely to smooth aw difficulties, to carry out the directions given to it by th Security Council; and to report how far the advice an directions, if any, of the Security Council have been carrie out.

(D) The Commission shall perform the functions described i Clause C:

1. In regard to the situation in the Jammu and Kashmir Sta set out in the letter of the representative of India addresse to the President of the Security Council, dated 1 Janua 1948, and the letter from the Minister of Foreign Affairs Pakistan addressed to the Secretary-General, dated 15t January 1948; and
2. In regard to other situations set out in the letter from th Minister of Foreign Affairs of Pakistan addressed to th Secretary-General, dated 15th January 1948, when th Security Conncil so directs.

(E) The Commission shall take its decision by majority vote. shall determine its own procedure. It may allocate among i members, alternate members, their assistants, and its personnel suc duties as may have to be fulfilled for the realization of its mission an the reaching of its conclusions.

(F) The Commission, its members, alternate members, the assistants and its personnel shall be entitled to journey, separately together, wherever the necessities of their tasks may require, and, i particular, within those territories which are the theatre of the even of which the Security Council is seized.

(G) The Secretary-General of the United Nations shall furnis the Commission with such personnel and assistance as it ma consider necessary.

In the interests of orderty discussion I think it would be well fo the moment to keep the debate as far as possible within th framework of the draft resolution.

Finally, may I pay tribute to the co-operative and helpful spirit of both parties. I am sure that the Council, for its part, will be eager to show the same readiness.

5.7. Speech* on Draft Resolution in Security Council Meeting by N. Gopalaswami Ayyangar, Representative of India, January 20, 1948

I wish to submit that whether or not we retain the words "on the Jammu and Kashmir question" in the heading of this draft resolution, the resolution can relate only to the Jammu and Kashmir question. I thought that was clearly understood. The item on the agenda which we are now considering is headed "The Jammu and Kashmir question". In the course of the discussions we have had with the President of the Security Council during the last two days, we did consider the question of widening the scope of the functions of this commission. The representative of Pakistan was in favour of including matters which did not relate to the Jammu and Kashmir question. After a good deal of argument and discussion, it was decided that while the Commission was being appointed primarily for the Jammu and Kashmir question, if, later on, the counter complaint of Pakistan was brought on the agenda of the Security Council and, after discussion, it was decided that any matters in that complaint also required investigation, it would then be appropriate to refer such questions to the same Commission. With a view to arriving at an agreed arrangement, we decided to insert Clause D of this draft resolution.

Clause (D) says:

"D. The Commission shall perform the functions described in Clause C:

"1. In regard to the situation in the Jammu and Kashmir State set out in the letter of the representative of India addressed to the President of the Security Council, dated 1 January 1948, and in the letter from the Minister of Foreign Affairs of Pakistan addressed to the Secretary-General, dated 15th January 1948; and

* SCOR, 3rd Year, Mtg. no. 230, p. 135-136.

> "2. In regard to other situations set out in the letter from the Minister of Foreign Affairs of Pakistan addressed to the Secretary-General, dated 15th January 1948, when the Security Council so directs."

Those matters can relate only to Jammu and Kashmir. We conceded that if, later on, the Security Council came to the conclusion that other matters in the counter-complaint—which is not yet on agenda of the Security Council—had to be referred to a Commission at all, we should have no objection to their being referred to this same Commission.

In so far as the draft resolution is concerned, the Security Council can pass this resolution only with regard to the item entered on the agenda. But I particularly wish to stress the fact that we attach the greatest importance to the urgeney and the immediacy of dealing with the situation in Kashmir. Our first efforts should be directed toward the Commission's taking such steps as may be necessary to resolve this particular dispute and to bring about the stoppage of fighting there. If in the coure of such investigations, the Security Council should become seized of the other matter and should also, come to the conclusion that any items connected with that matter require investigation, then the Security Council can certainly give a directive to this Commission, and the Commission can consider the matter.

Personally, I think the heading as entered in the draft resolution before us is correct, but as the President has ruled that those words "on the Jammu and Kashmir question" should be omitted from the heading, I have no objection. But it makes no difference at all with regard to the substance of what we are really contending-this resolution can relate only to the item that is now on the agenda.

The main contention is whether we are investing this Commission today with jurisdiction to deal not only with matters connected with the Jammu and Kashmir situation but also with matters outside that situation which have been brought to the notice of the Security Council by Pakistan. Those matters have been brought to the Security Council's attention in Document II, which was attached to the letter of my friend, Sir Mohammed Zafrullah Khan, addressed to the Security Council (Document S/646), and which requested that Document II be placed before the Security Council.

It is true that Document II has been received by the Security Council, but I do not think that document II has yet been placed before the Security Council for its consideration.

In the first place, we have yet to state our case on the matters referred to in Document II. I may mention to the Security Council, for its information, that Document II covers such wide ground that our case pertaining to those matters will take a little time to be presented to the Security Council.

In the second place, although Document II was included amongst those which were sent as enclosures to the Pakistan Foreign Minister's letter, the spokesman for Pakistan before the Security Council confined himself to the Jammu and Kashmir issue in the two speeches that he delivered before this body (228th and 229th meetings). We also have confined ourselves in our statement only to the Jammu and Kashmir issue. It is necessary that issue should be dealt with quickly and promptly and put out of the way as soon as possible.

In the third place, let me mention that on a very cursory reading of Document II, which I have already referred to, I am in a position to state that several matters mentioned in that Document are no longer disputes between India and Pakistan. There are other matters with which, by friendly negotiations between the two Dominions, we are already dealing outside the Security Council.

In the fourth place, it seems to me that there is hardly any matter mentioned in Document II which is likely to endanger international peace and security. Other opinions may be expressed on that particular point, but that will be one of the contentions which we may have to raise on that counter-complaint.

I mention these facts in order to show that the Security Council is not in a position today to state whether any of the matters referred to in Document II could be made the subject of an inquiry by a commission, or whether it will be necessary for the Security Council to proceed with an inquiry into such matters.

We hope to be able to convince the Security Council, once we have dealt with the Kashmir question, there will probably not be anything of substance which will divide India and Pakistan to the extent of endangering international peace and security. From the facts, as we look upon them, it seems to me that it will not be right for us to say that this Commission will necessarily deal with such matters which are not now before the Security Council. Whether such matters have to go to a Commission at all will have to be decided later on.

However, we have conceded that, if the Security Council should reach a decision that any of those matters should be referred to a Commission, this particular Commission may deal with them. That is the agreement at which we have arrived. Therefore, it is not possible for us to agree to the position that we are now setting up a mere instrument of the Security Council for the purpose of dealing with whatever matters the Security Council may choose to refer to that Commission. We first set up a Commission for the purpose of dealing with the Jammu and Kashmir issue. We agree that, if the Security Council later comes to the conclusion that other matters should be referred to a Commission, that Commission may deal with those matters. That is the position on which India necessarily has to stand at this stage.

5.8. Speech* on Draft Resolution in Security Council Meeting by Sir Mohammed Zafrullah Khan, Representative of Pakistan, January 20, 1948

With reference to what was said by the Representative of India, it is well known, of course, as must be the case under the circumstance, that the resolution represents a compromise between the parties. The original paint I raised was merely that the language in the title of the resolution should run in accordance with that compromise. The representative of India has chosen to put his own gloss upon the language of the resolution, whereas all the President's efforts were directed towards making sure that the language of the resolution should represent what had been agreed upon. I regret that any gloss should have been necessary, and that makes it necessary for me to make one or two observations with regard to that aspect of the case.

It is true that it was insisted on the one side that the language of the resolution should have reference only to the Jammu and Kashmir matter. It was equally insisted on the other side that the resolution, in scope, should embrace all the matters that were disturbing the friendly relations between the two States, and which had been brought to the notice of the Security Council, and of which the Security Council is now seized, irrespective of the fact that discussion

* SCOR, 3rd Year, Mtg. no. 230, p. 133-135

was proceeding at the moment only with regard to one of them.

When too much insistence was laid on the Indian side on the fact that the discussion had not yet reached the other items, it will be re-called that we then suggested that our conversations should be postponed until, in due course, the Security Council had reached the discussion of the other matter also.

It was then pointed out that it would save time if, in the meantime – and before the Security Council could arrive at decisions with regard to any of these matters, whether those decisions are based upon an agreement between the parties or whether those decisions are decisions of the Security Council – the period that would elapse would be utilized in agreeing upon the personnel of the Commission and getting the Commission together, so that when the decision or decisions would be arrived at, the instrument would be ready, on the spot, if possible, to carry out those decisions.

When that stage was reached, after two or three attempts at drafting with regard to how that agreement should be expressed, the final draft was adopted. Clause D, therefore, represents the actual situation that the Kashmir matter being under discussion, the Commission would perform its functions with reference to that, and would go on to perform its functions with regard to the other matters when so directed by the Security Council.

Though we have here a machinery now agreed upon to carry into effect the directions that may be given to it by the Security Council, our main task still remains, and I desire to express the hope that whether by way of consultations between the parties under the leadership and guidance of the President, or by way of discussion of the matter before the Security Council, the question of a settlement – at least the principles upon which the working out of the settlement should be based – is the first question to which attention must be directed.

As will be seen from Clause C of the resolution, which defines the functions of the Commission, its functions are "to investigate the facts pursuant to Article 34 of the Charter"; that is to say, where a situation exists which "is likely to endanger the maintenance of international peace and security". That, we were told, is technically necessary, but is obvious in any case from the disputes which have been brought to the notice of the Security Council. The Commission is also invested with the function of exercising, "without interrupting the work of the Security Council, any mediatory influence likely to smooth away difficulties..." But its main function will be "...to carry out the directions given to it by the Security Council; and to report how far the advice and directions, if any, of the Security Council, have been carried out". That function still remains with the Security Council.

The machinery will be there, but the machinery will not come to life until the Security Council has arrived at some sort of decision with regard to the principle upon which the settlement is to be based, though it may be left to the Commission to carry it into effect or to settle its details, to make proposals back with regard to any of the details that might stand in need of clarification, and so on.

That is the only submission I would make at this time.

5.9. Second Resolution* Adopted at 230th Meeting of Security Council, January 20, 1948

The Security Council,

Considering that it may investigate any dispute or any situation which might, by its continuance, endanger the maintenance of international peace and security and that, in the existing state of affairs between India and Pakistan, such an investigation is a matter of urgency.

Adopts the following resolution:

(A) A Commission of the Security Council is hereby established, composed of representatives of three Members of the United Nations, one to be selected by India, one to be selected by Pakistan, and the third to be designated by the two so selected. Each representative on the Commission shall be entitled to select his alternates and assistants.

(B) The Commission shall proceed to the spot as quickly as possible. It shall act under the authority of the Security Council and in accordance with the directions it may receive from it. It shall keep the Security Council currently informed of its activities and of the development of the situation. It shall report to the Security Council regularly, submitting its conclusions and proposals.

* Adopted by 9 votes to none, with 2 abstentions (Ukrainian Soviet Socialist Republic, Union of Soviet Socialist Republics). Res. 39 (1948); Document No. 654

(C) The Commission is invested with a dual function: (1) to investigate the facts pursuant to Article 34 of the Charter of the United Nations; (2) to exercise, without interrupting the work of the Security Council, any mediatory influence likely to smooth away difficulties; to carry out the directions given to it by the Security Council; and to report how far the advice and directions, if any, of the Security Council have been carried out.

(D) The Commission shall perform the functions described in clause C: (l) in regard to the situation in the Jammu and Kashmir State set out in the letter of the representative of India addressed to the President of the Security Council, dated 1 January 1948, and in the letter from the Minister of Foreign Affairs of Pakistan addressed to the Secretary-General, dated 15th January 1948; and (2) in regard to other situations set out in the letter from the Minister of Foreign Affairs of Pakistan addressed to the Secretary-General, dated 15th January 1948, when the Security Council so directs.

(E) The Commission shall take its decision by majority vote. It shall determine its own procedure. It may allocate among its members, alternate members, their assistants, and its personnel such duties as may have to be fulfilled for the realization of its mission and the reaching of its conclusions.

(F) The Commission, its members, alternate members, their assistants, and its personnel shall be entitled to journey, separately or together, wherever the necessities of their tasks may require, and, in particular, within those territories which are the theatre of the events of which the Security Council is seized.

(G) The Security-General shall furnish the Commission with such personnel and assistance as it may consider necessary.

5.10. Letter from Sheikh Mohammed Abdullah to Home Minister of Government of India, January 31, 1948 (Excerpts)

There is an alternative possible for me and that is to withdraw the accession and that may kill the reference to the UNO because Indian Union will have no right to continue the proceedings before the Council if the Accession is withdrawn. The result may be a return to the position the State held before the Accession.

5.11. Letter from Maharaja Hari Singh to Sardar Patel, Home Minister of Government of India, January 31, 1948

The military situation as you know has been quite depressing since the arrival of the Indian troops. Except the first gains in the Kashmir Valley here has been a debt balance throughout so far as achievements are concerned.

The Indian troops arrived in the Valley on 27th October, at that time we were in possession of about 3/4th of Poonch and the whole of the Mirpur district. We had by then lost only small bits of Poonch and Muzaffarabad district. After the recapture of Baramulla and Uri, there has been a standstill. Two months have passed and the Indian troops are still at Uri. They attempted to venture to the town of Poonch and though they reached it, it was at a great cost and the road was eventually lost. In the Poonch Jagir, which was held by the State troops inch by inch, we had to withdraw and eventually lost the whole of the Jagir except the town itself, where about 40,000 people are besieged alongwith 4 battalions (3 State and 1 Indian). The situation is by no means satisfactory. I may mention that in the August disturbances, with two battalions of the State troops we cleared the whole of Poonch Jagir, peace was restored, the whole of the revenue was realised and the administration was functioning normally. It was only in the second week of October that trouble again began in Poonch and our troops resisted it till about the end of December. But as no help was given, they had eventually to fall back on Poonch town...

In Mirpur district, at the time when the Indian forces arrived, we are still holding Mangla and our territory along the Jehlum Canal bank, but during the past two months we have lost Mangla, Alibeg, Gurdwara, and the town of Mirpur, the town of Bhimber and the villages of Deva and Battala, the town of Rajouri and the whole of the area adjoining Chhamb, Naoshera. Jhangar, a key-place both for Mirpur and Kotli, was lost after a defeat. These defeats have been a heavy blow for us and have also undermined the prestige of the Indian forces. Not a single town has so far been recovered by the Indian troops. The people judge an army from results and not from propaganda carried on about it. On the Kathua-Sialkot border attacks have been intensified. Everyday there is one raid after another. A number of villages have been burnt, people have been looted, women abducted and there have been killings also. The result has been that all the border villages has been vacated and we have about 70,000 to 80,000 refugees in the city of Jammu. Crops, houses and valuables have been lost. Most of the people are also vacating Jammu and its suburbs and are going to West Punjab. The situation, therefore, is worsening everyday.

The name of the Indian Army is getting into the mud in spite of its brilliant record. I was a member of the War Cabinet. I travelled in war zones during the Great war. The name of the Indian Army was at its highest pitch and it pains me to see that the name of the Indian Army has become a topic of every tongue during these days and it is daily losing prestige. Some people think that it is not the fault of the Army but the fault of the policy that is being followed; others feel that it is the fault of the commanders who are quite new to the job. People who would have had to wait for 10 to 15 years to become generals have been put in charge of operations. Opinions differ, but the fact is that the name of the Army is in the mud. Sardar Baldev Singh was here for a day. He has heard from our politicians, members of the public and from me and my Prime Minister all that everyone had to say. He told me secretly that he had ordered certain actions to be taken. I told him that a mere order is nothing unless it is implemented. When you kindly spent two days with us here, a number of decisions were taken and you gave instructions in certain matters. Since your departure nothing has been done and, as I have said, we had more serious attacks. The effort on the part of Pakistan is gaining ground everyday. Their morale owing to success is going up. They loot property, they take away cattle and women and when they go back to Pakistan, they incite people and tell them how much loot and what benefits there are to raid our territory. On the other hand, our morale is rapidly going down. So far the people are concerned, they are thoroughly demoralised and they start fleeing as soon as there is even a rumour of a raid. Even people living at distant places start fleeing when they see fire five or six miles from their villages. So far as the Indian forces are concerned, they do not leave their apportioned places to meet the raiders. There are no mobile columns to meet them. The work is felt to a few Home Guards or to a platoon or so of very tired State forces. How can it be possible for them to engage 500 or 1,000 raiders? Last time you ordered guerrillas to come into the State and take over this work. As far as I know, no guerrillas have arrived so far . . .

In the situation, therefore, my position as Ruler has become very anamolous and one of great perplexity. People in the State continue sending me telegrams and asking for help. Our civil administration is in the hands of the National Conference and military operations in the hands of the Indian Union. I have no voice or power either on the civil or military side. The State forces are under the Indian Army Commander. The result, therefore, is that I have just to watch the terrible situation in a helpless manner, to look on at the abduction of women, killing and loss of my people, without power to give them any redress whatever. People continue to approach me everyday and they still think that it lies in my power to give them relief and redress. You will realise that my position is getting most awkward every day, so long as the military situation is adverse to us and refugees continue pouring in the city and daily raiders from Pakistan keep on coming without any reply from us.

Apart from the military situation, the reference to the UNO and the proceedings that are hanging fire there are causing great uncertainty and perplexity not only to me but to every Hindu and Sikh in the State as well as to those who belong to the National Conference. The feeling is strongly gaining ground that the UN Security Council will take an adverse decision and that the State will eventually have to accede to Pakistan as a result of what the Security Council will decide. The Hindus and Sikhs have, therefore, started going away from the State, as they anticipate that the result of the UNO decision will be the same as what happened in West Punjab and therefore it is much better to clear out of the State before that eventuality arises. The National Conference leaders also feel that they may eventually be let down by accepting the decision of the Security Council and that would be disastrous for them.

My position in this matter is also precarious. You know I definitely acceded to the Indian Union with the idea that the Union will not let us down and the State would remain acceded to the Union and my position and that of my dynasty would remain secure. It was for this reason that I accepted the advice of the Indian Union in the matter of internal administration. If we have to go to Pakistan, it was wholly unnecessary to accede to India or to mould the internal administration according to the desire of the Indian Union. I feet that the internal administration or the question of accession is wholly foreign to the jurisdiction of the Security Council. The Indian Union only referred a limited question to the Security Council, but the whole issue has been enlarged and not only the matter of aggression by one Dominion over the other is being considered by the Security Council but internal questions of the formation of the Interim Government and the matter of accession have all been taken notice of by them. It was a wrong step in going to Security Council and then agreeing to the enlargement of the agenda before that Council. As soon as the Council enlarged the agenda, the Indian Union should have withdrawn the reference and ended the matter.

In the situation described above, a feeling comes to my mind as to the possible steps that I may take to make, so far as I am concerned, a clean state of the situation. Sometime I feel that I should withdraw the accession that I have made to the Indian Union. The Union provisionally accepted the accession and if the Union cannot recover back our territory and is going eventually to agree to the decision of the Security Council which would result in handing us over to Pakistan, then there is no point in sticking to the accession of the State to the Indian Union. For the time being, it may be possible to have better terms from Pakistan, but that is immaterial, because eventually it would mean an end of the dynasty and end of the Hindus and Sikhs in the State. There is an alternative possible for me and that is to withdraw the accession and that may kill the reference to the UNO, because the Indian Union will have no right to continue the proceedings before the Council, if the accession is withdrawn. The result may be return to the position the State held before the accession. The difficulty in that situation, however, will be that the Indian troops ...have to work as volunteers to help the State. I am prepared to takeover command of my own forces along with the forces of the Indian Army personally to help the State. I am prepared to lead the Army personally and to command, if the Indian Union agrees, also their troops. I know my country much better than any of your generals will know it even during the next several months or years and I am prepared to take the venture boldly rather than merely keep on sitting here doing nothing. It is for you to consider whether the Indian Union will accept this in both the situations, whether after the withdrawal of the accession or even if the accession continues. I am tired of my present life and it is much better to die fighting than watch helplessly the heartbreaking misery of my people.

Another alternative that strikes me is that if I can do nothing, I should leave the State (short of abdication) and reside outside so that people do not think that I can do anything for them. For their grievances they can hold the civil administration responsible or the

Indian forces who are in charge of the defence of the State. The responsibility will then clearly be either of the Indian Union or of the administration of Sheikh Abdullah. If there is any criticism, those responsible can have it and the responsibility for the suffering of the people will not be mine. Of course, I well anticipate that, as people started saying when I left Kashmir only on Mr. Menon's advice, that I had run away from Srinagar, they will say that I have left them in their hour of misery, but it is no use remaining in a position where one can do nothing merely to avoid criticism. Of course, if I go out of the State, I will have to take the public into confidence and tell them the reasons why I am going out.

The third alternative in the situation that has arisen is that the Indian Dominion discharges its duty on the military side effectively and makes an all-out effort to stop the raids from Pakistan and to drive out of the State not only the raiders but also all rebels. This can only be done if the Dominion really fights. It has avoided fighting so far. Two or three courageous battles will more or less end this situation, and, if it is delayed, there is bound to be a catastrophe. Pakistan is more organised against Kashmir than the Indian Dominion, and as soon as snow melts it will start attacking Kashmir on all sides and the province of Ladakh will also come into the hands of the enemy and the Valley and the whole border will be raided and even double the number of troops at present in Jammu and Kashmir will not be able to save the situation. What should have been done and achieved a month before can still be achieved during the next month, but if matters are delayed and if owing to the UNO reference and the attitude of compromise, the situation remains at a standstill, it would become terribly grave after the expiry of the month. Therefore, unless the Indian Union makes up its mind to fight fully and effectively, I may have to decide upon the two alternatives mentioned above.

5.12. Reply from Sardar Patel to Maharaja Hari Singh, his letter of January 31, 1948, February 9, 1948

I fully realise what an anxious time you must be having. I can assure you that I am no less anxious about the Kashmir situation and what is happening in the UNO, but whatever the present situation may be, counsel of despair is entirely out of place.

5.13. Speech by Sheikh Mohammed Abdullah (India) in Security Council, 241st Meeting, February 5, 1948

I have heard with patience, attention and respect the statements made by the representative of Pakistan and members of the Security Council, as well as the statements made on various occasions by the members of my own delegation. The Security Council will concede that I am probably the one man most concerned in this dispute because I happen to come from that land which has become the bone of contention between the two Dominions of India and Pakistan.

I have been quoted profusely on either side, and rightly so, because I have had the fortune—or, should I say, misfortune— of leading my countrymen to freedom from 1931 onwards. In this task, I have suffered a great deal. I have been imprisoned not once or twice, but seven times, and the last imprisonment carried with it an aggregate sentence of nine years.

There are many troubles in Kashmir. I have heard patiently to the debate in the Security Council, but I feel that I am rather confused. After all, what is the point in dispute? The point in dispute is not that the sovereignty of the Prince is in question, as the representative of Pakistan stated yesterday. After all, I have suffered the punishment of being sentenced to nine years' imprisonment for saying what the representative of Pakistan said with regard to the Treaty of Kashmir of 1846. I am glad that he said it in the Security Council, where he is immune from any punishment. Therefore, I am not disputing that point, and that it is not the subject of the dispute before the Security Council.

The subject of the dispute before the Security Council is not the maladministration of the Princely State of Kashmir. In order to set right that maladministration, I think I have suffered the most, and today, when, for the first time, I heard the representative of Pakistan supporting my case, it gave me great pleasure.

After all, what is the dispute between India and Pakistan? From what I have learned from the complaint brought before the Security Council by my own delegation, the dispute revolves around the fact that Kashmir acceded legally and constitutionally to the Dominion of India. There was some trouble about the democratization of the Kashmir administration within the State, and the tribesmen from across the border have poured into my country. They have been helped and are being helped by the Pakistan Government, with the result that there is the possibility of a greater conflagration between India and Pakistan. India sought the help of the Security Council so that Pakistan might be requested to desist from helping the tribesmen, and to desist from supporting the inside revolt, should I say, against the lawful authority.

I should have understood the position of the representative of Pakistan if he had come boldly before the Security Council and maintained: "Yes, we do support the tribesmen; we do support the rebels inside the State because we feel that Kashmir belongs to Pakistan and not to India, and because we feel that the accession of Kashmir to India was fraudulent." Then we might have discussed the validity of the accession of the State of Kashmir to India. But that was not the position taken by the representative of Pakistan. He completely denied that any support was being given by the Government of Pakistan to either the tribesmen or those who are in revolt within the State against the constituted authority.

How am I to convince the Security Council that the denial is absolutely untrue? I am sitting before the Security Council at a distance of thousands of miles from my country. I have fought many battles, along with my own men, on the borders of Jammu and Kashmir; I have seen with my own eyes the support given by the Pakistan Government, not only in supplying bases but in providing arms, ammunition, direction and control of the tribesmen and I have even seen the Pakistan Army forces from across the border.

The denial has come so flatly that it becomes very difficult for me to disprove it here before the Security Council, unless the Security Council accedes to our request to send a Commission to the spot and to find out first whether the allegations brought before the Security Council with regard to the aid given by the Government of Pakistan are correct or incorrect. If they are incorrect, the case falls; if they are correct, then the Security Council should take the necessary steps to advise the Government of Pakistan to desist from such support.

But then, this simple issue has been confused. On the one hand, the Pakistan Government says: "We are not a party to the trouble within the State. The trouble within the State exists because the people are fighting against the maladministration of the Jammu and Kashmir Government." Yes, we are fighting. We have been fighting against the maladministration of that State since 1931; we have been demanding democratization of the Government there. But how is it that today Pakistan has become the champion of our liberty? I know very well that in 1946, when I raised the cry of "Quit Kashmir," the leader of the Pakistan Government, who is the Governor-General now, Mr. Mohammed Ali Jinnah, opposed my movement, declaring that this movement was a movement of a few renegades and that Muslims as such had nothing to do with the movement.

The Muslim Conference, which has been talked about so much, opposed my movement and declared its loyalty to the Prince. The representative of Pakistan now says that Sheikh Abdullah, once the supporter of "Quit Kashmir," has joined hands with the Maharaja of Kashmir, and that in one of my public speeches I declared that I wanted the Maharaja to be the Maharaja of Jammu and Kashmir – not the Maharaja of Jammu only, but the Maharaja of the entire State.

I should like to correct the misreporting of my speech. I did deliver that speech in Jammu, which is the winter capital of our country, but it was in a different context. As the members of the Security Council have already heard from the head of my delegation, some massacres did occur in the Jammu Province. After the Kashmir Province was raided by the tribesmen, and after thousands of Hindus and Sikhs were uprooted from the villages and towns in the Kashmir Province and found their way into the Jammu Province, there was some very bad retaliation. I could not go to Jammu Province to control that situation, because I was busy with the raiders in Kashmir Province. However, as soon as I had some time, I flew down to Jammu Province, addressed a gathering of 60,000 Hindus and Sikhs in Jammu City, and gave them some plain advice.

I told them clearly that this policy of retaliation would bring no good to them as Hindus and Sikhs and would bring no good to their leader, because while they could retaliate in one or two districts where they formed the majority, and could even wipe out the Muslim population in these one or two districts, the State happens to have a population which is 80 per cent Muslim, and it would be impossible for them to wipe out the entire Muslim population. The result would be that the Prince, whom they wanted to support, would remain the Prince of only two districts, and not of the entire State of Jammu and Kashmir. I told them that, if they wanted him to be Prince of Jammu and Kashmir, they would have to change their behaviour. That was the speech I delivered, and that was the context in which it was made.

However, I have already stated how this trouble started. It is probable that the representative of Pakistan would admit that, when India was divided into two parts, my colleagues and I were all behind prison bars. The result of this division of India was start of massacres on either side. Where Muslims in West Punjab formed the majority, the killing of Hindus and Sikhs started, and this was retaliated in East Punjab: All along our border, massacres of Hindus and Sikhs, on the one hand, and Muslims, on the other hand, were a daily occurrence. But the State of Jammu and Kashmir, and its people, kept calm. The result was that thousands of refugees, both Muslims and Hindus, sought refuge in our State and we rendered every possible help to all of them.

Why was that so? It was because I and my organization never believed in the formula that Muslims and Hindus form separate nations. We do not believe in the two-nation theory, nor in communal hatred or communalism itself. We believed that religion had no place in politics. Therefore, when we launched our movement of "Quit Kashmir" it was not only Muslims who suffered, but our Hindu and Sikh comrades as well. That created a strong bond of unity between all the communities, and the result was that while Hindus, Sikhs and Muslims were fighting each other all along the border, the people of Jammu and Kashmir State – Muslims, Hindus and Sikhs alike – remained calm.

The situation was worsening day by day and the minority in our State was feeling very nervous. As a result, tremendous pressure was brought to bear upon the State administration to release me and my colleagues. The situation outside demanded the release of workers of the National Conference, along with its leader, and we were accordingly set free.

Immediately we were liberated from prison we were faced with the important question of whether Kashmir should accede to Pakistan, accede to India, or remain independent, because under the partition scheme these three choices were open to us as, indeed, they were open to every Indian State. The problem was a very difficult one, but I advised the people of my country that although the question was very important to us, it was a secondary consideration. The all-important matter for us was our own liberation from the autocratic role of the Prince, for which we were fighting and had been fighting for the past seventeen years. We had not achieved that goal, and therefore I told my people that we must do so first. Then, as free men we should have to decide where our interests lay. Being a frontier State, Kashmir has borders with both Pakistan and India, and there are advantages and disadvantages for the people of Kashmir attached to each of the three alternatives to which I have referred.

Naturally, as I have indicated, we could not decide this all-important issue before achieving our own liberation, and our slogan became "Freedom before accession." Some friends from Pakistan met me in Srinagar. I have a heart-to-heart discussion with them and explained my point of view. I told them in plain words that, whatever had been the attitude of Pakistan towards our freedom movement in the past, it would not influence us in our judgement. Neither the friendship of Pandit Jawaharlal Nehru and of Congress, nor their support of our freedom movement, would have any influence upon our decision if we felt that the interests of our million Kashmiris lay in our accession to Pakistan.

I requested them not to precipitate this decision upon us but to allow us time, supporting our freedom movement for the while. I added that once we were free they should allow us an interval to consider this all-important issue. I pointed out that India had accepted this point of view and was not forcing us to decide. We had, in fact, entered into a Standstill Agreement with both Pakistan and India, but the leader of the Indian delegation has already explained to the Security Council what Pakistan did to us.

While I was engaged in these conversations and negotiations with friends from Pakistan, I sent one of my colleagues to Lahore, where he met the Prime Minister of Pakistan, Mr. Liaquat Ali Khan, and other high dignitaries of the West Punjab Government. He placed the same point of view before them and requested that they should allow us time to consider this vital question, first helping us to achieve our liberation instead of forcing us to declare our decision one way or the other. Then, one fine morning while these negotiations were proceeding, I received news that a full-fledged attack had been carried out by the raiders on Muzaffarabad, frontier town in the Kashmir Province.

The representative of Pakistan has stated that immediately upon my release I went down to Delhi to negotiate the accession of Kashmir to India. That is not a fact. He probably does not know that while in gaol I was elected President of the All India States People's Conference, and that immediately upon my release I had to take up my duties. Accordingly, I had called a meeting of the executive of that Conference in Delhi, a fact which I had conveyed to the Prime Minister of Pakistan. Indeed, I had told the Prime Minister of Pakistan that immediately upon my return from Delhi I should take the opportunity of meeting him personally to discuss my point of view with him. I did not go to Delhi to conclude any agreement on behalf of Kashmir because, although released, I was still considered a rebel.

I might inform the representative of Pakistan that although I am beyond doubt the head of the Administration of Kashmir State, I am not the Prime Minister. I am head of the Emergency Administration, and that not because the Maharaja of Kashmir wished it. In fact, I do not know whether the Maharaja wishes it even now. I hold the position because the people of my country wish me to be at the helm of affairs in Jammu and Kashmir State.

When the raiders came to our land, massacred thousands of people – mostly Hindus and Sikhs, but Muslims, too – abducted thousands of girls, Hindus, Sikhs and Muslims alike, looted our property and almost reached the gates of our summer capital, Srinagar, the result was that the civil, military and police administrations failed. The Maharaja, in the dead of night, left the capital along with his courtiers, and the result was absolute panic. There was no one to take over control. In that hour of crisis, the National Conference came forward with its 10,000 volunteers and took over the administration of the country. They started guarding the banks, the offices and houses of every person in the capital. This is the manner in which the administration changed hands. We were *de facto* in charge of the administration. The Maharaja, later on, gave it a legal form.

It is said that Sheikh Abdullah is a friend of Pandit Jawaharlal Nehru. Yes, I admit that. I feel honoured that such a great man claims me as his friend. And he happens to belong to my own country; he is also a Kashmiri, and blood is thicker than water. If Jawaharlal gives me that honour, I cannot help it. He is my friend. But that does not mean that, because of his friendship, I am going to betray the millions of my people who have suffered along with me for the last seventeen years and sacrifice the interests of my country. I am not a man of that calibre.

I was explaining how the dispute arose – how Pakistan wanted to force this position of slavery upon us. Pakistan had no interest in our liberation or it would not also have opposed our freedom movement.

Pakistan would have supported us when thousands of my countrymen were behind bars and hundreds were shot to death. The Pakistani leaders and Pakistani papers were heaping abuse upon the people of Kashmir who were suffering these tortures.

Then, suddenly, Pakistan comes before the bar of the world as the champion of the liberty of the people of Jammu and Kashmir. The world may believe this, but it is very difficult for me to believe.

When we refused the coercive tactics of Pakistan, it started full-fledged aggression and encouraged the tribesmen in this activity. It is absolutely impossible for the tribesmen to enter our territory without encouragement from Pakistan, because it is necessary for them to pass through Pakistan territory to reach Jammu and Kashmir. Hundreds of trucks, thousands of gallons of petrol, thousands of rifles, ammunition, and all forms of help that an army requires, were supplied to them. We know this. After all, we belong to that country. What Pakistan could not achieve by the use of the economic blockade it wanted to achieve by full-fledged aggression.

I had thought all along that the world had got rid of the Hitlers and Goebbels, but, from what has happened and what is happening in my poor country, I am convinced they have only transmigrated their souls into Pakistan.

We are being attacked daily. Thousands of armed men come across the Pakistan border and raze each and every village of our country to the ground. That is what is actually happening. We see it daily with our own eyes, and yet we are being told that Pakistan has nothing to do with this – that it is not at all interested.

What do we request? We request nothing more than that the Security Council should send some members to this area to see for themselves what is bappening there.

If Pakistan comes forward and says, "We question the legality of the accession," I am prepared to discuss whether or not the accession of Jammu and Kashmir to India was legal. However, now they say, "We want a plebiscite; we want to obtain the free and unfettered opinion of the people of Kashmir. There should be no pressure exerted on the people and they should make the free choice as to the State to which they wish to accede."

Not only is this the offer that was made by the people of Kashmir to Pakistan long, long ago, but it is the offer made by the Prime Minister of India at a time when, I think, he had not the slightest need for making it, as Kashmir was in distress.

We realized that Pakistan would not allow us any time, that we had either to suffer the fate of our kith and kin of Muzaffarabad, Baramula, Srinagar and other towns and villages, or to seek help from some outside authority.

Under those circumstances, both the Maharaja and the people of Kashmir requested the Government of India to accept our accession. The Government of India could easily have accepted the accession and could have said, "All right, we accept your accession and we shall render this help." There was no necessity for the Prime Minister of India to add the proviso, when accepting the accession, that "India does not want to take advantage of the difficult situation in Kashmir. We will accept this accession because, without Kashmir's acceding to the Indian Dominion, we are not in a position to render any military help. But once the country is free from the raiders, marauders and looters, this accession will be subject to ratification by the people". That was the offer made by the Prime Minister of India.

That was the same offer which was made by the people of Kashmir to the Government of Pakistan, but it was refused because at that time Pakistan felt that it could, within a week, conquer the entire Jammu and Kashmir State and then place the *fait accompli* before the world, just as happened some time ago in Europe. The same tactics were used.

But, having failed in those tactics, Pakistan now comes before the bar of the world, pleading: "We want nothing; we only want our people to be given a free hand in deciding their own fate. And in deciding their own fate, they must have a plebiscite." There is no dispute as to that. After all, this is the offer that was made by the Prime Minister of India and by the people of Kashmir.

They then continue and say: "No, a plebiscite cannot be fair and impartial unless and until there is a neutral administration in the State of Jammu and Kashmir." I have failed to understand this terminology with reference to a "neutral administration". After all, what does "neutral administration" mean?

The representative of Pakistan has stated that Sheikh Abdullah, because he is a friend of Jawaharlal Nehru, because he has had sympathy for the Indian National Congress, because he has declared his point of view in favour of accession to India, and because he is head of the Emergency Administration, cannot remain impartial. Therefore, Sbeikh Abdullah must depart.

Let us suppose that Sheikh Abdullah goes. Who is to replace

Sheikh Abdullah? It will be someone from amongst the 4 million people of the State of Jammu and Kashmir. But can we find anyone among these 4 million people whom we can call impartial? After all, we are not logs of wood; we are not dolls. We must have an opinion one way or the other. The people of Kashmir are either in favour of Pakistan or in favour of India.

Therefore, Pakistan's position comes down to this: that the 4 million people of that State should have no hand in running the administration of their own country. Someone else must come in for that purpose. Is that fair? Is that just? Do the members of the Security Council wish to oust the people of Kashmir from running their own administration and their own country?

Then, for argument's sake, let us suppose that the 4 million people of the State of Jammu and Kashmir agree to have nothing to do with the administration of their country; someone else must be brought into the country for this purpose. From where do the members of the Security Council propose that such a neutral individual may be secured? From India? No From Pakistan? No From anywhere in the world. No Frankly speaking, even if the Security Council were to request Almighty God to administer the State of Jammu and Kashmir during this interim period, I do not feel that he could act impartially. After all, one must have sympathy either for this side or that side.

If elections were to be held in the United Kingdom sometime after tomorrow, with the Labour Government in power, would anyone say to Mr. Attlee: "The elections are now going on. Because you happen to belong to the Labour Party, your sympathies will be in favour of the Labour vote. Therefore, you had better clear out. We must have a neutral man as Prime Minister until our elections are finished?"

However, we have been told that Sheikh Abdullah must walk out because he has declared his point of view in favour of India. Therefore, he cannot be impartial. We must have some impartial man; we must have some neutral man.

As I have submitted to the members of the Security Council, Sheikh Abdullah happens to be there because the people wish it. As long as the people wish it, I shall be there. There is no power on earth which can displace me from the position which I have there. As long as the people are bebind me, I will remain there. Once the people cease to have any faith in me, I will not be there.

We have declared, once and for all, that there shall be freedom of voting, and for that purpose we have said: "Let anyone come in; we have no objection. Let the Commission of the Security Council on India come into our State and advise us how we should take a vote, how we should organize it, and how it can be completely impartial. We have no objection." My Government is ready to satisfy, to the last comma, the impartiality of the vote.

But to have an impartial vote is one thing; to have a say in the administration of the State is a different thing entirely. After all, with what are we concerned? We are concerned only with the fact that no influence shall be exercised over the voters, either in one way or in another. The people shall be free to vote according to their own interests. We are ready to accede to that.

It is then said: "You cannot have freedom of voting as long as the Indian Army remains in the State of Jammu and Kashmir." It is probably very difficult for me to draw a full picture of what is going on in that country. There is absolute chaos in certain parts of the country; fighting is going on, and thousands of tribesmen are there, ready to take advantage of any weakness on the part of the State of Jammu and Kashmir.

Once we ask the Indian Army, which is the only protective force in Kashmir against these marauders, to clear out, we leave the country open to chaos. After all, one who has suffered for the last seventeen years, in attempting to secure the freedom and liberation of his own country, would not like an outside army to come in and to remain in the country.

However, what is the present situation? If I ask the Indian Army to clear out, how am I going to protect the people from the looting, arson, murder, and abduction with which they have been faced all these long months? What is the alternative? The Prime Minister of India long ago declared that the Government of India has no intention of keeping its army permanently stationed in Kashmir. He stated: "We are there only as long as the country is in turmoil. Once law and order are established, once the marauders and the tribesmen leave the country, we will withdraw our army." That pledge is already there.

There need be no fear, since the Indian Army is there, that this army will interfere in the exercise of a free vote. After all, a Commission of the Security Council will be there in order to watch. The Indian Army does not have to go into every village. It will be stationed at certain strategic points, so that in the event of danger from any border, the army will be there to protect that border. The army is there to curb disorders anywhere in the State; that is all. The army will not be in each and every village in order to watch each and every vote.

It is then said: "Can we not have a joint control? Can we not have the armies of Pakistan and India inside the State in order to control the situation?" This is an unusual idea. What Pakistan could not achieve through ordinary means, Pakistan wishes to achieve by entering through the back door, so that it may have its armies inside the State and then start the fight. That is not possible.

After all, we have been discussing the situation in Kashmir. I should say that we have been playing the drama of Hamlet without the Prince of Denmark. The people of Kashmir are vitally interested in this question. Four million people in Kashmir are keenly interested in this entire affair. I have sympathies with the peoples of Poonch and Mirpur. The representative of Pakistan will probably concede that I have suffered greatly for the people of Poonch as well as for the people of Mirpur. There is no difference on this part of internal democratization of the administration between me, my party and the people of Poonch. We are one, we want our own liberty, we want our own freedom, we do not want autocratic rule. We desire that the 4 million peopie in Jammu and Kashmir – Hindus, Sikhs and Muslims – shall have the right to change their destiny, to control their country, and to administer it as best they can. On that point there is absolutely no difference.

However, it is not a question of internal liberation. The Security Council should not confuse the issue. The question is not that we want internal freedom; the question is not how the Maharaja got his State, or whether or not he is sovereign. These points are not before the Security Council. Whether Kashmir has lawfully acceded to India – complaints on that score have been brought before the Security Council on behalf of Pakistan – is not the point at issue. If that were the point at issue, then we should discuss that subject. We should prove before the Security Council that Kashmir and the people of Kashmir have lawfully and constitutionally acceded to the Dominion of India, and Pakistan has no right to question that accession. However, that is not the discussion before the Security Council.

Indian and Kashmiri forces are ready to deal with the tribesmen, to come to an understanding with the people of Kashmir, and to establish a democratic form of government inside the State. We shall do all that. We do not want Pakistan to lend us support to suppress an internal revolt or to drive out the tribesmen. We do not seek any support from Pakistan in that connexion. Since Pakistan is a neighbouring country, we desire to remain on the friendliest possible terms with this sister Dominion. But we do ask that Pakistan shall have no hand, directly or indirectly, in this turmoil in Kashmir. The Government of Pakistan has said, "We have had no band in this turmoil". The only course left to the Security Council is to send out the Commission and to see whether or not Pakistan has had any hand in this turmoil. If Pakistan has had any hand in this turmoil, then the Government of Pakistan should be asked to desist from such activity. If Pakistan has had no hand in this turmoil, then that can be proved.

This issue has been clouded by very many other issues and interests. I suggested at informal talks that, according to my understanding, there are two points at issue: first, how to have this neutral, impartial administration; second, whether or not the Indian Army shall remain.

It is not at all disputed that we must have a plebiscite and that the accession must be ratified by the people of Kashmir, freely and without any pressure on this or that side. That much is conceded; there is no dispute about that. The dispute arises when it is suggested that, in order to have the free vote, the administration must be changed. To that suggestion we say, "No."

I do not know what course future events will take. However, I may assure the Security Council that, if I am asked to conduct the administration of this State, it will be my duty to make the administration absolutely impartial. It will be my duty to request my brothers, who are in a different camp at this time, to come to lend me support. After all, they are my own kith and kin. We have suffered together; we have no quarrel with them. I shall tell them: "Come on; it is my country; it is your country. I have been asked to administer the State. Are you prepared to lend me support? It is for me to make the administration successful; it is for me to make the administration look impartial." It is not for Pakistan to say: "No, we must have an impartial administration." I refuse to accept Pakistan as a party in the affairs of the Jammu and Kashmir State; I refuse this point blank. Pakistan has no right to say that we must do this and we must do that. We have seen enough of Pakistan. The people of Kashmir have seen enough. Muzaffarabad and Baramula and hundreds of villages in Jammu and Kashmir depict the story of Pakistan to the people of Jammu and Kashmir. We want to have no more of this.

In concluding, I again request that, in order to settle this issue of Kashmir, the Security Council should not confuse the point in dispute. The Security Council should not allow various other extraneous matters to be introduced. Very many extraneous matters have been introduced. The representative of Pakistan gave us the history of the Jammu and Kashmir State. He read to us some letters from Viceroys of India, asking the Maharaja of Jammu and Kashmir to behave, giving the Maharaja good advice, etc. However, we cannot forget that these States are the creation of British imperialism in India. Who has supported these States and this misrule for these 150 years? It is not going to convince me or the world for the representative of Pakistan to say: "These events have happened and these letters were written." We know how the Princes have acted, how the States were brought into existence, and how the Princes were supported. This was all a game in the British imperialist policy. But this legacy has now fallen upon us. We are not here to discuss whether or not the Maharaja lawfully became the ruler of the State, whether or not there is moral administration in this State, whether or not the Maharaja is sovereign and whether or not Kashmir has legally acceded to India. Those issues are not before the Security Council. The only issue before the Security Council is that Pakistan must observe its international obligations and must not support any outside raiders.

Pakistan should not encourage inside revolt. Pakistan has denied that it has. In order to verify the statements made by the representatives of India and Pakistan, the Security Council must send a Commission to the spot to see whether the complaint brought before the Security Council is valid or invalid. If the Security Council finds that the complaint brought before it by India is valid, then, Pakistan should be asked to desist, or India should be permitted to use its means to carry out the decision of the Security Council.

As far as I can speak on behalf of India, India does not want the help of the armies of Pakistan. What it wants from Patistan is that Pakistan should not supply bases to the raiders on Pakistan territory across the border from Jammu and Kashmir State. All along the border on Pakistan territory, there are huge concentrations of these tribesmen who are Pakistani nationals. We request Pakistan not to allow its territory to be used by these raiders.

Pakistan should not provide ammunition, arms, direction and control to these tribesmen. It should stop the passage of these tribesmen through its territory. Pakistan should not supply arms and ammunition to the people who are fighting within the State because all these matters fall under an international obligation. Therefore, Pakistan should desist from that practice. That is all.

We do not want any armed help from Pakistan. If Pakistan does what we have requested the Indian Army, I am quite sure, will be capable of driving out the raiders and tribesmen. If Pakistan does not meddle in our affair, we will be capable of solving all our own internal disputes with the Maharaja of Kashmir. However, as long as this unofficial war continues, it is very difficult for us to do anything. Our hands are tied.

What is happening? The raiders are concentrated just across the border. They enter our State in large number – four or five thousand strong. They raid four or five villages, burn them, capture them, they go back across the border. Our army cannot go across the border, and cannot fire a single shot across the border, because if it does, there is the immediate danger of a greater conflagration. So our hands are tied.

We did not want to create this difficult situation without informing the Security Council, and we felt honour-bound to inform it of the actual position. The Indian Army could easily have followed the raiders across the border and could have attacked the bases, which were all in Pakistan territory, but it desisted. We thought it would be better to inform the Security Council of the situation.

However, I did not have the slightest idea that, when the case came before the Security Council, the representative of Pakistan would so boldly deny that Pakistan supplied all this help. Everybody knows that Pakistan is aiding these raiders and tribesmen and the people who are fighting within the State. However, Pakistan chose boldly to deny all these charges.

What is left for me to do? After all, I do not have any magic lamp so that I might bring the entire picture of Jammu and Kashmir State, along with the borders of Pakistan, before the eyes of the members of the Security Council so that they might see who is fighting and who is not fighting. Therefore, somebody must go to the spot. Then at that time it would be for us to prove that the charges we have brought before the Security Council are correct to the last word. That is the only help, we want, and no other help.

5.14. Speech by Lopez (Colombia) in Security Council, 245th Meeting, February 11, 1948

In trying to be brief, I have omitted the two most relevant remarks that I had intended to make.

Firstly, we do not really have to decide upon the request, because we do not have the request for adjournment. When we started the discussion, the Indian delegation had already booked their passage to India. Notwithstanding all the very friendly and obliging requests that have been made by the Security Council, the Indian delegation have not so far agreed to stay here any longer, so that, really, we cannot say that they have made a request, but they have informed us of their determination to leave for India today. Therefore, I do not know if it would not be much better to inform the Indian delegation that we have taken due notice of their determination to go to India for consultation with their Government and their decision to have somebody else clothed with authority to represent them in the deliberation of the Security Council.

The second remark I wish to make is that, perhaps becausc we have not given him an opportunity—and I may be the most guilty—the Indian representative has not clarified this question in so far as he might find it advisable to do so in order to dissipate some of the doubts which I have expressed.

The representative of France made what I thought to be a very intelligent suggestion when he said be could not vote on the proposal before the Security Council until he knew whether or not the Indian delegation was going to remain for a few more days. I had already made a similar suggestion. However, I shall be content if the President agrees to my request that the Indian delegation be offered an opportunity, before the Security Council votes on this proposal, to provide some clarification of the various points which has been raised.

Finally, I wish to say that, after the remarks I made earlier today, my attention was called to the fact that the letter from the delegation of India does refer to the draft resolution submitted to the President last Sunday. Aside from that, my remarks stand.

5.15. Speech by President of Security Council in 269th Meeting, March 18, 1948

Part of the question raised by the representative of Colombia was put to me by the representative of Pakistan when he raised the question of procedure. I shall answer first the question asked by the representative of Pakistan. There are indeed a number of draft resolutions before the Security Council beginning with those introduced by the representative of Belgium [Documert S/667]. All those resolutions will be dealt with according to our rules of procedure.

In regard to the general handling of this question, the members of the Security Council will remember that I inherited the present method from my two predecessors. At the very first meeting this month which was devoted to this question, I consulted the members of the Security Council as to whether or not they wished that procedure to be continued. So far as I am concerned, I should welcome abandonment of the present procedure and adoption of the procedure which is used by the Security Council in connexion with all other questions.

I should like to add, however, that the draft resolution which I have presented today is the result of considerable consultation with the delegations of India and Pakistan. While it has not been found acceptable by both delegations, I think I am correct in saying that the representative of Pakistan did not say that the povisions of the resolution are unacceptable as far as they go. If I understood his criticism correcly, he meant that those provisions do not go far enough and do not provide adequate safeguards. He was not in favour of dropping any of the safeguards provided in the draft resolution. If my understanding is correet, his position was that he would accept the resolution if certain other provisions were added to it. Wish that I could have produced a draft resolution entirely acceptable to both parties.

My forecast is this: Whether the detailed work involved in this kind of preliminary survey and consultation is carried on by the President of the Security Council or by another member or by several members, it will be very difficult to produce a resolution entirely acceptable to both parties. I think the Security Council should aim at the maximum agreement possible between the two delegations. There will be a margin of disagreement. So far as that margin is concerned, I hope that in the end the two parties will accept what the sense of fairness of the Security Council recommends.

5.16. Third Resolution* Adopted at 286th Meeting of Security Council, April 21, 1948

The Security Council,

Having considered the complaint of the Government of India concerning the dispute over the State of Jammu and Kashmir.

Having heard the representative of India in support of that complaint and the reply and counter-complaints of the representative of Pakistan.

Being strongly of the opinion that the early restoration of peace and order in Jammu and Kashmir is essential and that India and Pakistan should do their utmost to bring about a cessation of all fighting.

Noting with satisfaction that both India and Pakistan desire that the question of the accession of Jammu and Kashmir to India or Pakistan should be decided through the democratic method of a free and impartial plebiscite.

Considering that the continuation of the dispute is likely to endanger international peace and security.

Reafirms its resolution 38 (1948) of 17th January 1948.

Resolves that the membership of the Commission established by its resolution 39 (1948) of the 20th January 1948 shall be increased to five and shall include, in addition to the membership mentioned in that resolution, representatives of**. . . and . . .,and that if the membership of the Commission has not been completed within ten days from the date of the adoption of this resolution the President of the Council may designate such other Member or Members of the United Nations as are required to complete the membership of five.

Instructs the Commission to proceed at once to the Indian subcontinent and there place its good offices and mediation at the disposal of the Governments of India and Pakistan with a view to

* Adopted by 7 votes to none, with 4 abstentions Belgium, Colombia, Ukrainian Soviet Socialist Republic, Union of Soviet Socialist Republics.
Res. 47 (1948), UN Document No. S/726.

** Belgium and Columbia were appointed vide Security Council Decision at 287th Meeting, April 23, 1948 facilitating the taking of the necessary measures, both with respect to the resolution of peace and order and to the holding of a plebiscite, by the two Governments, acting in co-operation with one another and with the Commission and further instructs the Commission to keep the Council informed of the action taken under the resolution; and, to this end.

Recommends to the Governments of India and Pakistan the following measures as those which in the opinion of the Council are appropriate to bring about a cessation of the fighting and to create proper conditions for a free and impartial plebiscite to decide whether the State of Jammu and Kashmir is to accede to India or Pakistan:

A. Restoration of place and order

1. The Government of Pakistan should undertake to use its best endeavours:

(a) To secure the withdrawal from the State of Jammu and Kashmir of tribesmen and Pakistani nationals not normally resident therein who have entered the State for purpose of fighting, and to prevent any intrusion into the State of such elements and any furnishing of material aid to those fighting in the State; and

(b) The make known to all concerned that the measures indicated in this and the following paragraphs provide full freedom to all subjects of the State, regardless of creed, caste, or party to express their views and to vote on the question of the accession of the State, and that therefore they should co-operate in the maintenance of peace and order.

2. The Government of India should:

(a) When it is established to the satisfaction of the Commission set up in accordance with the Council's resolution 39 (1948) that the tribesmen are withdrawing and that arrangements for the cessation of the fighting have become effective, put into operation in consultation with the Commission a plan for withdrawing their own forces from Jammu and Kashmir and reducing them progressively to the minimum strength required for the support of the civil power in the maintenance of law and order;

(b) Make known that the withdrawal is taking place in stages and announce the completion of each stage;

(c) When the Indian forces have been reduced to the minimum strength mentioned in (a) above, arrange in consultation with the Commission for the stationing of the remaining forces to be carried out in accordance with the following principles:

  (i) That the presence of troops should not afford any intimidation or appearance of intimidation to the inhabitants of the State;

  (ii) That as small a number as possible should be retained in forward areas; and

  (iii) That any reserve of troops which may be included in the total strength should be located within their present base area:

3. The Government of India should agree that until such time as the Plebiscite Administration referred to below finds it necessary to exercise the powers of direction and supervision over the State forces and police provided for in paragraph 8, they will be held in areas to be agreed upon with the Plebiscite Administrator.

4. After the plan referred to in paragraph 2 (a) above has been put into operation, personnel recruited locally in each district should so far as possible be utilized for the re-establishment and maintenance of law and order with due regard to protection of minorities, subject to such additional requirements as may be specified by the Plebiscite Administration referred to in paragraph 7.

5. If these local forces should be found to be inadequate, the Commission, subject to the agreement of both, the Government of India and the Government of Pakistan, should arrange for the use of such forces of either Dominion as it deems effective for the purpose of pacification.

B. Plebiscite

6. The Government of India should undertake to ensure that the

Government of the State invite the major political groups to designate responsible representatives to share equitably and fully in the conduct of the administration at the ministerial level while the plebiscite is being prepared and carried out.

7. The Government of India should undertake that there will be established in Jammu and Kashmir a Plebiscite Administration to hold a plebiscite as soon as possible on the question of the accession of the State to India or Pakistan.

8. The Government of India should undertake that there will be delegated by the State to the Plebiscite Administration such powers as the latter considers necessary for holding a fair and impartial plebiscite including, for that purpose only, the direction and supervision of the State forces and police.

9. The Government of India should, at the request of the Plebiscite Administration, make available from the Indian forces such assistance as the Plebiscite Administration may require for the performance of its functions.

10. (a) The Government of India should agree that a nominee of the Secretary-General of the United Nations will be appointed to be the Plebiscite Administrator.

(b) The Plebiscite Administrator, acting as an officer of the State of Jammu and Kashmir, should have authority to nominate his assistants and other subordinates and to draft regulations governing the plebiscite. Such nominees should be formally appointed and such draft regulations should be formally promulgated by the State of Jammu and Kashmir.

(c) The Government of India should undertake that the Government of Jammu and Kashmir will appoint fully qualified persons nominated by the Plebiscite Administrator to act as special magistrates within the State judicial system to hear cases which in the opinion of the Plebiscite Administrator have a serious bearing on the preparation for and the conduct of a free and impartial plebiscite.

(d) The terms of service of the Administrator should form the subject of a separate negotiation between the Secretary-General of the United Nations and the Government of India. The Administrator should fix the terms of service for his assistants and subordinates.

(e) The Administrator should have the right to communicate directly with the Government of the State and with the Commission of the Security Council and, through the Commission with the Security Council, with the Governments of India and Pakistan and with their representatives with the Commission. It would be his duty to bring to the notice of any or all of the foregoing (as he in his discretion may decide) any circumstances arising which may tend in his opinion, to interfere with the freedom of the plebiscite.

11. The Government of India should undertake to prevent, and to give full support to the Administrator and his staff in preventing, any threat, coercion or intimidation, bribery or other undue influence on the voters in the plebiscite, and the Government of India should publicly announce and should cause the Government of the State to announce this undertaking as an international obligation binding on all public authorities and officials in Jammu and Kashmir.

12. The Government of India should themselves and through the Government of the State declare and make known that all subjects of the State of Jammu and Kashmir, regardless of creed, caste or party, will be safe and free in expressing their views and in voting on the question of the accession of the State and that there will be freedom of the press, speech and assembly and freedom of travel in the State, including freedom of lawful entry and exit.

13. The Government of India should use and should ensure that the Government of the State also use their best endeavours to effect the withdrawal from the State of all Indian nationals other than those who are normally resident therein or who on or since 15 August 1947 have entered it for a lawful purpose.

14. The Government of India should ensure that the Government of the State releases all political prisoners and take all possible steps so that:

(a) All citizens of the State who have left it on account of disturbances are invited, and are free, to return to their homes and to exercise their rights as such citizens;
(b) There is no victimization; and
(c) Minorities in all parts of the State are accorded adequate protection.

15. The Commission of the Security Council should at the end of the plebiscite certify to the Council whether the plebiscite has or has not been really free and impartial.

C. General Provisions

16. The Governments of India and Pakistan should each be invited to

nominate a representative to be attached to the Commission for such assistance as it may require in the performance of its task.

17. The Commission should establish in Jammu and Kashmir such observers as it may require of any of the proceedings in pursuance of the measures indicated in the foregoing paragraphs.

18. The Security Council Commission should carry out the tasks assigned to it herein.

The five members of the United Nations Commission for India and Pakistan were: Czechoslovakia (nominated by India on 10 February 1948); Belgium and Colombia (appointed by the Council on 23rd April 1948 – see the decision below); Argentina (nominated by Pakistan on 30th April 1948); United States of America (designated the President of the Council on 7th May 1948, in the absence of agreement between Argentina and Czechoslovakia on the member to be designated by them).

Decision

At its 287th meeting, on 23rd April 1948, the Council, pursuant to its resolution 47 (1948), appointed Belgium and Colombia as the additional members of the United Nations Commission for India and Pakistan.

5.17. Fourth Resolution* Adopted at 312th Meeting of Security Council, June 3, 1948

The Security Council

1. *Reaffirms* its resolutions 38 (1948) of 17th January, 39 (1948) of 20th January and 47 (1948) of 21st April 1948;

2. Directs the United Nations Commission for India and Pakistan to proceed without delay to the areas of dispute with a view to accomplishing in priority the duties assigned to it by resolution 47 (1948);

3. *Directs* the Commission further to study and report to the Security Council when it consider it appropriate on the matters

*Adopted by 8 votes to none with 3 abstentions (China, Ukrainian Soviet Socialist Republic, Union of Soviet Socialist Republic). Res. 51 (1948); UN Document No. S/819.

raised in the letter of the Foreign Minister of Pakistan, dated 15 January 1948, in the order outlined in paragraph D of Council resolution 39 (1948).

5.18. Resolution of United Nations Commission for India and Pakistan (UNCIP)*, August 13, 1948

The Resolution comprises a Preamble and three Parts.

Part I deals with the cease-fire, which was agreed by India and Pakistan and made effective on January 1, 1949. As a completion of this part of the Resolution a cease-fire line was agreed upon by two Governments under the auspices of the UNCIP in the Karachi. (Agreement of July 27, 1949.) The line was demarcated.

Part II, entitled "Truce agreement", outlined the way in which the demilitarization of the State should be carried out.

Part III is a reaffirmation of the will of the Governments of India and Pakistan that the future status of the State of Jammu and Kashmir shall be determined in accordance with the will of the people.

RESOLUTION

"Simultaneously with the acceptance of the proposal for the immediate cessation of hostilities as outlined in Part I, both Governments accept the following principles as basis for the formulation of a truce agreement, the details of which shall be worked out in discussion between their representatives and the Commission:

A

1. As the presence of troops of Pakistan in the territory of the State of Jammu and Kashmir constitutes a material change in the situation since it was represented by the Government of Pakistan before the Security Council, the Government of Pakistan agrees to withdraw its troops from that State.
2. The Government of Pakistan will use its best endeavour to secure the withdrawal from the State of Jammu and

* *see also* Chapter 7

Kashmir of tribesmen and Pakistan nationals not normally resident therein who have entered the State for the purpose of fighting.

3. Pending a final solution, the territory evacuated by the Pakistan troops will be administered by the local authorities under the surveillance of the Commission.

B

1. When the Commission shall have notified the Government of India that the tribesmen and Pakistan nationals referred to in Part II, A. 2 hereof have withdrawn, thereby terminating the situation which was represented by the Government of India to the Security Council as having occasioned the presence of Indian forces in the State of Jammu and Kashmir, and further, that the Pakistan forces are being withdrawn from the State of Jammu and Kashmir, the Government of India agree to begin to withdraw the bulk of its forces from that State in stages to be agreed upon with the Commission.
2. Pending the acceptance of the conditions for a final settlement of the situation in the State of Jammu and Kashmir, the Indian Government will maintain within the lines existing at the moment of the cease-fire those forces of its Army which in agreement with the Commission are considered necessary to assist local authorities in the observance of law and order. The Commission will have observers stationed where it deems necessary.
3. The Government of India will undertake to ensure that the Government of the State of Jammu and Kashmir will take all measures within its power to make it publicly known that peace, law and political rights will be safeguarded and that all human political rights will be guaranteed."

5.19. Speech by Mohammed Zafrullah Khan (Pakistan) in Security Council, 382nd Meeting, November 25, 1948

With reference to what the representative of India has said towards the end of his remarks, I would beg to submit that that has a tendency of opening a controversy on the merits of the question now pending before the Commission.

The representative of India has said: 'We do not decline to accept the resolution of 13 August.' Equally, and with complete justice, I might submit, we did not decline to accept the resolution of 13 August either. The resolution of 13 August provided for a cease-fire in Part I, for a truce agreement in Part II, and, with all respect to the Commission, if I might so describe it, a somewhat indefinite proposal in Part III with regard to what would happen after the truce. It was with regard to that Part that Pakistan put forward its proposal.

As the Council is aware, both sides had certain objections to the Security Council's resolution of 21 April. The Pakistan objections were put forward; the Indian objections were put forward; and the position which we took up before the Commission was that if the two sides continued to make demands on the basis of their objections with regard to the conditions which would secure a fair and impartial plebiscite, no progress would be possible after the truce. Therefore, what we put forward was that modifications of the Security Council's proposals contained in articles 6 to 15 of the resolution, or addition to them, might be possible, but could only be possible—as the Commission agreed—by agreement of the parties and the acceptance of those modifications or amendments by the Commission. And we said that the only way to make progress in that respect was for the two Governments to agree that the conditions for a fair and impartial plebiscite would be those laid down by the Security Council—even though each side had objections to them—subject to additions and modifications which might be agreed upon. That is the only condition that the Government of Pakistan put forward.

It took no objection to the proposals contained in the first and second parts. The issue had been clarified to the Pakistan Government in certain respects by the Commission. There appears a second condition in our reply to the Commission, but it is only a nominal condition. Certain clarification and elucidations had been given to us and, as the Commission had been discussing its proposals on an equal basis with both Governments, it was possible that certain clarifications had been given to the Government of India. It subsequently appeared that clarifications had in fact been given, and our second condition was only to the effect that the clarification and elucidations given to each side should be communicated to the other side and should be acceptable to it. This was inherent in the very nature of the negotiations themselves—it was not a condition.

The only condition that we put forward was that in default of any additions or modifications, or subject to any conditions or modifications which might be agreed upon, both sides should accept paragraphs 6 to 15 of the Security Council's resolution of 21 April. I am not seeking to raise a debating point; this is not a matter which we wished to raise here; it is not a matter which has urgency today. Ever since we had the honour of welcoming the Commission in Karachi on 7th July, we have been at all times not only agreeable but anxious to put an end to the fighting on the basis of an immediate cease-fire. We have never at any time put conditions upon that proposal or showed any hesitation about it.

The conditions of the truce as laid down in the second part of the Commission's proposals of 13 August are in themselves not a matter of objection to us. All that we have insisted upon is that there should be some kind of agreement, at least in principle, between the two Governments as to what is to happen after the truce, namely, that a fair and impartial plebiscite should be held and that the conditions should be such as would ensure a fair and impartial plebiscite.

I am prepared to agree here and now, once again, that if the Government of India is prepared to accept paragraphs 6 to 15 of the Security Council's resolution of 21 April—to which they had some objections and to which we had some objections—subject to any conditions or modifications which may be arrived at with the help of the good offices of the Commission, the whole matter can be settled now, before this meeting of the Security Council adjourns. There may be some difficulty in the way of the Government of India which prevents it from doing that. Again, I am not seeking to score a debating point; the difficulty may be very real and I am not trying to force it into that position at all; these things have to be ironed out. But I submit that we are ready and always have been ready for an immediate cease-fire without imposing any conditions upon anybody. Then, once the further conditions or principles are agreed upon, the truce proposals can come into effect and the preparations for a plebiscite can be taken in hand so that the whole thing can be settled. That is our position and has been all along.

5.20. Basic Principles for a Plebiscite Proposed by UNCIP to the Governments of India and Pakistan, December 11, 1948

The Commission reaffirms its resolution of 13th August 1948.

The Governments of India and Pakistan simultaneously accept supplementary to this resolution the following principles :

The question of the accession of the State of Jammu and Kashmir to India or Pakistan will be decided through the democratic method of a free and impartial plebiscite.

A plebiscite will be held when it shall be found by the Commission that the cease-fire and truce arrangements set forth in Parts I and II of the Commission's resolution of 13 August 1948 have been carried out and arrangements for the plebiscite have been completed.

(a) The Secretary-General of the United Nation will, in agreement with the Commission, nominate a Plebiscite Administrator who shall be a personality of high international standing and commanding general confidence. He will be formally appointed to office by the Government of Jammu and Kashmir;

(b) The Plebiscite Administrator shall derive from the State of Jammu and Kashmir the powers he considers necessary for organizing and conducting the plebiscite and for ensuring the freedom and impartiality of the plebiscite;

(c) The Plebiscite Administrator shall have authority to appoint such staff of assistants and observers as he may require;

(a) After implementation of Parts I and II of the Commission's resolution of 13 August 1948, and when the Commission is satisfied that peaceful conditions have been restored in the State, the Commission and the Plebiscite Administrator will determine, in consultation with the Government of India, the final disposal of Indian and State armed forces – such disposal to be with due regard to the security of the State and the freedom of the plebiscite; and

(b) As regards the territory referred to in A.2 of Part II of the resolution of 13th August, final disposal of the armed forces in that territory will be determined by the Commission and the Plebiscite Administrator in consultation with the local authorities.

All civil and military authorities within the State and the principal elements of the State will be required to cooperate with the Plebiscite Administrator in the preparation for and the holding of the plebiscite.

(a) All citizens of the State who have left it on account of the disturbances will be invited and be free to return and to exercise all their rights as such citizens. For the purpose of facilitating repatriation there shall be appointed two Commissions, one composed of nominees of India and the other of nominees of Pakistan. The Commissions shall operate under the direction of the Plebiscite Administrator. The Governments of India and Pakistan and all authorities within the State of Jammu and Kashmir will collaborate with the Plebiscite Administrator in putting this provision into effect.

(b) All persons (other than citizens of the State) who on or since 15 August 1947 have entered it for other than lawful purpose, shall be required to leave the State.

All authorities within the State of Jammu and Kashmir will undertake to ensure, in collaboration with the Plebiscite Administrator, that :

(a) There is no threat, coercion or intimidation, bribery or other undue influence on the voters in the plebiscite;

(b) No restrictions are placed on legitimate political activity throughput the State. All subjects of the State, regardless of creed, caste or party, shall be safe and free in expressing their views and in voting on the question of the accession of the State to India or Pakistan. There shall be freedom of the press, speech and assembly and freedom of travel in the State, including freedom of lawful entry and exit.

(c) All political prisoners are released;

(d) Minorities in all parts of the State are accorded adequate protection; and

(e) There is no victimization.

The Plebiscite Administrator may refer to the United Nations Commission for India and Pakistan problems on which he may require assistance, and the Commission may in its discretion call upon the Plebiscite Administrator to carry out on its behalf any of the responsibilities it has been entrusted.

At the conclusion of the plebiscite, the Plebiscite Administrator shall report the result thereof to the Commission and to the Government of Jammu and Kashmir. The Commission shall then certify to the Security Council whether the plebiscite has or has not been free and impartial.

Upon the signature of the truce agreement, the details of the foregoing proposals will be elaborated in the consultations envisaged in Part III of the Commission's resolution of 13th August 1948. The Plebiscite Administrator will be fully associated in these consultations.

5.21. Nomination of the Plebiscite Administrator, March 24, 1949

Paragraph (3) (a) of the Resolution of 5th January 1949 reads as follows :

> "The Secretary-General of the United Nations will, in agreement with the Commission, nominate a Plebiscite Administrator who shall be a personality of high international standing and commanding general confidence."

The Governments of India and Pakistan were consulted on names of personalities who would be acceptable as Plebiscite Administrator. Both Governments agreed that Fleet Admiral Chester W. Nimitz would be acceptable to them and on 24th March 1949, following the Commission's recommendation to the Secretary-General, the Commission was notified of his acceptance and nomination.

The Plebiscite Administrator will enter into his functions only when agreement will have been reached between the two parties on the completion of Part I and on the details for the implementation of Part II of the Resolution of 13th August 1948.

6

Article 370 of Indian Constitution, 1949 with Amendments (As on the 1st February, 1990)

6.1. [1][370. Temporary Provisions with Respect to the State of Jammu and Kashmir

(1) Notwithstanding anything in this Constitution, –

(a) the provisions of article 238 shall not apply in relation to the State of Jammu and Kashmir;

(b) the power of Parliament to make laws for the said State shall be limited to –

(i) those matters in the Union List and the Concurrent List which, in consultation with the Government of the State, are declared by the President to correspond to matters specified in the Instrument of Accession governing the accession of the State of the Dominion of India as the matters with respect to which the Dominion Legislature may make laws for the State; and

(ii) such other matters in the said Lists, as, with the concurrence of the Government of the State, the President may be order specify.

Explanation – For the purposes of this article, the Government of the State means the person for the time being recognised by the President as the Maharaja of Jammu and Kashmir acting on the advice of the Council of Ministers for the time being in office under the Maharaja's Proclamation dated the fifth day of March, 1948;

(c) the provisions of article 1 and of this article shall apply in relation to that State;

(d) such of the other provisions of this Constitution shall apply in relation to that State subject to such exceptions and modifications as the President may by order[2] specify:

Provided that no such order which relates to the matters specified in the Instrument of Accession of the State referred to in paragraph (i) of sub-clause (b) shall be issued except in consultation with the Government of the State:

Provided further that no such order which relates to matters other than those referred to in the last preceding proviso shall be issued except with the concurrence of that Government.

(2) If the concurrence of the Government of the State referred to in paragraph (ii) of sub-clause (b) of clause (1) or in the second proviso to sub-clause (d) of that clause be given before the Constituent Assembly for the purpose of framing the Constitution of the State is convened, it shall be placed before such Assembly for such decision as it may take thereon.

(3) Notwithstanding anything in the foregoing provisions of this article, the President may, by public notification, declare that this article shall cease to be operative or shall be operative only with such exceptions and modifications and form such date as he may specify:

Provided that the recommendation of the Constituent Assembly of the State referred to in clause (2) shall be necessary before the President issues such a notification.

Appendix I

6.2. [3]The Constitution (Application to Jammu and Kashmir Order, 1954

C.O. 48

In exercise of the powers conferred by clause (1) of article 370 of the Constitution, the President, with the concurence of the Government of the State of Jammu and Kashmir, is pleased to make the following Order:

1. (1) This Order may be called the Constitution (Application to Jammu and Kashmir) order, 1954.

(2) It shall come into force on the fourteenth day of May, 1954, and shall thereupon supersede the Constitution (Application to Jammu and Kashmir) Order, 1950.

2. [4][The provisions of the Constitution as in force on the 20th day of June, 1964 and as amended by the Constitution (Nineteenth Amendment) Act, 1966, the Constitution (Twenty-first Amendment) Act, 1967, Section 5 of the Constitution (Twenty-third Amendment) Act, 1969, the Constitution (Twenty-fourth Amendment) Act, 1971, Section 2 of the Constitution (Twenty-fifth Amendment) Act, 1971, the Constitution (Twenty-sixth Amendment) Act, 1971, the Constitution (Thirtieth Amendment) Act, 1972, Section 2 of the Constitution (Thirty-first Amendment) Act, 1973, Section 2 of the Constitution (Thirty-third Amendment) Act, 1974, Sections 2, 5, 6 and 7 of the Constitution (Thirty-eight Amendment) Act, 1975, the Constitution (Thirty-ninth Amendment) Act, 1975 the Constitution (Fortieth Amendment) Act, 1976, Sections 2, 3 and 6 of Constitution (Fifty-second Amendment) Act, 1985 and the Constitution (Sixty-first Amendment) Act, 1988 which, in addition to article 1 and article 370, shall apply in relation to the State of Jammu and Kashmir and the exceptions and modifications subject to which they shall so apply shall be as follows: –]

(1) The Preamble

(2) Part I

To article 3, there shall be added the following further proviso, namely: –

"Provided further that no Bill providing for increasing or diminishing the area of the State of Jammu and Kashmir or altering the name or boundary of that State shall be introduced in Parliament without the consent of the Legislature of that State".

(3) Part II

(a) This Part shall be deemed to have been applicable in relation to the State of Jammu and Kashmir as from the 26th day of January, 1950.

(b) To article 7, there shall be added the following further proviso, namely: –

"Provided further that nothing in this article shall apply to a permanent resident of the State of Jammu and Kashmir who, after having so migrated to the territory now included in Pakistan, returns to the territory of that State under a permit for resettlement in that State or permanent return issued by or under the authority of any law made by the Legislature of that State, and every such person shall be deemed to be a citizen of India".

(4) Part III

(a) In article 13, references to the commencement of the Constitution shall be construed as references to the commencement of this order.

[5]* * *

(c) In clause (3) of article 16, the reference to the State shall be construed as not including a reference to the State of Jammu and Kashmir.

(d) In article 19, for a period of [6][[7][twenty-five] years] from the commencement of this Order: –

(i) in clauses (3) and (4) after the words "in the interests of", the words "the security of the State or" shall be inserted;
(ii) in clause (5), for the words "or for the protection of the interests of any Scheduled Tribe", the words "or in the interests of the security of the State" shall be substituted; and
(iii) the following new clause shall be added, namely: –

'(7) The words "reasonable restrictions" occurring in clauses (2), (3), (4) and (5) shall be construed as meaning such restrictions as the appropriate Legislature deems reasonable.'

(e) In clauses (4) and (7) of article 22, for the word "Parliament", the words "the Legislature of the State" shall be substituted.

(f) In article 31, clauses (3), (4) and (6) shall be omitted; and for clause (5) there shall be substituted the following clause, namely:-

"(5) Nothing in clause (2) shall affect –

(a) the provisions of any existing law; or

(b) the provisions of any law which the State may hareafter make –

(i) for the purpose of imposing or levying any tax or penalty; or
(ii) for the promotion of public health or the prevention of danger to life or property; or
(iii) with respect to property declared by law to be evacuee property."

(g) In article 31A, the proviso to clause (1) shall be omitted; and for sub-clause (a) of clause (2), the following sub-clause shall be substituted, namely: –

(a) "estate" shall mean land which is occupied or has been let for agricultural purposes or for purposes subservient to agriculture, or for pasture, and includes –

(i) sites of buildings and other structures on such land;
(ii) trees standing on such land;
(iii) forest land and wooded waste;
(iv) area covered by or fields floating over water;
(v) sites of *Jandars* and *gharats*;
(vi) any *Jagir, inam, muafi* or *mukarrai* or other similar grant, but does not include –

(i) the site of any building any town, or town area or village *abadi* or any land appurtenant to any such building or site;
(ii) any land which is occupied as the site of a town or village; or
(iii) any land reserved for building purposes in a municipality or notified area or cantonment or town area or any area for which a town planning scheme is sanctioned.

[8][(h) In article 32, clause (3) shall be omitted.]

(i) In article 35 –

(i) references to the commencement of the Constitution shall be construed as references to the commencement of this Order;

(ii) in clause (a) (i), the words, figures and brackets "clause (3) of article 16, clause (3) of article 32" shall be omitted; and

(iii) after clause (b), the following clause shall be added, namely: –

"(c) no law with respect to preventive detention made by the Legislature of the State of Jammu and Kashmir, whether before or after the commencement of the Constitution (Application to Jammu and Kashmir) Order, 1954, shall be void on the ground that it is inconsistent with any of the provisions of this Part, but any such law shall, to the extent of such inconsistency, cease to have effect on the expiration of [9][[10][twenty-five] years] from the commencement of the said Order, except as respects things done or omitted to be done before the expiration thereof."

(j) After article 35, the following new article shall be added, namely: –

"35A. *Saving of laws with respect to permanent residents and their rights* – Notwithstanding anything contained in this Constitution, no existing law in force in the State of Jammu and Kashmir, and no law hereafter enacted by the Legislature of the State, –

(a) defining the classes of persons who are, or shall be, permanent residents of the State of Jammu and Kashmir; or

(b) conferring on such permanent residents any special rights and privileges or imposing upon other persons any restrictions as respects –

(i) employment under the State Government;
(ii) acquisition of immovable property in the State;
(iii) settlement in the State; or
(iv) right to scholarships and such of other forms of aid as the State Government may provide,

shall be void on the ground that it is inconsistent with or takes away or abridges any rights conferred on the other citizens of India by any provision of this Part".

(5) Part V

[11][(a) For the purposes of Article 55, the population of the State of Jammu and Kashmir shall be deemed to the sixty-three lakhs.

(b) In Article 81, for clauses (2) and (3), the following clauses shall be substituted, namely: –

"(2) For the purposes of sub-clause (a) of clause (1) –

(a) there shall be allotted to the State six seats in the House of the People;
(b) the State shall be divided into single member territorial constituencies by the Delimitation Commission constituted under the Delimitation Act, 1972, in accordance with such procedure as the Commission may deem fit;
(c) the constituencies shall, as far as practicable be geographically compact areas, and in delimiting them regard shall be had to physical features, existing boundaries of administrative units, facilities of communication and public convenience; and
(d) the constituencies into which the State is divided shall not comprise the area under the occupation of Pakistan.

(3) Nothing in clause (2) shall affect the representation of the State in the House of the People until the dissolution of the House existing on the date of publication in the Gazette of India of the final order or orders of the Delimitation Commission relating to the delimitation of parliamentary constituencies under the Delimitation Act, 1972.

(4) (a) The Delimitation Commission shall associate with itself for the purpose of assisting it in its duties in respect of the State, five persons who shall be members of the House of the People representing the State.

(b) The persons to be so associated from the State shall be nominated by the Speaker of the House of the People having due regard to the composition of the House.

(c) The first nominations to be made under sub-clause (b) shall be made by the Speaker of the House of the People within two months from the commencement of the Constitution (Application to Jammu and Kashmir) Second Amendment Order, 1974.

(d) None of the associate members shall have a right to vote or to sign any decision of the Delimitation Commission.

(e) If owing to death or resignation, the office of an associate member falls vacant, it shall be filled as soon as may be practicable by the Speaker of the House of the People and in accordance with the provisions of sub-clauses (a) and (b)."]

[12][(c) In Artical 133, after clause (1), the following clause shall be inserted, namely: –

'(1A) The provisions of Section 3 of the Constitution (Thirtieth Amendment) Act, 1972, shall apply in relation to the State of Jammu and Kashmir subject to the modification that references therein to "this Act", "the commencement of this Act", "this Act had not been passed" and "as amended by this Act" shall be construed respectively as references to "the Constitution (Application to Jammu and Kashmir) Second Amendment Order, 1974", "the commencement of the said Order", "the said Order had not been made" and "as it stands after the commencement of the said Order"].

[13][(d)] In Article 134, clause (2), after the words "Parliament may", the words "on the request of the Legislature of the State" shall be inserted.

[13][(e)] Articles 135, [14]*** and 139 shall be omitted,

[15]***

[16][(5A) Part VI

[17][(a) Articles 153 to 217, Article 219, Article 221, Articles 223, 224, 224A and 225 and Articles 227 to 237 shall be omitted.]

(b) In Article 220, references to the commencement of the Constitution shall be construed as references to the commencement of the Constitution (Application to Jammu and Kashmir) Amendment Order, 1960.

[18][(c) In Article 222, after clause (1), the follwoing new clause shall be inserted, namely:-

(1A) Every such transfer from the High Court of Jammu and Kashmir or to that High Court shall be made after consultation with the Governor'.]

(6) Part XI

[19][(a) In Article 246, for the words, brackets and figures "clauses

(2) and (3)" occurring in clause (1), the word, brackets and figures "clause (2)" shall be substituted, and the words, brackets and figures "Notwithstanding anything in clause (3)," occurring in clause (2) and the whole of clauses (3) and (4) shall be omitted.]

[20][[21] [(b) For Article 248, the following article shall be substituted, namely: –

"248. *Residuary powers of legislation* – Parliament has exclusive power to make any law with respect to –

[22][(a) prevention of activities involving terrorist acts directed towards over-awing the Government as by law established or striking terror in the people or any section of the people of alienating any section of the people or adversely affecting the harmony amongst different sections of the people;]

[23][aa)][24][prevention of other activities] directed towards disclaiming, questioning or disrupting the sovereignty and territorial integrity of India or bringing about cession of a part of the territory of India or secession of a part of the territory of India from the Union or causing insult to the Indian National Flag, the Indian National Anthem and this Constitution, and

(b) taxes on –

(i) foreign travel by sea or air;
(ii) inland air travel;
(iii) postal articles, including money orders, phonograms and telegrams."

[25][*Explanation* – In this article, "terrorist act" means any act or thing by using bombs, dynamite or other explosive substances or inflammable substances or firearms or other lethal weapons or poisons or noxious gases or other chemicals or any other substances (whether biological or otherwise) of a hazardous nature.];

[26][(bb) In Artical 249, in clause (1), for the words "any matter enumerated in the State List specified in the resolution," the words "any matter specified in the resolution being a matter which is not enumerated in the Union List or in the concurrent List" shall be substituted.]]

(c) In Article 250, for the words "to any of the matters

enumerated in the State List", the words "also to matters not enumerated in the Union List" shall be substituted.

[27]* * *

(e) to Article 253, the following proviso shall be added, namely:-

"Provided that after the commencement of the Constitution (Application to Jammu and Kashmir) Order, 1954, no decision affecting the disposition of the State of Jammu and Kashmir shall be made by the Government of India without the consent of the Government of that State".

[28]* * *

[29][(f)] Article 255 shall be omitted.

[29][(g)] Article 256 shall be re-numbered as clause (1) of that article, and the following new clause shall be added thereto, namely: –

"(2) The State of Jammu and Kashmir shall so exercise its executive power as to facilitate the discharge by the Union of its duties and responsibilities under the Constitution in relation to that State; and in particular, the said State shall, if so required by the Union, acquire or requisition property on behalf and at the expense of the Union, or if the property belongs to the state, transfer it to the union on such terms as may be agreed, or in default of agreement, as may be determined by an arbitrator appointed by the Chief Justice of India."

[30]* * *

[31][(h)]] In clause (2) of Article 261, the words "made by Parliament" shall be omitted.

(7) Part XII

[32]*

[33][(a)] Clause (2) of Article 267, article 273, clause (2) of Article

283 [34][and Article 290] shall be omitted.

[33][(b)] In Articles 266, 282, 284, 298, 299 and 300 references to the State or States shall be construed as not including references to the State of Jammu and Kashmir.

[33][(c) In Articles 277 and 295, references to the commencement of the Constitution shall be construced as references to the commencement of this Order.

(8) Part XIII

[34]***In clause (1) of Article 303, the words "by virtue of any entry relating to trade and commerce in any of the Lists in the Seventh Schedule" shall be omitted.

[35]* * *

(9) Part XIV

[36][In Article 312, after the words "the States", the brackets and words "(including the State of Jammu and Kashmir)" shall be inserted.]

[37][(10) Part XV

(a) In clause (1) of Article 324, the reference to the Constitution shall, in relation to elections to either House of the Legislature of Jammu and Kashmir be construed as a reference to the Constitution of Jammu and Kashmir.

[38][(b) In Articles 325, 326, 327 and 329, the reference to a State shall be construed as not including a reference to the State of Jammu and Kashmir.

(c) Article 328 shall be omitted.

(d) In Article 329, the words and figures "or Article 328" shall be omitted.]

[39][(e) In Article 329 A, clauses (4) and (5) shall be omitted.]]

(11) Part XVI

[40]* * *

[41][(a)] Articles 331, 332, 333, [42][336 and 337] shall be omitted.

[41][(b)] In Articles 334 and 335, references to the State or the States shall be construed as not including references to the State of Jammu and Kashmir.

[43][(c) In clause (1) of Article 339, the words, "the administration of the Scheduled Areas and" shall be omitted.]

(12) Part XVII

The provisions of the Part shall apply only in so far as they relate to–

(i) the official language of the Union;

(ii) the official language for communication between one State and another, or between a State and the Union; and

(iii) the language of the proceedings in the Supreme Court.

(13) Part XVIII

(a) To Article 352, the following new clause shall be added, namely: –

[44][(6)] No Proclamation of Emergency made on grounds only of internal disturbance or imminent danger thereof shall have effect in relation to the State of Jammu and Kashmir (except as respects Article 354) [45][unless–

(a) it is made at the request or with the concurrence of the Government of that State, or

(b) where it has not been so made, it is applied subsequently by the President to that State at the request or with the concurrence of the Government of that State.]"

[46][(b) In clause (1) of Article 356, references to provisions or provision of this Constitution shall, in relation to the State of Jammu and Kashmir, be construed as including references to provisions or provision of the Constitution of Jammu and Kashmir.

(c) Article 360 shall be omitted.]

(14) Part XIX

[47]* * *

[48][(a)] [49][Article 365] shall be omitted.

50* * *

[48][(b)] To Article 367, there shall be added the following clause, namely: –

"(4) For the purposes of this Constitution as it applies in relation to the State of Jammu and Kashmir –

(a) references to this Constitution or to the provisions thereof shall be construed as references to the Constitution or the provisions thereof as applied in relation to the said State;

[51][(aa) references to the person for the time being recognised by the President on the recommendation of the Legislative Assembly of the State as the Sadar-i-Riyasat of Jammu and Kashmir, acting on the advice of the Council of Ministers of the State for the time being in office, shall be construed as references to the Governor of Jammu and Kashmir;

(b) references to the Government of the said State shall be construed as including references to the Governor of Jammu and Kashmir acting on the advice of his Council of Ministers:

Provided that in respect of any period prior to the 10th day of April, 1965, such references shall be construed as including references to the Sadar-i-Riyasat acting on the advice of his Council of Ministers;]

(c) references to a High Court shall include references to the High Court of Jammu and Kashmir :

52* * *

[53][d)] references to the permanent residents of the said State shall be construed as meaning persons who, before the commencement of the Constitution (Application to Jammu and Kashmir) Order, 1954 were recognised as State subjects under the laws in force in the State or who are recognised by any law made by the Legislature of the State as permanent residents of the State; and

[54][(e)] references to a Governor shall include references to the Governor of Jammu and Kashmir:

Provided that in respect of any period prior to the 10th day of April, 1965, such references shall be construed as references to the person recognised by the President as the Sadar-i-Riyasat of Jammu and Kashmir and as including references to any person recognised by the President as being competent to exercise the powers of the

Sadar-i-Riyasat.]"

(15) Part XX

[55][(a)] [56][To clause (2) of Article 368], the following proviso shall be added, namely:—

"Provided further that no such amendment shall have effect in relation to the State of (New Delhi) and Kashmir unless applied by order of the President under clause (1) of Article 370."

[57][(b) After clause (3) of Article 368, the following clause shall be added, namely:—

"(4) No law made by the Legislature of the State of Jammu and Kashmir seeking to make any change in or in the effect of any provision of the Constitution of Jammu and Kashmir relating to—

(a) appointment, powers, functions, duties, emoluments, allowances, privileges or immunities of the Governor; or

(b) superintendence, direction and control of elections by the Election Commission of India, eligibility for inclusion in the electoral rolls without discrimination, adult suffrage and composition of the Legislative Council, being matters specified in Sections 138, 139, 140 and 150 of the Constitution of Jammu and Kashmir, shall have any effect unless such law has, after having been reserved for the consideration of the President, received his assent."]

(16) Part XXI

(a) Articles 369, 371, [58][371A], [59][372A], 373, clauses (1), (2), (3) and (5) of Article 374 and [60][Articles 376 to 378A and 392] shall be omitted.

(b) In article 372—

(i) clauses (2) and (3) shall be omitted;

(ii) references to the laws in force in the territory of India shall include references to *hidayat, ailans, ishtihars*, circulars, *robkars, irshads, yadashts*, State Council Resolutions, Resolutions of the Constituent Assembly, and other instruments having the force of law in the territory of the State of Jammu and Kashmir; and

(iii) references to the commencement of the authority

functioning as the Privy Council of a State shall be construed as a reference to the Advisory Board constituted under the Jammu and Kashmir Constitution Act, 1996 and references to the commencement of the Constitution shall be construed as references to the commencement of this Order.

(17) Part XXII

Articles 394 and 395 shall be omitted.

(18) First Schedule.

(19) Second Schedule.

[61]* * *

(20) Third Schedule

Forms V, VI, VII and VIII shall be omitted.

(21) Fourth Schedule

[62]**[(22) Seventh Schedule**

(a) In the Union List –

(i) for entry 3, the entry "3. Administration of cantonments." shall be substituted;

[63][(ii) entries 8, 9 [64][and 34], [65]*** entry 79, and the words "Inter-State migration" in entry 81 shall be omitted;]

[66]* * *

[67][(iii) in entry 72, the reference to the States shall be construed, –

(a) in relation to appeals to the Supreme Court from any decision or order of the High Court of the State of Jammu and Kashmir made in an election petition whereby an election to either House of the Legislature of that State has been called in question, as including a reference to the State of Jammu and Kashmir;

(b) in relation to other matters, as not including a reference to that State]; [68][and] [69][(iv) for entry 97, the following entry shall be substituted, namely: –

[70][97, Prevention of activities –

(a) involving terrorist acts directed towards overawing the Government as by law established or striking terror in the people or any section of the people or alienating any section of the people or adversely affecting the harmony amongst different sections of the people;

(b) directed towards disclaming, questioning or disrupting the sovereignty and territorial integrity of India or bringing about cession of a part of the territory of India or secession of a part of the territory of India from the Union or causing insult to the Indian National Flag, the Indian National Anthem and this Constitution, taxes on foreign travel by sea or air, on inland air travel and on postal articles, including money orders, phonograms and telegrams.

Explanation – In this entry, "terrorist act" has the same meaning as in the Explanation to Article 248.]]

(b) The State List shall be omitted.

[71][(c) In the Concurrent List –

[72][(i) for entry 1, the following entry shall be substituted, namely: –

"1. Criminal law (excluding offences against laws with respect to any of the matters specified in List I and excluding the use of naval, military or air forces or any other armed forces of the Union in aid of the civil power) in so far as such criminal law relates to offences against laws with respect to any of the matters specified in this List."];

[73][[74] (ia) for entry 2, the following entry shall be substituted, namely: –

"2. Criminal procedure (including prevention of offences and Constitution and organisation of criminal courts, except the Supreme Court and the High Court) in so far as it relates to, –

(i) offences against laws with respect to any matters being matters with respect to which Parliament has power to make laws; and

(ii) administration of oaths and taking of affidavits by diplomatic and consular officers in any foreign country."

(ib) for entry 12, the following entry shall be substituted, namely: –

"12. Evidence and oaths in so far as they relate to, –

(i) administration of oaths and taking of affidavits by diplomatic and consular officers in any foreign country; and

(ii) any other matters being matters with respect to which Parliament has power to make laws.];

(ic) for entry 13, the entry "13. Civil procedure in so far as it relates to administration of oaths and taking of affidavits by diplomatic and consular officers in any foreign country." shall be substituted;]

[75]* * *

[76][[77][(ii)] for entry 30, the entry "30. Vital statisties in so far as they related to births and deaths including registration of births and deaths." shall be substituted;]

[78]* * *

[79][(iii) entry 3, entries 5 to 10 (both inclusive), entries 14, 15, 17, 20, 21, 27, 28, 29, 31, 32, 37, 41 and 44 shall be omitted;

(iiia) for entry 42, the entry "42. Acquisition and requisitioning of property, so far as regards acquisition of any property covered by entry 67 of List I or entry 40 List III or of any human work of art which has artistic or aesthetic value." shall be substituted; and]

[80][(iv) in entry 45, for the words and figures "List II or List III", the words "this List" shall be substituted.]

(23) Eighth Schedule

[81]**[(24) Ninth Schedule**

[82][a)] After entry 64, the following entries shall be added, namely: –

[83][64A.] The Jammu and Kashmir State Kuth Act (No. I of Svt. 1978).

[83][64B] The Jammu and Kashmir Tenancy Act (No. II of Svt. 1980).

[83][64C] The Jammu and Kashmir Alienation of Land Act (No. V of Svt. 1995)

[84]* * *

[85][64D] The Jammu and Kashmir Big Landed Estates Abolition

Act (No. XVII of Svt. 2007)

[85][64E] Order No. 6-H of 1951, dated the 10th March, 1951, regarding Resumption of Jagirs and other assignments of land revenue, etc.

[86][64F] The Jammu and Kashmir Restitution of Mortgaged Properties Act, 1976 (Act XIV of 1976).

64G. The Jammu and Kashmir Debtor's Relief Act, 1976 (Act XV of 1976)].

[87][(b) Entries 87 to 124, inserted by the Constitution (Thirty-nine Amendment) Act, 1975, shall be renumbered as entries 65 to 102 respectively.]

[88][(c) Entries 125 to 188 shall be renumbered as entries 103 to 166 respectively.]

[89][**(25) Tenth Schedule**

(a) for the brackets, words and figures "[Articles 102(2) and 19(2)]". the brackets, word and figures "[Article 102(2)]" shall be substituted;

(b) in clause (a) of paragraph 1, the words "or the Legislative Assembly or, as the case may be, either House of the Legislature of a State" shall be omitted;

(c) in paragraph 2–

(i) in sub-paragraph (1), in sub-clasue (ii) of clause (b) of the *Explanation*, the words and figures "or as the case may be, article 188" shall be omitted;

(ii) in sub-paragraph (3), the words and figures "or, as the case may be, Article 188" shall be omitted;

(iii) in sub-paragraph (4) the reference to the commencement of the Constitution (Fifty-second Amendment) Act, 1985 shall be construed as a reference to the commencement of the Constitution (Application to Jammu and Kashmir) Amendment Order, 1989;

(d) in paragraph 5, the words "or the Chairman or the Deputy Chairman of the Legislative Council of a State or the Speaker or the Deputy Speaker of the Legislative Assembly of a State", shall be omitted;

(e) in sub-paragraph (2) of paragraph 6, the words and figures "or, as the case may be, proceedings in the Legislature of a State within the meaning of article 212" shall be omitted;

(f) in sub-paragraph (3) of paragraph 8, the words and figures "or as the case may be article 194," shall be omitted.]

NOTES AND REFERENCES

1. In exercise of the powers conferred by this article the President, on the recommendation of the Constituent Assembly of the State of Jammu and Kashmir, declared that, as from the 17th day of November, 1952, 5th said Art. 370 shall be operative with the modification that for the *Explanation* in cl. (1) thereof, the following Explanation is substituted namely:
"*Explanation* – For the purposes of this article, the Government of the State means the person for the time being recognised by the President on the recommendation of Legislative Assembly of the State as the Sadar-i-Riyasat* of Jammu and Kashmir, acting on the advice of the Council of Ministers of the State for the time being in office."
2. See the Constitution (Application to Jammu and Kashmir) Order, 1954, (C.O.48), as amended from time to time in Appendix I.
3. Published with the Ministry of Law Notification No. S.R.O. 1610, dated the 14th May, 1954, Gazette of India, Extraordinary, part II, Section 3, page 821.
4. The opening words have been successively amended by C.O. 56, C.O. 74, C.O. 76, C.O. 79, C.O. 89, C.O. 91, C.O. 94, C.O. 98, C.O. 103, C.O. 104, C.O. 105, C.O. 108, C.O. 136 and C.O. 141 to read as above.
5. Omitted by C.O. 124 (w.e.f. 4-12.1985).
6. Subs. by C.O. 69, for "ten years".
7. Subs. by C.O. 97, for "twenty".
8. Subs. by C.O. 89, for cl. (h).
9. Subs. by C.O. 69, for "ten years".
10. Subs. by C.O. 97, for "twenty".
11. Subs. by C.O. 98, for cls. (a) and (b).
12. Ins. by C.O. 98.
13. Cls. (c) and (d) relettered as cls. (d) and (e) by C.O. 98.
14. The figures "136" omitted by C.O. 60.
15. Cls. (f) and (g) omitted by C.O. 56.
16. Ins. by C.O. 60 (w.e.f. 26-1-1960).
17. Subs. by C.O. 89, for cl.(*a*).
18. Subs. by C.O. 74, for cl.(*c*) (w.e.f. 24-11-1965).
19. Subs. by C.O. 66, for cl.(*a*).
20. Subs. by C.O. 85, for cl.(*b*).
21. Subs. by C.O. 93, for cl.(*b*).
22. Ins. by C.O. 122 (w.e.f. 4-6-1985).
23. Cl.(a) relettered as cl.(aa), *ibid.* (w.e.f. 4-6-1985).
24. Subs. *ibid.*, "Prevention of activities".
25. Ins. by C.O. 122 (w.e.f. 4-6-1985).
26. Subs. by C.O. 129, for Cl. (*bb*).
27. Cl.(*d*) omitted by C.O. 129.
28. Cl. (*f*) omitted by C.O. 66.

---

*Now "Governor" (Ministry of Law Order No. C.O. 44, dated the 15th November, 1952).

29. Cls. (*g*) and (*h*) relettered as cls. (*f*) and (*g*), ibid.
30. Cl.(*i*) omitted by C.O. 56.
31. Cl.(*j*) relettered as cl.(*i*) by C.O. 56 and again relettered as cl.(*h*) by C.O.66.
32. Cls.(*a*) and (*b*) inserted by C.O. 55 have been omitted by C.O. 56.
33. Cls.(*a*), (*b*) and (c) relettered as (*c*), (*d*) and (*e*) respectively by C.O. 55 have again been relettered as (*a*), (*b*), and (*c*) respectively by C.O. 56.
34. Subs. by C.O. 94, for "articles 290 and 291".
35. Brackets and letter "(*a*)" and cl. (*b*) omitted by C.O. 56.
36. Subs. *ibid.*, for the previous modification.
37. Subs. by C.O. 60 for sub-paragraph (10) (w.e.f. 26-1-1960).
38. Subs. by C.O. 75 for cls.(*b*) and (*c*).
39. Ins. by C.O. 105.
40. Omitted by C.O. 124 (w.e.f. 4-12-1985).
41. Cls.(*b*) and (*c*) relettered as clauses (*a*) and (*b*), by C.O. 124 (w.e.f. 4-12-1985).
42. Subs. *ibid.*, for certain figures and word (w.e.f. 4-12-1985).
43. Ins., *ibid.*, (w.e.f. 4.12-1985).
44. Subs. by C.O. 104, for "(4)".
45. Subs. by C.O. 100, for certain words.
46. Subs. by C.O. 71, for cl.(*b*).
47. Cl. (*a*) omitted by C.O. 74.
48. Cls. (*b*) and (*c*) relettered as cls. (*a*) and (*b*), *ibid.*
49. Subs. by C.O. 94 for "Articles 362 and 365".
50. Original cl.(*c*) omitted by C.O. 56.
51. Subs. by C.O. 74, for cl. (*b*).
52. Cl. (*d*) omitted by C.O. 56.
53. Cl. (*e*) relettered as cl. (*d*), ibid.
54. Subs. by C.O. 74, for cl. (*e*).
55. Numbered as cl. (*a*) by C.O. 101.
56. Subs. by C.O. 91, for "To article 368".
57. Ins. by C.O. 101.
58. Ins. by C.O. 74.
59. Ins. by C.O. 56.
60. Subs. *ibid.*, for "articles 376 to 392".
61. Modification relating to paragraph 6 omitted by C.O. 56.
62. Subs. by C.O. 66, for sub-paragraph (22).
63. Subs. by C.O. 85, for item (ii).
64. Subs. by C.O. 92, for "34 and 60".
65. The words and figures 'the words "and records" in entry 67' omitted by C.O. 95.
66. Original item (*iii*) omitted by C.O. 74.
67. Subs. by C.O. 83, for item (*iii*).
68. Ins. by C.O. 85.
69. Subs. by C.O. 93, for item (*iv*).
70. Subs. by C.O. 122, for entry 97 (w.e.f. 4-6-1985).
71. Subs. by C.O. 69, for cl. (*c*).
72. Subs. by C.O. 70, for item (*i*).
73. Ins. by C.O. 94.
74. Subs. by C.O. 122 for sub-clauses (*ia*) and (*ib*) (w.e.f. 4-1-1985).
75. Items (*ii*) and (*iii*) omitted by C.O. 74.
76. Ins. by C.O. 70.

77. Item (*iv*) renumbered as item (*ii*) by C.O. 74.
78. Item (*v*) and (*vi*) omitted by C.O. 72.
79. Subs. by C.O. 95, for item (*iii*).
80. Item (*vii*) renumbered as item (*iv*) by C.O. 74.
81. Subs. *ibid.*, for sub-paragraph (24).
82. Numbered by C.O. 105.
83. Renumbered by C.O. 98.
84. Omitted by C.O. 106.
85. Renumbered, *ibid.*
86. Ins., *ibid.*
87. Ins. by C.O. 105.
88. Ins. by C.O. 108 (w.e.f. 31-12-1977).
89. Ins. by C.O. 136.

7

United Nations Commission for India and Pakistan (UNCIP)*, 1948 and Cease-Fire 1949

7.1. Establishment of the Commission

The Commission was appointed by a resolution[1] adopted on January 20, 1948 at the 230th meeting of the Security Council by 9 votes to none, with 2 absention.

7.2. UNCIP Resolution, January 5, 1949

The text of paragraph 4 of the resolution of 5 January 1949 is as follows:

"(a) After implementation of Parts I and II of the Commission's resolution of 13 August 1948, and when the Commission is satisfied that peaceful conditions have been restored in the State, the Commission and the Plebiscite Administrator will determine, in consultation with the Government of India, the final disposal of Indian and State armed forces, such disposal to be with due regard to the security of the State and the freedom of the plebiscite."

(a) The Indian Government has maintained that the final disposal of Indian and State armed forces should be

---

1 Chapter 5, Para 5.9

Note : * *see also* Chapter 5, Para 5.18

determined by UNCIP (or the United Nations Representative) and the Plebiscite Administrator, in consultation with the Government of India, such disposal to be with due regard to the security of State and the freedom of the plebiscite.

(b) The Government of India considered that the expression "security of the State" was intended to connotate the security of Jammu and Kashmir against incursion by tribesmen, Pakistan nationals, and regular Pakistan forces, whether acting separately or in concert.

(c) The Pakistan Government considered that there should be a balance between the Indian forces and the State armed forces referred to in sub-paragraph 4(a), on the one hand, and the "Azad" Kashmir forces referred to in sub-paragraph 4 (b), on the other.

Paragraph 4 continues:

"(b) As regards the territory reffered to in A (3) of Part II of the resolution of 13 August, final disposal of the armed forces in that territory will be determined by the Commission and the Plebiscite Administrator in consultation with the local authorities."

(a) The Government of India has maintained that the withdrawal of the bulk of its forces referred to in Section B, paragraph 1, Part II of the 13 August 1948 resolution was conditioned on a large-scale disbanding and disarming of "Azad" Kashmir forces.

(b) The Government of Pakistan has contended that the disbanding and disarming of the "Azad" Kashmir forces was a matter to be dealt with when sub-paragraphs 4 (a) and (b) of the 5th January 1949 resolution were implemented.

7.3. Speech by UNCIP Chairman Korbel in Security Council, 399th Meeting, January 13, 1949

May I be allowed to say on behalf of the Commission that it feels highly honoured to appear today before the Security Council to present its second interim report. The first interim report (S/100) was presented to the Council on 25 November 1948 and covered the period of the Commission's activities in the sub-continent. The second interim report covers the Commission's work in Geneva, in Paris, and at Lake Success to the present date.

Members of the Security Council will remember that on 13 August last year, when in Karachi, the Commission passed a resolution consisting of three parts, which appears in its first interim report (S/100). In Part one it asked the Governments of India and Pakistan to stop fighting; in Part two it proposed certain principles for a truce; and in Part three it expressed in general terms its conviction that the future status of the State of Jammu and Kashmir should be decided by the free will of the people of that State.

The Government of India signified its acceptance of the Commission's resolution, and the Government of Pakistan attached to its acceptance certain conditions regarding mainly the question of conditions under which the plebiscite should be held in the State of Jammu and Kashmir.

On the basis of this, the Commission, when in Paris, suggested that two representatives of the Governments of India and Pakistan should take part in conversations regarding the conditions and the basic principles which should govern the holding of the plebiscite. Both Governments responded to this suggestion affirmatively. Thus, the Commission held several informal conversations with the representatives of India and Pakistan, these conversations being held partly by the Commission as a body and partly by individual members of the Commission.

These conversations led the Commission to formulate its final proposals, which were communicated to both Governments on 11 December. In the Commission's communication it was stated that the Commission hoped that those proposals would be accepted by both Governments in their entirety.

The main points of those proposals were: that the accession of the State of Jammu and Kashmir would be decided by way of a free and impartial plebiscite: that the Secretary-General of the United Nations would nominate, in agreement with the Commission, a Plebliscite Administrator who would be a person of high international standing and who would derive from the Government of Jammu and Kashmir the powers which he considered necessary to organize and conduct a free and impartial plebiscite. The Commission further proposed that all human and political rights should be re-established and guaranteed; that the return of refugees should be organized by two Commissions to be nominated by the Governments of India and Pakistan respectively; that the question of the final disposal of the armed forces which are in the State of Jammu and Kashmir should be solved by the Plebiscite Administrator and the Commission in consultation with both Governments and the competent authorities; finally, that the Plebiscite Administrator should report the result of the plebiscite to the Commissin and to the Government of Jammu and Kashmir, and that the Commission should inform the Security Council whether the plebiscite had been free and impartial.

The Commission put these proposals before the two Governments and decided to send one of its members to the sub-continent so that he might place his services at the disposal of both Governments, if any clarification or interpretation of the Commission's proposals were needed.

The representative of Colombia, Minister Lozano Agudelo, accompanied by his alternate, Mr. Samper Gomez, and the personal representative of the Secretary-General paid a short visit to both capital and held several conversations with officials of the Governments of Pakistan and India. In view of the clarifications which Minister Lozano offered to both Governments, I am highly privileged to announce that both Governments have accepted the Commission's proposals and, on the basis of these, have declared the cessation of hostilities in the territory of the State of Jammu and Kashmir as from 1 January 1949.

The Commission reconvened on 5 January at Lake Success, where the report of Minister Lozano Agudelo was considered and approved, where the second interim report to the Security Council was elaborated and approved, and where a resolution was adopted embodying the proposals accepted by both Governments. The Commission then resolved to return to the sub-continent in the immediate future.

If the Commission has succeeded in the first stage of its work, it is only thanks to Governments of India and Pakistan. The Commission has been working on these proposals in Paris in close contact with the representatives of both Governments, who have offered the Commission all possible help and assistance; and thus they have given proof of their desire to solve the problem of Kashmir in a peaceful way.

The Commission will return in a few days to the sub-continent in order to work in close co-operation with the two Governments on the implementation of Part I and Part II of its resolution of 13 August, and, at a later stage, it will elaborate the details of the Commission's proposals. The Commission sincerely believes that on returning to Lake Success it will be able to report to the Security Council that it has carried to a happy conclusion the honourable mission which has been bestowed upon it.

7.4. Speech by Benegal Rama Rau (India) in Security Council, 399th Meeting, January 13, 1949

May I first, on behalf of my Government, express appreciation of the very generous references made to the efforts of my Government to reach a satisfactory compromise with regard to this very difficult problem. I should also like to associate myself with the tribute paid by the President to the members of the Commission for the success they have in the first and most difficult step towards the establishment of peace between India and Pakistan. Everyone knows of the formidable difficulties with which they were faced, and this great achievement has revived the faith of many people in the utility and effectiveness of the Security Council and of the United Nations generally.

India has also demonstrated its faith in the United Nations by going very far to achieve this result. I am sure that this effort to reach agreement by peaceful methods will be an encouragement to all those who have attempted to reach satisfactory agreement in other spheres, in other parts of the world.

I should also like to take this opportunity, if I may, to thank the President personally for the part he has played in this matter. I do not wish to single out any particular member of the Security Council, but I should like to mention the great part played by the representative of China and his efforts to reach a satisfactory agreement. The consequences of all this are extremely important not only from the point of view of India and Pakistan, but also from the point of view of the whole of Asia because the future of Asia depends, to a large extent, on the friendly relations established between those two countries, and because, to some extent, those two countries are great stabilizing forces in Asia today. They inherited a well-ordered system of government from the British, and this administration has played a great part in maintaining law and order in the south of Asia.

I do not wish to make this an occasion for a lengthy speech. I shall only conclude by presenting my best wishes to the Commission for the further efforts they are likely to make at attempting to reach a satisfactory settlement of this very difficult and complicated problem. On behalf of my Government, I can give the assurance that it will not only co-operate to the utmost with the Commission itself towards a settlement in Kashmir, but also with the United Nations in securing peace everywhere, because it believes that this Organizatoin offers the only hope for peace for future generations, on a secure basis.

7.5. Speech by Shaffi (Pakistan) in Security Council, 399th Meeting, January 13, 1949

When I came to this meeting, I was not aware that I was to be given the privilege of speaking before the Security Council.

I should like, however, to take this opportunity to associate myself with the remarks of the President and the representative of India. I believe that it is impossible to overestimate the work which has been done by the Commission. I believe that the Commission's work may quite well be a milestone in the history of United Nations. My Government has always desired and hoped most earnestly that this question would be settled on an amicable basis. I believe that, thanks to the Commission's sterling work, there is every reason to look forward with optimism to the settlement of this whole dispute. Much still remains to be done, of course, and my Government hopes that the details of the carrying out of the agreement will be worked out so that the people of Kashmir may be firmly convinced that a free, unfettered and impartial plebiscite has been held. That is the earnest desire of my Government. It is for the people of Kashmir and Jammu, through the auspices of an impartial plebiscite, to decide for themselves in accordance with the democratic way of life whether they wish to accede to India or to Pakistan.

I think there remains little more to say except to thank the Security Council for its forbearance in this matter. I know that the arguments have on occasion dragged on almost interminably, and I think the patience of the Council has sometimes been strained almost to the breaking point. I also know that, on occasions, the work of Commission has been hard and arduous; but its tenacity and good faith all round have undoubtedly contributed largely toward bringing us to the stage which we have now reached.

7.6. Truce Terms* Transmitted to Governments of India and Pakistan by UNCIP, April 15, 1949

I. CEASE-FIRE LINE

(A) The cease-fire line will be the line fixed by the Commission and, except as noted below, traced in yellow on the map annexed, and based upon the factual positions occupied on 1 January 1949 by the forces under the control of the Indian and Pakistan High Commands. Based also upon the same factual considerations, the line between Chakothi and Tithwal and from Chorwan to the north of Dras, shall be demarcated as soon as possible by the Military Adviser of the Commission. The cease-fire line shall eleminate all no-man's lands and shall be demarcated on the ground by agreement between the respective local Commanders, assisted by the Commission's Military Observers. The line shall, to the greastest extent possible, follow easily recognizable features on the ground.

(B) The Commission's Military Adviser shall decide, without appeal, local adjustments of the cease-fire line in cases where no agreement is reached between the local Commanders.

(C) The Commission will have observers stationed where it deems necessary throughout the State of Jammu and Kashmir.

(D) Observers will advise the Commission and/or the Plebiscite Administrator regarding developments in the sparsely populated and mountainous region of the territory of Jammu and Kashmir in the north. Without prejudice to the provisions of point 8 of resolution of 5 January 1949, should the Commission and/or the Plebiscite Administrator conclude upon advice from the Observers, or upon resports from the Government of India, that it is necessary for the defence of the area, the Commission and/or the Plebiscite Administrator may request the Government of India to post garrisons at specified points.

---

* UN Document No. S/AC. 12/195.

II. WITHDRAWAL OF TROOPS

A. The Government of Pakistan Agrees

1. To withdraw its troops from the territory of the State of Jammu and Kashmir in seven weeks as follows:

(a) During the first three weeks twenty infantry battalions, plus the corresponding proportion of artillery and supporting units;
(b) During the following fortnight the remainder of the Pakistan troops, with the exception of eight infantry battalions; and
(c) By the end of the seventh week, all Pakistan troops, including their ammunition, stores and material, will have left the territory of the State.

2. That, having secured the withdrawal of the tribesmen from the territory of the State of Jammu and Kashmir, it shall secure the withdrawl of Pakistan nationals still in the territory of State and not normally resident therein, who have entered the State for the purpose of fighting.

B. The Government of India Agrees

1. To withdraw the bulk of its forces from the State of Jammu and Kashmir in stages submitted by the Commission for the agreement of the Government of India. The withdrawal will begin as soon as the Commission shall have notified the Government of India that the tribesmen and Pakistan nationals, not normally resident in Jammu and Kashmir territory who have entered the State for the purpose of fighting, have withdrawn, and that the Pakistan troops are being withdrawn from the State of Jammu and Kashmir.

2. That the schedule of the withdrawal of Indian forces will be made public by the Commission with the schedule of the withdrawal of Pakistan forces immediately after the acceptance of these terms by both Government.

C. The operations mentioned in the above paragraphs A and B will be carried out under the surveillance of the Commission through its Military Adviser.

III. GENERAL PROVISIONS

(A) The territory evacuated by the Pakistan troops will be administered by the local authorities under surveillance of the Commission.

(B) Immediately upon the acceptance of these terms, the Commission would enter into consultations with the Government of India regarding the disposal of the Indian and State armed forces, and with the local authorities regarding the disposal of the armed forces in the territory to be evacuated by Pakistan troops, with a view to initiating implementation of point 4(a) and (b) of the Commission's resolution of 5 January 1949.

(C) If, before expiration of the seven weeks contemplated in point II. A., decisions are reached in the consultations for the initial implementation referred to in III. B, above, the schedule of withdrawal of Pakistan Army, as provided for in II A. above, may be extended to three months, in order to facilitate the implementation of decisions relating to point 4(b) of the Commission's resolution of 5 January 1949.

(D) All prisoners of war will be released within one month.

(E) The land mines to be immediately lifted by the sides which sows them.

(F) It will be made publicly known throughout the State of Jammu and Kashmir that peace, law and order will be safeguarded and that all human and political rights will be guaranteed.

(G) These terms are without prejudice to the territorial integrity and the sovereignty of the State of Jammu and Kashmir.

(H) These terms do not prejudice the functions and powers of the Plebiscite Administrator.

(I) These terms will become effective and will be published by the Commission immediately upon their acceptance by both Governments.

7.7. Agreement* between Military Representatives of India and Pakistan regarding Establishment of a Cease-fire Line in the State of Jammu and Kashmir, July 27, 1949

I. INTRODUCTION

(A) The military representatives of India and Pakistan met

*UN Document No.S/AC. 12/TC.4.

together in Karachi from 18 July to 27 July 1949 under the auspices of the Truce Sub-committee of the United Nations Commission for India and Pakistan.

(B) The members of the Indian delegation were: Lieutenant General S.M. Shrinagesh, Major General K.S. Thimayya, Brigadier S.H.F.J. Manekshaw. As observers: Mr. H.M. Patel, Mr. V. Sahay.

(C) The members of the Pakistan delegation were: Major General W.J. Cawthorn, Major General Nazir Ahmad, Brigadier M. Sher Khan. As observers: Mr. M. Ayub, Mr.A.A. Khan.

(D) The members of the Truce Sub-committee of the United Nations Commission for India and Pakistan were: Mr. Hernando Samper (Colombia), Chairman; Mr. William L.S. Williams (United States); Lieutenant General Maurice Delvoie, Military Adviser; Mr. Miguel A. Marin, Legal Adviser.

II. AGREEMENT

(A) Considering:

1. That the United Nations Commission for India and Pakistan, in its letter dated 2 July 1949 (annex 25), invited the Governments of India and Pakistan to send fully authorized military representatives to meet jointly in Karachi under the auspices of the Commission's Truce Sub-committee to establish a cease-fire line in the State of Jammu and Kashmir, mutually agreed upon by the Governments of India and Pakistan;

2. That the United Nations Commission for India and Pakistan in its letter stated that "The meetings will be for military purposes; political issues will not be considered," and that "They will be conducted without prejudice to negotiations concerning the truce agreement";

3. That in the same letter the United Nations Commission for India and Pakistan further stated that: "The cease-fire line is a complement of the suspension of hostilities, which falls within the provisions of Part I of the resolution of 13 August 1948, and can be considered separately from the questions relating to Part II of the same resolution";

4. That the Governments of India and Pakistan, in their letters dated 7 July 1949 to the Chairman of the Commission, accepted the Commission's invitation to the military conference in Karachi;

(B) The delegations of India and Pakistan, duly authorized, have reached the following agreement:

1. Under the provisions of Part I of the resolution of 13 August 1948, and as a complement of the suspension of hostilities in the State of Jammu and Kashmir on 1 January 1949, a cease-fire line is established.

2. The cease-fire line runs from Manawar in the south, north to Keran and from Keran east to the glacier area, as follows:

(a) The line from Manawar to the south bank of the Jhelum River at Urusa (inclusive to India) is the line now defined by the factual positions about which there is agreement between both parties. Where there has hitherto not been agreement, the line shall be as follow:

(i) In Patrana area: Kohel (inclusive to Pakistan) north along the Khuwals Kas Nullah up to Point 2276 (inclusive to India), thence to Kirni (inclusive to India).

(ii) Khambha, Pir Satwan, Point 3150 and Point 3606 are inclusive to India, thence the line runs to the factual position at Bagla Gala, thence to the factual position at Point 3300.

(iii) In the area south of Uri the positions of Pir Kanthi and Ledi Gali are inclusive to Pakistan.

(b) From the north bank of the Jhelum River the line runs from a point opposite the village of Urusa (NL, 972109), thence north following the Ballaseth Da Nar Nullah (inclusive to Pakistan), up to NL 973140, thence northeast to Chhota Quzinag (Point 10657 inclusive to India), thence to NM 010180, thence to NM 03721, thence to Point 11825 (NM 025354, inclusive to Pakistan), thence to Tutmai Gali (to be shared by both sides, posts to be established 500 yards, on either side of the Gali), thence to the northwest through the first "R" of Burji Nar to north of Gadori, thence straight west to just north of Point 9870, thence along the black line north of Bijidhar to north of Batarasi, thence to just south of Sudpura, thence due to the Kathaqazinag Nullah, thence along the Nullah to its junction with the Grangnar Nullah, thence along the latter Nullah to Kajnwala Pathra (inclusive to India), thence across the Danna ridge (following the facual positions) to Richmar Gali (inclusive to India), thence north to Thanda Katha Nullah, thence north to the Kishanganga River. The line then follows the Kishanganga River up to a point situated between Jargi and Tarban, thence (all inclusive to Pakistan) to Bankoran, thence norht-east to Khori, thence to the hill feature 8930 (in Square 9053), thence straight north to Point 10164 (in Square

9057), thence to Point 10323 (in Square 9161), thence northeast straight to Guthur, thence to Bhutpathra, thence to NL 980707, thence following the Bugina Nullah to the junction with the Kishanganga River at Point 4739. Thereafter the line follows the Kishanganga River to Keran and onward to Point 4996 (NL 975818).

(c) From Point 4996 the line follows (all inclusive to Pakistan) the Jamgar Nullah eastward to Point 12124, to Katware, to Point 6678, then to the northest to Sarian (Point 11279), to Point 11837, to Point 13090, to Point 12641, thence east again to Point 11142, thence to Dhakki, thence to Point 11415, thence to Point 10301, thence to Point 7507, thence to Point 10685, thence to Point 8388, thence south-east to Point 11812. Thence the line runs (all inclusive to India) to Point 13220, thence across the River to the east to Point 13449 (Durmal), thence to Point 14586 (Anzbari), thence to Point 13554, thence to Milestone 45 on the Burzil Nullah, thence to the east to Ziankal (Point 12909), thence to the southeast to Point 11114, thence to Point 12216, thence to Point 12867, thence to the east to Point 11264, thence to Karo (Point 14985), thence to Point 14014, thence to Point 12089, thence following the track to Point 12879. From there the line runs to Point 13647 (Karobal Gali, to be shared by both sides). The cease-fire line runs thence through Retagah Chhish (Point 15316), thence through Point 15889, thence through Point 17392, thence through Point 16458, thence to Marpo La (to be shared by both sides), thence through Point 17561, thence through Point 17352, thence through Point 18400, thence through Point 16760, thence to (inclusive to India) Dalunang.

(d) From Dalunang eastwards the cease-fire line will follow the general line Point 15495, Ishmam, Manus, Gangam, Gunderman, Point 13620, Junkar (Point 17628), Marmak, Natsara, Shangruti (Point 17531), Chorbat La (Point 16700), Chalunka (on the Shyok River), Khor, thence north to the glaciers. This portion of the cease-fire line shall be demarcated in detail on the basis of the factual position as of 27 July 1949 by the local commanders, assisted by United Nations Military Observers.

(C) The cease-fire line described above shall be drawn on a one-inch map (where available) and then be verified mutually on the ground by local commanders on each side with the assistance of the United Nations Military Observers, so as to eliminate any no-man's land. In the event that the local commanders are unable to reach agreement, the matter shall be referred to the Commission's Military

Adviser, whose decision shall be final. After this verification, the Military Adviser will issue to each High Command a map on which will be marked the definitive cease-fire line.

(D) No troops shall be stationed or operate in the area of the Burzil Nullah from south of Minimarg to the cease-fire line. This area is bounded on the west by the ridge leading northeast from Dudgaikal to Point 13071, to Point 9447, to Point 13466, to Point 13463, and on the east by the ridge running from Point 12470, to Point 11608, to Point 13004, to Point 13976, to Point 13450. Pakistan may, however, post troops on the western of the above ridges to cover the approaches to Kamri Bal Pass.

(E) In any dispositions that may be adopted in consequence of the present agreement troops will remain at least 500 yards from the cease-fire line except where the Kishanganga River constitutes the line. Points which have been shown as inclusive to one party may be occupied by that party, but the troops of the other party shall remain at a distance of 500 yards.

(F) Both sides shall be free to adjust their defensive positions behind the cease-fire line as determined in paragraphs A through E, inclusive, subject to no wire or mines being used when new bunkers and defences are constructed. There shall be no increase of forces or strengthening of defences in areas where no major adjustments are involved by the determination of the cease-fire line.

(G) The action permitted by paragraph F above shall not be accompanied or accomplished by the introduction of additional military potential by either side into the State of Jammu and Kashmir.

(H) Except as modified by paragraph A to G, inclusive above, the military agreements between the two High Commands relating to the cease-fire of 1 January 1949 shall continue to remain operative.

(I) The United Nations Commission for India and Pakistan will station Observers where it deems necessary.

(J) The delegations shall refer this agreement to their respective Government for ratification. The documents of ratification shall be deposited with the United Nations Commission for India and Pakistan not later than 31 July 1949.

(K) A period of thirty days from the date of ratification shall be allowed to each side to vacate the areas at present occupied by them beyond the cease-fire line as now determined. Before the expiration of this thirty day period there shall be no forward movement into areas to be taken over by either side pursuant to this agreement, except by mutual agreement between local commanders.

In faith whereof the undersigned sign this document in three original copies.

Done in Karachi on 27th July 1949.

For the Government of India:

(Signed) S.M. Shrinagesh

For the Government of Pakistan:

(Signed) J.Cawthorn
Major General

For the United Nations Commission for India and Pakistan:

(Signed) Hernando Samper
M. Delvoie

7.8. Speech by UNCIP Chairman Samper in Security Council, 457th Meeting, December 17, 1949

I am honoured to represent the United Nations Commission for India and Pakistan before the Security Council and, on behalf of the Commission, I wish to express our appreciation for the Council's reception.

The members of the Security Council will recall that, when the Council received the Commission in Paris in November 1948 (382nd meeting), conversations were underway looking towards an agreement the Government of India and Pakistan on the principles relating to a free and impartial plebiscite in the State of Jammu and Kashmir, and that the result of these conversations was sbsequently embodied in the Commission's resolution of 5 January 1949 (S/1196, paragraph 15).

The Security Council is aware that the Governments of India and Pakistan, on their own initiative and before the Commission had reached the Sub-Continent again, made the cease-fire order effective as of 1 January 1949. The Commission is pleased to report that the high commands of the Indian and Pakistan Armies made every effort to avoid incidents and violations of the cease-fire during the very difficult time when no line as such existed, and that it was due largely to their attitude of conciliation and understanding that the military conference in Karachi in July of this year led to the agreement on a line. The task of demarcating the line was achieved through the assistance of United Nations military observers under the

Commission's Military Adviser. The immediate and vital objective of the Security Council – namely, the cessation of hostilities in the State of Jammu and Kashmir – has thus not only been achieved, but ensured, through the co-operation and the goodwill of the two Governments.

The Commission, unfortunately, cannot inform the Security Council that substantial progress has been made in the implementation of the succeeding parts of the Commission's resolutions of 13 August 1948 (S/1100, paragraph 75) and 5 January 1949. After eight months of negotiations, the Commission has deemed it advisable, having in mind the importance of continuing an active movement towards a solution of the problem, to refer the matter back to Security Council. We believe that the parent body will more easily find means for making the adjustments and modifications which today have becomes necessary for the execution of the commitments and agreements entered into by the two Governments.

The Commission's third interim report (S/1340 and S/1430/Add. 1 and Add. 2) has been before members of the Security Council for several days now, and I do not believe it will be necessary to take up the time of the Council by going into a lengthy expose of its contents. Members of the Council are aware that, throughout eight months, the Commission endeavoured to mediate the differences which existed in the way of implementing Part II of the first resolution dealing with the truce and principally concerned with the withdrawl of troops (S/1100, paragraph 75). The Commission maintained direct contact with the two Governments individualy in New Delhi and in Karachi. It instituted sub-committees. It drafted truce terms of its own, which were presented to the two Governments and which, in the light of the response of the two Governments, were modified in so far as this was possible, keeping in mind the framework and the principles which were our guides. The Commission also suggested a joint political meeting of the two Governments for the purpose of reaching agreement on the truce; this meeting was subsequently cancelled by the Commission. Finally, in a last endeavour, the Commission asked the two Governments if they would be willing to submit to arbitration the differences arising between them as regards the implementation of Part II of the resolution of 13 August 1948.

The third interim report endeavours to set forth objectively, impartially and comprehensively the reasons for the unsuccessful outcome of the negotiations, which cover the period from February to September 1949. It has been the Commission's intention to show how the strict letter of previous commitments has become more and more rigid in a changing and dynamic situation, and how questions which, in the light of the over-all problem and of the objective pursued by the two Governments and by the United Nations in the dispute, might be considered as of lesser importance have, in fact, impeded positive action on the part of the two Governments, in spite of their desire to proceed to a settlement.

The facts of the case are clear. The main issues stand well defined. The Commission believes that three of these issues are the most important: first, the withdrawal of troops from the State, which is essential for the creation of conditions for a free and impartial plebiscite; secondly, and closely linked, the disposal of the *Azad Kashmir* forces in the western part of the State of Jammu and Kashmir; and thirdly, the administration and defence of the northern areas of the State.

With this information at hand, gathered from the past experience of the Commission, it is our hope that future action under the auspices of the United Nations and with the co-operation of India and Pakistan may be facilitated. Should this prove to be the case, the Commission will then have served an important and useful purpose in furthering the solution of this dispute.

In the conclusions of the report, the Commission has described the spirit which animated it in drafting that report. It also has expressed the belief that the present pattern, as it stands, is outmoded and unsuited in respect of question of timing and method, and that this pattern should be made freer and more ample for mediation to be effective. The Commission is of the opinion that a single individual can now more expeditiously undertake what might be termed the third phase of the Kashmir dispute. It has so recommended to the Security Council and hopes that consultations with the representatives of India and Pakistan will take place to this end.

I have the privilege formally to present for the consideration of members of the Security Council the third interim report of the United Nations Commission for India and Pakistan. The report was prepared in Geneva and was signed there by four of the five members: the representatives of Argentina, Belgium, Colombia and the United States of America. The representative of Czechoslovakia reserved his position at the time of discussion of the report until a later date. At a meeting of the Commission held yesterday afternoon at Lake Success, the representative of Czechoslovakia presented his delegation's minority views. (S/1430/Add.3).

Before concluding these brief remarks, may I express the Commission's gratitude to the Governments of India and Pakistan for the courtesy, consideration and warm hospitality which they have extended to the Commission during its stay on the Sub-Continent. We are convinced that both Governments wish to find a peaceful and a final solution of this dispute and that it is the intention of the Governments of India and Pakistan to continue to co-operate with the United Nations for this purpose.

The Commission and its Rapporteur, the Belgian representative, of course remain at the disposal of the Security Council and its President.

8

Resolutions Adopted and Speeches in Security Council, 1950–1957

8.1. Fifth Resolution* Adopted at the 470th Meeting of the Security Council, March 14, 1950

The Security Council,

Having received and noted the reports of the United Nations Commission for India and Pakistan established by its resolutions 39 (1948) of 20 January and 47 (1948) of 21 April 1948.

Having also received and noted the report of General A.G.L. McNaughton on the outcome of his discussions with the representatives of India and Pakistan which were initiated in pursuance of the decision taken by the Security Council on 17 December 1949.

Commending the Governments of India and Pakistan for their statesman like action in reaching the agreements embodied in the United Nations Commission's resolutions of 13 August 1948 and 5 January 1949 for a cease-fire, for the demilitarization of the State of Jammu and Kashmir and for the determination of its final disposition in accordance with the will of the people through the democratic method of a free and impartial plebiscite, and commending the parties in particular for their action in partially implementing these resolutions by (1) the cessation of hostilities effected 1 January 1949, (2) the establishment of a cease-fire line on 27 July 1949, and (3) the

---

*Adopted by 8 votes to none, with 2 abstentions (India, Yugoslavia). Res. 80 (1950); UN Document No. S/1469.

agreement that Fleet Admiral Chester W. Nimitz shall be Plebiscite Administrator.

Considering that the resolution of the outstanding difficulties should be based upon the substantial measure of agreement on fundamental principles already reached, and that steps should be taken forthwith for the demilitarization of the State and for the expenditious determination of its future in accordance with the freely expressed will of the inhabitants.

1. *Calls upon* the Governments of India and Pakistan to make immediate arrangements, without prejudice to their rights or claims and with due regard to the requirements of law and order, to prepare and execute within a period of five months from the date of this resolution a programme of demilitarization on the basis of the principles of paragraph 2 of General McNaughton's proposal or of such modification of those principles as may be mutually agreed;

2. *Decides* to appoint a United Nations Representative for the following purposes who shall have authority to perform his functions in such place or places as he may deem appropriate:

(a) To assist in the preparation and to supervise the implementation of the programme of demilitarization referred to above and to interpret the agreements reached by the parties for demilitarization;

(b) To place himself at the disposal of the Governments of India and Pakistan and to place before those Government or the Security Council any suggestions which, in his opinion, are likely to contribute to the expeditious and enduring solution of the dispute which has arisen between the two Governments in regard to the State of Jammu and Kashmir;

(c) To exercise all of the powers and responsibilities devolving upon the United Nations Commission for India and Pakistan by reason of existing resolutions of the Security Council and by reason of the agreement of the parties embodied in the resolution of the United Nations Commission of 13 August 1948 and 5 January 1949;

(d) To arrange at the appropriate stage of demilitarization for the assumption by the Plebiscite Administrator of the functions assigned to the latter under agreements made between the parties;

(e) To report to the Security Council as he may consider

necessary, submitting his conclusions and any recommendations which he may desire to make;

3. *Requests* the two Governments to take all necessary precautions to ensure that their agreements regarding the cease-fire shall continue to be faithfully observed, and calls upon them to take all possible measures to ensure the creation and maintenance of an atmosphere favourable to the promotion of further negotiations;

4. *Extends its best thanks* to the members of the United Nations Commission for India and Pakistan and to General A.G.L. McNaughton for their arduous and fruitful labours;

5. *Agrees* that the United Nations Commission for India and Pakistan shall be terminated, and decides that this shall take place one month after both parties have informed the United Nations Representative of their acceptance of the transfer to him of the powers and responsibilities of the United Nations Commission referred to in paragraph 2 (c) above.

8.2. Sixth Resolution* Adopted at the 539th Meeting of the Security Council, March 30, 1951

The Security Council,

Having received and noted the report of Sir Owen Dixon, the United Nations Representative for India and Pakistan, on his mission initiated by Security Council resolution 80 (1950) of 14 March 1950.

Observing that the Governments of India and Pakistan have accepted the provisions of the United Nations Commission for India and Pakistan resolutions of 13 August 1948 and 5 January 1949 and have reaffirmed their desire that the future of the State of Jammu and Kashmir shall be decided through the democratic method of a free and impartial plebiscite conducted under the auspices of the United Nations.

Observing that on 27 October 1950 the General Council of the "All Jammu and Kashmir National Conference" adopted a resolution recommending the convening of a Constituent Assembly

---

* Adopted by 8 votes to none with 3 abstentions (India, Union of Soviet Socialist Republics, Yugoslavia).
Res. 91 (1951); UN Document No. S/2017/Rev. 1.

for the purpose of determining the "future shape and affiliations of the State of Jammu and Kashmir"; observing further from statements of responsible authorities that action is proposed to convene such a Constituent Assembly and that the area from which such a Constituent Assembly would be elected is only a part of the whole territory of Jammu and Kashmir.

Reminding the Governments and authorities concerned of the principal embodied in its resolutions 47 (1948) of 21 April 1948, 51 (1948) of 3 June 1948 and 80 (1950) of 14 March 1950 and the United Nations Commission for India and Pakistan resolutions of 13 August 1948 and 5 January 1949, that the final disposition of the State of Jammu and Kashmir will be made in accordance with the will of the people expressed through the democratic method of a free and impartial plebiscite conducted under the auspices of the United Nations.

Affirming that the convening of a Constituent Assembly as recommended by the General Council of the "All Jammu and Kashmir National Conference" and any action that Assembly might attempt to take to determine the future shape and affiliation of the entire State or any part thereof would not constitute a disposition of the State in accordance with the above principle.

Declaring its belief that it is the duty of the Security Council in carrying out its primary responsibility for the maintenance of international peace and security to aid the parties to reach an amicable solution of the Kashmir dispute and that a prompt settlement of this dispute is of vital importance to the maintenance of international peace and security.

Observing from Sir Owen Dixon's report that the main points of difference preventing agreement between the parties were:

(a) The procedure for and the extent of demilitarization of the State preparatory to the holding of a plebiscite, and

(b) The degree of control over the exercise of the functions of government in the State necessary to ensure a free and fair plebiscite,

1. *Accepts,* in compliance with his request, Sir Owen Dixon's resignation and expresses its gratitude to Sir Owen for the great ability and devotion with which he carried out his mission;

2. *Decides* to appoint a United Nations Representative for India

and Pakistan in succession to Sir Owen Dixon:

3. *Instructs* the United Nations Representative to proceed to the subcontinent and, after consultation with the Governments of India and Pakistan, to effect the demilitarization of the State of Jammu and Kashmir on the basis of the United Nations Commission for India and Pakistan resolutions of 13 August 1948 and 5 January 1949;

4. *Calls upon* the parties to co-operate with the United Nations Representative to the fullest degree in effecting the demilitarization of the State of Jammu and Kashmir;

5. *Instructs* the United Nations Representative to report to the Security Council within three months from the date of his arrival on the subcontinent; if, at the time of this report, he has not effected demilitarization in accordance with paragraph 3 above, or obtained the agreement of the parties to a plan for effecting such demilitarization, the United Nations Representative shall report to the Security Council those points of defference between the parties in regard to the interpretation and execution of the agreed resolutions of 13 August 1948 and 5 January 1949 which he consider must be resolved to enable such demilitarization to be carrieds out;

6. *Calls upon* the parties, in the event of their discussions with the United Nations Representative failing in his opinion to result in full agreement, to accept arbitration upon all outstanding points of difference reported by the United Nations Representative in accordance with paragraph 5 above, such arbitration to be carried out by an arbitrator, or a panel or arbitrators, to be appointed by the President of the International Court of Justice after consultation with the parties;

7. *Decides* that the military observer group shall continue to supervise the cease-fire in the State;

8. *Requests* the Governments of India and Pakistan to ensure that their agreement regarding the cease-fire shall continue to be faithfully observed and calls upon them to take all possible measures to ensure the creation and maintenance of an atmosphere favourable to the promotion of further negotiations and to refrain from any action likely to prejudice a just and peaceful settlement.

9. *Requests* the Secretary-General to provide the United Nations Representative for India and Pakistan with such services and facilities as may be necessary in carrying out the terms of this resolution.

8.3. Seventh Resolution* Adopted at the 566th Meeting of the Security Council, November 10, 1951

The Security Council,

Having received and noted the report of Mr. Frank Graham, the United Nations Representative for India and Pakistan, on his mission initiated by Security Council resolution 91 (1951) of 30 March 1951, and having heard Mr. Graham's address to the Council on 18 October 1951.

Noting with approval the basis for a programme of demilitarization which could be carried out in conformity with the previous undertakings of the parties, put forward by the United Nations Representative in his communication of 7 September 1951 to the Prime Ministers of India and Pakistan.

1. *Notes with gratification* the declared agreement of the two parties to those parts of Mr. Graham's proposals which reaffirm their determination to work for a peaceful settlement, their will to observe the cease-fire agreement and their acceptance to the principle that the accession of te State of Jammu and Kashmir should be determined by a free and impartial plebiscite under the auspices of the United Nations;

2. *Instructs* the United Nations Representative to continue his efforts to obtain agreement of the parties on a plan for effecting the demilitarization of the State of Jammu and Kashmir;

3. *Calls upon* the parties to co-operate with the United Nations Representative to the fullest degree in his efforts to resolve the outstanding points of difference between them;

4. *Instructs* the United Nations Representative to report to the Security Council on his efforts, together with his views concerning the problems confided to him, not later than six weeks after this resolution comes into effect.

---

* Adopted by 9 votes to none, with 2 abstentions (India, Union of Soviet Socialist Republics)
Res. 96 (1951); UN Document No. S/2392.

8.4. Eighth Resolution* Adopted at the 611st Meeting of the Security Council, December 23, 1952

The Security Council,

Recalling its resolution 91 (1951) of 30 March 1951, its decision of 30 April 1951 and its resolution 96 (1951) of 10 November 1951.

Further recalling the provisions of the United Nations Commission for India and Pakistan resolutions of 13 August 1948 and 5 January 1949 which were accepted by the Governments of India and Pakistan and which provided that the question of the accession of the State of Jammu and Kashmir to India or Pakistan would be decided through the democratic method of a free and impartial plebiscite conducted under the auspices of the United Nations.

Having received the third report, dated 22 April 1952, and the fourth report, dated 16 September 1952, of the United Nations Representative for India and Pakistan.

1. *Endorses* the general principles on which the United Nations Representative has sought to bring about agreement between the Governments of India and Pakistan.

2. *Notes with gratification* that the United Nations Representative has reported that the Governments of India and Pakistan have accepted all but two of the paragraphs of his twelve-point proposals;

3. *Notes* that agreement on a plan of demilitarization of the State of Jammu and Kashmir has not been reached because the Governments of India and Pakistan have not agreed on the whole of paragraph 7 of the twelve-point proposals;

4. *Urges* the Governments of India and Pakistan to enter into immediate negotiations under the auspices of the United Nations Representative for India and Pakistan in order to reach agreement on the specific number of forces to remain on each side of the cease-fire line at the end of the period of demilitarization, this number to be between 3,000 and 6,000 armed forces remaining on the Pakistan side of the cease-fire line and between 12,000 and 18,000 armed forces remaining on the India side of the cease-fire line, as suggested by the United Nations Representative in his

---

* Adopted by 9 votes to none, with 1 abstention (Union of Soviet Socialist Republics)
Res. 98 (1952); UN Document No. S/2883.

proposals of 16 July 1952, such specific numbers to be arrived at bearing in mind the principles or criteria contained in paragraph 7 of the United Nations Representative's proposal of 4 September 1952;

5. *Records its gratitude* to the United Nations Representative for India and Pakistan for the great efforts which he has made to achieve a settlement and requests him to continue to make his services available to the Governments of India and Pakistan to this end;

6. *Requests* the Governments of India and Pakistan to report to the Security Council not later than thirty days from the date of the adoption of this resolution;

7. *Requests* the United Nations Representative for India and Pakistan to keep the Security Council informed of any progress.

8.5. Ninth Resolution* Adopted at the 765th Meeting of the Security Council, January 9, 1957

The Security Council,

Having heard statements from representatives of the Governments of India and Pakistan concerning the dispute over the State of Jammu and Kashmir.

Reminding the Governments and authorities concerned of the principle embodied in its resolutions 47 (1948) of 21 April 1948, 51 (1948) of 3 June 1948, 80 (1950) of 14 March 1950 and 91 (1951) of 30 March 1951, and the United Nations Commission for India and Pakistan resolutions of 13 August 1948 and 5 January 1949, that the final disposition of the State of Jammu and Kashmir will be made in accordance with the will of the people expressed through the democratic method of a free and impartial plebiscite conducted under the auspices of the United Nations.

1. *Reaffirms* the affirmation in its resolution 91 (1951) and declares that the convening of a Constituent Assembly as recommended by the General Council of the "All Jammu and Kashmir National Conference" and any action that Assembly may have taken or might attempt to take to determine the future shape and affiliation of the entire State or any part thereof, or action by the parties concerned in support of any such action by the assembly,

* Adopted by 10 votes to none, with 1 abstention (Union Soviet Socialist Republics).
Res. 122 (1957); UN Document no. S/3779.

would not constitute a disposition of the State in accordance with the above principle.

2. *Decides* to continue its consideration of the dispute.

8.6. Speech by Krishna Menon (India) in Security Council, 769th Meeting, February 15, 1957

Mr. President, I believe you reminded the Council this morning that its proceedings would centre around the draft resolution [S/3787], or at least I gathered that impression. Since there have been reasonably long debates on the general issue, I propose to confine myself to the draft resolution initiated by the United Kingdom and the United States and sponsored by Cuba and Australia in addition.

The operative part of this draft resolution requests the President of the Security Council, the representative of Sweden, to examine the Governments of India and Pakistan proposals; to visit so far as we are concerned, India for this purpose; and invite the Government of India to cooperate.

Before I enter into the substance of this matter and in order that the position of my delegation, my Government and my people should be understood not only in the Security Council but in the outside world, I should like to state here and now that so far as we are concerned, Mr. President, your counsel, your country, the high office you held and your person are held in high respect in India, and you would be welcome at any time. But the question of the functional character of the operations you propose to undertake would be another matter, which we would have to discuss in substance. Therefore, the traditional hospitality of our country would not be disregarded, even in the face of a Security Council resolution with which we may find ourselves in disagreement.

Having got that out of the way, I would like now to refer to the subject matter that is before us this afternoon. There have been several speeches. The majority of them, if not all of them purport to be based upon the statements made by India and Pakistan and, for the greater part, refer to the statement that I made in this Council. Therefore, it becomes necessary for me to deal with them paragraph by paragraph. First of all, I do not have the script with me and, secondly it will become interminably long. After that I will try to examine the draft resolution before the Council and deal with its more important aspects as far as the text concerns us.

Next I will try to convey to the Security Council what its consequences would be. I do not mean the short-term consequences of how members of the Council vote. What would be its consequences with respect to peace and stability in our part of the world, with respect to public opinion not only in India but in South East Asia, with the exception of parts of Pakistan and with respect to the purported objective of the draft resolution itself? These are obligations I owe to the Council. Some of them may not be welcome to those who are the authors of certain observations. But my duty here is not to reflect the will of other Governments but to reflect, as far as I can, the will of my people and my Government and to convey to you the state of affairs.

It is not so long ago that, for the sake of peace and in order not to drive certain issues to differences, we came to an agreement with the then British Government of the day to station a boundary force under a supreme command on the Indo-Pakistan frontier in the West. It was one of the great tragic decisions we took, largely buying that time in the necessities of the situation. I do not think either of our countries had made a more sad decision because as the result of that came the great slaughter of 1947, with respect to which my Prime Minister decided to dissolve the force.

The first statement by a Council member was made by the representative of the United Kingdom, for whom we have very great respect. With his country we had relations of one kind, and we have relations of another kind today. Those relations have been strained considerably by the British adventure in the Middle East and now their adventure in regard to Kashmir, but, so far as we are concerned, we would do our best not to allow these individual actions on the part of the United Kingodm Government—not of its people, fortunately—to come in the way of the more substantial relations that should exist between our countries. But I would be doing no service to this Council, or indeed to the United Kingdom or to the very many friends that we have there and with whom we have been in such close relationship if I did not indicate to them the enormous, deep and very vehement feelings in India at the present time in regard to the United Kingdom. The United Kingdom might easily retaliate by saying: "We felt somewhat like that when you took a certain position in another matter." Of course, that is one way of looking at it.

Sir Pierson Dixon, after tracing the history of this matter, said that finally, after the failure of various missions, to which I shall come back in a minute, including that of Mr. Graham, whose absence from this table my delegation regrets – even though there is nothing very much in Mr. Graham's report that assists the statement of the position that we made, because he did not examine that – the breakdown of the direct negotiations was due to extraneous causes. We had, during the course of this debate, largely because of our concern in regard to Indo-American relations and to avoid introducing issues of the "cold war" outside the Kashmir question and, what is more, in the hope that the present lapse from fortitude and wisdom in this matter is temporary, not reffered to them, but the extraneous consideration to which Sir Pierson Dixon refers is the military agreement between the United States and Pakistan.

Our views on this matter are very well known, and there is no doubt – and again one must state the facts of the case – that the added military strength of Pakistan by the supply of very considerably quantities of war material to that country, of which we have some knowledge, has certainly altered the situation. But it would be equally wrong to say that that was the only changed condition, or indeed the reason for the direct talks between Mr. Mohammed Ali, the former Prime Minister of Pakistan, and afterward someone else, and the Prime Minister of India. It did weigh considerably, there is no doubt about it. What is more, we at that time said that with relation to Kashmir we could not consider the United States as being neutral, and for that reason, and with the utmost politeness, we suggested that observers of United States nationality were not the best people to serve on the cease-fire line. They responded with equal politeness, and we resolved that situation as between two countries who have no desire to exaggerate a difficulty. I regret that this matter has come up, because I have been at great pains to avoid it, but it was referred to by a close ally of the United States, and it is not my practice to run away from any argument that has been put forward. So that is that. So this extraneous relationship, if it is one of the factors, was not the factor that led to the breakdown of the negotiations.

Sir Pierson Dixon made other statements. I picked out that speech because that is the keynote speech, as they call it in this country. The other speeches follow more or less that line with the exception of the speech from Colombia. That is, they lay stress on what is called demilitarization. This word "demilitarization" for this purpose must be interpreted with the connotation that it has derived through the years, by negotiation.

In spite of the Security Council having heard my voice for so long, perhaps the members would be so kind, even if they did not read one per cent of the papers before them, which is impossible because there are so many of them, as to at least refer to the resolutions of the Commission and point out to me any place where there is reference to demilitarization. Demilitarization is a phase and a problem, as it is now pinpointed, which arose as one of the methods for creating the conditions under Part II of the resolution of 13 August 1948 (S/1100, para. 75). It is very important for us to refer to this in view of the other suggestions to be covered by demilitarization, but we are prepared to face this in this way.

When either the United States or the United Kingdom, speaks to us about the importance of demilitarization, they have to take into account certain factors. In Kashmir, which the legitimate Government of Kashmir administers, there are units of the Indian Army. I want to explain this. The Indian Army in Kashmir is not a foreign army any more than we have a foreign army in Bombay. The Kashmiris pay for it like everybody else. That is, certain units of the Army of the Indian Union are in the Constituent State of Kashmir. They are easily identifiable. They have no uniforms that are not Army uniforms. Their divisions and their numbers are well known. In addition to this, we have in Kashmir approximately 6,000 men belonging to the Kashmir militia, who are a kind of territorial force, a State force, largely of an armed police character, intended for internal security and the like. That is the total strength of our military position in Kashmir, far below what it was at the time of the cease-fire. These are published figures or, if they are not, I shall publish them, and I take the responsibility for doing so.

On the other side, according to our information, which normally is reliable, in regard to Pakistan military dispositions, there are forty-five battalions of the "Azad" Kashmir forces. There were thirty-five at the time of the cease-fire. Now there are forty-five battalions of the "Azad" Kashmir forces, officered by men of the Pakistan Army. If the Security Council has any doubt about it, we shall some day be willing to furnish you their names, their ranks and their particulars from available sources. They are officered, trained and equipped by the Pakistan Army. They are well-trained soldiers. There are artillery regiments, cavalry, a tank corps, and so on. There were thirty-five, and now there are approximately forty-five battalions of these troops. In addition, as Mr. Firoz Khan Noon admitted the other day by implication, the Pakistan Army itself is there, because he said he would withdraw it, and you cannot withdraw what is not there. Therefore, in addition, there is the Pakistan Army itself. When we speak about demilitarization, we have to think of this military element and what is demilitarizable.

Add to that two other factors. There are the commandos that are being trained, of which there are 800 in school at all times. When they are finished, they are thrown back into the population. They are another military element in the situation just across our border, mainly in the population. This is not in the whole of the Pakistan-occupied area, because over the whole of the Pakistan-occupied area, in Gilgit, Baltistan and so on, these factors do not apply so much, but in this small area where there are half a million people.

In addition to that, as I pointed out the other day, there is today an army in Pakistan which is out of proportion to the relations established at the time of partition. Pakistan has well over 200,000 men equipped not only with the normal equipment that comes from the United Kingdom under the usual purchase arrangements, but with the considerable supply of military material that comes from the United States in pursuance of military agreements, which are not directed against us, so far as the United States is concerned – and we accept that situation so far as the United States is concerned. They are within very short distances of our frontier. I gave the Security Council the mileages the other day. (764th meeting, paras 119 and 162).

Therefore, when we speak about demilitarization we must take all these elements into consideration and set them side by side with two other factors. You gentlemen here representing the Member States are not merely concerned about passing resolutions but about their vast social, political and world consequences. Let us set these factors side by side with two others.

One of these constitutes the remarks made by the representative of Pakistan outside his printed text when he first spoke here. He stated:

> "Here I would like to say that it is sometimes argued by India that everything is peaceful, so why bother about Kashmir? But I

warn you" – he warns the Security Council – "that is a calm before the storm. Everything is not peaceful. We have just seen a telegram which states that, on 11 January, our Minister for Information, Mr. Amir Azam Khan, made a statement in Karachi that the Indians have massed their troops on our border." (761st meeting, para. 105) – a statement which I contradicted the other day.

The representative of Pakistan then went on to say:

"Please do not be misled by the fact that we are peaceful and that we want a peaceful solution." (*Ibid*., para. 106).

This is exactly the pattern, and there may be those who remember this fact, that occurred in 1947. We were told: "Wolf, wolf – " – at that time – "it is coming, it is coming; after all we cannot stop it". And then it came and the Pakistan Army came afterwards.

The "Daily Telegraph" of London – a paper which is not friendly to India – carried on 11 February 1957 an interview with Sardar Abdul Quiyum Khan, President of the "Azad" Government. I shall not read the whole of the interview, but this is a part of what he said:

"It is coming to a fight in Kashmir" – this is issued not from 'Azad' Kashmir, but from the Ministry of Kashmir affairs in Karachi – "whether the people like it or not. We have no alternative left and I have told the Pakistan Government this. I had expected we should be fighting by December or January but certain factors intervened." – The fact of the United States elections, and therefore the Security Council was put off, "I now think it is certain there will be fighting this year, perhaps even in a few weeks."

When the correspondent raised the plebicite issue, the President said:

"Recent Security Council notes were encouraging politically" – that is a also borne out by the testimonial to the United Kingdom Government by the Pakistan Prime Minister, to which I shall refer in a moment – "but Kashmiris want to see some results at last, if not by diplomacy then by war. India will

> never agree to a free plebiscite. India had occupied most of Kashmir and had poured money into her organization there. She knew that Kashmiris on a free vote would never opt for India, so Nehru would be crazy to agree to a plebiscite. I don't think he is crazy." – That is the only part of it that is true. – "It will be a people's war: we know our country. In Kashmir we can give the Indians hell. We are much better equipped" – this is another truthful fact, – "now than in the former fighting when we often had not more than five rounds per man."

The President went on to point out that "Azad" Kashmir was not a party to the cease-fire agreement – this again is the pattern of 1947 – and therefore was not bound by it. He said:

> "If the United Nations would leave the matter in the hands of 'Azad' Kashmir fighting men for just a few weeks, the question would be solved. Nehru only understands that kind of language. He would come running to the United Nations begging them to intervene on his behalf. We can turn both flanks of the India."

This is only a sample of what is going on. I want to report to the Security Council that this type of wild statement is being made at a time when a vast election campaign is going on in India, where we are addressing, as I stated the other day, an electorate of 200 million people. I state to the Security Council in all conscience that the efforts of our leaders at the present moment are to exercise restraint upon the people so that they should not become inflamed. I could quote to the Council, if there was time, the speeches made by the Prime Minister in this connexion, when he said that if misfortune should befall us by way of attack, we should meet it with fortitude and calm, but there was no need to get excited.

Normally this does not very much matter, but we had a dress rehearsal and we have a performance afterwards, so that this is a repeat performance. When the Security Council passes resolutions which have the effect of unsettling events – unsettling events in Pakistan, in the occupied areas, in Jammu and Kashmir and in the whole of India – then it takes upon itself a responsibility which, fortunately for itself, it will not have to shoulder, while the people of India will have to shoulder it. I hope that my good friend, General Carlos Romulo, the representative of the Philippines will not say that

I was admonishing the Council. I shall come to that in a moment.

That is the background of what the representative of Pakistan refers to as the decrease in tension. Unless this is measured in reverse terms with the whole thermometer upside down, I do not see how this can mean a decrease in tension. There is a decrease in tension between Pakistan and India in certain other matters, particularly between India and Eastern Pakistan in respect of which we have concluded trade agreements and where the populations are less inflamed by these matters. Therefore, when we speak about demilitarization and a decrease in tension, these matters have to be understood.

While I am on this point, I might deal with one other matter, because my Government is very anxious and very concerned that no statement of ours or any errors of omission or commission should afterwards be charged up to us as a commitment. We have suffered by moderation. We have suffered by reasonableness in our proceedings before this Council. Every time we considered a hypothetical proposition and every time we have agreed to embark upon an exploration, it has been charged up against as a commitment. Therefore, I want to say here and now that whatever mathematical calculations were made with regard to 6,000 or 3,000 or 12,000 or 21,000 in the various previous negotiations, these no longer hold true, because no offer, that is not accepted, is a binding contract, either in the case of individuals or in the case of nations. Otherwise we should have a number of floating commitments, and no country would know where it stood, In the course of long negotiations, all kinds of offers are made. If the Secretary-General were to be committed to the many suggestions which he must have made in the past sixty days then he would be in an awkward position. The same thing is true with respect to a government.

Therefore, I want to say here and now, Mr. President, that if you were to go to India, or if anyone else were to go, it would be no use telling us that we agreed to this and that that time and that "now therefore you are committed to it." We agree to nothing – we discuss all these proposals. They must all be considered, as with any problem, in the context of the time. We agree to things to which we are parties.

That brings me to the next propositions put forward by the representative of the United Kingdom. He said, quite rightly, that it is common ground between Pakistan and India that the only obligations appearing in this matter are the resolutions of 13 August 1948 and 5 January 1949 (768th meeting, para. 13). But Sir Pierson Dixon would feel flattered by the fact that I was educated in a system for which he has very great appreciation and therefore I take care to be precise in language. I said that the only obligations we "had" undertaken – and, although English is rather sparse in grammar, it does have tenses – were these two resolutions. It is quite true that my distinguished colleague put it differently. I do not say that his language is more precise, but he has more friends around this Council than I have, and therefore he does not have to be so much forewarned. And I suppose that General Romulo would say that I am, by nature, suspicious. Of course, he is wrong.

At any rate, we say that these resolutions of 13 August 1948 and 5 January 1949 are our only engagements – and I use the word "engagements" very deliberately. I said that they could be elevated to the form of treaties if they were fromal. But what we said was that the only international engagements are the two resolutions of the Commission – and this is recounting history at the present time. I do not object to the statement made by the distinguished representative, but it bears the inference that this thing stands by itself, without any further progress in that matter or any past history. Those engagements have to be understood in the context of all that was said at that time. That becomes necessary because someone is likely to say: "Well, here are these resolutions. It is quite true that you did not get anywhere with them. Why don't we start on them tomorrow morning? Well, tomorrow is Saturday, and on Sunday we go to church, so we will start on Monday". That would not work because you have to take all the surrounding circumstances into account. And that is why it is necessary to repeat very briefly the fact that the position of the Government of India, as stated the other day by the Prime Minister in a speech at Allahabad, is that Pakistan has violated the cease-fire agreement. That is a far more grievous charge, and we make that deliberately: that Pakistan has violated the cease-fire agreement by the introduction of military personnel and materials into the area and by the annexation of territory. And therefore, when the first part of the agreement stands violated, the consideration of the second part becomes very, very, very subsequent. That is very bad English – but it becomes very subsequent.

Therefore, the observation made by the representative of the United Kingdom must be taken in the context, first of all, of the explanations that I submitted on behalf of my Government and the fact that, since the conclusions of that agreement, there have been violations of the Part I by the accentuation of the forces on the other side of the cease-fire line and by the assimilation of territory.

The President of the Council is what might be called an example of the European neutral. I would ask him, in all conscience, since I am entitled to address a question to the President: How is it that when the Constituent Assembly of Kashmir, under our constitutional procedures and using only the pen and not the sword, working over a period of five or six years and proceeding from a legal instrument about which you all say you are neutral – nobody has challenged it so far – writes a Constitution which does not alter any of the physical facts, that is called annexation, whereas the eleven members around this table never turned around and asked the Pakistan delegation under what title its Government annexed these territories of 42,000 square miles? The latter was barefaced annexation.

Here I propose to cite to you assurances, documents and statements made in the Security Council time after time, that the sovereignty of the Jammu and Kashmir Government remains inviolate and that neither the Commission nor the Council will do anything to alter it.

That leads me to the third point, Sir Pierson Dixon referred to engagements. He is a friend of mine, and I am sure he will forgive me for centring the argument around him (in a sense, it is an expression of great esteem). I said the other day that this engagement bound our two countries. Since this is probably my last main intervention during this episode of the discussion of this item, I should like to say that there are three parties engaged in this whole process.

The Security Council is a party to the resolution of 13 August 1948, and we of the Government of India have the privilege and the right to ask the Security Council what it is going to do about the violation of Part I. The Council is very quick in passing resolutions about the Constituent Assembly and being misled into acceptance of what was put out in a "crisis atmosphere". How is it that no question had been asked by the eleven nations represented round this table – I ask this question only because my people will ask and because the Security Council does not represent only these eleven countries but, as we understand it, all the Member States of the United Nations – about this apparent, gross, obvious, continuous, persistent and flagrant violation of the cease-fire agreement, of international law, of commitments contained in Security Council resolutions and Commission resolutions, and solemn understandings given by representatives of Member States to our Government, which are in writing and which have been made public?

The shoe is on the other foot. That is to say, the annexation is on the other side. The Security Council would be justified in asking us why we have not requested a meeting in order to complain about this annexation. The answer is two-fold. My Government proceeds on the basis that this problem – and that is what it is; it is not a dispute – is one of extreme complexity, which involves India-Pakistan relations and various other world factors. The solution of it, which was supposed to be proximate on 1 January 1949, is still far from being at hand. We consider that we have a duty not to re-agitate matters and therefore we have let sleeping dogs lie so far as the actual stage of affairs is concerned, without in any way permitting the Security Council or anyone else to obtain our assent – and it is repeated so many times – to any change or alteration in the status of this territory.

The representative of Colombia had referred to these matters (768th meeting). He probably has a first-hand knowledge of the question, because some of these assurances were given by Mr. Lozano. The Secretary-Geneal has an easy way of ascertaining the facts in this connexion, because some of the members of the Commission's staff at that time are still members of the Secretariat here. These assurances are not hanging in the air; they are part of the resolutions. I deal with them more specifically today in view of the observations of the representative of Colombia,

To place demilitarization in the centre of the present draft resolution is, in our opinion, a misreading of the entire situation. It is this aspect which has bedevilled the question since the time of General McNaughton. It is a matter of great regret to us that suggestions made, in a spirit of good will, by two persons from countries which are members of our Commonwealth should have been ultra vires of every decision and of the principles of the Security Council. Sir Owen Dixon is a distinguished judge; he is now Chief Justice of Australia. With great respect, I must say that Sir Owen Dixon seems to have approached this problem as though Kashmir were the Australian bush of 200 years ago – and, if Mr. Walker objects to that idiom, if it is one, I shall withdraw it – as though Kashmir belonged to no one and, therefore, a United Nations government or some other government could be set up in gross violation of the Security Council's express commitment.

My Government is entitled to ask this question: why is it when we have committed no violations whatsoever, that there is all this talk about violations by us? The Secutiry Council itself – a party to this agreement – is remiss in not drawing the other party's attention to violations; the Security Council is remiss in not asking for the withdrawal of the other party from that area; the Security Council's representatives make proposals to us which are in gross violation of the commitments. Why is there no unanimity about these violations?

In fact, we would not have discussed the 13 August 1948 resolution if there had been any suggestion that the soverignty of the Jammu and Kashmir Government and India's competence as regards the defence of its frontiers – which are on the western and nothern side of Kashmir – were in question.

I do not know whether the Security Council wishes me to go on citing these documents. The documents are before the Council, as I have said time and time again.

Mr. Korbel, the Czechoslovak representative, who was Chairman of the Commission in August 1948, said that the sovereignty of the territory was not to be changed. In a letter which the Prime Minister of India sent to Mr. Korbel on 20 August 1948, the Prime Minister wrote:

> "If I understood you (Mr. Korbel) correctly, A, 3 of Part II of the resolution does not envisage the creation of any of the conditions to which we have objected in paragraph 3 (1) of this letter. In fact, you made it clear that the Commission was not competent to recognize the sovereignty of any authority over the evacuated areas other than that of the Jammu and Kashmir Government." (S/1100, para.71).

Now, there was only one Jammu and Kashmir Government then, and there is only one Jammu and Kashmir Government now. I ask the representative of Cuba, who is so attached to the idea of sovereignty and freedom from intervention in internal affairs, how he reconciles that position with this one in respect of Kashmir.

In reply to the above-mentioned letter, Mr. Korbel wrote to the Prime Minister of India as follows:

> "The Commission requests me to convey to Your Excellency its view that the interpretation of the resolution as expressed in paragraph 4 of your letter coincides with its own interpretation." [*Ibid*, para. 79.]

In a letter dated 16 April 1949, the Vice-Chairman of the Commission, who, I believe, was a United States citizen, wrote:

> "It has consistently been the view of the Commission, as well as the Security Council, that pending the determination of the will of the people as regards the accession of the State of India or Pakistan neither body"—and this means neither the Security Council nor the Commission, nor India or Pakistan—"Will recognize any new sovereignty in the State. To do so would constitute a prejudgement of the will of the people."

I read out all these documents because they have a relation to the draft resolution sponsored by the United State and the United Kingdom. They have a resolution to the violation of our municipal law and the principles of the law of those two countries—and this particularly concerns the representative of the United Kingdom, for it is from the United Kingdom that we claim the heritage of this law. What is more, they have a relation to the violation fo international law—and I shall return to this aspect in a moment.

I should like now to read out the following excerpt from the Commission's third interim report:

> "The territory evacuated by the Pakistan troops will be administered by the local authorities"—and the expression "local authorities" is intended to mean persons who are not a governemt, who are operating in the area de facto—"under the surveillance of the Commission and without prejudice to the sovereignty of the State."

Hence, there can be neither a Pakistan nor an "Azed" nor a "Gilgit" government, nor any other government in this area. The other day, I read out to the Council the Commission's agreement that we were entitled to station garrisons there for the protection of the trade routes from the north and the northwest (763rd meeting, para. 62).

I continue to quote from the Commission's third interim report :

> "These provisions are without prejudice to the territorial integrity" – and, when part of the country has been annexed, that is certainly a violation of territorial integrity – "and the sovereignty of the State of Jammu and Kashmir."

I could go on quoting from these documents – and there are so many of them.

In the Security Council, General McNaughton – who, I believe, was President of the Council at the time of which I am speaking – approached this problem as though this territory really did not belong to anyone, as though two parties were fighting over it; he tried to place us both on an equal status.

Sir Benegal Rau, who was then a member of the Security Council, wrote the following to General McNaughton in this connescion:

> "It has been admitted all along that the sovereignty of the Jammu and Kashmir State should be accepted over the whole area of the State." – that is a statement of our position – ."If Pakistan irregular forces, such as the Gilgit or the Baltistan Scouts, remain in the northern area, the sovereignty of the State will be violated militarily. – This, again, is a point which has an immediate bearing on the suggestion made by the United States and the United Kingdom. – "Further, if, as suggested, the administration of this area is to remain in the hand of the existing local authorities, which have been created by Pakistan and are aided by Pakistan officials, the sovereignty of the Jammu and Kashmir State in this area will be equally violated in the administrative field."

That was said in reply to General McNaughton's suggestion for the creation of a new situation, disregarding the basis of the procedures.

Members of the Council will thus be able to understand why the Government of India has to be extremely wary. A suggestion is put to us, and we are told: "No, you are not asked to accept it, you are only asked to look at it". But the next day we shall be told, "You looked at it, and did not think it was a profanity to do so; if it is not profane, then it must be sacred, and therefore it is binding on you". That is the kind of argument that we have heard.

Sir Benegal Rau also said the following with regard to the question of sovereignty, on 7 February 1950:

> "...accession does not mean dissolution: the acceding State remains intact and fully sovereign in its own field even after accession; it continues as a single unit. If, therefore, the plebiscite is to be held for the State as a whole, it must not be disrupted beforehand." (463rd meeting, para. 12).

I turn now to a memorandum which the representative of India transmitted to the United Nations Representative, Mr. Graham, on 11 September 1952. I allude to this later period in order to show that this is not old history. In that memorandum, the representative of India said that the Government's position was the following:

> "The administration of this area would, under paragraph 3 of Part II of the resolution of 13 August 1948, vest in local authorities to be established or recognized for the purpose; to these local authorities, under the same resolution, only local administrative functions have been assigned...To give them any armed force equivalent to troops would not be consistent either with their status or with their function and would be a violation of the soverignty of the Union of India and the Jammu and Kashmir State. In the very nature of things, therefore, these local authorities can be entrusted only with a civil armed force." (S/2783 and Corr. 1, annex 5, sect. 1).

In a letter to Mr. Graham dated 17 February 1953, we stated:

> "The Government of India are unable to agree to the retention of any military force in the socalled 'Azad' Kashmir territory. Not only would this be contrary to the assurance given by UNCIP to India" – and I contend that every assurance given by the United Nations Commission for India and Pakistan to India is an assurance given by Security Council to the Government of India – "that the resolution of 13 August should not be interpreted, or applied in practice, so as to bring into question the sovereignty of the Jammu and Kashimr Government over

the portion of their territory evacuated by Pakistan troops..." (S/2967, annex IV, para. 2).

Of course, the evacuation never took place.

That is the position with regard to sovereignty.

The observation that I shall now make has relation to the whole conception which is now sponsored by the United States and the United Kingdom in regard to United Nations forces. There are also other matters connected with it. My distinguished friend, Mr. Lodge, United States Ambassador, has told us at the 768th meeting that we are only being asked by the Security Council to consider this idea of United Nations forces, but it is not right to ask a sovereign Government to consider something that is against international law, against its own sovereign rights, and in violation of the agreement with the Security Council. It is unethical, inequitable and, what is more, it would not lead to a settlement. I am afraid that Mr. Lodge made a slip when, in explaining the draft resolution, he used the words "specifically the United Nations force", so that it was not just one of those things that are innocent. He said that the core of this draft resolution was the United Nations force and, Mr. Lodge being a man of, if I may say so with great respect, great simplicity of mind and frankness and candour of expression, let this out. No doubt his speech had been very carefully looked into and the words had been put there. Since in a year from now these words may be quoted against us, I do not want to make any mistake of my not having something to show to you about that.

The United States representative has addressed a request to the Government of India to receive the President of the Security Council very cordially. We appreciate this request and accept it in the spirit in which it is made, but, as I said a while ago, so far as hospitality is concerned the present President is almost half a native of India. I do not mean this in a disrespectful way; you are always welcome.

In the statement of the representative of the United States—perhaps I might make this general—there is no reference whatsoever to the people on the other side. My colleague from Cuba has spoken about rights, about self-determination about the people and about all those things that we value (768th meeting, paras. 87 to 90), but why is it we have not heard the voice of Cuba in connexion with the freedom of the people who are under the suppression and tyranny of Pakistan authorities on the other side of our cease-fire line? Why is it that we have not heard that in ten years these people have not seen a ballot paper? Why is it that they are streaming into our part of the territory? Why is it they are under conditions of economic degradation? Why is it that when the five-years plan is making vast strides in the State of Jammu and Kashmir, there is no such thing at all, or even a semblance of it, anywhere in the Pakistan-occupited area? Why is it there are still wild tracts? What is more, why is it that the very men who are the accredited representatives of the organizations of this area make representations to the Pakistan Constituent Assembly and say: "We are but helots, we are but slaves, we have no voice in our own country"? With what voice can either the Security Council, or anyone coming before it, demand a plebiscite for people on our side who exercise their franchise, who have freedom of speech, who function under scores of local bodies, who have freedom of dicussion, who have newspapers, who have economic development? With what voice, with what strength of argument can Pakistan come before the Security Council and ask about freedom of choice for those people who have no freedom at all? We say that Part I of the resolution of 13 August 1948 stands violated and therefore, Pakistan should have no say at all. It is my bounden duty to request the Security Council – not, my friend from the Philippines, to admonish – to give me an answer to these questions.

Our people are dedicated to the Charter. Their emotional reactions, as the Secretary-General will bear witness – I am not making him a party to our dispute – are dedicated to the Charter. They feel that here everything works in terms of justice, equity and fair play. How is it that in all these nine years of discussion no one has asked these questions? All the argument has been about the people who have rights, asking us – and that is putting it at its best – why do they not have more. In other words, if there were a plebiscite when the conditions are satisfied, when it will not create an upset, and when the security of India is not in danger, if we are, by the lack of the conditions that are necessary for a fair settlement, put into the position of handing these unfortunate men who have exercised their freedom into the helotry that prevails on the other side, then it would be a sin against the United Nations Charter.

My colleague from Australia later reminded us of very valid

examples, as he described them, and very salutary examples. He said that we had recently had a case where we sent out a United Nations force (768th meeting, para. 53). It is my recollection, although I may be wrong, that the representative of Australia did not support that proposition at the time, but that is by the way. It is misleading and it is unfair to us, at any rate, whatever you may think of it yourself, to draw an analogy between the United Nations Emergency Force in which we participate and which is in Egypt and any suggestion of the kind that is now being made. In one case, the territory of Egypt was invaded by France, the United Kingdom and Israel, and there was no question of having to find out about the invasion. Nobody ever denied that it was an invasion, and the purposes of this Force were two-fold, and my Government has insisted that these purpose should remian two-fold. The purposes of this Force are described in paragraph 12 of the Report of the Secretary-General on the plan for an Emergency International United Nations force. In that paragraph it is stated that the functions of the Force are to supervise the cease fire and to supervise the withdrawal. Is anybody suggesting that a United Nations force should go into the Pakistan-occupied areas in order to supervise their misdoings or to stop their misdoing and to supervise their withdrawal, and then to go away? That is not the idea at all. Therefore, it is not possible to draw an analogy between the two cases. In one case, the United Nations Emergency Force had to go to the defence of those who were aggressed against, and in the other case it would go to stand by the aggressor. As Sir Pierson Dixon, with the candour we expect of him, has pointed out, that is what Pakistan has asked for and that has been espoused. Any attempt to draw this parallel is, in my humble submission, a challenge to the political intelligence of the Member States of the United Nations, because the analogy bears no relation to facts whatsoever. As the film writers would say, such resemblances as there may be are purely coincidental. Therefore, do not let us draw this analogy, which comes ill from the representative of Australia, who initially refused to have anything to do with this business of sending a force to Egypt in order to implement the purposes of the Charter. I will come back to this and say where we stand with regard to the Charter.

We agree in the main with what has been said by the representative of Colombia, who had the advantage of having one of his countrymen on the Commission who spent hours and hours with the Heads of Government and high officials both in Pakistan and in

India.

We have circulated documents for your information, and we hope that you have read them. We hope that if you have not yet read them, you will read them in the future. If I may say so with respect I would not feel any sense of umbrage if people did not read them fully, because I myself find it difficult to get from one end of these documents to the other, but a reading of them is necessary.

The representative of Cuba started from a basic problem that was worthy of the great philosopher, Jean-Jacques Rousseau, about the sovereign will of the people. He then went into history and, if I may say so, he misunderstood what I said in the Security Council, but that may have been my fault. I said that the capital of Kashmir, Srinagar, was founded 2,300 years ago. I did not say at that time that through the millennia this was a separate State. Actually, the history of Kashmir goes back 5,000 years before the Christian era. It comes into mere modern history, in the Buddhistic period. After a short period of Buddhist rule, a succession of Hindu dynasties ruled in Kashmir until the end of the twelfth centruy. Then it came under Moslem rule and was subsequently reconquered by a Moslem emperor, Akbar of India, and became part of the Indian Empire. For sixty-three years, on account of the row with the English, the Afghans then occupied it. There were difficulties between the Afghans and the British at various times but not now—they are very good friends, and we are happy they are. There are only few episodes in the long history of Kashmir when it had been outside of the mainland of India. My colleague from Pakistan the other day refuted the "purchase" of Kashmir and I gave the answer to it.

The argument of the representative of Cuba is that the accession by the King is not acceptable. With great respect to his legal knowledge, which is very considerable so far as I am concerned—I mean the respect—no other accession would have been valid, and I call as witness the representative of the United Kingdom or his legal experts. Even if the four and a half million people in Kashmir had signed a memorandum saying: "We accede", on that day in 1947, that accession would not be worth the paper it was written on. It might have political value. It has political value and it has social value. The British Parliament laid down that the accession was to be by the King. This does not mean that we could trick a King into giving an accession against the will of the people. If that is the argument that is in the mind of the representative of Cuba, then I think it is a valid argument and I humbly refer him to the answer I made to the Pakistan 'Foreign Minister in regard to the allegation of fraud. Therefore, there is no question that, over and above that, the first thing we did was to seek, and in the end obtain, the consent of the only national movement there was which for twenty-five years has resisted the Maharaja's rule and the members of the national movement agreed and they head the government today. We agree with the representative of Cuba that we must honour commitments, but we equally submit that the Security Council has an obligation to honour, commitments, and commitments are what are in the documents and what is in the spirit of those documents in all the surrounding circumstances.

That takes me to the question of the plebiscite which has been referred to constantly. It appears to me to be comparatively simple. The resolution of 13 August 1948 was adopted by the Commission at its 40th meeting. I want to submit to you as responsible members representing Member States that just because a word appears in a document or a resolution and it is repeated a million times over, it does not add to its legal, political, moral or other values. It is quite true that we have talked about the plebiscite, but what is the place of it in this document? I have read this many times, but I will read it again. Part III of the resolution reads:

> "The Government of India and the Government of Pakistan reaffirm their wish" – not their resolve, not their commitment, but their wish – "that future status of the State of Jammu and Kashmir shall be determined in accordance with the will of the people and to that end, upon, acceptance of the truce agreement" – here my colleague from the Philippines comes in – "upon acceptance of the truce agreement, both Governments agree". Agree to what? They agree "to enter into consultations with the Commission to determine fair and equitable conditions..."(S/1100, para 75).

We did not say that when a plebiscite has been organized we would enter into consultation after it was over. Perhaps it was our mistake that we entered into consultation before because we thought we were going very, very fast. It may be a lesson for the future, but I submit it is not a reason for misunderstanding the position of my Government in regard to international commitments. We agreed "upon acceptance of the truce agreement...to enter into consultations with the Commission". What for? To determine "fair and equitable conditions". Now how about this propaganda which has been going on for the last seven or eight years and which shows no sign of abatement and, what is more—it is not only aided and abetted—which is inspired by responsible leaders and members of the Government of Pakistan, which is part of their national policy. In those circumstances, I submit to you that we had to create the conditions, that is, the first conditions necessary.

A plebiscite is a peaceful process, and you cannot force this peaceful process. It is like some people using the machinery of democracy in order to destroy it. So, similarly, the word "plebiscite" embodies the great idea of self-determination and it simply is not to be misinterpreted. We stand by Part III of the resolution. Two parts have not been satisfied. Our undertaking is to confer in order to find "fair and equitable conditions". Are conditions equitable when there is a compaign of hatred? Are conditions equiable when the treaty is in the place of an annex? Are conditions equiable when the Pakistan Government both privately and openly says the purpose of its military programme with the United States is in order to arms against India? If I am challenged on this, I will produce the evidence. That is with regard to the plebiscite, so I say with great respect to my friend from Cuba that we are not running away from any conception. But I submit that it is wrong, that it is against international law, that it is against the commitments of the United Nations, that it is against any possibility of the Charter's being respected and that it is a violation of the dignity and work of those people who believe in the United Nations, to say that just because these words appear somewhere that that is therefore a contract. That would be like my colleague the other day who accused some little Moslem boy of quoting the Koran only in one part. Therefore, that is the position of the plebiscite.

I have been asked why we take up one position in regard to Algeria and another in regard to Kashmir. First of all, in regard to Kashmir, the conditions have been laid down here, a whole plan has been laid down here. We agreed to the principles. By the way, Sir Pierson Dixon also referred to the resolution of 5 January 1949. I should like to refresh his memory. It refers to the principles on which a plebiscite has to be carried out—it Parts I and II of the resolution of 13 August operate. After Part I and Part II, then Part III begins to function by negotiation. When that is all ready, then there is a plan on the chessbord. You cannot start from the other end. That is how things are.

With regard to Algeria there has been a conquest, and that is not denied by anybody. I do not want to go outside the realm of this discussion, but I did not raise this question. There was a conquest and there was a national movement to replace that conquest. There is no such thing in Kashmir. I told you the other day that the best evidence and the most convincing argument before the Security Council, irrespective of all legal doctrine, would have been if the marauders that came into Kashmir, and later the Pakistan Army, had been welcomed as liberators by the people. They were not. They committed rapine and plunder and there was no question of religion because the Christians and Moslems were equally sufferers. They were not welcomed as liberators by the local populations. So when the representative of Iraq refers to the great brotherhood, he must take this into account. We are also part of a greater brotherhood, namely, the human brotherhood, and therefore it is not as though the two things were on a par. There may be a great deal of argument in favour of not implementing self-determination in Algeria or implementing it. That is another matter. But the two things are not on all fours.

In regard to the statement of the representative of Cuba there is one other matter which I want to dispose of, and that is the reference of my Prime Minister. I have, both for reasons of propriety and political reasons, the obligation to put everybody right on this matter.

There were two suggestions, one of which I answered at a previous meeting (767th meeting, para 88), apparently without carrying conviction. One was a telegram sent by the Prime Minister early in October 1947 to Mr. Liaquat Ali Khan, of whom he was an intimate friend, suggesting that the two countries together should come before the Security Council and that the matter should be settled by plebiscite, by the United Nations and so on. This was long before there was any proof that the Pakistan Army was invading. That was at the time when Pakistan was denying that there was complicity on its part. That was at the time when we had just parted company; and I pointed out that, so far as the political and the documentary parts of the problem were concerned, whatever might have been the commitments, if they had been accepted, they would be binding; if they were not accepted, they were not even escrows;

they had lapsed and, therefore, we started from the Security Council because the letter of 22 December 1947 from my Prime Minister to Mr. Liaquat Ali Khan said that nothing had happened and proposed to take our remedy under the Charter of the United Nations. And we came here and said; "We are invaded. In order to protect ourselves we may have to invade Pakistan. We do not want to do so; therefore, please stop them from doing that."

The second declaration is the one to which the representative of Cuba had kindly given authority. It comes from an organ called "United Project" which is not run by the Indian Government and we have no responsibility for its policy. It was a massage that came on 6 February 1957 from Allahabad in which, according to the report. Mr. Nehru listed the following conditions for agreeing to the plebiscite: withdrawal of Pakistan troops from "Occupied Kashmir", the "legal Government" of Kashmir must take over the entire State. I believe that this massage came to the United Nations between four and five O'clock. Between five and six O'clock, thanks to the reputable agency Reuter's, we get another version of it, which was published all over the world, and which we have not contradicted, and this was what the Prime Minister said: "We have been charged in certain quarters" – that is, over here – "with having backed out of our commitment to hold a plebiscite in Kashmir." I would like to draw the attention of those who are making this charge against us to the prerequisite condition of the plebiscite. The condition was that Pakistan would withdraw its forces from that part of Kashmir which it occupies. Has Pakistan fulfilled that condition? Mr. Nehru said: "A grave injustice has been done to India in regard to Kashmir. The basic point that Pakistan committed aggression in Kashmir has been ignored altogether." And the representatives around this table have done it this morning. The Prime Minister said: "Kashmir has made tremendours progress in the last nine years and no steps should be taken which would disturb the peace of that State." Outside of all controversy. I ask the Council to believe that that is our overwhelming concern about the re-agitation of a situation which can lead to civil war all the way round and conflicts of a character which I shall describe in a moment.

In view of the time, I shall try to make the remainder of the observations very brief.

Mr. Romulo said that I had "admonished" the Security Council (768th meeting, para 107). Normally speaking, I would let this pass, but it is not something which I wish to leave on the record, coming from the distinguished personality who occupied the Chair at that time. I believe this rises from that fact that he was listening to a very long speech, and like everybody else, sometimes he gets tired of it. What did I say? I said that our basic position was aggression. Our basic position is the complaint that we brought forth here on 1 January 1948. From that, we have never moved. From that, we did not move when we came here in those days, not with General McNaughton, not with Sir Owen Dixon, not with Mr. Graham, not with you, not with anybody in the world. That position we have never moved from. But I went on to say that, at the same time, representatives of States members of the Security Council, calling me before them, could not just regard themselves as Rip Van Winkles, as though nothing had happened here in nine years. In spite of that basic position, I have the responsibility to address myself to the draft resolution before the Council. That puts a totally different complexion upon my admonition. Do I look like the kind of person who would admonition this august body? I leave it to the Council to judge.

We have great confidence, in spite of the present attitude of the Security Council, that when these facts become more and more known – and that is why we keep on bringing the Council's attention to them – representatives will begin to have doubts in that matter.

Now we come to the draft resolution before the Council (S/3787). There were two suggestions made by the President in his capacity as representative of Sweden. I have not referred to the observations made by the representative of Iraq except to say that the presentation he has made does not represent the facts of the situation. It ignores the circumstances but, at the same time, I pay tribute and express my appreciation of his desire to be kindly on the side on which he is not neutral; and that is all I can say. One must stick to the truth even when one wants to be polite. The representative of Sweden, who is the President, speaking here said:

> "As we see it, there are, in principle, two courses open to us along which progress may be made towards the ultimate goal which, it seems to us, must be an agreement between the parties on a political basis..." (Para. 39 above.)

This is a matter which I shall have to deal with when I come to the basic position of the Security Council under the terms of the Charter, and particularly Chapter VI. There is no settlement in this matter that is possible except by agreement between the parties; and, so far as my Government is concerned, we have done everything we can, up till now—but I said "up till now": we have not written the end of history. We have made a solemn declaration, and we repeat it, that we shall at no time, on any issue, however much it may be against us, refuse to negotiate, refuse to seek conciliation, but we cannot be called upon to surrender our sovereignty beforehands; and we cannot be called upon by the Security Council to forgo the charge of aggression upon our sovereignty. We cannot be called upon to ignore a complaint which we have submitted in terms of the provisions of the Charter.

Mr. Romulo said—as was said by someone else the other day—that there were counter-charges (768th meeting, para 104). I submit that there were no counter-charges on Kashmir. There may have been counter-charges on other matters. The Security Council decided not to discuss them, we would be willing to answer. In regard to Kashmir, so far as I can recollect, it is only paragraph 3 of the document submitted by Pakistan (S/1100, annex 6 document 1) that is relevant, and the answer was a denial. It was not even what the lawyers call a traversing of the facts; it was a denial, saying that we had not invaded. That denial was denied afterwards by the Commission, and, therefore, what remains is invasion, and aggression.

When General McNaughton was President of the Council and when Mr. Graham and earlier when members of the Commission, whom we did not invite—in fact we did not invite the Commission, but we said, ours is a hospitable country: you can come—came and talked and talked—and in our part of the world it is very rude not to answer people's questions—and asked questions, we answered them. But we also asked some questions ourselves. So, would it have been right for us to come before General McNaughton and to say; no, we will not talk until you decide this question of aggression? This very Council, with great legitimacy—I may say, with total legitimacy—would have told us that we were being unreasonable. But what could we do? We reserve our position today; and, by reserve, we mean, do not put it on the shelf.

In other words, if the position put forward by General Romulo and, the other day, by Mr. Tsiang is to be accepted, it becomes a crime to negotiate, because once a charge of aggression is decided, what is there left to negotiate? We are prepared to negotiate without prejudice to that, and that is what the Commission said all along. Therefore, Mr. President, it is in your hands; it is your responsibility to address yourself to this position.

It is easy for me to be dismissed, as one person; you cannot however dismiss the 400 million people in our country when a question of this kind comes before them. This is a problem which has deeply agitated our people, and it is only the strength of our leadership, which is based in the masses, which is based in trust and confidence, that has been able to restrain the kind of excitment which might lead to a hatred which could not be controlled afterwards. It is only that which has prevented them from developing the wrong kind of feeling in regard to certain other countries, which has prevented them from getting into a kind of war fever. The second course suggested, therefore, so far as that is concerned, is one by which as a general principle or as a universal premise my country alsways stands – indeed, I submit all countries stand committed by it – under the Articles of the Charter.

There are underlying problems of a legal character. Becuase I have tried to be precise in regard to the position, becuase if the accession is complete and legal all these problems become comparatively simple. I have never asked the Security Council to pronounce on these legal issues since from the very beginning our position has been that we cannot ask the Council to do so because it is not a court of law. At the same time, the Council is working in the context of international law and justice and cannot depart from that, and that is why I have pointed it out to you.

The President, speaking as representative of Sweden, has thrown out the suggestion that it might be useful to have certain underlying problems of a legal character progressively clarified in order to create better conditions for an agreement. I suppose the real meaning is that a look should be taken at the legal claims which we make and which are basic to our position. If it means nothing more, in terms of any provision of the Charter, I believe the President will agree that I am justified in saying that he would want to see this in greater clarity and would want it to have full consideration by our Government and with our legal advisers – indeed, the United Nations would want to do that – for we cannot at any time turn our face against the law. That is our position, whatever the consequences are; that is our position in regard to these suggestions and there it is.

The President went on to say that some legal aspects of the matter might perhaps be referred to the International Court of Justice for an advisory opinion. However, it all depends upon what questions are referred to the Court; we ought to have the opportunity to consider them in order to see whether the problem is referred to the Court in its necessary ambit and scope. Therefore, so far as the Government of India is concerned at the present moment, we simply say that we do not reject any of these ideas, because if we did we should be doing wrong. You would fall foul of us, and even apart from that we should ourselves feel uneasy in our minds. We are therefore prepared to give consideration to these matters, and indeed the Government of India knows the views of the Swedish Government and is prepared to take them into consideratian, but we cannot go into any deep consideration of policy until the general elections are over.

That deals with the statements. Now I come to the draft resolution (S/3787) and I will not take very long over it.

The first paragraph of the preamble recalls previous resolutions. It is one of those habits that we have formed, to recall resolutions, but I would like the draftsmen who assists the representatives of the United States and the United Kingdom to have a look at these resolutions. Some of them you can recall as a matter of historical interest, but you cannot implement them. For instance, one of them says that the Commission ought to go to India and Pakistan or something like that; so it is not possible of implementation. This is probably a very obvious instance but there are parts of these resolutions that have been worn out by time.

Therefore, when the representative of the Philippines made a criticism of my Prime Minister's statement—he did not say so, but he implied it—I want to say that we stand by that statement. I had a copy of the first draft of this resolution half an hour after I started speaking and the only alteration which was made in it was to the advantage of Pakistan. Secondly, when I finished speaking that evening I said to the President, who was the representative of the Philippines, that I had then made that part of my statement in order that he need not feel perturbed that some D-Day, some zero hour was approaching not that I had finished the argument. In fact, I stated expressly that I had still to argue the case. What is more, those who know the facts of this matter know very well that what my Prime

Minister says represents the truth.

Therefore, recalling these resolutions is merely an exercise, the sort of thing that often happens; and my delegation and my Government would find it difficult to understand why the resolution of 24 January 1957 (S/3779) has greater significance than the resolution of 17 January 1948, and I would be glad if the representative of the United Kingdom would tell me. If the Council would insist upon adherence to the resolution of 17 January 1948, we could forget all these other resolutions and I think we would have made a beginning in solving this problem.

On 17 January 1948, the Council asked both parties not to aggravate the situation, not to introduce war material and things of that character. That stands violated. This is what was said:

> "*The Security Council*,
>
> "*Having heard* statements"—and may I remind the representative of the United Kingdom that in those days they said: "having heard statements"—"on the situation in Kashmir from the representatives of the Governments of India and Pakistan".
>
> "*Recognizing* the urgency of the situation"—and then comes the operative part:
>
> "*Calls upon* both the Government of India and the Government of Pakistan to take immediately all measures within their power...calculated to improve the situation,"—and "Jehad" is not an instrument of improving the situation: and the calumny and the base words ultered about my Prime Minister and the head of my Government and of my country and of our traditions that is going on in West Pakistan at the moment is something not in consonance with this—"and to refrain from making any statements and from doing or causing to be done or permitting any acts which might aggravate the situation;
>
> "*And further requests* each of those Governments to inform the Council immediately"—I want to repeat this, if I can have the attention of the Council for one moment—"of any material

> change in the situation which occurs or appears to either of them to be about to occur while the matter is under the consideration of the Council..."

The matter has been under the consideration of the Council from that time until now and Pakistan did not inform the Council that it had introduced troops. I say it acted behind the Security Council's back and concealed facts from the Security Council and I think all our sins would be washed out in the face of that. And I ask my colleague Sir Pierson Dixon why the resolution of 17 January 1948 has less sanctity than any other resolutions. Insofar as they are recalled, and if they have any meaning, that is a helpful situation. I say that if the resolution of 17 January 1948 was adhered to by Pakistan, then we would have had the beginning of a solution.

May I preface my next observation by saying that I recognize that I have no part in the draft resolution before the Council (S/3787) either by saying that I support it or that I oppose it because I am not a member of the Security Council, but I believe that I am invited to offer observations.

The second paragraph of the preamble reads:

> "*Having taking into consideration* the statements of the representatives of the Governments of India and Pakistan".

With great respect I would submit that this is a slight overstatement because, although the statements have been heard, the case is so complex and has been argued at such great length, and there are so many documents on the matter and so many cross currents in it, it would be more accurate to say "having heard what we have to say", this would be nearer the truth and more nearly in conformity with previous resolutions. This gives the impression of a great deal of deliberation on this matter before coming to the next conclusion and I submit that I believe that we would like member Governments, not just one individual in the Security Council, but member Governments, to go into this situation, which is one of the most important situations in the world.

The draft resolution continues :

> "*Concerned* at the lack of progress in settling the dispute".

This word "dispute" was introduced by te Security Council without our assent. The only two resolutions to which we agree are those of 17 January 1948 and 20 January 1948 and the two resolutions of the Commission. You will find that in these resolutions the word "dispute" does not occur. The word is "situation –and it is not quibbling with words–we have head the legal aruments–and law is the essence of civilized language, so we cannot just ignore it–but we definitely think that the introduction of the word "dispute" means a political change.

Sir Gopalaswami Ayyangar, speaking before this Council, said in categorical terms that this is not a dispute over territory–there is no dispute over our territory; the territory is a Constituent State of the Union of India. In the exercise of its sovereignty, for any political reason, it can consent, it can initiate, it can order an act of cession. That is a different question. Therefore, there is no dispute over territory. I submit this frequent reintroduction of the word "dispute" is an attempt on the part of the framers of these resolutions to weight these things against us–because this is a "situation", it is not a territorial dispute. How can it be a territorial dispute when the sovereignty of Jammu and Kashmir was recognized by the Security Council when you say neither the Security Council nor the Commission can change it, when you say that it is the duty of the Union of India to look after the security of this territory? It can station garrisons on the western and north-western frontiers to guard the passes that come into India.

I read the next paragraph :

> "*Considering* the importance which it has attached to the demilitarization of the State of Jammu and Kashmir. . ."

I submit the word "demilitarization" has a particular connotation. It is not only just a plain smite. It means much more. And if you will use the word "demilitarization" in the context where a party who has no legal, no moral, nor any other title under any semblance of law, is in occupation of the part of territory, to speak about demilitarization in regard to that area, is a mockery of justice and of international law. And so far as we are concerned, what the Security Council is doing is to expose our vast territory to the insecurity of a neighbour who is not showing from the west the friendly intentions that we expect. Therefore "demilitarization" in terms of counting, in quantum of troops and whether they shoot pistols; or revolvers, or shotguns or machine guns, those problems are not the important problems.

The first element in demilitarization is the removal of those people who have no business and no title to be present on the soil of Jammu and Kashmir. That is in the 13 August 1948 resolution, that is in the 5 January 1949 resolution, that is in every resolution of the Council. And what is more, that is in every assurance given by Mr. Korbel, given by Mr. Lozano and given by Mr. Huddle – the United States representative who was also Chairman – that irrespective of personalities, those were the assurances given to us, not in secret, not whispered into our ears, but they are part of the public documents which are in the records of the Security Council. If for any reason the Council on a subsequent date gave an assurance or the Pakistan side, which they can interpret in another way, the responsibility does not lie on the heads of the Government of India. Therefore, we would object to this word if we were parties to the resolution. We insist, because this is throwing the whole thing out of its context; that is to say, you are asking the President of the Security Council to do what Mr. Graham has been trying to do for five years, what Sir Owen Dixon tried to do, and at the end said that this is not the problem, this is something else which he has not been asked to do – and so on. The whole reference – that clause – I submit is misconceived. It is the wrong context, the wrong thing. We are talking about something that has no real relation. I do not say it is irrelevant. The relevance of it is not essential. That is, there is no essentiality about this because that is not the problem.

The next paragraph reads :

> "*Noting* that demilitarization preparatory to the holding of a free and impartial plebiscite under United Nations auspices has not been achieved."

Now there, I think it should also have been noted that one of the conditions of holding a free and impartial plebiscite is the cessation of religious propaganda. Under our law, which is copied from the British law, at least the essence of it, it is an unlawful practice (and some other legal phraseology, which I have forgotten) to appeal to religion, to say to voters that they are Catholics, therefore they ought to vote for the Catholic candidate; or that they are Protestants, therefore they ought to vote for the Protestant candidate; or that they are Moslems, that they ought to do this; or that they are Hindus and they ought to do that, or the wrath of God would be visited upon them. In any way, to make use of religion in order to obtain a political end in an election in our law is an unlawful practice which would disqualify the person concerned. The holding of a free and impartial plebiscite therefore is possible only when there is the preparatory condition,

Now, I submit to the two representatives who are responsible for the initiating of this draft resolution, is it fair to ask for the adoption of a method, which in its general essence, which in its genesis, which in its purpose is peaceful, but enable it to be surrounded, if not rooted, in hatred? Therefore, until that is cleared away, how can one get anywhere at all; and even with the passing of nine years, it has not been cleared away, and what is more, is being accumulated. I cite the evidence of the statement of the distinguished Foreign Minister who warned the Security Council, who professed in his first speech, in what in effect amounts to an ultimatum. And this camaign of "Jehad" that goes on – we are still in the days of the holy wars.

The next paragraph is the crucial part :

"*Noting* the proposal of the representative of Pakistan for the use of a temporary United Nations force in connexion with demilitarization."

It may be argued that it is right to note anything. There is no crime in stating that something has been said. But when in a resolution something is noted and something is not noted – for example, it has not been noted that the Government of India says that the country has been illegally occupied, that there is an enormous influx, accumulation of arms and forces, that there is hatred propaganda and all the other things I have told you, those things are equal, or even of greater value and they have not been noted. – So this selection, this invidious selection, lends a political importance to it. The Security Council, this august body which is seriously minded, noted something in relation to its value. Therefore a greater value is placed on this than on other things. It is this suggestion that has come out of "noting the proposal of the representative of Pakistan". I submit that the proposals ought really to come from the Security Council. That, of course, is a matter for you gentlemen and not for me.

We come to the next paragraph.

> "*Believing that*, insofar as it might contribute towards the achievement of demilitarization as envisaged in the resolutions of the United Nations Commission for India and Pakistan and towards the pacific settlement of the dispute, the use of such a force would deserve consideration".

We should like to offer observations on three parts of this paragraph. First we should like to comment on the words "might contribute towards the achievement of demilitarization". Facts deny this. How would a United Nations force contribute to the achievement of demiliterization when there are forty-five battalions of the "Azad" army on the other side and large numbers of irregulars and commandors who cannot be traced. What would be the practical size of any United Nations force that goes in there? Would a United Nations force in the conditions of the world at the present time be in a position to disarm any soldier of any other country? I can understand their performing police duties. I can understand their going into a place where we are sure they would not be fired at. But would you say that in the conditions that obtain in these areas any United Nations force that you can get to go would be able to achieve demilitarization? Would they be able to exercise the degree of supervision that was necessary? All this is on the basis that some agreement has been reached about it.

Furthermore, I would say that it is not necessary to have a United Nations force to achieve demilitarization. All that has to be done is for the Pakistan Army to withdraw and, in order to create conditions of security, for it to give an international guaranty that it will not move out of its cantonments beyond the spaces which can be permitted with security; and for the Indian Army in Kashmir, which is in a constituent part of its territory, to be deployed only in conditions of peace. That is what we have done. Therefore, the question of sending somebody to disarm does not arise.

With great respect I wish to say we have not in our country

attuned our minds to the conception of any foreign forces. United Nations or otherwise, disarming our soldiers or disbanding them. That is a function of our sovereign Government. So far as we are concerned, if we gave an undertaking to withdraw them, as indeed we have done; we have, without any commitment, withdrawn very large numbers of troops from this area.

In this connexion, I would like to contradict what was said by the Foreign Minister of Pakistan the other day. It is a statement of the same character as I contradicted the other day, which he has not repeated afterwards, that the Government of India is concentrating troops on the Indo-Pakistan border. This is an entirely untrue statement, and I am authorized by my Government to deny it. There has been no addition of military strength either on the Punjab frontier or any other Indo-Pakistan frontier. The Indian Army moves along according to the normal routine of its manoeuvres, of its practice. There has been no accumulation of forces anywhere, and no addition to their strenght. This is, I believe, a story somebody picked up somewhere, which was printed in the newspapers and was believed.

The second idea in this is "demilitarization as envisaged in the resolutions of the United Nations Commission". With great respect to the authors of the draft resolution, I submit that this is a misstatement of fact. What is envisaged in the resolutions is the disbanding and disarming of "Azed" forces, the total withdrawal of the Pakistan Army and, at a subsequent stage when that is achieved, the withdrawal of the bulk of the Indian forces. It is quite true that we have discussed at various times a simultaneous synchronized operation. I submit, however, that as this has not been accepted, it ceases to have value. It cannot have. Hereafter, my Government will not agree to any commitment hanging over its head because we find that we have been the suffers in this. There is no room not to be on one's guard. Therefore, we submit that we have no commitments in this direction apart from what is in the resolution of 13 August 1948. Consequently, the second idea is not strictly accurate.

The last part is the most important, it says "deserve consideration". I ask my colleague from the United Kingdom, who is a scholar of great repute, to explain to me what that means, apart from saying that this has merit. This is the Security Council which is composed of Member Governments of the United Nations, and they make a proposition which not only does not deserve consideration but which is contrary to the Charter, contrary to the interests of peace and contrary to the friendship that exists between my country and the United States on the one hand, and my country and the United Kingdom on the other. It is contrary to all the canons of international behaviour that must be respected. Therefore, it does not deserve consideration.

I say the proposal is contrary to the Charter because the United Nations has no authority to place any Pakistan soldiers in our territory under Chapter VI, and I want to make this perfectly clear. In this connexion, when I say "our territory", any Pakistan soldier that sets foot in the any area of the State of Jammu and Kashmir is violating the sovereignty of the Indian Union because, according to your decisions, according to the commitments we have with you, it is part of Jammu and Kashmir. So it is not as though you can make an arrangement with Pakistan and feel that you have not violated any law. It is a violation of Charter.

The other day the Secretary-General, in another connexion, pointed out that it was only under Chapter VII that troops could be placed anywhere, without consent. Now, sameone said that this consent should be forthcoming. I have no desire to sound uncooperative or even worse. The Government of India will in no circumstances permit foreign troops on its soil. That is a categorical statement I am asked by my Government to make to this Council. We will in no circumstances in this context permit the stationing of foreign troops on our soil. The only condition on which we shall have our troops go on foreign soil, as we told the Secretary-General publicly and privatly, on which we shall accept foreign troops ourselves is in pursuance of the Charter.

The Security Council is asking us, not deliberately, to accept a situation which in our view, is contrary to the provisions of the Charter, a violation of our sovereignty and calculated to disturb the peace. That is the legal part of it.

More than that, I would ask the representative of the United Kingdom, who has much more access to information about India than anyone else because of past connexions with us and many present connexions, to cognitate on the situation. What volume of troops would be required to keep order in the State of Jammu and Kashmir on both sides when our security troops are withdrawn, considering the vast amount of opposition there is even to the past resolutions of the Security Council, the enormous amount of public demonstrations of disapproval and public anger and the intensity of the feeling in the country with regard to this matter? On our side, how many troops would be required by the United Nations, assuming there were no legal or other difficulties? Equally, the moment this is published in Pakistan as a great victory for their side, there will be enormous hopes aroused and all these forces, about which I read to you—the man who asserts he will do it by force—will be altered. Therefore, any conception that this is deserving of consideration—I suggest that this is a chimerical proposition, an impractical proposition, a proposition that goes against the purposes of the Charter and the purposes of settlement.

There is a statement about the people of Kashmir—that is to say, the part that is not taken over by the enemy. This comes from an authority which will appeal to my colleague from Australia. It is a conservative paper which I believe has had very adverse comments on our policy. It is "The Sydney Morning Herald", and its correspondent Mr. Morrisby is now in Kashmir. This is what he wrote and said to the people on 11 February 1957, that is to say, a fortnight after 26 January. (This report is partly in direct narration and partly in indirect narration) :

> "The people of Kashmir have given their full support to the State's new Constitution, as this Constitution enshrines the sovereign will and has, therefore, special significance for all of them', said Edwin Morrisby of 'The Sydney Morning Herald' of Australia in Srinagar, 7 February 1957, in an informal meeting with the local newspapermen. Morrisby, who was giving his impressions of four days' tour of Kashmir, added that the State enjoyed semi-autonomous status in the Indian Republic, and so the people enjoyed more freedom than in other States of India. The enthusiasm with which the people had rallied to the call for active participation in the implementation of development plans 'provide irrefutable evidence of the popularity of the Government and their leaders' he said."

Then there is another quotation from Mr. Morrisby :

> "They have made it cleaı that they would under no circumstances tolerate any attempt to disturb the peace and stability of the State which has been achieved after great trials

and sufferings', he added.

> "Morrisby who went to some remotest corners of Kashmir Valley said : 'As I told you the other day, there are no restrictions on foreign travellers to Kashmir, apart from the fact that they must be able to pay their way'. He went on to say: 'There is nothing abnormal in the State. The people are quite contended and busy in their business of life, just like in the rest of India."

We did not ask Mr. Morrisby to write that. As we say this is not an Indian newspaperman. I usually do not quote newspapers, because, after all, they are not authoritative in this sense, but this is the latest opinion we have received from an independent source and it deserves consideration.

On this point about deserving consideration, I should like to request the representatives who are responsible for this draft resolution to address their minds to the history of this proposition. This is not a new suggestion. This suggestion was first made as early as 1948. If representatives will look at the transactions at that time, I would refer to the statements made by the Minister for Foreign Affairs of Pakistan, Sir Mohammed Zafrullah Khan, in a memorandum dated 19 August 1948 which was published in the first interim report of United Nations Commission for India and Pakistan. I shall read the relevant part :

> "In particular, the Pakistan Government would be glad to know whether the Commission intend to secure the services of an international or neutral force for this purpose and, if so, what the strenght of such a force would be." (S/1100, annex, 26, appendix, para 5)

So as far as Pakistan is concerned it is an old suggestion which has been reported time after time. The Commission's reply was this :

"In drawing up the resolution of 13 August 1948, the Commission did not and could not proceed on the assumption that one or the other party would violate the truce. The implementation of the resolution presupposes good faith and co-operation between the two parties."—That fact is still true because without that we could not have any implementation.

> "As the Government of Pakistan is aware, the United Nations does not have at its disposal an international froce. The use of a neutral force has not been contemplated by the Commission. However, the Government of Pakistan will have noted that the resolution provides for neutral military observers. . ." (*Ibid*., annex 27, appendix, para 5).

The United Kingdom and the United States, if I may say so without any disrespect, are not original in this suggestion. They came out with this on 21 February 1951. The joint effort in relation to us is of long standing in this matter. In the United States and United Kingdom draft resolution of 21 February 1951, contained in document S/2017, this is said :

> "4. *Authorizes* the United Nations Representative to take into account in his discussions"—the same things as now—"with the two Governments and in considering the arrangements for demilitarization and for the holding of the plebiscite : . . .
>
> "(ii) The possibility"—it was less at that time—"that any forces required for the purpose"—at that time it did not say that it must be this one. It only said: "If you want someone: we shall send someone."—"of facilitating demilitarization and the holding of the plebiscite might be provided from member States of the United Nations or raised locally." (S/2017).

I remember that the same suggestion was made by the Prime Minister of Australia in informal conversations. Our reply was made by Sir Benegal Rau, a man whose memory is revered and who cannot be accused of any overstatement of any sentiment :

> "We are wholy unable to accept any entry of foreign troops in the State or in any other part of India."—that was in 1951, and we repeat that.—"In view of the provision made by the resolutions of August 1948 and January 1949, there is no occasion for the use of foreign troops or of special local levies recruited by outside agency. Nor, in view of the detalied provisions contained in the resolution of January 1949 to ensure a fair and impartial plebiscite, can we accept a supersession of the lawful Government of the State or any

interference with its normal functions." (533rd meeting, para 40).

He was asked about it again a few meetings later, and Sir Benegal Rau's answer appears in the report of the 536th meeting held on 9 March 1951 :

> "My friend has asked whether India agrees to the principle of having United Nations forces in Kashmir. I have already stated India's position in this matter and given our reasons for it : first, we are wholly unable to accept any entry of foreign troops in the State or in any other part of India; secondly, in view of the provision made by the resolutions of August 1948 and January 1949, there is no occasion for the use of foreign troops (. . .) (536th meeting, para. 26).

Then something happened which I hope will happen this time also. On 21 March 1951 the United Kingdom and the United States dropped this suggestion in their revised resolution (S/2017/Rev. 1). The same proposal was revived by Mr. Graham in India, and this was contained in his second report to the Security Council (S/2448). In paragraph 5 (c) of the questionnaire addressed to us, this was one of the questions :

> "If not, is the Indian Government ready to accept forces to be provided by the United Nations in order to safeguard the security of and to maintain law and order in the whole State of Jammu and Kashmir as long as the United Nations, in consultation with the Governments of India and Pakistan, seems necessary" (S/2448, annex 3, p. 17).

Our answer, given by the Prime Minister at that time, was this :

> "As regards the suggestion for the bringing of United Nations forces into the States, it has been made clear more than once on behalf of the Government of India that the replacement of Indian security forces by foreign troops, howsover constituted, can under no circumstances be accepted. We do not understand why this suggestion is being repeated." (*Ibid.*, annex 9, para. 10).

With very great respect, I repeat that last sentence of the Prime Minister : "We do not understand why this suggestion is being repeated".

Then I have a paragraph from my old friend, Sir Gladwyn Jebb's observation was rather nostalgic, in a way of getting the troops back, but I do not share that view, and so I shall leave it.

On this draft resolution – and I ask Sir Pierson Dixon not to take this in the wrong way – our minds, not only mine but also those of people sitting around here, go back to those 300 years from Clive to Wellesley, from Wellesley to Dalhousie, from Dalhousie to Canning, from Canning to Minto – referring to the partition of India – from Minto to Linlithgrow. During all that period we have served to liberate our land from the presence of foreign feet on its soil with arms. The Security Council dare not ask us to accept the introduction of foreign troops on our sacred territory. Therefore, the history of our country being what it is, one of the conditions we have always asked was that there should be no foreign troops on our soil. If this brings back these sentiments to us and even to those of us who are comparatively uninstructed – I say this perhaps with lack of modesty – what kind of sentiments will come back to the masses of our people? Therefore, any suggestion of this kind would be unwelcome in India.

I wish to add, before I leave that the introduction of United Nations forces, which presumably would be constituted of volunteers of Member States, unless the United Nations proposes to form a foreign legion, would, in my submission, not only be a violation of the Charter; it would be a violation by each Member State that contributes troops, because we have bilateral relations with them. If a Member State were to send its troops to our country in violation of the Charter, then they are not protected by the Charter. Their protection disappears on account of the illegality.

I come now to the operative paragraphs of the draft resolution. I shall make this very brief. As regards the representative of Sweden, who is the present President of the Security Council, we have already expressed our views. Perhaps we should not say any more, because it might embarrass him. Someone might suggest that the President of the Security Council is too well liked by India. It is true that he was the Minister of his country in India, but, at the same time, I believe that he was Minister in Pakistan. I note that he is indicating that he was not, so I may be wrong on that. At any rate, so far as we are concerned, whether one has been to India or not, our Government would never refuse hospitality to anyone who comes from the United Nations, or indeed anyone who is satisfied with the kind of modest hospitality that we can offer. But when it comes to discussion of propositions, we have to look at what he has. However, in the general context of never declining conciliation, in that, India will not be found wanting.

This draft resolution, in our submission, is totally vitiated by its Preamble and by its introduction of United Nations forces. I would ask the United Kingdom and the United States to consider that in the way in which they have presented their proposal, they have established what a lawyer would call a *Prima facie* case, that is they have already given them a good certificate – it is a *laissez-passer* for this matter. Of course it could be argued that it deserves consideration by the Government of India. That is a possible explanation. But I have given the answer : we have considered it for many years and we have rejected it. Therefore, so far as that is concerned, that draft resolution will be of no value. Secondly, it will not meet the purposes for which it is required.

Sir Pierson Dixon, with characteristic sincerity, has asked us to believe that his country was a common friend of ours – and I have forgotten the fact that he forgot us in the numbering the other day, and I accept that in the way it is offered. But I would be failing in my duty if I did not convey to the Security Council and to him that the developments of the last few days and the promotion of the Pakistan proposals, either by or with the assistance of the United Kingdom, have not served to soothe the difficult relations that have arisen as a result of many other matters. My Government will not throw the baby out with the bath water. We are a conservative people, even though all of us do not belong to the Conservative Party. We are a people who are attached to the peoples of the United Kingdom by many ties. But the basis of all that is mutual respect, and once that disappears other things become difficult.

I would be failing in my duty and it would be inaccurate to suggest that the reception of this idea on the other side is in the same way. Here is a report of the view of the Prime Miniter of Pakistan. As everyone knows, he has sent his congratulations and his appreciation and gratitude to the representative of the United States. After that he stated – this is a report taken from the newspaper "Dawn", and I do not say that it is an offical paper; it was founded by the founder of

Pakistan and is considered to be the leading paper – I hope I am not making invidious distinctions in Karachi:

> "The Prime Minister of Pakistan paid a tribute to the role played by the United Kingdom in the Security Council deliberations, and said that the United Kingdom had lent a great deal of assistance in the Kashmir question, which was again responsible for the support received from the United States."

I am afraid that this is not very flattering to the United States, but I am not reading out my opinions; this is the opinion of the Prime Minister of Pakistan. Of course, it may well be that he is so pleased with the matter that he attributes reasons in other ways. The United Kingdom is entirely free in this matter to take whatever position it wishes as a sovereign nation and as a permanent member of the Security Council. But so much has been made in this debate of our being two peas in a pod, of our common and equal relations, and so on.

I was High Commissioner in London for five years and I had a great deal to do with the relations of the United Kingdom and India. I also had a great deal to do with our military organization, as far as it concerned the United Kingdom in connexion with supplies and so on. It would take much more than normal circumstances for me to believe that there has being any occasion on which we have been the object of any particularly favourable treatment. We never asked for it and we never got it. But we have always been treated kindly, courteously and with respect, and I am sure that this position will continue.

But I would beg of Sir Pierson Dixon not to ask us to convey the view to our people that the attitude of the United Kingdom on this draft resolution is one of impartiality as between Pakistan and India. This does not mean that the United Kingdom is not impartial on the question according to its own lights. As far as we can see it, however, it would not be so regarded by our public opinion.

I express my thanks to the Council for the courteous way in which this difficult problem has been presented. This very bitter pill has been coated with a lot of jam, but nevertheless the pill is very bad. It is not only bitter, it is poisonous – sheer poison so far as peace is concerned.

Concern was expressed in the Security Council by the representative of Cuba for the people of Kashmir. My Prime Minister stated the same thing. The People of Kashmir do not necessarily have to be separated from the people of India for this. It is their future, it is their economic and political stability, their rights of freedom and their hopes of the future. They have waited for a long time to have their difficulties settled and they have taken things into their own hands. Any attempt to interfere in this or not to allow this question to be solved by direct negotiation between our two people in conditions in which Pakistan and India can mutually respect and trust each other, would be wrong. That cannot be done by resolutions of the Security Council or by resolutions of any other organ. That is a matter to which we have to make our contribution; I say with equal respect that Pakistan has to make its contribution in a greater measure to make up for its defaults of the past.

The first element would be to call off the dogs of hatred, the campaign of hatred. Our country will not tolerate threats and we shall not sit down under them. My Prime Minister stated yesterday that if it came to that, we would perform our duty under the Charter of the United Nations, that is : defend the soil of our country. We are not cowed down by these threats, nor are we going to fall a victim to them by creating a war atmosphere in our country. We shall reject the attempt to introduce war elements in the way of a United Nations force, following upon the military pacts and other war apparatus on our frontiers, which have extended whold realm of the "cold war" right into the heart of our country.

Will you say, Mr. President, that a responsible Government like ours does not have the primary duty for the security of our country, which in the last 800 years or so has been time after time invaded through the north-western passes, and which for 300 years has lain at the feet of the conqueror? Are these not the primary duties that we owe to the Council and to ourselves? Or are we to be intimidated by the press propaganda, calling us an immoral people? We are the judges of morality. Morality is not a matter of voting. You cannot vote prople into morality. If we acted against international morality, that would be on our conscience and the action would show.

India pleads not guilty and denies all charges of any attempt at violation. It begs of the representative of the United Kingdom not to throw aspersions upon our determination to observe these obligations. It begs of the Security Council to take into account that if we have any engagements, those engagements are conditional. They are the foundation upon which the commitment is built. On Part I, then on Part II; on Parts I and II, then on Part III – that is how it is. Therefore, those conditions are fundamental.

Therefore, if we have addressed ourselves to this matter at length, it is not because we want to win a resolution or to ask you to accept or reject a resolution. This is a time of great political excitement and activity, when we have this barrage of propaganda from the north-west – thank God, not from the north-east – and all these misstatements of fact about concentrations of the Indian Army. I ask you : how do we concentrate these armies without having to pay for them? We have a Parliament, we have a budget – we have to find the money. Where do we get the extra troops? What is more, there are observers on the cease-fire line : if we concentrated troops, they would know it and they would report to the Secretary-General.

Therefore, we cannot proceed in that context. I beg of you not to take a step which will aggravate the situation. There is always room for good men, men of wisdom, to find ways and means. But these are not the ways. It is implied that we are wriggling out of a commitment. Newspapers are led to believe that India is backing out of a commitment that was made, and the world is not told the truth – the simple truth – that must be accepted by every Member of the United Nations. How did Pakistan get into Kashmir? There is only one way that she got in, and that was by invasion. And is there anywhere in the Charter any provision for exercising by the use of arms a right over a territory over which a country has no claim – over which it may establish one in the future, but over it now has no claim?

I submit that after nine years there is a bounden duty lying at the door of the Security Council to look back at the resolution of 17 January 1948 and subsequent resolutions and at the concealment of facts, not only when the Commission went there but subsequently, time after time. The accumulation of arms today and the continuous concealment of the increase in armed strength, in the air and on the ground and everywhere – these are not only violations of the Charter, but they are a threat. And those threats do not come from us. We, as a country, have given evidence of our loyalty to the Charter. With our meagre resources, we have contributed to the safeguarding of peace. In the course of doing that , we have incurred hostility from various sides.

Without introducing any element of controversy, I should like to conclude on this note : my country has deliberately chosen the path of an independent foreign policy. No pressures will elbow us into an alignment in one direction or another. We serve our people and the cause of international peace as enshrined in the Charter of the United Nations.

8.7. Speech by Noon (Pakistan) in the Security Council, 770th Meeting, February 18, 1957

This morning I have to answer two speeches of the representative of India, but please do not be afraid that my statement will be inordinately long. I shall try to be as brief as possible.

I am at a loss to decide where to begin my remarks and where to end them. I have listened very carefully to the representative of India. I do not know what the members of the Security Council feel about it, but I have had three lectures – too many on the words "accession", "aggression" and "sovereignty". All these matters, as the Council is well aware, have already been considered and decided, and I fail to see why the representative of India has dwelt constantly on these three words. I can find no reason for it except this that probably he believes, as Hitler in "Mein Kampf", that if one goes on repeating a thing a million times, perhaps people will begin to believe in it. Otherwise, the time of the Security Council has been completely wasted by discussing these three words because such discussion is quite irrelevant. Therefore, I do not wish to waste any more of the Council's time in dwelling on them.

Mr. Krishna Menon picked out these three words from the speeches, but he has forgotten – although he may have mentioned the word "plebiscite" once or twice – that the draft resolution now before the Council (S/3787) was presented mainly for the purpose of holding a plebiscite, and through all his speeches he has never diverted either the Council's attention or his own to the question of a plebiscite. He has always talked of irrelevant things and tried to establish confusion – with all due respect to Mr. Krishna Menon – so that in that confusion the question of a plebiscite might be forgotten.

I must reiterate at the very beginning that the question which is before the Security Council is how to implement the international agreement that subsists between India and Pakistan for deciding the question of the accession of the State of Jammu and Kashmir to India or to Pakistan. The Security Council and the parties to this dispute agree that demilitarization of the disputed area is an essential pre-requisite to the holding of the plebiscite. It has not so far been possible to bring about demilitarization of the State in accordance with the terms of the international agreement for a plebiscite. It is, therefore, most essential that the Security Council should devote its attention to the problem of demilitarization in order that the agreed objective of a free and impartial plebiscite may be reached quickly. This is also the purpose of the present draft resolution.

Before I proceed to make my submission about the draft resolution which is under consideration. I must say a few words with regard to some points that the representative of India made in the course of his address to the Security Council on 8 February 1957 (767th meeting). My sole object in doing so is to keep the record straight. I will limit myself to the main points and will leave aside the rest. That does not mean that we accept either the validity of the other arguments used, or in any way subscribe to them. I am leaving them aside because in our view those matters are completely irrelevant to the issue that is engaging the attention of the Security Council. I think that such matters as the so-called secularism of India or the propaganda which is carried on in the vernacular Press of India and Pakistan against each other, of who in India or in Pakistan had suffered imprisonment, or what Sheikh Abdullah does or does not want, or the claim of India that, because Kashmir has prospered under its control, Kashmiris should be denied the right of self-determination, are all irrelevant to the issue which is under consideration.

The statement of the representative of India seems to imply that India accepted the resolution of the United Nations Commission for India and Pakistan, dated 13 August 1948 [S/1100, para. 75], about a week after it was presented, and accepted the second proposal of the Commission, dated 11 December 1948 [S/1196, annex 3], on 23 December 1948. What happened actually was that the Commission framed a resolution on 13 August 1948 and presented it to the parties. The Government of India signified its acceptance of the resolution. The Government of Pakistan also signified its acceptance of the resolution, subject to certain conditions. The Commission could not at that stage accept those conditions of the Government of Pakistan, chief amongst which was that the resolution should specify the conditions that should govern the final resolution of the dispute by means of a free and impartial plebiscite to be conducted under the auspices of the United Nations. Thereupon, the nagotiations for a cease-fire and a truce fell through and the Commission went back to Geneva and submitted its first report [S/1100] to the Security Council.

After some time, the Commission again took up negotiations with the representatives of India and Pakistan and succeeded in securing their agreement to certain proposals for a plebiscite. These proposals were, as pointed out by the then Foreign Minister of Pakistan in his letter to the Commission dated 25 December 1948 [S/1196, annex 5], in amplification of the resolution of 13 August. The proposal were put to the two Governments on 11 December 1948 and were accepted by the Governments of India and Pakistan after certain assurances and clarifications had been given to them on 23 and 25 December respectively. These proposals, after acceptance, were embodied in a resolution by the Commission, which was adopted on 5 January 1949 [S/1196, para. 15].

The entire agreement for a cease-fire, a truce and a plebiscite was thus accepted by the Government of India on 23 December 1948 and by the Government of Pakistan on 25 December 1948. The agreement constitutes one entity. Each part of it is linked-up with the other. There was to be a cease-fire first, which was to be followed by a truce, which in turn was to be followed by the plebiscite. The entire agreement stands or falls together.

It is very significant to note here that whereas Pakistan took a little time, a month or two, in asking for clarifications and then accepting, along with India, the resolution *in toto,* Mr. Krishna Menon tried to create trouble because of this two or three months' delay. Then we accepted. On the other hand, his country, for eight or nine years, having accepted those resolutions, has not carried them out and had evaded them, and that waste of time does not concern him at all.

The Indian representative has said that India accepted the two resolutions of the Commission on the basis of certain clarifications that were given to the Government of India by the Commission. I beg to submit that the Government of Pakistan also accepted these resolutions on the basis of certain assurances that were given to it by the Commission. The Indian representative has mentioned only the assurances that were given to the Government of India by the Commission. I am afraid I have not been able to trace the authority for all of these assurances. He has put them in a context which makes them completely different from what they were intended to mean.

For instance, it has been claimed by the Government of India that the Commission had assured it that there would be large-scale disbanding and disarming of the "Azad" Kashmir forces. We accept this as being correct, but the point is, when will such disbanding and disarming take place? I have clearly shown in my opening address [761st meeting] that according to the terms of the resolutions of the Commission as well as the various assurances that were given to us and the qualifications that were given to the Government of India, indeed according to the Government of India's own admission the disbanding of "Azad" Kashmir forces is to take places at the plebiscite stage.

In his letter to the Commission dated 18 February 1949, the Secretary-General of the Ministry of External Affairs and Commonwealth Relations of the Government of India stated :

> "The disarming of 'Azad' forces is really a matter of chronology. First, there must be a cease-fire and, after that, a truce, as envisaged in Parts I and II of the Commission's Resolution of 13 August 1948. After that, the condition precedent to arragements for the holding of a plebiscite is the creation of conditions in which Kashmir nationals can return to the area now in the occupation of 'Azad' Kashmir forces. So far as non-Muslims are concerned, such a movement will not take place untill large-scale disarming of these forces has beed carried out."

Today, the Government of India says that such disbanding is a prerequisite to the withdrawal of the bulk of their forces from the State, always putting meaning into sentences, which meaning is not there.

I would like to mention only a few of the assurances given to us by the Commission : one that no officer, either civil or military, of the Government of India or of the State Government will be allowed to cross the cease-fire line or allowed to exercise any authority in the "Azad" Kashmir area; two, that the "Azad" Kashmir forces will not be disbanded or disarmed in the truce stage; three, that synchronization of the withdrawal of the bulk of the Indian Army with the withdrawal of the Pakistan Army will be arranged by the

Commission in consultation with the two High Commands; four that the Commission will be free to hear the views of the Government of Pakistan with regard to the withrawal of the bulk of the Indian forces from the Indian side of the cease-fire line; five, that the expression "the Plebiscite Administrator will be formally appointed to office by the Government of Jammu and Kashmir" does not mean that he will be an employee of the Government of Jammu and Kashmir or subject to its control; six, that by the expression "the Plebiscite Administrator shall derive from the State of Jammu and Kashmir the powers he considers necessary" is meant that the Plebiscite Administrator will be competent to exercise such powers as he considers necessary for organizing and conducting the plebiscite and for ensuring its freedom and impartiality, and he shall be deemed to have derived those poweres from the authorities concerned. The organizing and conducting of the plebiscite shall be the responsibility exclusively of the Plebiscite Administrator. The Plebiscite Administrator could not derive his authority either from India or from Pakistan since there was no accession of the State to either one. Nor did the sovereignty of the State vest in either India or Pakistan. Therefore, the imaginary fountainhead of the Plebiscite Administrator's authority was mentioned as the State of Jammu and Kashmir, the dissolution of whose powers to the Plebiscite Administrator was thus presumed. The Commission did not deliberately use the phrase "Government of Jammu and Kashmir" stated in this context.

These and other assurances which are not mentioned, are contained in the three reports of the Commission to the Security Council : document S/1100 dated 9 November 1948, document S/1196 dated 10 January 1949 and document S/1430 dated 9 December 1949.

Thus it will be seen that it is not only the Government of India that was given assurances with regard to the provisions of the two resolutions of the Commission. The Government of Pakistan was equally interested in the framing of these resolutions. Although we do not claim to have as much ingenuity of thought as my Indian colleague has, we also took some care to see that our viewpoint was heard by the Commission and the provision for it was made in the resolutions.

While dealing with the text of the resolution of 13 August 1948, the distinguished and ingenious representative of India had tried to import into one of its clauses a meaning which it is utterly incapable of bearing. I refer to Part II, section B, paragraph 2 of the resolution. I will read it once again :

> "Pending the acceptance of the conditions for a final settlement of the situation in the State of Jammu and Kashmir, the Indian Government will maintain within the lines existing at the moment of the cease-fire the minimum strength of its forces which in agreement with the Commission are considered necessary to assist local authorities in the observance of law and order. The Commission will have observers stationed where it deems necessary." [S/1100, para. 75].

The representative of India has argued that because the phrase "local authorities" is used, it is meant to allude to the area which is under the control of the "Azad" Kashmir Government. I would beg of the members of the Security Council to mark the phraseology of the clause which says the Indian Government will be allowed to maintain within the lines existing at the moment of the cease-fire the minimim strength of its forces which in agreement with the Commission are considered necessary to assist local authorities in the observance of law and order.

Now, you will want to know why the words "truce lines" and not "truce line" are used. As a matter of fact there are two of these lines, one is in the northern area which runs from south to north-east, and the other runs on the borders of the Punjab—our Punjab—which runs from north-west to south-east. Therefore, when the word "lines" is used it is two truce lines and not one. Now, with regard to the word "authorities". Mr. Krishna Menon took a great deal of trouble in pointing out to you that the word "authorities" means the authority on the occupied Kashmir side, and the authority on the "Azad" Kashmir side—and therefore the word "authorities" is used [767th meeting, para. 124]. He tried to give us a talk on the English language and the implication of this word. Well, I do not pretend to know the English language because it is a foreign language to me; but I tried to look it up in the Oxford Dictionary. I found that since the year 1611 the words "authority" and "authorities" are used in the following sense. When the word is used in the abstract sense, the "authority" of law or "authority" of government, it is singular —"authority". When it is used in the concrete sence, that is : the municipal "authorities" then it is used in the plural, not in the singular. Therefore, when it is used here, "authorities", it is used in the concrete sense which means "authorities" on the Indian side of the cease-fire line and "authority" on our side of the cease-fire line. Therefore, the meaning that Mr. Krishna Menon tried to put into the word "authorities" is not what the English language means.

English is a very difficult language, even the English themselves probably do not understand it, and we in the East are particularly in a very difficult situation. So you see, for us to come and lecture you people here who know the English language much better than we do, I will not say it is presumptuous, but it is very daring.

The cease-fire lines were established on 27 July 1949. The Government of India can maintain within the lines existing at the moment of the cease-fire a certain number of its forces. Could it be claimed that the Government of India is authorized by this clause to cross the cease-fire line and post its froces in "Azed" Kashmir territory? No further proof is required for rebutting this novel piece of reasoning. If, however, any futher proof of the true import of the clause is required, I would respectfully draw the attention of the Security Council as well as of my distinguished colleague from India, to the Commission's summary report, dated 21 August 1948, of a meeting held between the United Nations Commission and the Government of India headed by the illustrious Prime Minister of India in person to discuss the Commission's resolution of 13 August 1948 in New Delhi at 3 p.m. on 17 August 1948. This forms part of the first interim report of the Commission to the Security Council [S/1100, annex 12].

I shall now read out to the Council extracts from this very interesting document which show what the Commission thought about the proposal of the Government of India to post forces on the "Azad" Kashmir side of the cease-fire line. (The Commission's view was apparently accepted by the Government of India, as no further mention of this demand appears in either the letter dated 20 August 1948 [S/1100, para. 78], or the letter dated 23 December 1948 [S/1196, annex 4], from the Government of India to the Commission, or in any one of the two aides memoires which formed appendices to the letter of 23 December.)

"Mr. Korbel (Czechoslovakia) replied that the Commission fully recognized the concern of the Government of India for security, but that in all frankness he had to tell the Prime Minister that the

Government of Pakistan was equally fearful of invasion by the Indian forces. The Commission, he said, could not assure either country on this question of security. The present document, he said, was a first step in that direction. If the Commission could succeed in obtaining the withdrawal of Pakistan troops, it would have the obligation, while on the sub-continent, of watching over Pakistan. Once the Kashmir problem had been satisfactorily settled, it would then be the duty and right of the Government of India, should the State finally be placed under the sovereignty of that country, to take all necessary measures for the security of that area.

"The Prime Minister reiterated his fears of possible infiltration with or without the knowledge of the Government of Pakistan and mentioned that the strategic points previously enumerated to the Commission which the Government of India considered that its forces must hold in order to ensure the security of Kashmir. Mentioning Domel in particular, he remarked that, if Government of India forces held that point, a natural boundary between the two would be established along the line of the river, and that Pakistan would, in no sense, be threatend through the occupation of that point by the forces of the Government of India inasmuch as Pakistan was from twenty-two to twenty-six miles distant.

"Mr. Korbel commented that such a readjustment of the front line went beyond the cease-fire and said frankly that the Commission, after giving careful consideration to the Indian point of view in that respect, had not been able to accept the view." [S/1100, annex 12, pp. 103 and 104].

And here is a perfectly clear and specific statement by the Commission with regard to the state of fear that will prevail in the area which will be evacuated by the Pakistan Army:

> "Part III, Section G of the document entitled "Truce terms transmitted to the Governments of India and Pakistan by the Commission", recognizes that the Commission cannot prejudge the sovereignty and integrity of the State as a whole. It should not be construed as envisaging the introduction into the area to be evacuated by Pakistan troops of civil or military officials of the Governments of Jammu and Kashmir or of the Governments of India for the purpose of administration or control."

The representative of India has asserted that the withdrawal of troops as contemplated in this resolution was unconditional. The facts, however, as I showed in my opening speech [76 1st meeting] are quite otherwise. The Commission assured us that the withdrawal of the Pakistan Army would be synchronized with the withdrawal of the bulk of the Indian Army. Besides, the phraseology of the 13 August 1948 resolution itself clearly showed that a certain action has to be taken by the Governments of Pakistan on its side, while the corresponding action has to be taken by the Governments of India on its side. It is not that the Pakistan Army would withdraw and then nothing would happen on the Indian side of the cease-fire line. When the Pakistan Army is beginning to withdraw from the State, the Government of India is equally bound to withdraw the bulk of its forces from that State.

Then it has been alleged that the Government of Pakistan has incorporated certain areas of the Kashmir State into Pakistan. I wish to state categorically that this is entirely incorrect. I would quote to the Security Council Article 203 of the Constitution of Pakistan which reads as follows:

> "When the people of the State of Jammu and Kashmir decide to accede to Pakistan, the relationship between Pakistan and the said State shall be determined in accordance with the wishes of the people of that State."

With the existence of this definite provision in our Constitution, when Mr. Krishna Menon made the remark in my presence that Pakistan had incorporated the Kashmir State already, I was quite a little surprised. What does this show? Does it show what we have incorporated certain areas of the State into Pakistan, or that the relationship of Jammu and Kashmir with Pakistan can be determined only after the question of the accession has been solved?

In this connexion I would like to mention the case of Chitral once again. The Indian representative has stated that Chitral is part of the State of Jammu and Kashmir. We deny it. I do not propose to go into the histroy of Chitral in order to prove that it was a State which acceded to us lawfully, because the question of Chitral is not before the Security Council. But if Mr. Krishna Menon claims that Chitral is part of Kashmir, would he be willing to count the votes of the people of Chitral in a plebiscite for the determination of the question of accession of the State of Jammu and Kashmir to India or Pakistan? If that were the case I am sure he would speak for another four hours as to why those votes should not be counted on the Pakistan side.

Allied to this is another matter which I may deal with before passing on to other points. I am amazed that the representative of India should accuse us of not allowing elections to be held in "Azed" Kashmir. Although we have had elections in all the provinces of Pakistan on an adult franchise basis, why have no elections been held in "Azad" Kashmir? The reason is not far to seek. We have scrupulously refrained from interfering with the administration of "Azad" Kashmir; it is the responsibility of the local authorities. If they want to hold elections they are at liberty to do so, but that is a question they have to decide. In adopting this attitude I claim that we have upheld the directive of the Security Council contained in the resolution of 17 January 1948 "to refrain from...doing or causing to be done or permitting any acts which might aggravate the situation". It is unfortunate that the very fact of compliance with the directions of the Security Council is being pleaded against us before that very body.

I think it would be interesting to point out to the Council that Mr. Krishna Menon of course claims the credit that whereas there have been no elections on the "Azad" Kashmir side, there have been elections on the occupied Kashmir side. But I think you will be pleased to notice that in that so-called election not a single vote was cast. All the seventy-five members put up under this dictatorial order of the Indian Government were returned unopposed and that is what Mr. Krishna Menon was pleased to call an election. It is a very strange election in which not a single vote is cast and yet India tries to spread it about in the world that elections have been held in the occupied Kashmir side.

Mr. Krishna Menon has pointed out that according to the electoral laws of his country people are forbidden to appeal to religion when asking for votes. It is clear that it might interfere with the freedom of an election if ecclesiastical condemnation and religious fiats were issued threatening with damnation a particular candidate or those who might support him. Mr. Krishna Menon on this occasion tried to take credit for the fact that in his country there is a law by which religious interference is not permited and the elections are free. But I think it is ungenerous of him not to admit that this law was framed by the British in the year 1920 and not by the present Congress Governments and that law was framed not only for the Indian side of the people in India but that the same law exists in Pakistan also, where similar rules exist regarding the freedom of elections; and we both inherited that law from the British. Therefore, for him to claim credit for something which was dome by the British and then come before an international body and try to be so generous was rather surprising to me.

It would be perfectly legitimate in the case of a plebiscite to draw attention to religious, cultural, linguistic, economic, geographic, strategic and other ties, affinities and considerations that might sway the choice. So long as nothing has been done to incite lawlessness or to exercise correction, the exercise of all considerations that might affect the choice would be legitimate.

I think that Mr. Krishna Menon – and I bow before him for his knowledge of the English language – forgot to differentiate between the word "election" and the word "plebiscite". Whereas in an election it is the duty of a Governments to see that it is free and no religious arguments are brought in, the matter of a plebiscite, wherever it is held, it is held because of religious differences or of ethnic differences or of geographic, linguistic or other differences. Therefore in a plebiscite it is quite legitimate for people to appeal to the electorate for these reasons before they decide whether to accede to one side or the other. In the matter of an election, it is quite different. I am very sorry that Mr. Krishna Menon is not here today to listen to my views personally and that he is not well. I hope he will soon recover. We must realize that we are now dealing with the question of a plebiscite and not an ordinary election, and we must not be confused by the arguments that he advances on this point. In fact, the Prime Minister of India himself emphasized this principle in the telegram of 22 September 1947 to the Government of Pakistan when he characterized the acceptance by that Governments of the accession of Junagadh as being "in utter violation of the principles on which partition was agreed and effected". These were the words of the Prime Minister, Mr. Nehru that Pakistan's action in accepting the accession of Junagadh was against all the accepted principles on which India and Pakistan were agreed. But he forgets all those arguments when he applies the facts to the Kashmir case – that is to say, the principle of separating contiguous Muslim majority areas from non-Muslim majority areas and constituting them respectively into the sovereign States of India and Pakistan.

The word "Junagadh" has reminded me of the fact that in both of my speeches I emphasized the case of Junagadh, which is still on the file of the Security Council and which India has forcibly annexed; and the State of Hyderabad, which was also annexed by invasion. Not a single word has Mr. Krishna Menon said in his speech in defence of the action of his country in invading and annexing these two States.

The representative of India persists in referring to the question of the so-called accession of the State of Jammu and Kashmir to India. I will simply state that this matter has been disposed of. No party to the dispute can now claim that Kashmir has acceded to it so long as the international agreement subsists, and there is nothing that the party can do to break that agreement unilaterally. The question of the accession of the State of Jammu and Kashmir to India or to Pakistan must be decided by the democratic method of a free and impartial plebiscite.

There are other matters in the speech of the representative of India which are important. But I will pass over them to save the time of the Security Council, especially as these points have been made in this forum *ad nauseum*, and replies to each one of them are already on the record of the Security Council.

There is only one point out of these which I would submit to the Security Council. In trying to impress on the Council the importance of the Commission's resolution of 13 August 1948, the representative of India said quite a lot about the comings and goings and the palavers and conferences that preceded the framing of the resolution and its acceptance by the parties. He said that the resolution was a very carefully drafted document. Immediately thereafter, he ran into some difficulties with regard to the meaning of the resolution of 5 January 1949, especially paragraph 4, which dealt with the question of the demilitarization of the State in the plebiscite stage. Speaking about the paragraph, the representative of India said :

> "As members of the Council know, the word 'disposal' has been used with regard to the Governments of India forces in the sense of disposition, not in the sence of throwing away." [767th meeting, para. 147].

Here, again, we have had quite a lecture on the English

language, on the meaning of the word "disposal". He says that the word "disposal" means locating the troops in various areas and not the dissolution or demobilization of the forces. That is what he is trying to do.

If my memory does not fail me, the members comprising the Commission which drafted the very carefully-worded document of 13 August 1948 also drafted the proposals of 1 December 1948, which were later incorporated in the resolution of 5 January 1949. Surely the representative of India should have thought of some better argument in support of his interpretation of the term "final disposal". The word "disposal" is used in both parts of the paragraph and governs the armed forces both of India and of "Azad" Kashmir. If Mr. Krishna Menon reads the meaning in this word regarding his side of the cease-fire line in the sense that the word means location of troops and not demobilization, then the same meaning shall be read into that word used in connexion with the "Azad" troops on their side, which is mentioned in the very next sub-paragraph; and that will mean that Mr. Krishna Menon contemplates the continuance of "Azad" troops on their side of the cease-fire line. I am sure that nothing is farther from his mind than this interpretation which he placed on this word without realizing the consequences. I hope that I have made myself clear.

Paragraph 4 says:

"4. (a) After implementation of Parts I and II of the Commission's resolution of 13 August 1948, and when the Commission is satisfied that peaseful conditions have been restored in the State, the Commission and the Plebiscite Administrator will determine, in consultation with the Government of India, the final disposal of Indian and State armed forces, such disposal to be with due regard to the security of the State and the freedom of the plebiscite;

"(b) A regards the territoy referred to in A. 2 of Part II of the resolution of 13 August"—which means the 'Azad' Kashmir territory—"final disposal of the armed forces in that territory will be determined by the Commission and the Plebiscite Administrator in consultation with the local authorities". [S/1196, para. 15].

If Mr. Krishna Menon says that the word "disposal" here means location of troops and not their demobilization, then the argument that he has been putting before the Security Council that the "Azad" Kashmir forces must be demobilized is contradicted by the interpretation which is put here, because if the word "disposal" means location, then this clause contemplates the continued location of "Azed" troops also, which I am sure is very far from his mind when he talks in that manner. But when arguments are made in haste and people are carried away by their rhetoric, then the consequences of those arguments are perhaps not realized momentarily.

The representative of India has said a great deal about the provisions of the resolution of the Commission dated 5 January 1949. But the most misleading statement made by him is to the effect that this resolution gives way to Part III of the previous resolution of 13 August 1948, in which India and Pakistan reaffrm "their Wish" that the future of the State shall be determined by the will of the people of the State. Much is made of this by Mr. Krishna Menon, and he seeks to characterize India's undertaking regarding a plebiscite as a mere wish – not a resolve, not a commitment, but a wish. Nothing is said by the representative of India about the further and unequivocal undertaking of paragraph 1 of the resolution of 5 January 1949, which reads as follows:

> "The question of the accession of the State of Jammu and Kashmir to the India or Pakistan will be decided through the democratic method of a free and impartial plebiscite." (*Ibid.*)

> I am afraid that the copy of the resolution that he has been reading does not contain this very important paragraph.

I do not contest Mr. Krishna Menon's right to talk about the conditions of a plebiscite in the State, but perhaps it is not entirely relevant to the question that is engaging our attention at this stage, which is the problem of demilitarization of the State preparatory to the plebiscite. Whether a certain type of propaganda will or will not be allowed, how and when the refugees will go back to the State, what measures will be taken to ensure to them the right of legitimate political activity, what will happen if local authorities on the two sides of the cease-fire line do not do those things which they are called upon to do under the terms of the resolutions – these are all matters for discussion with the Plebiscite Administrator when he assumes office. He alone has the authority to discuss these matters with those concerned and to take decisions on them. It is not because we have no views on these subjets that I steer clear of them at this stage, it is only because the Pakistan Government does not wish to prejudice these issues beforehand.

The representative of India has pleaded forcefully against any "unsettlement". He said:

> "Any unsettlement can only be based on the appeal to non-secularity; it can only be based on this appeal to religious prejudice." (767th meeting, para. 232.)

I have searched a lot whether we have made such an appeal and to whom, and I admit that I have not been able to find it. What is it that Pakistan has been demanding about Kashmir? It is not that Kashmiris should be disposed of like goods and chattels to suit the whims and fancies of either the Government of India or the Government of Pakistan. We have always maintained that Kashmiris and Kashmiris alone can decide their own future in a free and impartial plebiscite – and when we say Kashmiris we mean all Kashmiris without distinction of religion.

The representative of India has levelled certain charges of breaches of international agreements against Pakistan. This is indeed a serious matter, and I would be failing in my duty if I did not refer to them.

The first so-called breach on the part of Pakistan was, and I quote from Mr. Krishna Menon's speech, "withholding information from the United Nations that it was a combatant and that it was a party to the invasion" (767th meeting, para. 193)

I submit that this matter has been considered and disposed of by the Security Council. The Security Council adopted a resolution on 17 January 1948 which called upon the Governments of India and Pakistan to take all measures within their power calculated to improve the situation, and to refrain from doing or causing to be done or permitting any acts which might aggravate the situation. Both Governments accepted this resolution of the Security Council. In utter violation of this resolution of the Security Council and of its acceptance of the resolution, the Government of India mounted an offensive in the State of Jammu and Kashmir some time in the Spring of 1948. It was to meet this offensive, and to a threat to Pakistan, that a certain number of Pakistan forces were moved into the State of Jammu and Kashmir in the first week of May 1948 in sheer self-defence. When the Government of India mounted their offensive in the State, did it or did it not amount to an aggravation of the situation? Did they infrom the Security Council about their troop movements?

Again, the representative of India has cited Sir Owen Dixon in support of his contention that Pakistan was an aggressor in Kashmir. I shall, with the permission of the Security Council, read out what Sir Owen Dixon said on the subject in his report:

> "Upon a number of occasions in the course of the period beginning with the reference on 1 January 1948 of the Kashmir dispute to the Security Council, India had advanced not only the contention to which I have already referred that Pakistan was an aggressor, but the further contention that this should be declared. The Prime Minister of India, at an early stage of the meeting, made the same contention and he referred to it repeatedly during the conference. I took up the positions, first that the Security Council had not made such a declaration: secondly that I had neither been commissioned to make nor had I made any judicial investigation of the issue; but thirdly that, without going into the causes or reasons why it happened, which presumabaly formed part of the history of the sub-continent. I was prepared to adopt the view that when frontier of the State of Jammu and Kashmir was crossed, on, I believe, 20 October 1947, by hostile elements, it was contrary to international law, and that when, in May 1948, as I believe, units of the regular Pakistan forces moved into the territory of the State, this too was inconsistent with international law.
>
> "I therefore proposed that the first step in demilitarization should consist in the withdrawal of the Pakistan regular forces commencing on a named day. After a significant number of days from the named day, then other operations on each side of the cease-fire line should take place and as far as practicable, concurrently. What number of days should be fixed as significant was a matter of detail for them to settle.

> "The Prime Minister of Pakistan expressed strongly his dissent from the third of the three positions I took up, that is to say the third of the positions stated above. But he expressed his readiness to accept, in compliance with my request, the proposition that as a first step in demilitarization the withdrawal of the regular forces of the Pakistan Army should begin on a specified day and that a significant number of days should elapse before the commencement of any operation involving forces on the Indian side of the cease-fire line," (S/1791, paras 21 to 23.)

To put this in very plain language, here was this gentleman looking into this case and trying to hold a plebiscite. Each time he mentioned the word "plebiscite", India, instead of getting down to brass tacks and talking about a plebiscite, always said: "Pakistan is an aggressor; please declare that Pakistan is an aggresor", which was quite irrelevant. The Indian team must have repeated this question of aggression so many times that this gentleman must have got sick and tired of it and said : "For God's sake stop. Let us take for granted that there was an aggression and let us get on with the plebiscite now." Having mentioned those words which were out of context, the Government of India representative came here and said : "So and so reported that there was aggression." I do not understand the sense of this logic, when people try to get rid of a certain gentleman because he is talking too much by saying: "All right, take it for granted for the sake of argument that what he says is true, and now let us get on to the real point", and goes on to say : "Now you have admitted there was an aggression."

In the same way, there has been a discussion here about aggression and sovereignty, and so on, for seventeen hours. I do not know what the feeling of the Security Council is. Personally I think you would be prepared to say that we are so sick of hearing this that I would say : "All right, let us take for granted that all these things have happened. What about the agreement for a plebiscite? Why not get on with the plebiscite?" Then the Indians will come tomorrow and say that the Security Council decided that there was complete accession, and there was aggression, and there was sovereignty, and therefore there can be no plebiscite. This sort of argument has gone on for so long, for the last eight years, that I am sure we are tired of it, if the Security Council is not.

I have quoted what Sir Owen Dixon said in his report. What does this really mean? According to my understanding of the English language, which I must admit is imperfect, it only means one thing. That is this : for the purpose of getting the agreement of the Government of India to a plan of demilitarization, Sir Owen Dixon was prepared to assume, only for the sake of argument, that when the tribesmen entered Kashmir that was a breach of international law and that the entry of Pakistan troops was also a breach of international law. It meant nothing more than this. In fact, Sir Owen Dixon himself made it more than clear that the Security Council had not made any declaration on the question of aggression, nor had he been asked by the Security Council to go into that question, nor had he himself made any study or invesigation of that matter, and therefore he was not in a position to pronounce upon it.

It is quite clear that Sir Owen Dixon was prepared to make a mere assumption in order to put one side the question of aggression, so that progress could be made towards the agreed plebiscite. The representative of India had taken the words out of their context in order to twist them to mean what clearly they do not mean. Incidentally, it is rather amusing to note that the distinguished jurist from Australia was such in the estimation of the representative of India only in respect of this single observation, although according to his own admission, he was neither asked to examine the question of agression nor did he undertake such an examination; but when he formulated his plans of demilitarization and ultimately came to the conclusion that India's agreement would never be obtained to them, he fell from grace and became quite a different personality in the eyes of India.

The next so-called violation is with regard to the non-withdrawal of the Pakistan Army from the State. I repeat that the withdrawal of the Pakistan Army from the State is to be synchronized with the withdrawal of the bulk of the Indian forces on the other side of the cease-fire line. The Government of Pakistan is only too anxious to withdraw all its forces from the State. May I ask if the Government of India is equally willing to honour its international agreement with regard to the withdrawal of its Army and forces?

Then comes an astounding statement which is utterly incomprehensible to me:

"Not only has the Pakistan Army not withdrawn, but the

> changed conditions in view of the imbalance of forces created by rearmament is such that withdrawal has become practically impossible." (767th Meeting, para. 194.)

I really to not understand what this means. Even if the Pakistan Army should have become stronger, when it withdraws it will leave the State with all its equipment. I wonder whether he was referring to the Pakistan Army in "Azad" Kashmir or to the Pakistan Army in our own territory. If he meant the Pakistan Army in "Azad" Kashmir has become stronger, which is not the case, then why should be worry, because we say that when we withdraw, this whole army will go back? Why weep about it? Besides, what has the strength of the Pakistan Army within the borders of Pakistan to do with the question of the demilitarization of Jammu and Kashmir under the terms of an international agreement between India and Pakistan on deciding the question of accession by means of a plebiscite? However, if Mr. Krishna Menon is referring to the fact that our Army has become stronger, let us say in West Pakistan, that has nothing to do with the dimilitarization in the Kashmir State. Perhaps only Mr. Krishna Menon himself knows to what he was really referring.

Pakistan has accepted military aid in order to strengthen its defences. It has been repeatedly asserted that this military aid, and for that matter, any equipment that we may have, will not be used for aggressive purposes. The Government of India is also strengthening its armed forces. The only difference is that whereas Pakistan is receiving military aid, India is taking economc aid and diverting its funds and resources to the procurement of military supplies. This is a very interesting point and I should like once and for all to place it before the Security Council. I am referring to the allegation of India that Pakistan is becoming stronger and stronger.

India itself has recently placed an order for the purchase of sixty-five Canberras in the United Kingdom. The Canberra, as members of the Council know, is a long-range bomber which is used only for offensive purposes. Why is India purchasing these bombers and who are they going to be used against? It is only Pakistan and nobody else. India has also placed an order in the United Kingdom for 300 of the best and the largest tanks. Against which country are these 300 tanks going to be used? It is not against China and Soviet Russia I know that. They will not look towards those countries. Water does not flow up the hill; it always flows down the hill. He dare not look towards Peking or Moscow because they are too big for him. He looks only towards the smaller countries, like the poor Hyderabad State, Junagadh and Kashmir. If we had been equally weak, he probably would have started a war against us by now. All the armaments that India is receiving and preparing are against Pakistan.

Mr. Krishna Menon complained that the British Government was not very kind to his country. But where has India placed these orders? Who has supplied it with all the equipment? It is the United Kingdom. It takes these things from the United Kingdom and then abuses it. From whom is India buying aircraft carriers? It is buying them from the United Kingdom, and then it comes here and abuses the United Kingdom for nothing.

I want to point out that at the time of partition, all the gun factories, the tank factories, the armoured car factories, airplane repair shop factories, were all inside the territory which is today India. Most of the large underground installations of army stocks and munition dumps were in the territory which is now India. Members will recall that the British left the country within two months. They were the quickest quitters that anybody has ever seen in the whole history of mankind. They left all those armaments in the hands of the Indians. Having withdrawn, they said : "Now, gentlemen, you divide it amongst yourselves." Do you think that India was going to give us a single thing out of those armaments, part of which was our share? It has swallowed all those armaments and they are still in India. It is proceeding to purchase more from Canada, from the United Kingdom and from all over the world. The Americans give the money, bags full of dollars, and say: "Oh, you poor boys; you take this money to help yourselves." By obtaining that money, India makes a reduction in its budget, and with the money saved, purchases things from the United Kingdom and Canada.

The position today with regard to armed forces is the following : Air Force – ours is one-third the size of India's, Navy – ours is one-thrid the size of India's; Army – ours is one-third the size of India's. The money that India is spending on its defence forces, or offence forces, is four times the amount that we are spending. We are spending 75 per cent of our national revenue on defence forces. India, with a budget four or five times larger, is spending 40 to 50 per cent. This is published in its budget. The last time I made this statement, Mr. Krishna Menon tried to deny it. In the latest budget published by India, 40 per cent of the total revenue is going to its defence forces. Why is India trying to build up all these defence forces? Against whom? They will never be used against China, I can assure you.

At the time of the partition, the British had their forces in Tibet; they had their battalions, their political officers, their public works officers to look after the roads, and their post and telegraph officers – that all belonged to the British. That country was looked after by the British. It was almost a part of British India, like any of the other States. But when the Chinese Government paid a little attention to Tibet, my friends there said : "Oh yes; these people look like you; this is your country, by all means come and take it." Behind that request was the might of China, and not the Prime Minister of a small country like Pakistan.

The Security Council must realize these matters. It is responsible for the security and peace of the world. It is the highest authority today in the International organization and these things must be brought to its notice.

I am told that in oder to attack a country one must have at least three times the strength of the other country. If today we have one armoured division and we want to attack India, which had three armoured divisions, in order to win we would need nine armoured divisions. How can we increase our strength from one armoured division to nine armoured divisions over-night in order to fight against India?

When India comes before the Security Council and pretends that there is a danger of and it fears an attack from Pakistan, I am reminded of a little story of the wolf and the lamb that were drinking water from the same stream. The lamb was downstream from the wolf, and the wolf turned round and said : "Why are you polluting my water?" The lamb replied : "Sir, I am drinking down here below you and you are above me; I cannot be polluting your water." The wolf then said : "You dare to contradict me and call me a liar", whereupon he grabbed the lamb and ran off with him. That is the type of argument which India is now putting forward with regard to the defensive strength of Pakistan, a small country which has practically nothing at all in comparison with what India has, when it claims that we are going to attack it. I think that the world has better sense than to agree to such a flimsy argument.

I assert that the Indian armed might is not there for show. Even as I am speaking before this august body, the Indian war machine is being mobilized and concentrated along the frontiers of Pakistan. We had a press release here concerning the mobilization of the Indian Army on our frontier, and Mr. Krishna Menon said, "There are observers in Kashmir and we have mobilized no army in Kashmir". The mobilization of the Army is outside Kashmir on the borders of West Pakistan. I shall give the Council the official details on this matter. If I say that India possesses a knife in its right hand, Mr. Krishna Menon says, "Come and look, my right hand is quite empty, there is no knife in it"; but he has got a big sword on his left hand side. He then says, "But you never said anything about the left hand side." He is trying to hoodwink the Security Council by saying that they have done nothing in Kashmir. They may have done nothing there, that is not our allegation. Our allegation is that they have mobilized troops on our borders in West Pakistan.

Significant troop movements have taken place on the Indian side of West Pakistan since the recent discussion of the Kashmir question in the Security Council began. The information that I am going to give the Council is based on a telegram which I received from my Government, and the telegram is based on army intelligence reports and other reports which our Government possesses about the troop movements of India on our borders. We released this information by way of a press release here, and it was based on this official telegram and not on newspaper information which was conveyed to us. This is official Government information.

> The principal moves were as follows:
>
> "(1) 166th Brigade (5th Division) has been moved from Dalhousie (Punjab, India) to Pathankot on the Indo-Pakistan border;
>
> "(2) 77th Infantry Brigade (5th Division) from Dharamsala to Amritsar"—which is within thirteen miles of our border—"relieving 123rd Brigade (27th Division) which is now being deployed in the Khemkaran-Rajoke area between Ferozpur and Wagah"—That is also on our border.
>
> "The net result of these movements is that India now has two complete divisions, plus one independent brigade, on the East

Punjab – West Pakistan border, and, in addition, one division, the 4th Division, at Ambala, and two independent armoured brigades at Patiala.

"Thus the over-all position is that India now has three divisions, plus three detached brigades, on the Jammu and Kashmir border."

Now these are the figures in Kashmir State:

"Three divisions, plus three detached brigades, on the Jammu and Kashmir border, three divisions, plus one independent brigade and an armoured brigade on the East Punjab border, making a grand total of six divisions and four brigades, plus an armoured brigade, against West Pakistan.

"There are indications that one armoured division is also moving from its present location at Jhansi-Babina."

In view of these developments, my Prime Minister broadcast to the people of Pakistan on 16 February and I quote in part from his statement, as follows:

"Whatever may be reasons for these movements, the action of India will have dangerous consequences. So many troop movements along the border, digging trenches, taking up strategic positions, may provoke border incidents which may become serious. I have issued instructions to our Army and our people not to be provoked under any circumstances. Clashes on the border will suit India, and may even be engineered by it in an attempt to prevent the United Nations from considering the matter coolly and calmly. We have, therefore, to be all the more careful that we do not get excited and that we do not fall into a trap laid for us."

I should at this stage, like to point out very earnestly to the Security Council that question is very serious. You do not know, gentlemen, the danger that you are facing, and it is really the duty of the Security Council to take some definite steps to resolve this dangerous situation. Otherwise, the whole of this area will get into a position which we will all regret hereafter. So, something has to be done, and has to be done quickly, and you, gentlemen, have got to stop this progressive deterioration between these two countries. I should not say more. I think you know what the position is, and if you do not take any action, well, it is your responsibility.

Mr. Menon again said, "Now there are forty-five battalions of the 'Azad' Kashmir forces..., officered, trained and equipped by the Pakistan Army" (769th meeting, para. 58). The conclusion which it is sought to draw from this is that demilitarization of the 'Azad' Kashmir area is not possible. I am sorry, but I have not been able to understand that argument. I would, first and foremost, like to state categorically that the "Azad" Kashmir forces do not number forty-five battalions. I have said before, and I repeat, that not one soldier has been added to the strength of the "Azad" Kashmir forces since the time the cease-fire became effective.

So, when this area is demilitarized, what will happen? The Pakistan Army will withdraw from the State, taking out all its equipment and personnel. The link between the Pakistan Army and the "Azad" Kashmir forces will thus be broken. What will be left in "Azad" Kashmir will be the people of the area itself. There will be no officer of the Pakistan Army in command of any "Azad" Kashmir forces when the Pakistan Army withdraws from Kashmir. The reason that there are some Pakistan officers in top positions in the "Azad" Kashmir forces is that, in agreement with "Azad" Kashmir Government, the Pakistan High Command is in over-all command of all the forces that are now in that area.

Then a reference was made to the alleged violation by Pakistan of the cease-fire agreement. The cease-fire agreement was concluded on 27 July 1949. According to the terms of that agreement, all violations of the cease-fire are reported to the two States and to the United Nations Military Observers Group. There is a procedure laid down for that purpose. The Security Council receives periodical reports from the United Nations Military Observers Group. Let it declare after reference to those reports, whether the allegations made in this respect by the representative of India are correct. I assert that those allegations are completely baseless.

The representative of India has more than once quoted from the third interim report of the Commission words to the effect that, while the situation in the State has changed, the resolutions remain unchanged. That report was submitted by the United Nations

Commission for India and Pakistan on 9 December 1949. All that the Commission said, I submit, was – and I quote from paragraph 283:

> "The period of investigation has been completed. Within the framework of its terms of reference, following in its endeavours the provisions contained in its resolutions of 13 August 1948 and 5 January 1949, the Commission feels that the possibilities of mediation open to it have been exhausted. Over a prolonged period, in a changing and dynamic situation and restricted by long-standing related clarifications which proved to be a real impediment to reaching agreement, the framework of the resolution of 13 August has become inadequate in the light of the factual conditions in the State. The Commission has been unable, therefore, to mediate much beyond what is today a rather outmoded pattern. The State of Jammu and Kashmir has not been demilitarized, as was envisaged in Part II of the resolution of 13 August, and until this is achieved the conditions necessary to the holding of plebiscite cannot begin to be established. As has been seen from those parts of the report entitled 'The "Azad" Kashmir forces, and "Withdrawal of forces", the Commission believes that the problem of demilitarization must be treated as a whole, and that the distinctions relative to demilitarization which exist in the division of the problem into truce and plebiscite periods as visualized in the original plan of demilitarization has proven one of the most difficult obstacles in achieving agreement on the problem. It is evident that the presence of large number of troops in the State is not conducive to the creation of a peaceful atmosphere. The demilitarizatoin of the State is essential to permit the holding of a free and unfettered plebiscite."

> "Two recent demonstrations of mob violence against myself and another British correspondent here were carefully 'fixed' by a high quarter of the Kashmir Government. I have good grounds for believing. Demonstrations were intended to impress on me the pro-Indian feeling of the people here and also the degree of hatred and bitterness felt against the British, the United Nations and the West generally for favouring the Pakistan request for a plebiscite. They were also intended to

try to scare me off talking to those who oppose integration with India. They undoubtedly exist, stifled though they are."

Another correspondent who visited the area was Mr. Stephen Harper of the *Daily Express*. This is what he said about his experiences in Srinagar in a dispatch published in the *Daily Express* on 5 February 1957:

"In this capital city of the 'Valley of Fear', I learned today how a plot was laid to set the mob against me. The 'Valley of Fear' is in Kashmir – where India's Premier Nehru keeps a puppet Government in power with the support of 80,000 Indian troops.

"The puppet Premier is Bakhshi Ghulam Muhammed. He had declared 'the irrevocable accession' of Kashmir to India without Kashmir's 4 million people having a say in the matter.

"I had scarcely arrived in the Srinagar capital last week when a mob swarmed round my car. They shouted 'Murder him – we don't want British reporters here." Car doors and canopy were ripped off. Hands grabbed and tore at my clothes. Little baskets of charcoal – carried around for heat – were poured over me and burned my face.

"Today I discovered that the mob gathered as a result of a telephone call from a Government official to the home of the brother of the puppet Premier Bakhshi.

"The idea was to try to convince me that the people of Srinagar favour integration with India, as Bakhshi has decreed.

Secondly, assembling of the mob was an attempt to try to frighten me out of trying to contact opponents of the Bakhshi regime. In both ways the plot failed.

"I now have evidence that Sheikh Abdullah – hustled out of premiership and jailed in 1953 – is still the darling of Kashmir, and a party called the Kashmir Political Conference carries on secret meetings in mosques.

> "Besides my sources for this news, I have heard of two other attempts to contact me. Last night I was warned that I am a target for the mob because my paper is critical of Premier Nehru. News of the *Daily Express* campaign urging a fair deal for Kashmir has spread to this remote valley."

I am mentioning these recent incidents because Mr. Krishna Menon has chosen to inform the Security Council of what an Australian correspondent was reported to have told Indian newspapermen in Srinagar on 7 February. The fact, however, is that India's policy has consistently been to screen off the area from foreign correspondents. Whenever, under pressure of world opinion, India has allowed foreign correspondents to go to Srinagar, we have had reports on conditions which would interest this Council.

A correspondent of the London "Economist" made the following report in a dispatch which appeared on 20 August 1955:

> "As things are, the average Kashmiri has no desire to be assaulted by the paid bullies of the present Kashmir Government's so-called 'Peace Brigade' or to be arrested on some specious charge and to be locked up without trial. His resentment smoulders, but it seldom bursts into flame. Kashmir is quite a well-run Indian colony...Bakhshi Ghulam Mohammed, the present Prime Minister of Kashmir, looks like a moustached Mussolini and often talks like one."

The London *Times* of 14 October 1955 published the following report from its correspondent in India:

> "The Government of India is still practising censorship by refusing to allow British correspondents to visit Kashmir. Representatives of the *Daily Telegraph* and *Daily Express* have failed to obtain the necessary permits and have left the country."

The London *Daily Telegraph* of 14 October published a dispatch from its correspondent, Mr. George Evans, which said, in part:

> "This morning when I withdrew my application after a vain eighteen-day wait for an entry permit to Kashmir, a New Delhi

Government spokesman insisted that my application had not been refused. It was merely 'delayed'.

"This statement was made despite the fact that since my application was first submitted the India Ministry of Defence, which controls the issue of permits, had given one to a Japanese correspondent within two days of his application."

In its issue of 21 October 1955, the London *Daily Telegraph* published another dispatch from the same correspondent, Mr. George Evans, writing from Muzaffarabad, "Azad" Kashmir – that is, from the free side of Kashmir. In this dispatch, Mr. Evans said:

"Recent reports of disaffection in 'Azad' Kashmir emanating from India and not in accordance with the actual conditions which I have observed in the course of a two-day visit here.

"The most striking contrast is that, while Mr. Nehru's Government excludes observers from Indian-occupied Kashmir whom it suspects might voice criticism of conditions there, no such discriminatory censorship is applied this side of the cease-fire line...

"Permission to enter 'Azad' Kashmir is necessary, but it seldom takes more than a few hours to get it. The day after applying, I drove unconducted across the frontier."

A correspondent of the London *Times* who secured permission to go to Srinagar sent a long dispatch to his newspaper, dealing with the activities of the "Peace Brigade" in Anantnag. This correspondent of the London *Times* said:

"One man had torn nostrils and another claimed that his teeth had been knocked out by members of the 'Peace Brigade'. Two shopkeepers complained that they had been robbed during unofficial searches and others said their shops had been looted. A women in a highly hysterical state said that she was afraid to go home because of constant harassment. She was the widow of a Muslim killed during the tribal invasion while escorting Hindu refugees, and she alleged that compensation awarded to her had not been paid because she was a supporter of Sheikh Abdullah.

"Mr. Beg said that physical injuries were inflicted on two occasions when his brother, G.M. Beg, was publicly welcomed after his release from prison and when shopkeepers declared *hartal* last week after one of their member alleged that he had been beaten and robbed by members of the 'Peace Brigade'.

"One of the town's leading traders appeared before this correspondent with bruised and bandaged face. To top all this, the correspondent himself was approached by a member of the 'Peace Brigade', who demanded information such as his name, address, nationality and purpose of his visit.

"The Indian Government often behaves as if its moral duty is to defend dependent peoples, and it is therefore surprising that so little attention is given to the political welfare of 4 million Kashmiris for whom it is ultimately responsible.

"Generous Indian economic aid and indeed the intelligent development programme of the Kashmir Government tend to conceal the methods of that Government that are totalitarian in concept and occasionally border on outright terrorism in practice."

May I also recall to the Security Council the beating administered to Mr. Ashoka Mehta, a prominent member of the Indian Parliament who, on a visit to the Kashmir State, had the audacity of suggesting a fair deal to the people of Kashmir. This incident was fully reported pratically in every important Indian newspaper.

Then the Council has before it the testimony of such a distinguished Indian social worker as Miss Mridula Sarabhai with regard to the conditions prevalent in Indian-held Kashmir. She was an inmate of the Gandhi Ashram for years and later became Assistant Secretary-General of the Indian National Congress. After she had written the letters which have been circulated to the members of Security Council, the Indian Prime Minister has her thrown out from the New Delhi Constitution House, a Government hostel, where she had stayed for a number of years. It was recently reported in the Indian Press that the Indian Prime Minister had her ejected from a meeting of the Congress, at which she was present and which Mr. Nehru was addressing. I have requested that her letters be released as a United Nations document as well as the letter of Sheikh Mohammed Abdullah, the veracity of which has been admitted by Bakhshi Ghulam Muhammed, the present Prime Minister of Kashmir. This is what has happened to a lady of very high rank. She is a daughter or sister of one of the biggest textile manufacturers of India, and she has spent her whole life in social service for the benefit of the people. She has been in the forefront of the Congress Party—that is Mr. Nehru's party. The moment she utters a word in favour of the people of Kashmir, Mr. Nehru throws her out of the hostel in New Delhi, which is a Government building, and he ejects her from the meeting in which she is sitting. To give that treatment to a woman of status, position, a woman who is a friend, a friend's daughter; it can only happen in India.

Mr. Krishna Menon had been trying to create an impression, here and outside, that it is entirely immaterial what world opinion thinks of Pandit Nehru's attitude in Kashmir, of his intransigence and defiance of this international body created by the Charter, to which India has subscribed.

At this stage I should like to refer to a speech that Mr. Nehru made on 3 February 1957 in connexion with the election campaign. Having seen that his Government was being condemned by the Press of the whole world for not allowing the plebiscite in Kashmir, and being convinced of his position, that he had fallen in the eyes of the whole civilized world in this matter, he made a remarkable speech at this public meeting. He said:

> "Gentlemen, I am told"—I suppose he referred to the world Press and world political opinion—"that I have fallen in stature. But what does it matter what the whole world thinks? My stature depends on you, my people."

That is the value that Mr. Nehru attaches to world opinion, to the Security Council, to the United Nations and to the world Press. He says, "Let them say what they like. So long as my people, you people, are with me, I do not care for world opinion". When you are dealing with a man like that, I do not know what method you can employ in order to incline him to honour his pledges given to the United Nations and to the Security Council, when the man does not care for public opinion, the public opinion of the whole world. I think that Mr. Krishna Menon wasted your time when he came here and argued his case for seventeen hours when his Prime Minister has no intention of carrying out his international obligations.

I am sure that members of the Security Council have seen some of the comments that have appeared in the Press the world over which have severely taken Pandit Nehru to task for his Kashmir policy. Among these are such distinguished papers as the *Manchester Guardian* and the *New Statesman and Nation* of London, both of which are great admires of Pandit Nehru. Mr. Kingsley Martin, who is the world-renowned editor of the *New Statesman and Nation* of England, is a fast friend of Pandit Nehru and has been such for the last twenty or thirty years. Mr. Kingsley Martin has brought out a leading article against Mr. Nehru, his friend, condemning him for not allowing a plebiscite in Kashmir and for dishonouring his international agreement. What further proof do you need of world opinion in this direction? In the face of Mr. Nehru's wholly unreasonable attitude in Kashmir, the World Press has been forced to revise its estimate of Mr. Nehru. Such distinguished papers or magazines as *The New York Times*, the *Christian Science Monitor*, the *Washington Post*, the *New York Herald Tribune*, *Life* and *Time* in the United States, the *Times*, Observer, the *Daily Telegraph*, the *Daily Mail*, the *Economist*, to mention only a few of the British papers, and leading newspapers in Canada, France, Switzerland, Norway, Sweden, Australia, Burma, Indonesia, South America and other countries have expressed views on this matter which are wholly uncomplimentary to the Indian Prime Minister.

I have with me a very interesting cartoon. I think that if Mr. Krishna Menon were here he would regret having referred to one newspaper correspondent on whom he tried to pin his faith. I have here the latest edition of *Punch*, the periodical. Here on this page – I will pass it on – we see a cartoon where Mr. Nehru has one body; he has two heads. On one side of his head, in one hand, he is holding a dove of peace and a little twig. On the other side of his body near his face there is a big sword and underneath is written on the sword side "Kashmir"; on the dove side "Suez Canel".

I would venture to say that on no single issue has world opinion expressed itself so clearly and so vigorously as in the case of Kashmir, and the Council would agree with me that almost the entire volume of this opinion is critical of Pandit Nehru's policy in Kashmir. Mr. Menon advises the Security Council to disregard this expression of public opinion the world over. We have compiled some of these comments and editorials, and although these are only a fraction of what the world Press has said, I would request that the compilation be circulated as a United Nations Document.

I, of course, agree with the representative of India that the resolutions of the United Nations Commission for India and Pakistan dated 13 August 1948 and 5 January 1949 are "the only international agreements that exists". Since these are international agreements, and binding international agreements, there is no relevance to Mr. Menon's laboured discussion of the present effect of unaccepted offers by the Government of India to hold a plebiscite in Kashmir. These offers, and for that matter the 20 August 1953 agreement between the Prime Ministers of India and Pakistan that a fair and impartial plebiscite was the most feasible method fo ascertaining the wishes of the people, as far as the Security Council is now concerned, are simply demonstrative of India's long-standing announced, intention to hold a plebiscite in the State. What is now before the Security Council is the implementation of the international agreement between the Council, India and Pakistan to hold that plebiscite.

No change has taken place as may absolve the Government of India of its international commitment to a plebiscite. Any change that may have taken place is due to unilateral action taken by the Government of India in clear violation of the provisions of the International agreement. Even these changes are such as can be easily undone without causing any harm to either side.

The representative of India has reminded the Council that it is not a legal tribunal. Surely he does not mean by this that the Security Council is unable to appreciate the nature of the obligation embodied in the international agreement – an obligation which he says his Government and his people "have no intention and...shall at no time violate" (767th Meeting, para. 85). What is the nature of that obligation? Mr. Menon points out that the holdings of the plebiscite must await the demilitarization of the State of Jammu and Kashmir. This is undoubtedly correct. With respect, I should like to point out that Mr. Menon's further argument, that because demilitarization has not been accomplished the obligation to hold a plebiscite falls, is utterly untenable. In fact, it is an attempt by India to take advantage of its own default. The settlement of the Kashmir dispute, according to the international agreement, must proceed step by step. The step that must now be taken is to secure the demilitarization of the State. It was with regard to this next step that my original remarks on 16 January were addressed (761st Meeting). We have tried every method recommended by the Charter, by the Security Council and by the Commission and by the United Nations representatives – and Kashmir is still not demilitarized. There is now before the Council a draft resolution (S/3787) which addressed itself to the next step.

I do not understand Mr. Krishna Menon's dissatisfaction with the supporters of this draft resolution and the manner in which he has expressed that dissatisfaction. It is interesting to note what Mr. Krishna Menon has said. He has accused Sir Pierson Dixon – or is it the Government of the United Kingdom? – of a "lapse from fortitude and wisdom" (769th meeting, para. 53). Mr. Krishna Menon has taunted the representative of the United States with having proposed something that is against international law, unethical and inequitable, although he does not impung Mr. Lodge personally, whom he regards as a man "of great simplicity of mind" – I do not know whether Mr. Lodge will consider that as a compliment – "frankness, and Candour of expression" (*Ibid.*, para. 99). Mr. Krishna Menon charges the representative of Cuba with not having understood history, political philosophy or the record of the Security Council in respect of Kashmir. The representative of Iraq was chided for having committed the offence of referring to the brotherhood of Islam. Mr Krishna Menon contrasted it with human brotherhood. If he had read the *Koran*, from which he is often fond of quoting, he would have known that the concept of the brotherhood of man and of tolerance for all peoples, irrespective of race, creed, colour or caste, is fundamental in Islam. It is one thing to put these things down in a Constitution and quite another thing fully to comprehend them. A little later in his speech Mr. Krishna Menon plainly accused the representative of Iraq of having departed from the truth.

Here, I should like to make a few comments. When Mr. Krishna Menon was commenting on the speech of the representative of Iraq, his last sentence was: "One must stick to the truth even when one wants to be polite." (769th meeting, para. 119). That means to say that the representative of Iraq had strayed from the truth. And that is a point which I feel that the Security Council cannot pass over lightly.

If an advocate before a High Court Judge, a Supreme Court Judge, or even an ordinary Magistrate, accuses the Judge or the Magistrate of departing from the truth, that is an insult which, when offered to a judicial authority, would bring the confiscation of a lawyer's licence to a practise. If a sentence like that accusation—and a false accusation—were uttered by a Member of Parliament, the Speaker would call upon that Member to withdraw that word. Otherwise, that Member of Parliament would be expelled from the House. I feel that it is commensurate with the dignity and honour of the Security Council that the parties who come before it to argue their cases must control their language and speak in a respectful manner which is in consonance with the high office which the Council holds; and I hope that it is for the Council now to take steps to defend its own honour and prestige so as not to set an example by which, in future, parties who come before it can insult it on its face in the manner in which the representative of Iraq has been insulted.

When dealing with other representatives on the Security Council, Mr. Krishna Menon has employed a technique which is well known to us in India and Pakistan, but which may not be well known to the Council. He began to criticize Sir Pierson Dixon very strongly, and when he saw a smile—as I did—on the face of Sir Pierson Dixon, he must have realized that the days when he could accuse the British in India, and they were frightened of us, had gone and we are now a free country, and that Sir Pierson was probably thinking: "Well, my friend, you are a free country; you must now look after yourself." Mr. Krishna Menon must have felt immediately that he had made a mistake in attacking Sir Pierson, and so he softened. He tried to cajole him: "When I was High Commissioner for India in London, the British gave us a lot of supplies and arms, and so on and we have been friends; we are in the Commonwealth, and we are a sister country, and we are brothers." Then he proceeded almost as if he was kissing him on both cheeks. This sort of conduct of a party using strong language against representative on the Security Council and then changing to another sort of language, thinking that the representative might get angrry, a language to cajole him, is an advocacy which I have very seldom come across.

I could have said a good deal about the remarks Mr. Krishna Menon has made about each representative—about the representative of Cuba, the representative of the United States, and so on—simply because if a representative on the Council does not agree with him he resorts to these personal attacks. However, I believe that representatives can defend themselves.

Instead of examining personalities, let us examine what the representatives on the Council have said about the draft resolution. This document has been explained exhaustively by the sponsors. My Government takes note of the following clarifications of the draft resolution that were offered by the sponsors in the course of the debate on 15 February 1957 (768th meeting).

The representative of the United Kingdom said:

> "As regards other conditions for progress towards the settlement, perhaps I should indicate what we have in mind in including this in the draft.
>
> "...This, then, is one condition for progress which indeed should be examined—the need for a decrease in tension—and there are doubtless other matters. I think, for instance, of clarification of the position of the Plebiscite Administrator, which the President may think would repay examination with the two Governments. But all this examination is governed by the phrase 'having regard to the previous resolutions of the Security Council and that of the United Nations Commission for India and Pakistan'. That point is fundamental.
>
> "...The draft resolution, therefore, provides for a procedure which, we trust, will enable progress to be made, but not through the medium of public debate, during the next few weeks. Yet, the need to make progress is pressing, and for that reason the draft resolution proposes a definite time-limit within which the President should report to the Security Council; for the Council cannot fail to take up its task again at the earliest possible moment." (768th meeting, paras 16 to 19).

The representative of the United States said:

> "The draft resolution which has been introduced by the Governments of Australia, Cuba, the United Kingdom and the United States (S/3787) builds upon these points of agreement.

It thus lays considerable stress on the importance of achieving demilitarization. Four of the preambular paragraphs refer to this problem.

"The task which we are suggesting that the Security Council assign to its President also emphasizes the efforts to achieve demilitarization. In this connexion, a proposal has already been put forward as a suggestion by which the present deadlock might be broken. This was the proposal of the representative of Pakistan at the 761st meeting, to the following effect:

"The functions of protecting the State and ensuring internal security should be intrusted by the Council to a United Nations force which should be introduced into the area at once." (761st meeting, para. 112).

"We have thought it desirable to note this proposal by the representative of Pakistan for the use of a temporary United Nations force in connexion with demilitarization."

"As I indicated earlier, the United State believes that we must build upon the gains which have been made before. The President, in undertaking this mission, is accordingly to do so having regard to the resolutions which have been adopted on Kashmir by the Security Council and the United Nations Commission for India and Pakistan. He is also to bear in mind the statements of the parties and specifically the proposal for a United Nations force. As the President of the Council, he will also no doubt bear in mind the statements of the members of the Council." (768th meeting, para 32 to 36).

The representative of Cuba said the following:

"The Cuban delegation therefore believes that this draft resolution would lead to the holding of a plebiscite...

"...Therefore for us...the problem of the plebiscite is something that has been definitely settled and agreed upon by the parties. All that has to be done is to bring about conditions in which the plebiscite can be held.

"From the Indian representative's statement here and also from the statements I have quoted, it seems clear that India has at no time tried to retract its promise to hold the plebiscite, since it laid down conditions under which Parts I and II must be complied with before Part III can be carried out; and there would be no reason to speak of the fulfilment of conditions for a plebiscite if no plebiscite were to be held. This, in our opinion, is crystal clear. We therefore believe that the draft resolution we have submitted is an attempt, by entrusting the President of the Council with this task, to bring about the conditions which will allow the holding of a plebiscite." (*Ibid.*, paras. 95 to 99).

The representative of Australia stated the following:

"The Council has all along attached great importance to the adaption of appropriate measures of demilitarization in the State of Jammu and Kashmir as a necessay step towards the holding of a free and impartial plebiscite. It is well known that negotiations on detailed practical measures to bring about such demilitarization have not in the past been sucessful. This is the most immediate problem to which, in our view, the Security Council should bend its present efforts.

"The draft resolution refers to the proposal of the representative of Pakistan for the use of a temporary United Nations force to facilitate agreement on effective arrangements for demilitarization. The idea is perhaps not a new one, but it gains interest and importance from the recent experience of the United Nations in the establishment and operations of the United Nations Emergency Force in Egypt. Without drawing any parallel between the situation that led to the General Assembly's decision to establish that Force and the problem of securing appropriate measures of demilitarization of Kashmir as a preliminary step towards holding a free and impartial plebiscite, it would seem to us very difficult for anybody to deny that the use of such a force, in so far as it might contribute towards demilitarization, would, in the words of the draft resolution 'deserve consideration'. It is the hope of the Australian delegation that this proposal will receive full and

> sympathetic consideration by the Council and the parties." (*Ibid.*, paras 52 and 53).

Apart from these clarifications and explanations as to its objective offered by the sponsors, my Government also notes the following from the speeches of the representative of the Philippines, China and Iraq with regard to their understanding of the contents of the resolution and its objectives.

The representative of the Philippines said:

> "Although the representative of India has dealt with the question of aggression anew, I do not thing that the Council is called upon to make any finding as to whether there has been aggression and by whom it was committed. It should be recalled that the charge and counter-charge of aggression ceased to be relevant the moment both sides agreed to the resolutions of the United Nations Commission for India and Pakistan of 13 August and 5 January 1949." (*Ibid.*, para. 104).

The representative of the Philippines then went on to say:

> "The will of the people of Jammu and Kashmir, according to the resolutions of the United Nations Commission for India and Pakistan of 13 August 1948 and 5 January 1949, which have been accepted by both India and Pakistan, is to be ascertained by the democratic method of a free and impartial plebiscite conducted under the auspices of the United Nations. The other provisions of the resolutions mentioned are clearly subordinated to that end. The provisions relating to the cease-fire and the truce arrangements are aimed simply at the creation of condition to enable the free and orderly attainment of the prime objective. Whatever changes may have occurred in the situation since the resolution of the Security Council were passed, it is submitted that the principle underlying those resolutions cannot be changed because it is unchangeable." (*Ibid.*, para.110).

The representative of the Philippines, further on in his statement, went on to say the following:

"The draft resolution before us meets all the requirements of the situation and without departing from the sound and practical course heretofore followed by this organ of the United Nations, opens the way realistically to a settlement which, if the parties are minded to co-exist in peace, should be final and conclusive.

"The proposal does not deviate from the course we have followed, it recognizes the absolute necessity of demilitarizing the disputed region as a condition precedent to any genuine plebiscite. None of us here will dispute the proposition that no plebiscite is possible in a setting of war like appearances. The first and most important condition to a free election is that the people should be able to go to the polls without fear in their hearts. Any sign of coercion would make the true expression of the people's will impossible. Those of us who have been used to the democratic way of life will readily admit that any plebiscite worth its name must be conducted under conditions of absolute peace if it is to be regarded as valid and conclusive.

"We can assume that one of the principal concerns of our President when he goes to the sub-continent is that the ground is properly laid for the untrammelled exercise of popular suffrage when the plan of a plebiscite, which is the Security Council's decision, is actually carried out.

"Finally, the reference in the draft resolution to the proposal made by the representative of Pakistan that a United Nations force be assigned to Jammu and Kashmir as a temporary means towards the achievement of demilitarization is in line with my Government's views that the idea merits full consideration." (*Ibid*., paras 118 to 121).

I must apologize for the these quotations, but I am going to draw a conclusion from them as regards the draft resolution. That is my only reason for quoting them.

The representative of China said:

"Therefore, what this draft resolution tries to do is to further the implementation of the resolutions which the Council or the Commission has already adopted. The co-sponsors have told us and the language of the draft resolution states that all those resolutions stand.

"...So we have to devise a scheme to take care of these two requirements: first, the peace and security of the State during the plebiscite; and second, that the force that maintains peace and security should not coerce or intimidate or give the appearance of intimidating the voters. These are the two reqirements that we must always keep in mind in solving this problem of demilitarization.

"I do not know of a better way of meeting those two requirements simultaneously. With the temporary use of a United Nations force in Kashmir, we can contribute to the maintenance of peace and security in that State during the plebiscite. In the second place the stationing of a temporary United Nations force in Kashmir cannot be suspected by anybody of intimidating or coercing the voters to vote in favour of either of the two parties. Therefore, I find that this idea of a temporary United Nations force really deserves consideration," (*Ibid.*, paras, 124 to 130).

The representative of Iraq said the following – and this is the last quotation:

"The whole issue centres around one major question, namely, that of the establishment of conditions under which a free and impartial plebiscite could be conducted. It will have been realized that all the resolutions, negotiations and reports were endeavours to promote such conditions. It could therefore be said that this problem, which was from its very beginning a clear one, at times had been obscured by the introduction of a number of elements foreign to it and sometimes quite irrelevant." (769th Meeting, para. 17).

The representative of Iraq then said:

"The passage of time has neither changed the principles upon

> which the future of Kashmir was to be decided nor has made the method of plebiscite less applicable now then it was eight years ago." (*Ibid.*, para. 21).

The representative of Iraq concluded his statement as follows:

> "We believe that the draft resolution submitted by Australia, Cuba, the United Kingdom and the United States (S/3787) contains all the elements necessary at the moment for taking certain positive steps in the solution of the Kashmir dispute." (*Ibid.*, para. 27).

The Government of Pakistan is grateful to the members of the Security Council for the clarifications of the draft resolution which they have been kind enough to give publicly. In view of these clarifications, I take great pleasure in informing the Securing Council that my Government would accept the draft resolution that is now before the Security Council and has authorized me to assure the Security Council that the distinguished President of the Council will receive all possible co-operation from the Government of Pakistan in his difficult and responsible task.

My Government has complete confidence in the ability and impartiality of the President of the Security Council, Mr. Gunnar V. Jarring, Ambassador of Sweden. Let us hope that his mission, which is to bring about demilitarization of the State of Jammu and Kashmir, preparatory to the holding of a plebiscite under the auspices of the United Nations to determine the question of the accession of the State to India or Pakistan, shall succeed.

My Government is happy that the Security Council has noted the proposal that a United Nations force be sent to the State of Jammu and Kashmir in order to facilitate its demilitarization in accordance with the terms of the international agreement. I would humbly submit, once again, that in our view this is a good way of making progress towards the agreed objective, namely, the plebiscite. Over the course of the last eight years the Government of India has rejected, one after another, eleven proposals to bring about the demilitarization of the State. The various procedures laid down in Chapter VI of the Charter have been tried without success. If the situation is not to erupt into a catastrophe, something positive must be done to demilitarize the State thus making it possible for the plebiscite to be held without further delay.

> Mr. Menon has said, and I quote him:
>
> "The Government of India will in no circumstances permit foreign troops on its soil." (769th meeting, para. 153).
>
> I submit, Mr. President, that Kashmir is not Indian soil. The question of any foreign troops going on Indian soil does not therefore arise.

Mr. Krishna Menon is a clever lawyer. He has left sufficient scope in these words to argue when he returns, after having agreed to everything, to say, "The meaning of my words were 'our territory', which was Indian territory but not Kashmir territory—which was not our territory." Therefore we should not be dismayed by the use of these words by Mr. Menon because he has left a loop-hole for himself.

The distinguished representative of India has also raised objections with regard to the United Nations force on the score that it may not succeed in demilitarizing the area. We have never suggested that the force will go round the army barracks in Kashmir and force the troops to surrender their arms. The disarming and disbanding of forces is under the terms of the international agreement the responsibility of the representative or the Plebiscite Administrator, as the case may be. The object of the entry—and I specially draw the attention of the honourable member of the Soviet Union of a United Nations force is simply to create confidence in the minds of the two sides which should enable them to proceed without fear to the discharge of their obligations under the international agreement. As soon as the United Nations force enters Kashmir both sides must, strictly according to the terms of the international agreement, start withdrawing their forces, which operation would be followed by disbandment of the "Azad" Kashmir forces and further reduction in the forces on the Indian side of the cease-fire line.

Now, this thing must be clearly understood, that this United Nations force is going into Kashmir with the consent of both parties in the sense that both parties have agreed to demilitarize and both parties have agreed to withdraw their forces. It is in pursuance of that agreement which has been made by India and Pakistan before you here, for demiliarization, that this force is going. Therefore, for anyone to think or imagine that this force is going against the wishes of the people of Kashmir, or India, or of Pakistan, would be wrong.

If India said today : "We will not admit the force", then it would be going against its agreement made before the Council that they will demilitarize. This force is now being sent there from the Pakistan side to occupy the frontiers, to prevent war between the two, and to remove fear from the mind of each that the other will invade if they withdraw. Therefore, when this United Nations force has gone to the cease-fire line, then India, having already agreed to withdraw its forces according to the resolution – international treaty, I call it – must withdraw. Therefore if anybody argues, and I want to address this point to Mr. Sobolev, that these troops are going there – forced on India – he is wrong. We are agreeing to it, and India has already agreed to demilitarization, therefore its consent is presumed.

Consequently I think the only way of ensuring peace now in that area is that the United Nations troops should go there, and we allow them to go to our area to occupy our cease-fire line. In which case, India already having agreed, and now I am sure it will again – when the President goes there – that if our troops go, it will be willing to go. If we confirm the original agreement, then Indian agreement can also be presumed, then the troops can go in. But we ourselves do not want to hand over the cease-fire to a few policemen from the United Nations, and then tomorrow India may invade our side and be a danger to Pakistan. The troops are sent and will be sent only when there is a presumption that both parties are willing to agree to demilitarize and accept these troops. We are giving our acceptance now. India is acceptance, the President will secure, I hope, when he goes to New Delhi.

Therefore the question of forcing the troops into that area does not arise. If anybody has been arguing – especially the Russian delegate – I hope he will bear in mind my interpretation of the request for troops : that is the willingness of the parties to receive the troops that will take the troops there. If India is fighting to go there, then we may not be willing to allow our troops to move out in order to make room for the United Nations troops unless India has also agreed. Therefore we must help the President in solving this problem. We must give him a chance. We must give him this authority. When he has been to New Delhi, then he will return to report to you and there will be sufficient time for every member of the Security Council to reconsider this matter in connexion with the troops. At the moment we are only authorizing the President to go and to negotiate with India to find out whether India is willing to receive the troops or not, and if so, on what conditions; and if it is not, how are they going to implement the international treaty?

Nothing is going to happen with regard to these troops until the President returns and reports to you on the opinion of India with respect to this subject. Then the Council will have plenty of time to assess the situation and consider this point. I am saying this because yesterday a certain rumour was spread by a certain quarter—which did not come from the Soviet Union, I know. That is why I felt it necessary to explain the question in this way since I did not have an opportunity of seeing the representative of the Soviet Union to explain this to him before. The troops are not being forced, and after the President returns the Council will have the time to consider this.

The Council also has before it the amendments proposed by the Soviet Union with respect to the draft resolution (S/3789). The decision on these amendments as well as the draft resolution is, of course, one for the Security Council. We have given careful consideration to these amendments and suggest, with due respect, that if adopted, the Soviet Union amendments would remove from the resolution an authoritative and valuable pronouncement on the present status of the dispute and the lines along which a solution must be sought. The significant area of agreement between India and Pakistan which the Security Council is seeking to build would be overlooked if the Soviet Union amendments were accepted, the usefulness of the purpose of a United Nations force which, though unexplored, has certain distinct possibilities, would be ignored.

Further, these amendments would severely restrict the authority of the President of the Security Council in seeking to develop proposals for the demilitarization of the State. The draft resolution speaks of examining proposals which in the Presidents opinion are likely to contribute to the achievement of demilitarization. The amendments restrict the President to examining the present situation and the progress that can be made. The Soviet Union amendments would unfortunately remove the deadline date for the President's report of demiltarization—a provision which my Government considers vital inview of the present mounting tension over this dispute.

Mr. Krishna Menon, in the course of his last intervention, has tried to differentiate between the case of Algeria and Kashmir (769th meeting, para. 112), but I cannot follow his arguments. Did he mean to convey to the Security Concil that because Algeria was conquered by the French some 130 years ago it has earned the right of liberation and self-determination, whereas Kashmir was conquered by Indian troops only nine years ago and therefore the struggle for liberation by these people cannot be rated on a par with the struggle for liberation of the Algerian people? Or is it that because the people of Kashmir, having placed their faith in the Security Council, have, under great provocation, refrained from reacting violently against the Indian forces of occupution, Mr. Menon does not consider them to be human beings worthy of the name? Is Mr. Menon waiting for Kashmir to erupt like Algeria before he will concede that the move for liberation by the people of that area is on the march?

The fact is that Kashmir did erupt some nine years ago but failed to engulf India because the Security Council solemnly promised to its people a fair and just solution through peaceful means. If that promise is not kept and if that solution is not allowed to go through, then it is much to be feared that Kashmir may rival or even outrun Algeria in respect of the heart-rending happenings in the latter country.

I am most grateful to the President and the members of the Council for having listened to me patiently, because I fully realize that my speech has been quite a long one this morning which is unusual, and which the Council does not expect from me.

8.8. Tenth Resolution* Adopted at the 774th Meeting of the Security Council, February 21, 1957

The Security Council

Recalling its resolution 122 (1957) of 24 January 1957, its previous resolutions and the resolutions of the United Nations Commission for India and Pakistan on the India-Pakistan question.

1. *Requests* the President of the Security Council, the

* Adopted by 10 vates to none, with 1 abstention (Union of Soviet Socialist Republics)
Res. 123 (1957); UN Document no. S/3793.

representative of Sweden, to examine with the Governments of India and Pakistan any proposals which, in his opinion, are likely to contribute towards the settlement of the dispute, having regard to the previous resolutions of the Security Council and of the United Nations Commission for India and Pakistan; to visit the subcontinent for this purpose; and to report to the Security Council not later than 15 April 1957.

2. *Invites* the Governments of India and Pakistan to cooperate with him in the performance of those functions.

3. *Requests* the Security-General and the United Nations Representative for India and Pakistan to render such assistance as he may request.

8.9. Eleventh Resolution* Adopted at the 808th Meeting of the Security Council, December 2, 1957

The Securtiy Council,

Having received and noted with appreciation the report of Mr. Gunnar V. Jarring, the representative of Sweden, on the mission undertaken by him pursuant to its resolution 123 (1957) of 21 Feburary 1957.

Expressing its thanks to Mr. Jarring for the care and ability with which he has carried out his mission.

Observing with appreciation the expression made by both parties of sincere willingness to co-operate with the United Nations in finding a peaceful solution.

Observing further that the Governments of India and Pakistan recognize and accept the provisions of its resolution 38 (1948) of 17 January 1948 and of the resolution of the United Nations Commission for India and Pakistan dated 13 August 1948 and 5 January 1949, which envisage in accordance with their terms and determination of the future status of the State of Jammu and Kashmir in accordance with the will of the people through the democratic method of a free and impartial plebiscite, and that Mr. Jarring felt it appropriate to explore what was impending their full implementation.

---

* Adopted by 10 votes to none, with 1 abstention (Union of Soviet Socialist Republices)
Res. 126 (1957); UN Document no. S/3922.

Concerned over the lack of progress towards a settlement of the dispute which his report manifests.

Considering the importance which it has attached to demilitarization of the State of Jammu and Kashmir as one of the steps towards a settlement.

Recalling its previous resolutions and the resolutions of the United Nations Commission for India and Pakistan on the India-Pakistan question.

1. *Requests* the Government of India and the Government of Pakistan to refrain from making any statements and from doing or causing to be done or permitting any acts which might aggravate the situation, and to appeal to their respective peoples to assist in creating and maintaining an atmosphere favourable to the promotion of further negotiations.

2. *Requests* the United Nations Representative for India and Pakistan to make any recommendations to the parties for further appropriate action with a view to making progress towards the implementation of the resolutions of the United Nations Commission for India and Pakistan of 13 August 1948 and 5 January 1949 and toward a peaceful settlement.

3. *Authorizes* the United Nations Representative to visit the subcontinent for these purposes.

4. *Instructs* the United Nations Representative to report to the Security Council on his efforts as soon as possible.

9

Statements of Sheikh Mohammed Abdullah 1958 and 1962

9.1. Statement of Sheikh Mohammed Abdullah after His Release, Issued from New Delhi, February 17, 1958

Since my release after 4-1/2 years' detention, I have tried to explain my viewpoint and possible solution in regard to various problems facing the political future of the State. With sufficient clarity, I hope, I have succeeded in elucidating the following points:-

(a) So long as final decision about the future disposition of Jammu and Kashmir State is not arrived at, the political uncertainty, economic distress and other mental strain and miseries which the people of the State are facing at present, cannot terminate.

(b) The existing strained relations between India and Pakistan are not only a source of great danger to the solidarity of Asia, but also contribute to the ruin of the people of the State. The dispute over Kashmir is one of the main contributing factors to these strained relations.

(c) The ultimate decision with regard to the future affiliation of the State vests with the people and can only be achieved by allowing them to exercise their right of self-determination under impartial international supervision, in accordance with the universally recognized methods as has been already agreed to by the parties concerned or is otherwise acceptable to all.

I am deeply sorry that in order to befog my views from the public, interested people have resorted, right from 1953, to a campaign of falsehood and every attempt is being made at misrepresentation and distortion. These people wish to keep the Kashmir issue hanging in order to exploit it to serve their own ends in spite of the fact that the progress of their Motherland and international peace and amity insistently demand its immediate solution.

Those who are opposed to a satisfactory final settlement of this problem falsely charged me, five years ago, as having conspired with a foreign power. Now since my release a compaign bas been started by these very people to depict me as a communalist for obvious reasons. As the charge of foreign conspiracy could not be substantiated, despite expiry of five years, an attempt is now being made to fabricate the charge of communalism against me so that public opinion in India and elsewhere may be deceived afresh, and the people's feeling and sympathy for me as a victim of persecution may be affected.

Another object seems a futile attempt on the part of these people to intimidate and coerce me into silence. I am conscious of the fact that these people have at their command services of the press, power, money and other resources with the help of which they are able to present falsehood as truth. On the other hand such facilities are denied to me. Even so I have no doubt in any mind that my effort to end this long-standing dispute about Kashmir can have no relation to communalism. This effort, in fact, is a great service to all those who have been facing untold miseries during the last ten years because of this dispute having remained unsolved. Who can deny the reality that failure to end this dispute is not only a source of distress and misery to the Muslims of Jammu and Kashmir but is a cause of anxiety and uncertainty to the entire population of the State? A solution of this dispute will not only contribute to the strengthening of peace and security throughout Asia but will heal up a festering sore which has been seeping into the very vitals of India and Pakistan. It is, therefore, for any intelligent man to judge whether it is fair to equate with communalism any endeavour to help solve this dispute. I firmly believe that real secularism is the soul of democracy but I am unable to understand how the demand for the final settlement of the dispute in regard to the accession of the Jammu and Kashmir State in accordance with the wishes of the people does in any way infringe any principle of secularism.

It is not the first time that I am charged with communalism. During the last 27 years a large section of the press in North India often brought such charges against me and every time facts and events proved them false. Many incidents in the Freedom Movement of our State bear witness to the fact that in 1931 this section of the press went so far as to allege that I aspired to be the Sultan of Kashmir and that a crown was ready in the Jamia Masjid, Srinagar, to be placed on any head at the opportune moment. Ultimately however, truth triumphed and the National Movement spread throughout the State. Later, these charges were repeated during the "Quit Kashmir Movement". But when the practical test came in 1947, these were proved not only false and malicious but the world also came to appreciate that the attitude taken up by the Muslims of Kashmir in safeguarding life, honour and property of their non-Muslim brethren was unparalleled throughout the sub-continent. Today in 1958, the same disruptive elements are again at their old game, and surprisingly, they include even those whose hands were besmeared, in 1947, with the innocent blood of their neighbours and who celebrated with great joy and distribution of sweets the brutal assassination of Mahatma Gandhi. Nevertheless, I feel sure that even this fresh attempt to malign me will also end in failure and fellow country-men belonging to the minorities will find me, as ever, their best friend, well-wisher and protector of their legitimate rights. My past record should be a sufficient guarantee for any one to judge my future behaviour. I do not, therefore, wish to waste my time and that of my country-men in putting up a defence against these slanderous accusations. When the dust raised by the propaganda of the interested people settles down, my fellow country-men will view me in the light of their past experience of me and events which have now become part of history, and will refuse to fall a prey to such a nefarions propaganda. The real secularism consists in safeguarding the legitimate rights of both the majority and minority communities. Happily the majority community in the State never considered the protection of the minorities as communalism and I hope and trust that the minority communities of this State will similarly not view the protection of the legitimate rights of the majority community as communalism.

I am being accused of break of pledge in support of the accession of the State to India. With all the force at my command, I repudiate this allegation and submit that the responsibility for the breach of the pledges rests elsewhere. A pledge is not a one-sided process; in regard to the accession of Kashmir the Governments of India and Kashmir accepted certain responsibilities and obligations but, unfortunately, the former did not fulfil their share in spite of the best endeavours of the Kashmir Government to persuade them to do so. When the charge of the breach of faith is, therefore, levelled against me, I have a right to pose the question as to where lies the responsibility for not implementing the promises and assurances given by the Government of India to the State of Jammu and Kashmir from the date of tribal raid till my arrest in 1953 .

Much propaganda is being made out of the fact that in November 1947, 1 pledged my support to Pandit Nehru in a mass meeting held at Lal Chowk in Srinagar. But with this, one should not forget what Panditji said a few minutes earlier. Explaining the Government of India policy, he stated that : "It must be remembered that the struggle in Kashmir is a struggle of the people of Kashmir under popular leadership against the invader. We have come to your help at this critical hour. Our forces are here simply to defend your country against the raiders and as soon as Kashmir is free from the invader, our troops will have no further necessity to remain here and you will be free to determine your future in accordance with your wishes..."

A few days before the Lal Chowk meeting, announcing the Government of India policy, Prime Minister Pandit Jawaharlal Nehru, in his broadcast from New Delhi on the 2nd November, 1947, said : "We are anxious not to finalize anything in a moment of crisis and without the fullest opportunity to be given to the people of Kashmir to have their say. It was for them ultimately to decide: And let me make it clear that it has been our policy all along that where there is a dispute about accession of a State to either Dominion, the accession must be made by the people of that State. It was in accordance with this policy that we have added a proviso to the Instrument of Accession of Kashmir."

When the Constitution of India was finalized, the State of Jammu and Kashmir was given the status of an autonomous State in all matters except (a) Defence, (b) Foreign Affairs and (c) Communications (Section 370 of the Indian Constitution). This was an inviolable pledge.

May I ask, as to where all these promises and assurances stand today and who is responsible for breaking them ? My illegal and unconstitutional dismissal from Premiership and my long detention without trial are in themselves the most glaring examples of the value attached to pledges and solemn assurances.

I am also blamed by my detractors as to why I do not consider the decision taken by the Kashmir Consembly regarding the accession as final. In this connection, the reality should not be lost sight of that the Government of India themselves have not accepted the decision of the Consembly regarding accession as final. The late Sir B.N. Rao in the capacity of the leader of the Indian Delegation before the Security Council declared on March 12th, 1951 : "My Government's view is that while the Consembly may, if it desires, express an opinion on this question, it can make no decision on it." And again on 29th March, 1951 he declared that "the Consembly cannot physically be prevented from expressing its opinion on this question if it so chooses, but this opinion will not bind my Government nor prejudice the position of this Council." Consequently the Security Council passed the following resolution on 30th March, 1951 :

> "Observing that the Governments of India and Pakistan have accepted the provisions of United Nations Commission for India and Pakistan (UNCIP) resolutions of 13th August, 1948, and 5th January, 1949, and have reaffirmed their desire that the future of the State of Jammu and Kashmir shall be decide through the democratic method of a free and impartial plebiscite conducted under the auspices of United Nations;
>
> "Observing that on 27th October, 1950, the General Council of the All Jammu and Kashmir National Conference adopted a resolution recommending the convening of a Constituent Assembly for the purpose of determining the future shape and affiliations of the State of Jammu and Kashmir; observing further from statements of responsible authorities that action is proposed to convene such a Constituent Assembly and that the area from which such a Constituent Assembly would be elected is only a part of the whole territory of Jammu and Kashmir;
>
> Reminding the Governments and Authorities concerned of the principle in the Security Council resolutions of 21 April 1948, June 1948 and 14 March 1950 and the United Nations Commission for India and Pakistan resolutions of 13 August

> 1948 and 5 January 1949, that the final disposition of the State of Jammu and Kashmir will be made in accordance with the will of the people expressed through the democratic method of a free and impartial plebiscite conducted under the auspices of the United Nations;
>
> "Affirming that the convening of a Constituent Assembly as recommended by the General Council of the All Jammu and Kashmir National Conference, and any action that Assembly might attempt to take to determine the future shape and affiliation of the entire State or any part thereof, would not constitute a disposition of the State in accordance with the above principle."

Pandit Jawaharlal Nehru, while answering a question on the subject in the Indian Parliament in 1955, declared the decision of the Constituent Assembly regarding the accession as unilateral and, therefore, of no consequence to resolve this international dispute on Kashmir. The decision of this Assembly cannot, moreover, be viewed in isolation and out of context of historical events that followed. The question is not about the decision but as to what were the means by which it was secured. A period of five years elapsed between the date of convening of the Consembly and taking a final decision on the accession issue. The Consembly which enjoyed popular support in 1951 on this side of the "Cease-fire Line" forfeited the confidence due to the events that took place on 9th August, 1953, and thereafter. The front rank members of the body were put in prison and debarred from participating in the proceedings of the House. Those who were not in prison were forced into submission by threats of persecution and imprisonment and irresistible temptations were thrown in their way. Consequently, the masses lost faith in them as there was no contact between those members and their constituents. The fact cannot be ignored that before the Constitution was finalised, the Leader of the House was arrested under a deeply-laid conspiracy and when the masses protested against this illegal and unconstitutional act, a reign of terror was let loose and hundreds of men, women and children were shot down in cold blood and this continued for months together. A period of four years was spent in making the members of the Assembly to toe the line of the *coup* stagers. Such of the members as did not submit were kept in jail and the Constitution declared passed.

Even though in detention, yet led by national interests, from time to time I tried to warn all concerned against the dangerous consequences of allowing the Constituent Assembly to be used for group conflicts of the National Conference. In telegram on 30th September, 1951 , I asked the President of the Constituent Assembly to allow me to be heard by the Assembly before the "vote of confidence" in *coup* stagers was considered. Then again when the Constitution was going to be finalised, on 16th August, 1956 I wrote to him saying:

"By 9th August action as well as by the long record of black deeds in and outside the House, the present Government and the Assembly have completely forefeited the confidence of the electorate and they no longer represent the political and economic aspiration of the people. It will be the height of treachery if such a body sits to frame a fundamental law for the people and their future generations. Nothing can be worse betrayal of their aspirations. I feel therefore. duty-bound to ask you to desist from such a course of action . . ."

In view of these circumstances, I fail to understand why and how my refusal to accent these decisions of the Consembly could be taken as treasonable.

One of the most important objects underlying the entire political movement in the State has remained to secure the right of self-determination for the people of the State. Expression of the will of the people through a plebiscite is the one formula which has been agreed upon by the parties concerned and in a mass of disagreements about details, this common denominator has held the field so far. The Security Council, also, has held that a plebiscite, conducted in a fair and free atmosphere under its own auspices, is a just solution of the problem consistent with the provisions of the United Nations Charter. This commitment has repeatedly been reaffirmed by the parties concerned.

The people of the State consider the formula of plebiscite as a clear interpretation of their long cherished aspirations and as a lasting solution of the complicated problem which is facing them since 1947. Their political outlook is the product of the last 27 years' struggle whose sheet-anchor has ever remained the conviction that "sovereignty vests with the people". A State which was sold away for a cash consideration and remained in slavish subjugation for a century, naturally gave this demand the foremost importance and made the right of self-democratic set-up as its cardinal creed.

The Indian National Congress has throughout raised its voice in support of our demand and it was on the basis of this principle that the leaders of the Congress, is general, and Pandit Nehru in particular, extended cooperation and help to the Freedom Struggle of the State from its very inception. I may refer in this connection to the resolutions passed and the speeches delivered at the Annual Session of the All Jammu and Kashmir National Conference held at Sopore in 1945, in which Pandit Jawaharlal Nehru, Maulana Azad, Khan Abdul Ghaffar Khan, Khan Abdul Samed Khan and other top-ranking Congress leaders participated. In this session the people's demand for the right of self-determination formed the central theme of the resolutions passed.

The Congress leaders not only supported , all along, our demand for the right of self-determination, but also helped in organizing me in the "Quit Kashmir Case". Pandit Jawaharlal Nehru did not only court arrest as a mark of his support to our struggle , but went to the extent of appearing as my council in the case, in collaboration with the late Mr. Asaf Ali and others. Subsequently, when the sub-continent was partitioned and the tribal raid took place, it was again in defence of this very right of self-determination that Government of India agreed to send its armed forces to Kashmir. Simultaneously, Government of India while accepting the Instrument of Accession signed by Maharaja Hari Singh on 26th October, 1947, laid down the condition that the accession was subject to ratification by the people.

Then came a period when Governments of India and Pakistan tried to solve the Kashmir dispute by direct negotiations. In May, 1953 we in "National Conference were asked to weigh and suggest the various alternate proposals for the solution. On 9th June the following unanimous decision was taken by a High Level Committee of the National Conference and communicated to Panditji :

"As a result of discussion held in the course of various meetings, the following proposals only emerge as possible alternatives for an honourable and peaceful solution of the Kashmir dispute between India and Pakistan :

(a) Overall plebiscite with conditions as detailed in the minutes of the meeting dated 4th June 1953;
(b) Independence of the whole State;
(c) Independence of the whole State with joint control of

foreign affairs and defence; and

(d) Dixon plan with independence for the plebiscite area.

"Bakhshi (Ghulam Mohammed) Sahib was emphatically of the opinion that the proposal (d) above should be put up as first and the only practicable, advantageous and honourable solution of the dispute. Maulana Sayeed, however, opined, that the order of preference as given above should be adhered to."

Unfortunately, the authorities at the helm of affairs could not appreciate the value of this and no further progress took place. In the meantime, events took an ugly turn and 9th August *coup* was staged, story of which need not be related here:

It was as late as August, 1953, after my detention, that the two Prime Ministers of India and Pakistan, after deliberating for a number of days in Delhi as to how-best to resolve this dispute, reiterated in a joint communique their "firm opinion that this (Kashmir Question) should be settled in accordance with the wishes of the people of that State... The most feasible method of ascertaining the wishes of the people was by fair and impartial plebiscite."

Bakhshi Ghulam Mohammed, as Prime Minister of the State, in a press statement issued by him on 21st August, 1953, declared : "I welcome the declaration of the two Prime Ministers in regard to the future disposition of the State of Jammu and Kashmir on the basis of the principle of self-determination. This declaration was finalized on behalf of the Government of India with our concurrence and has our unqualified support." The holding of a plebiscite is thus a solution which is not only consistent with the objectives of the Freedom Struggle of Kashmir and the Independence Movement of the Indian people but is one to which all concerned with the dispute have unequivocally committed themselves, time and again.

APPENDIX TO ABOVE STATEMENT

(a) "...The Princes being the creation of British Imperialism and the British having quitted India, the people in the States were their own masters and the Kashmiris must, therefore, decide, without any coercion or show of it, from within or without, to which dominion they should belong."

(Mahatma Gandhi, 1947)

(b) "...I have repeatedly stated that as soon as the raiders have been driven out of Kashmir or have withdrawn and peace and order have been established, the people of Kashmir should decide the question of Accession by plebiscite or referendum under international auspices such as those of the United Nations... By this declaration I stand."

(Pandit Jawaharlal Nehru,
November 21, 1947)

(c) "...Whether she (Kashmir) should withdraw from her accession to India, and either accede to India or remain independent with a right to claim admission as a member of the United Nations—all this we have recognized to be a matter for unfettered decision by the people of Kashmir after normal life is restored there.

(Sir Gopalaswami Ayyangar, leader of
the Indian Delegation, before the
Security Council, January 15, 1948)

(d) "...We have declared that the fate of Kashmir is ultimately to be decided by the people. The pledge we have given, and the Maharaja has supported it, not only to the people of Kashmir but to the world. We will not and cannot back out of it. We are prepared when peace and law and order have been established to have referendum held under international auspices like the United Nations..."

(Pandit Nehru's broadcast from New Delhi
on November 2, 1947)

9.2. Kashmir Conspiracy Case : Written Statement of Sheikh Mohammed Abdullah Submitted in the Sessions Court, Jammu, August 31, 1962

Mr. Judge,

We are charged with conspiracy to overawe the lawful Government of the Jammu and Kashmir State, a conspiracy alleged to have begun in 1953 and to have continued until 1958. This raises the issue of where the lawful government was to be found. In 1953 I was the Prime Minister of the State. I had the unanimous support of the Legislative Assembly. On the night of the 8/9th of August, I was summarily dismissed by the Sadar-i-Riyasat. I was then imprisoned without charge or trial under the Public Security Act/the Preventive

Detention Act. This dismissal was wholly unconstitutional and, as I shall submit, unlawful. It follows that the so-called government which was thereinafter installed was improperly appointed and had no lawful authority. On this ground alone the Prosecution must fail.

Even though I have regarded the government as being without lawful authority, I have never sought its destruction by resort to violence. Indeed throughout my political career which extends back for more that 30 years I have been a believer of non-violence – a principle which I learnt from Gandhiji. I have lived up to it throughout all phases of the political struggle.

I am alleged to have entered into this conspiracy as early as 1953. If the evidence for the Prosecution is to believed they were fully informed of the progress of the conspiracy in 1955. Yet I was unconditionally released on the 8th of January, 1958, and it was not until the 23rd October, 1958, that I was charged with these offences.

Except for a brief period of less than nearly 4 months, I was in detention throughout the period of the alleged conspiracy, heavily guarded by the Army and the Armed Constabulary of Government of India and thus completely under the lock and key of the Prosecutors. This very fact alone negatives any possibility of conspiring or executing the conspiracy as alleged.

At the very initial stage I told the committing Magistrate, and later the Hon'ble High Court, that the issues involved in this case are so vital and grave and the personalities interested are of such high status and position that a tribunal highly independent with unquestionable integrity who can withstand political and other pressures, alone can inspire confidence which is the bed-rock or a civilised judiciary. Unfortunately my protestations did not avail anything. Minds seemed too much conditioned by formal technicalities of procedure to yield to actual considerations for doing real justice.

Four and a half years experience has convinced me in my apprehensions expressed then. From the complaint itself stem out the vital issues on which the fate and destiny of a people hang. It is a tragedy that the thoughtless Prosecutors and a mass of suborned witnesses have recklessly been allowed to play with that destiny. Throughout the enquiry it was manifest that the Presiding Officer hardly ever exercised his independent judgement and judicial discretion which could inspire even a semblance of confidence in the mind of the accused. Should patience and time permit, bare perusal of his voluminous committal order will bear me out.

The world will observe the circumstances in which this trial is being held. As long ago as 1955 the Indian Parliament passed the Criminal Procedure (Amendment) Act whereby for the first time accused persons were given the right to testify in their own defence. A similar Act was passed for the Jammu and Kashmir State in 1956 subject to the provision that it should only come into force from the day appointed by the Government. That day has never dawned. It follows that my friends and I charged as we are with crimes of the utmost gravity, are to be denied the right to give evidence which would be accorded to us in India, in all parts of the Commonwealth and other civilised countries. We have no doubt that the reason why the Statute has never been brought into force is that authorities behind the Prosecution do not wish us to give our own account of the events of the last nine years as witness or allow speedy trial enjoined by the new Act.

It is just over nine years since I was first arbitrarily imprisoned. It is very nearly four years since I was first charged with these offences. This inordinate delay is not confined to the present case. Seven of my co-accused were charged with murder in the Hazratbal Case. They were committed for trial in October, 1958. The trial has not yet commenced. It follows that they must go through the present proceedings with capital charge still hanging over their heads. Another of my co-accused was charged in 1957 with a capital offence under the Enemy Agents Ordinance. The trial of this case by a Speical Court began on the 5th of October, 1957. This trial has not yet been concluded. These delay are without precedent and the only explanation is that the prosecuting authorities are determined for political reasons to keep the accused involved in criminal proceedings for the maximum possible time.

At every stage the government of the State has harassed the Defence and those who were seeking to assist the accused. Two of the counsel for the Defence were detained for periods of about a year under the Preventive Detention Act. Miss Mridula Sarabhai who sought to assist the Defence here was detained and later externed from the State in February, 1961, and frobidden to re-enter. What happened to Shri Balraj Puri merely for greeting me in court on the court record. The treatment meted out to him was not denied when questions were asked in the Indian Parliament. Very many of our friends and those who believe in political freedom have been detained for various periods under the Preventive Detention Act.

My personal and private documents fell into the hands of the *coup* stagers of 9th August 1953, and whatever was left was seized by the Police from my residence on the 29th of April, 1958. Most of these documents have not been produced in this case by the Prosecution nor have they been handed back to me, the obvious motive being to thwart my defence.

A very heavy burden is being cast on those members of the bar who have so far appeared for me and my co-accused. At the inception of the inquiry, I, therefore, made strenuous efforts to get the services of other suitable counsel in this case. The Prosecution got a hint from my correspondence which passes through censor that I was about to engage the services of Shri Nageshwar Prasad of Patna. They immediately got in contact with him, offered him fabulous fees and other amenities and engaged him as Chief Prosecution Counsel. This robbed me of a defence counsel of my choice from within the country. It may not be out of place to mention here that the Prosecution had already deprived us of the service of many prominent lawyers of Jammu and Srinagar Bar by engaging them in advance in various cases (including the instant one) instituted against me and my colleagues.

Shri Porus Mehta, an eminent Advocate from Bombay and Sardar Amar Singh Ambalvi, Advocate from Punjab, who appeared on behalf of my colleagues in other cases were not spared the harassment of being constantly shadowed by the Intelligence people during their visits to Kashmir.

The general environment in and around this Court premises is so infested by the Police and Intelligence Officers that free judicial atmosphere has well-high been destroyed. Amongst the Prosecutors and their Assistants there are those who have conducted investigations which is the other term for third-degree methods in Kashmir or have made interrogation of witnesses or taken a leading part in tutoring them. Their continued presence in and around the court room is a standing terror for any Prosecution witness who under the influence of such an atmosphere can hardly be a free agent even while in the witness box.

The court below refused to summon witnesses who were and are essential to the proper conduct of the defence.

Pursuant to the *coup* of 9th August, 1953, I and my government were overthrown by sheer use of forces, completely subverting the

Constitution whose sanctity everybody concerned had solemnly affirmed to respect. A new Government was brought into office. This "government" therefore, is not a technical complainant as understood in common parlance in criminal administration. It is personally "aggrieved" and a hostile party in these proceedings– avowedly inimical to the accused.

In a democratic set up, the only hope of a citizen to escape the tyranny of the executive is an independent judiciary. Where processes of law are employed by the executive for power politics, the very basis of democracy is completely undermined.

Under ordinary circumstances an accused would always welcome to have an opportunity of defending himself in order to prove his innocence. The present case and the circumstances which led to its institution are, however, very peculiar. The Prosecution has launched this case against me, I believe, not that they really feel that I am guilty of the offences mentioned in the complaint, but to serve entirely a different purpose. This is apparent from the fact that the prosecutors shifted their ground from time to time, vis-a-vis the accusations levelled against me. In 1953, they started with the allegation that I had entered into a conspiracy with United States of America, in order to establish an independent State of Kashmir and make it a war base for U.S.A. A virulent propaganda was set afoot here and abroad to that end, but the story was too grotesque to carry conviction. Moreover, they had second thoughts about it. Therefore, suddenly the "conspiracy" was switched over and Pakistan made the substitute for U.S.A. The bitterness of the Partition had not yet died down. Hence the Prosecutors thought it convenient and helpful for their purpose to tag me with Pakistan and thus obliterate my past services and unblemished record in the freedom movement.

I am now accused of having conspired with Pakistan to overthrow the so-called Kashmir government by the use of force in order to facilitate the State's wrongful annexation by that country. In these circumstances the evidence so laboriously assembled over the last nine years, particularly where it is the evidence of approvers, accomplices and spies should be probed with utmost care.

The prosecution has produced C.I.D. reports of some of my speeches and also copies of some letters to my friends from jail. I have admitted the authorship of these letters and have also not denied having delivered the speeches. For lack of proficiency in Urdu and complete ignorance of Arabic and Persian, the reporter has very often missed the content and purport of my speeches.

As regards the letters exhibited in the case, they were sent out from the jail duly censored by the concerned and competent authorities. The inferences drawn by the Prosecution from the text of these speeches and letters are wholly unwarranted and untenable. They militiate with the whole spirit of the subject-matter. It only needs an impartial mind, free from prejudice and possessed with adequate knowledge of Islamic history, the Quran and the Hadith to interpret them correctly. My misfortune is that neither the Magistrate nor the reporter and the translator who both figured as important witnesses against me could justifiably lay any claim to the knowledge of these subjects. On the contrary their examination revealed their stark ignorance. It was a case of blind leading the blind.

A few days back I was pained to listen to the arguments of the learned Chief Counsel for the Prosecution, Shri G.S. Pathak, when he moved for amendment of charges against me and others. He sought to add now a new charges of waging war to the charge already framed and in support quoted cases launched during British regime against some of the outstanding Indian patriots and freedom fighters like Vir Savarkar, M.N. Roy and others who had suffered long periods in jail to throw off the British yoke and free the motherland.

I had hoped that we had succeeded in terminating the British colonial rule with all its legacies but I am afraid Shri Pathak's reliance with gusto solely on the bad traditions of that rule puts one in doubt if the freedom has really been gained.

For the last 15 years the Indo-Pakistan dispute over the accession of J&K State had led the two neighbours to take to divergent paths, dividing them into hostile camps. The dispute first resulted in a shooting war which has now subsided to the worst type of cold war. Campaign of hate, bitterness and sinful vilification is at its height of which the main victim, unfortunately, is common man. The present case is being used by our prosecutors as a lever to aggravate the process of this cold war. The very contents of the complaint, evidence of the tutored winesses and the arguments advanced by the Prosecution, all lead to that single purpose. A vested interest has been created which adds fuel to this cold war. They seem to be convinced that they can make hay only so long as the two peoples of India and Pakistan stand at loggerheads. It is, however, my firm conviction that the continuance of this campaign of hate and bitterness will not only harm both India and Pakistan, but may exterminate our State in the process.

In this cold war and inflated tensions, it is most regrettable that the right of self-determination of 5 million people of J&K State is made the first casualty. The onslaught is vehemently carried on all fronts so as to divert the attention of the world from the basic issue confronting the people of the State and side-track into other channels.

Ever since the Kashmir freedom movement was launched in 1931 the people of the State have gone through blood and tears in order to achieve their basic right to shape their own destiny freely and without any coercion. This right had been usurped from them and they were enslaved for centuries suffering all sorts of indignities, that has always been the lot of an enslaved nation. Many of their spasmodic efforts to liberate themselves from the shackless of bondage and slavery had been ruthlessly suppressed in the past by the powers that be. In 1931 destiny left it to me to spearhead the movement for their emancipation and I have accordingly dedicated my life to that cause.

This is a political trial. I and my friends have been detained over many years and we are here today because of the principle for which we have stood – namely, the right of the people in Jammu & Kashmir State to be masters of their own destiny. It has been conveyed to me several times that not only could I go free immediately but I could also resume the Premiership of the State if I was prepared to accept the present status of Jammu & Kashmir State. This I have refused to do. That is why I and my friends stand in the dock today.

I, of course, plead not guilty to these false and fantastic charges. But in this case – not the first time in history – it is the accusers who are on trial. They have denied the Kashmiri people the right to determine their own future. They have maintained and still maintain a reign of terror. They have misused their powers in order to suppress and persecute their political opponents. Now they are seeking by manifestly perjured evidence to pervert the ends of justice. It is they who should be in the dock today. I await not only your verdict but the verdict of history.

Thank you.

Jammu,
Dated 31st August 1962.

Sd/-
Sheikh Mohammed Abdullah

10

Joint Talks between India and Pakistan, 1963

10.1. Statement in the Lok Sabha by Prime Minister Jawaharlal Nehru on Indo-Pakistan Talks on Kashmir, August 13, 1963

On the 7th of May last I made a statement in this House in which I referred to the joint talks on Kashmir and other related matters between India and Pakistan which had then still not concluded.

These talks originated from a joint statement issued on November 29, 1962, announcing our agreement to make a renewed effort to resolve the outstanding differences between India and Pakistan on Kashmir and other telated matters, so as to enable the two countries to live side by side in peace and friendship. On the 30th November I made a statement in the House in regard to this joint statement and referred to the discussions which I had had with Mr. Duncan Sandys, Minister for Commonwealth Relations of the U.K. and Mr. Averell Harriman, Assistant Secretary of State of the United States.

In pursuance of the joint statement our delegation led by Sardar Swaran Singh, Minister of Railways, participated in six rounds of talks. In all these six talks, spread over nearly five months, Pakistan showed no readiness to discuss anything apart from Kashmir.

As I have stated on many occasions previously, it has always been, and continues to be, India's policy to seek friendly and cooperative relations with Pakistan. The lack of such friendly and cooperative relations between the two countries would not only be unfortunate but would do violence to the long standing ties of geography, history and culture between the two countries. We are convinced that the only proper course for the two countries to adopt is to develop cooperative and friendly relations and live as good neighbours. In the larger interest of the two countries, we have been anxious to bring about a settlement of all Indo-Pakistan differences, including Kashmir, on a rational and realistic basis. It was in this spirit that we agreed to have joint talks but, as the House is aware, in spite of every effort made by Sardar Swaran Singh to arrive at an equitable and honourable settlement, these talks ended in failure.

From the very beginning, the Pakistan Government took various steps which came in the way of a settlement. On the eve of the first round of talks in Rawalpindi, Pakistan announced its so-called "agreement in principle" with China on Kashmir's border with Sinkiang. The timing of this statement was apparently intended to provoke India to refuse to start the talks the next morning. We felt that this was a bad augury for the future for the talks. Nevertheless, because of our earnest desire to arrive at some settlement, we decided to continue with the talks.

During the first plenary meeting, the Pakistan representative expressed his disinclination to discuss any of the Indo-Pakistan differences other than the Kashmir question which, he insisted, must be settled first. Sardar Swaran Singh in his opening speech listed various subjects which required to be discussed. But Mr. Bhutto insisted on confining himself to Kashmir only. Even on Kashmir, because of Pakistan's insistence, considerable time was spent in friendly but futile discussions on the old idea of plebiscite which, chiefly because of Pakistan's own acts of obstruction and non-implementation of the U.N. Commission's resolutions, had already proved to be impracticable, particularly in the light of irreversibly changed conditions in the last fifteen years.

This was followed by the signing of the Sino-Pakistan agreement under which Pakistan gave away as much as about two thousand square miles of our territory to China. The fact that this was done in the course of our talks indicated how little importance Pakistan attached to our talks. It was extraordinary that while these talks were taking place, Pakistan was busy handing over a large part of our territory to China which had invaded our country. The object apparently was to present us with a *fait accompli* in one part of our territory of Jammu and Kashmir while keeping her hands free to negotiate for the remaining part of the State. We might have been justified in not proceeding with the talks at this stage. Nevertheless, we proceeded with them after recording our strong protest.

The Rawalpindi talks, despite Pakistan's preliminary agreement with China had ended with the leaders of the two delegation issuing an appeal for moderation in mutual criticism. The joint appeal had hardly been made by the leaders of the two delegations in December when Pakistan launched an unprecedented compaign of vilification against India not only in Pakistan, but also in the capitals of Europe through their responsible officers. Thus it appeared cleary from the beginning that Pakistan was interested not so much in a settlement of outstanding differences or even of the Kashmir problem, but only in making political capital out of the situation created by Chinese aggression against India.

When the Pakistan delegation shifted from a futile discussion of plebiscite to the consideration of a possible political settlement, they began to put forward astonishing proposals. Pakistan claimed the catchment areas and the water-sheds of the three Western, rivers, the Chenab, the Jhelum and the Indus, in Jammu and Kashmir on the ground that these rivers had been allotted to Pakistan under the Indus Waters Treaty. Our delegation pointed out that the Indus Waters Treaty protected Pakistan's interests fully and gave her no ground to claim any territory in Jammu and Kashmir on the basis of the use and development of waters. If every lower riparian claimed the territory of the upper riparian on the pretext of its water requirements, the maps of many countries in the world would have to be drastically revised. By that argument, the lower riparian might even claim Tibet because the Indus and the Brahmaputra start in Tibet. No less absurd was another of Pakistan's claims to Jammu and Kashmir namely, that they must have the State to protect their Grand Trunk Road and their railway line, the security of which, our delegation was told was essential to ensure, what Pakistan called, its "defence in depth". Finally, Pakistan claimed Kashmir on the basis of its Muslim majority. This was a vicious communal approach repugnant to the entire spirit animating our national struggle for independence, and contrary to our Constitution and to our whole attitude to the problem of relationship between the State and the individual.

Pakistan's objective was obviously not a rational and realistic solution of the problem. They were just out to claim the entire State of Jammu and Kashmir, leaving to India, as it happened, in a forgotten moment of generosity, an insignificant area in the extreme south, roughly coinciding with the district of Kathua. Even more astonishing was the offer, obviously induced by their awareness of India's need for the defence of Ladakh against China, that Pakistan would be willing to agree to an interim arrangement in the Valley for a period of six months or a year, to enable India to deal with the Chinese. All that this could mean was that India might continue to commit its men and resources for the defence of Ladakh against the Chinese threat, but that once its effort and sacrifices had liberated Ladakh, India should abandon the State in favour of Pakistan. Another proposal was the so-called internationalisation of the Valley, again for a period of six months followed by some method of ascertaining the wishes of the people. This was the old and discarded idea of a plebiscite, without Pakistan having to implement the conditions laid down in the UNCIP Resolutions.

Faced with this deadlock, when a breakdown to the talks seemed inevitable on the last day, our delegation again offered a No-War agreement, together with a practical and immediate disengagement of troops, thus hoping to reassure our neighbour that our efforts to strengthen our defence against the Chinese aggression constituted no threat to Pakistan. A No-War agreement, we said, could include a specific undertaking that the two countries should continue to seek peaceful solutions of the problem, because we did not want the problem frozen. Such an agreement could be registered with the United Nations to give it an international backing. Pakistan rejected this offer. Their delegation also refused to agree to remit the matter to the two Government for a review and for considering other appropriate steps towards a peaceful settlement. Thus, Pakistan achieved what it had aimed at from the very beginning, that is, a non settlement and a deadlock on every-thing that should have been covered by the phrase "Kashmir and other related matters". This is where the Ministerial level talks with Pakistan ended.

In the early part of May, Mr. Dean Rusk, U.S. Secretary of State, and Mr. Duncan Sandys paid a visit to Delhi. In the course of discussions, the question of Kashmir came up again. We assured them of our earnest desire to have a settlement provided this was fair and equitable. As an earnest of this desire or ours, we said that we would be prepared to have the good offices of a mutually accepted personality, even through previously we had declined a similar proposal. Pakistan, however, continued to make quite impossible demands. In the first week of June, the President of Pakistan said at

Sargodha that no useful purpose would be served by the adoption of such procedure. Other Pakistan spokesmen have been suggesting impossible terms of reference. They wanted a time-limit, suspension of arms supply to India during this period, etc.

We used to be told by many friends, even by leaders in Pakistan, that a settlement of the Kashmir issue was essential in the interest of joint defence of the two countries. At one time, Pakistan made a grievance of the fact that while she was offering joint defence to us, we were not willing to accept it. That the proposal of joint defence was no more than a propaganda stunt, has now been made perfectly clear by the statements of Pakistan leaders. They have publicly declared that even if the Kashmir issue was settled amicably, Pakistan will not go either to the defence of India against China or change her friendly relations with Peking. On July 17th last, Mr. Bhutto is reported to have said in the Pakistan National Assembly that an "attack from India on Pakistan today is no longer confined to the security and territorial integrity of Pakistan", but "involves the territorial integrity and security of the largest State in Asia". He also said that if India were to turn her guns against Pakistan, the latter would not be alone in that conflict. He was obviously referring to China. The fact that India had no intention whatever of threatening the security of Pakistan or of turning any guns towards her, was ignored and the repeated offers of a No-War pact were forgotten. Pakistan today has only one object, and that is to malign India and to damage us in every way. They do not want to see us strong enough to stand up to China, They would like us to remain weak and helpless against the Chinese threat. They do not like to be told that the arms aid to India has nothing to do with Kashmir.

We have made it clear that while we are, and shall continue to be, anxious as ever on a settlement of our problems with Pakistan, based on rational and realistic considerations, there is no question of our considering any proposals for internationalsing, or division of the Valley, or joint control of Kashmir, and the like. If and when a settlement is arrived at, it must obviously be a peaceful one, not affecting the stability and progress already achieved, and must strengthen the friendship between the peoples of India and Pakistan. Without this, no settlement has any meaning.

During the talks, India not only exercised great patience and restraint, but also offered generous concessions, though in vain, in the hope of winning Pakistan's friendship and opening a new chapter of fruitful cooperation between the two countries. While we continue to cherish this hope there is little possibility of a settlement so long as Pakistan persists in its irrational animus against India. The concessions which we offered to Pakistan are no longer open, and they must be treated as withdrawn. We do not wish our neighbour to be treated by its Government as a jumping off ground for further claims. While the break in the talks is a matter of deep regret, we have to accept the facts, and we must wait for a more opportune moment for a settlement of all our differences with Pakistan.

11

Speeches of M.C. Chagla (India) and Z.A. Bhutto (Pakistan) in the Security Council, 1964

11.1. Speech by M.C. Chagla (India) in Security Council, 1088th Meeting, 1964

The Security Council is perhaps the most important organ of the United Nations. Every Member State has a right to approach it. But they must approach it with a due sense of responsibility, it is not intended as a platform for propaganda against any Member State. Nor is it obviously meant for creating tensions in a world where there are already more than enough difficulties and problems. I propose to satisfy you that there was no justification whatsover for Pakistan to have taken up the time of this Council, Pakistan's application constitutes the culmination of the campaign of hatred that it has ceaselessly carried on against India. The basic principle of its international policy is opposition to India on every front and, as *The Times* of London recently observed, "The load-stone of every aspect of Pakistan's foreign policy is bad relations with India." Its approach to the Council is purely an agitational approach. Its desire is to use the forum of the Security Council to carry on its agitation against my Government and my country.

We sat at this Council table yesterday listening patiently to the statement of the Minister for External Affairs of Pakistan to find some reason for the convening of this meeting and into what its deliberations are likely to lead. I confess that after having heard the statement of the representative of Pakistan, my delegation and my Government continue to hold the view that there was no reason for convening the Security Council, because no new situation has arisen to aggravate the existing conditions in Jammu and Kashmir. Pakistan's application reads like a horror story. We are told that the Muslim majority in Kashmir is in great peril by India's attempt at so-called integration or annexation of Kashmir; that large Muslim crowds have been demonstrating against India and in favour of a plebiscite; that Kashmir is in "open rebellion"; that the Kashmiris are being crushed under the heel of India and that terrible things will happen there unless something is done immediatly. I shall satisfy you that all this is a figment of a vivid imagination.

Pakistan has pretended to show a great solicitude for the Muslims living in India, and its Foreign Minister has stated that hundreds of thousands of Indian Muslims have been pushed out into East Pakistan. When Pakistan talks of the Muslim minority, it gives one the impression that we are dealing with a few thousands or a few hundred thousands of people in a large country tucked away in some far corner and surrounded by a large mass of Hindu population. Now let me inform the Council that the Muslims are not a minority in the ordinary sense of the term. They constitute 50 million of India's population. India is the third largest Muslim State in the world – the first being Indonesia and the second Pakistan. They are sons of the soil, they are Indian by race and they enjoy all the rights of citizenship. Every office is open to them, and in fact many of them hold the highest offices in the land. Our civilization is a synthesis of many diverse cultures and the Muslim contribution is one of the most significant. Ours is a secular State and an egalitarian society where everyone enjoys equal rights and equal opportunities and equal protection of the law. We have no official religion. Hindus, Muslims, Christians, Buddhists, Sikhs, Parsis and others have full freedom of worship and fundamental rights under Constitution are guaranteed to every citizen. We have no first-class or second-class citizenship. Before the law everyone is equal.

Much of our differences with Pakistan are due to the fact that there is this basic difference between our policy and that of Pakistan. While we have based our State on secularism, which means that there is no established *church* and everyone is entitled to profess and practise his religion without let or hindrance from the State. Pakistan is a theocratic State. When the leaders of the Muslim League demanded a partition of the country, the demand was based on the two-nation theory. Their contention was that Hindus and Muslims were separate nations, and were each entitled to have a homeland of their own. We recognize India and Pakistan as two nations, but we have repudiated the two-nation theory based on religion and it is abhorrent to us. If Hindus and Muslims constitute two-nations, then the inevitable result must follow that the 50 million Muslims in India are aliens in their own homes. We refuse to subscribe to the theory that religion can be the sole basis of nationality. We believe in a multiracial, multicommunal and multilinguistic society, and according to us, peace and goodwill in this world depend upon the success of such a society. I am sure that this sentiment will strike a sympathetic chord in the hearts of many African countries which have recently achieved independence. Most of them have populations which practise different religions. The same is the case with many Middle East countries, and in the United States itself a brave attempt is being made to consolidate and integrate its different racial groups.

Is it not extraordinarily that while Pakistan is shouting itself hoarse as a self-appointed guardian of Indian Muslims, Muslim opinion in India has always strongly endorsed the policy of my Government? May I, with the President's permission, read three quotations from Muslim newspapers in India. They were written in Urdu, but I have the translations. The first is from the *Siasat-e-Jadid*, of Kanpur, dated 16 January, 1964, which states:

> "The Pakistani authorities and journalists make an exhibition of great sympathy for the Indian Muslim minority and bewail their plight through speeches and writings, without ever realizing that it is for their verbal and written intemperances and provocations that the Muslims have to suffer. Indian Muslims . . . want to tell these foolish friends frankly that they should for God's sake leave them alone."

The *Nai Duniya* of 21 January states:

> "Pakistani newspapers, leaders and radio played up the theft of the holy hair in a manner so as to excite the feelings of the majority. If the newspapers, the radio and the leaders of Pakistan had not behaved in this irresponsible manner, the mischief-mongers of Khulna and Jessore would never have dared to attack the life and property of Hindus."

These two places are in East Pakistan. The third quotation is from the *Musalman* of Madras, of 18 January, which says that:

> "The trouble which started in Kashmir following the theft of the sacred hair should have remained localized but it is to be regretted that Pakistani citizens thoughtlessly created disturbances over it and subjected the innocent non-Muslim minority there to tyranny. This led to Hindu-Muslim riots in Calcutta, and the innocent Muslim minority of Calcutta had to suffer."

One might ask oneself what does Pakistan seek to achieve by its anti-Indian crusade, its campaign of scurrilous abuse and hatred of India? Is it helping the Muslims of India, is exciting communal passions, fanning the flames of fanaticism and intolerance and is preaching "jehad"—holy war—helping the cause of Muslims in India? May I observe in passing that no war is holy and that evey war is cruel, bloodthirsty and the cause of terrible suffering and distress. No, I do not think Pakistan is so unsophisticated as all that. It wants to see discord and turmoil in India, it wants India to be politically and economically weakened so that it can get an opportunity to continue further its present illegal occupation of a part of territory which by international law is as much a part of Indian territory as Bombay or Delhi is. It is already thereby playing the Chinese game of weakening India internally and undermining its defence against China. I wish to make it clear on behalf of my Government that nothing, and I repeat, nothing will induce any Government of India, whatever be its party affiliations, to sign the death warrant of the unity, integrity and solidarity of the country.

I said earlier that nothing has happened recently to justify Pakistan's approach to the Security Council. We are told in the letter addressed to the President of the Security Council dated 16 January 1964 (S/5517), that a grave situation had arisen in the State of Jammu and Kashmir and this was the direct consequence of the unlawful steps that the Government of India was continuing to take in order to destroy the special status of the State of Jammu and Kashmir, that this was a part of India's design to annex Jammu and Kashmir to India and that the Government of India was deliberately set on defying the Security Council and on integrating Jammu and Kashmir with the Indian Union. This is not a new complaint. A similar complaint was made by Pakistan in June 1949 following a decision of the Constituent Assembly of India to reserve four seats for the representatives of Jammu and Kashmir in the Indian Parliament. The United Nations Commission for India and Pakistan had then refused to take any action in the matter on the ground that is was difficult to oppose the measure of the Government of India on purely legal grounds. Similar complaints had been made by Pakistan every time some changes were made. In regard to the present complaint, it is relevant to point out that this had already been conveyed to the Security Council by the permanent representative of Pakistan in a letter dated 9 October 1963. India replied to this letter on 13 November 1963. The permanent representative of Pakistan addressed another letter on 5 January 1964 raising the same complaints. Nothing new has happened since then to justify the demand contained in the letter of the Foreign Minister of Pakistan of 16 January 1964 for an immediate meeting of the Security Council to consider the grave situation that has arisen in the State of Jammu and Kashmir.

Let me deal, at some length, with this charge of Pakistan that we are trying to "annex" or "integrate" Kashmir into the Indian Union. It is beyond doubt that legally and constitutionally when the Ruler of Kashmir executed the Instrument of Accession to India and Lord Mountbatten, the then Governor-General of India, accepted the Instrument, the whole of Kashmir became an integral part of the Union of India. It is necessary to look at the political and constitutional position prevailing in the subcontinent of India on the eve of independence. There was British India over which the United Kingdom exercies complete sovereignty. There were also more than 560 princely States which were semi-independent and which wer protected by the United Kingdom by a doctrine known as paramountcy. The meaning of this doctrine was that the King of England and Emperor of India was the paramount lord as far as these princes were concerned and, in return for the fealty pledged by them, the King-Emperor gave them protection.

When the Indian Independence Act of 1947 was passed by the British Parliament power transferred to the people of India, as far as British India was concerned, and Britain also put an end to paramountcy, leaving it to the princes to arrive at such arrangements as they thought proper with the Government of India and Pakistan. But the present Government of India was successor Government to the Government of the United Kingdom. Pakistan was a new State which came into existence. It was also provided that it was open to every princely State to accede either to India or to Pakistan. The law did not provide that the Instrument of Accession could be conditional. Once the accession was accepted either by the Governor-General of India or of Pakistan, the particular princely State became an integral part of one or the other of the two Dominions. It is significant to note that there was no provision for consulting the people of the princely State concerned. Nor was there any provision that the accession had to be ratified by ascertaining the wishes of the people of the acceding State. Leaving aside for a movement the question of Jammu and Kashmir, several princely State under this law acceded to India or Pakistan. It has never been suggested either by India or Pakistan that these accessions are, in any way, incomplete or require some action to be taken before they become conclusive. It is only in the case of Jammu and Kashmir that Pakistan has shown such laudable zeal in the sacred cause of democracy and self-determination.

It has also to be remembered that the partition of India was confined to British India and that in drawing the lines of the frontier, questions of Muslim majority provinces were taken into consideration only with regard to British India. There was no question whatsoever with regard to the religious complexion of the population of the princely States. The question whether one princely State should accede to India or Pakistan was left to the determination of the Rular of the State. Pakistan has often put forward a proposition that the State of Jammu and Kashmir, by reason of its large Muslim majority and of the fact that Pakistan came into existence as a Muslim State, should naturally form part of Pakistan. This is a wholly erroneous view of a legal and constitutional position.

The British Government had made it quite clear that the partition was only of British India and that this principle did not apply to States, such as Kashmir and several hundred others, which were ruled by Indian princes. I quote from the British Government's announcement of 3 June 1947, which said:

> "His Majesty's Government wish to make it clear that the decisions announced above" – about partition – "relate only to British India and that their policy towards Indian States

contained in the Cabinet Mission Memorandum of 12th May, 1946 remain unchanged."

The Cabinet Mission's memorandum reads, *inter alia*, as follows:

'...His Majesty's Government will cease to exercise the power of paramountcy. This means that the rights of the States which flow from their relaionship to the Crown will no longer exist and that all the rights surrendered by the States to the paramount power will return to the States. Political arrangements between the States on the one side and the British Crown and British India on the other will thus be brought to an end. The void will have to be filled either by the States entering into a federal relationship with the successor Government or Governments in British India, or failing this, entering into particular political arrangements with it or them."

Provision for accession was made in the Government of India Act of 1935 as adapted under the Indian Independence Act, 1947:

"An Indian State shall be deemed to have acceded to the Dominion if the Governor-General has signified his acceptance of an Instrument of Accession executed by the Ruler thereof..."

These were Acts of the British Parliament which created the Dominions of India and Pakistan. None of the provisions of these Acts can be questioned, at least by India, Pakistan or the United Kingdom which were parties to this agreement.

It was entirely for the Ruler of Jammu and Kashmir to decide taking all factors into consideration—the factor of contiguity, the factor of communications, the factor of economic ties and others—whether it would be beneficial for the State to be part of one Dominion or the other. The question of religion did not come into play at all. As a matter of historical fact, although the communal question assumed a large and unfortunate proportion in British India and was the platform on which the Muslim League based its policy, the people of the princely States, particularly Kashmir, although they suffered from many other disabilities and infirmities, did not suffer the disastrous consequences of religious hatred or intolerance.

Therefore, there is no substance in the suggestion that the

accession of Jammu and Kashmir was not complete and absolute because the people of that State had not been consulted nor been given opportunity to express their choice. It is clear that international law does not require that a treaty concluded by the ruler of a State, and with the mutual consent of the contracting parties, a treaty which is otherwise valid and binding, should be referred to the will of the people before it takes effect. There is no doubt, and I do not think Pakistan can dispute it, that the Government of the Maharaja of Kashmir was recognized by Pakistan. It was with this Government that Pakistan concluded a "standstill agreement" by the exchange of telegrams on 12 and 16 August 1947. At that time the Government of Pakistan had not questioned whether the Government of the Maharaja was capable of expressing the will of the people, nor had it doubted the validity of the agreement. It is thus clear that international law does not require that the party to an agreement should look behind a recognized Government with whom it contracts to see that the agreement has been arrived at by prior consultation with the people. In fact, as I shall mention later, the accession was also supported by the largest political party in Kashmir.

I shall briefly deal with the subsequent events and developments in Jammu and Kashmir and see whether these have, in any way, affected the legal and contitutional position. I hope to satisfy the Council that they have not, in the slightest degree. Jammu and Kashmir became an integral part of India when the Instrument of Accesssion was signed and accepted, and from that day till today it continues to occupy the same position *vis-a-vis* the Indian Union, and no question can possibly arise of annexing Kashmir or further integrating it into the Indian Union. You cannot make more complete which is already complete.

The distinguished Foreign Minister of Pakistan has said nothing new on the legal aspect of the accession of Jammu and Kashmir to India. He has repeated the same mixture of misstatements, omissions of material facts and the refusal to face up to the clear provisions of the Indian Independence Act. I do not wish to enter into the details of our case, which is well known to the Security Council. It was last set out at length in 1962. I shall content myself with drawing attention to salient points.

Unlike most of the rulers who had acceded to India or Pakistan before 15 August 1947, the Ruler of Kashmir did not make up his mind. Pending a decision on accession, he asked for a standstill agreement both with India and with Pakistan in regard to communications, supplies and post and telegraph arrangements which had always been interlinked with British India. Pakistan concluded the standstill agreement, but before a standstill agreement with India could be concluded, tribal raids started. Despite the standstill agreement, Pakistan cut off communications and stopped the supplies of essential commodities, thereby putting undue pressure on Kashmir. When this pressure failed armed invasion by nationals of Pakistan and tribal raiders followed. The Ruler's appeals to Pakistan were of no avail. The raiders caused havoc in different parts of Kashmir. The Kashmir State troops were incapable of offering effective resistance to such a large body of raiders. Events moved with great rapidity and the threat to the Valley of Kashmir became grave. Unable to prevent the raiders from committing large-scale killings, loot and arson, the Ruler requested of the Government of India that the State of Jammu and Kashmir should be allowed to accede to the Indian Dominion.

An appeal for help was also simultaneously received by the Government of India from the National Conference, which was the largest popular organization in Kashmir and which had fought for the peoples' rights and agitated for freedom of Kashmir from the rule of the Maharaja. The Conference also supported the request for the State's accession to India. May I draw the attention of the Council to what was stated by Sheikh Abdullah, who was then the leader of the National Conference, and about whom we have heard such laudatory remarks by the distinguished Foreign Minister of Pakistan? This is what he said:

> "When the raiders were fast approaching Srinagar, we could think of only one way to save the State from total annihilation – by asking for help from a friendly neighbour. The representative of the National Conference, therefore, flew to Delhi to seek help from the Government of India. But the absence of any constitutional ties between our State and India made it impossible for her to render any effective assistance in meeting the aggresor... But now, since the people's representative themselves sought an alliance, the Government of India showed readiness to accept it. Legally, the Instrument of Accession had to be signed by the Ruler of the State. This the Maharaja did."

A Sheikh Abdullah has come to judgement, I hope Pakistan will accept that judgement, both as to the consultation with the people of Kashmir and as to the fact that India did not put any pressure on Kashmir to accede to it.

As I have already stated, the Governor-General, Lord Mountbatten, accepted the Instrument of Accession. In answer to a letter of the Prime Minister of India, dated 22 December 1947, requesting Pakistan not to give aid or assistance to the raiders and not to prolong the struggle, the Prime Minister of Pakistan, on 30 December 1947, replid:

> "As regards the charges of aid and assistance to the invaders by the Pakistan, we emphatically repudiate them. On the contray, the Pakistan Government have continued to do all in their power to discourage the tribal movements by all means short of war."

On 1 January 1948, we approached the Security Council and, in our letter of that date, we stated:

> "Such a situation now exists between India and Pakistan owing to the aid which invaders, consisting of nationals of Pakistan and tribesmen from the territory immediately adjoining Pakistan on the north-west, are drawing from Pakistan for operations against Jammu and Kashmir...The Government of India request the Security Council to call upon Pakistan to put an end immediately to the giving of such an assistance which is an act of aggression against India."

It is an extremely significant fact, which is often over-looked because so much time has passed since that event, that we were the complainants before the Security Council, and that we complained of aggresion by Pakistan. On 15 January 1948, the Foreign Minister of Pakistan again emphatically denied that the Pakistan Government was giving aid and assistance to the invaders or had committed any act of aggression against India. On the contrary, the Foreign Minister stated, his Government had continued to do all in its power to discourage the tribal movement by all means short of war. He stated that the allegations made by the Indian Government that the Pakistan Government was affording aid and assistance to the tribal forces, or that these forces had bases in Pakistan territory or were being trained by the Pakistan Army, were utterly unconfirmed. Pakistan never contended that India had no right to be in Kashmir.

This categorical denied by Pakistan of being behind the tribal raid is the most important and significant aspect of the whole Kashmir issue. It is significant that, at that stage, Pakistan never tried to justify its presence in Kashmir or to claim any right to be there. Pakistan was obviously quite aware of the fact that its presence in Kashmir was contrary to international law and was fully conscious of the illegality of its action. That is why Pakistan could not admit its presence in Kashmir and that is why there was a total and straight denial of its presence. Incidentally, the facts just stated by me clearly show that the plea now put forward that Pakistan went to Kashmir in support of a liberation movement is clearly an after thought designed to create a false moral justification for its invasion of Kashmir. Subsequent admissions by Pakistan, to which I shall presently refer, have made clear that this was not merely an equivocation but a deliberate falsehood.

In its reply to the Government of India's complaint dated 1 January 1948, Pakistan, on 15 January, cast doubts on the legality of the accession of Jammu and Kashmir to India by suggesting that the accession has been obtained by fraud and violence. It is clear that in law, if fraud and violence was not established as vitiating it, the accession was perfectly legal and binding. On the question of fraud and violence, it may be stated that Lord Mountbatten had told the Maharaja of Kashmir, on behalf of the Government, that he might accede to Pakistan if he wished, and it would not be taken as an unfriendly act. It is also an admitted fact that not a single Indian soldier was sent to Kashmir to fight against the raiders before the accession. If any violence was used at all against the State of Jammu and Kashmir and the Maharaja, it was by Pakistan. If the Ruler of Jammu and Kashmir was forced to accede to India, it was not because violence was used by India but because it was used by Pakistan and therefore, strangely enough, the fraud and violence which Pakistan was complaining of was fraud and violence used not by India, but by itself, and it does not require a very deep knowledge of law to understand that a party cannot challenge or vitiate the legality of a contract by pleading its own unlawful acts.

The Foreign Minister of Pakistan has stated that India obtained the signature of the Ruler on the Instrument of Accession at a time when the people of Jammu and Kashmir had risen in rebellion against the Ruler and had ousted his authority from the State. This is a complete and utter distortion of facts. It was the tribal raiders and Pakistan nationals, aided and abetted by the Pakistan Government, who carried fire and sword into Kashmir, whose fate is now of such great concern to Pakistan, and compelled the Ruler to turn to Sheikh Abdullah, whose testimony is of great importance becaue it is the testimony of a witness who is speaking about contemporary events:

> "When for the first time the people of Srinagar saw the income planes from India and the tanks of the Indian Army passing through the streets here, their disappointment and anguish was turned into joy and happiness. The people here, Muslims, Hindus and Sikhs, heaved a sign of relief, knowing that their honor and dignity could now be safeguarded. We must not forget that time."

The Foreign Minister of Pakistan has also spoken of a despotic Maharaja having signed the Instrument of Accession. Are all the rulers of States who have acceded to Pakistan paragons of democratic virtue?

When the United Nations Commission for India and Pakistan visited Karachi in July 1948, Pakistan could no longer keep up the story that it had a blameless record as far as the invasion by the raiders was concerned, and Sir Mohammed Zafrullah Khan informed the Commission that three regular Pakistani Brigades had been fighting in Kashmir territory, since May 1948.

It is in this context that the Commission's resolutions of 13 August 1948 and 5 January 1949 which we accepted—and these are the only two resolutions, apart from the resolution of 17 January 1948, to which we have agreed—have to be understood and appreciated. The very foundation of these resolutions was that the presence of Pakistan in parts of Jammu and Kashmir was illegal, and that it must withdraw its troops and vacate the aggression against India. This is clear from the wording of paragraph 1 of Part II, section A, of the resolution of 13 August:

> "As the presence of troops of Pakistan in the territory of the State of Jammu and Kashmir constitutes a material change in the situation since it was represented by the Government of

Pakistan before the Security Council, the Government of Pakistan agrees to withdraw its troops from that State."

It was only on Pakistan's complying with this essential condition that the possibility of holding a plebiscite in Kashmir could arise. It is clear that the Security Council could not possibly have suggested to India the holding of a plebiscite so long as a gross illegality perpetrated by Pakistan and a deliberate violation of international law remined unrectified. The Security Council could not possibly countenance a naked aggression by one country against another.

It is often forgotten that, when Pakistan approaches the Security Council, it does so as an aggressor which has not vacated its aggression. My submission to you is that Pakistan has been guilty of gross contempt of this august body, and it has no right to be heard till it comes with clean hand. It has not only washed its hands and not only tries to justify its aggression but seeks to challenge the legal validity of an accession which has been accepted by the United Nations Commission for India and Pakistan and on the basis of which Pakistan's presence in Kashmir has been held to be illegal and contrary to international law. Memories are so short that I am sometimes surprised that Pakistan should be permitted to reverse the roles of itself and India before the Security Council. It comes here in the innocent garb of an aggrieved party making charges against us as if we were the aggressors. Throughout this Kashmir controversy, which in all conscience has be sufficiently long and protracted, Pakistan has continued to be an aggressor. Even today, it is guilty of continuing aggression and, in my submission, it has no *locus standi* whatsoever to make any complaint with regard to what India is doing in an integral part of its country.

It has been said that, notwithstanding the accession, assurances were given by several eminent Indian authorities that the wishes of the people of Jammu and Kashmir would be consulted with regard to that State's forming part of India. Those assurances which the Foreign Minister of Pakistan catalogued in his speech were given always in the context of the action of Pakistan's aggression and withdrawal of Pakistan from Kashmir as a condition precedent. The letter of Lord Mountbatten, the Governor-General of India, dated 27 October 1947 – a separate communication to the Ruler not forming part of the instrument of Accession – itself says:

> "...it is my Government's wish that as soon as law and order have been restored in Kashmir and her soil cleared of the invader, the question of the State's accession should be settled by a reference to the people."

I emphasize the words "as soon as law and order have restored in Kashmir and her soil cleared of the invader." Even today, sixteen years latter, the soil of Kashmir is not purged of the invaders who continue unlawfully to hold two-fifths of the State. Every time the authroities in India, the Prime Minister or someone else, talked of ascertaining the wishes of the people such remarks were always in the context of our demand for Pakistan's withdrawal from Kashmir.

A plebiscite is only a machinery for ascertaining the wishes of a people. There is nothng sacrosanct about it. There are other methods which are equally efficient. The British Government has, in the last twenty years, transferred power to a large number of its colonies, but it has never thought of ascertaining the wishes of these colonies by holding a plebiscite. In India itself no plebiscite was held to determine either whether the people of sub-continent of India wanted freedom or whether the majority of Muslims living in the country wanted partition. The United Kingdom came to the conclusion that independence should be given and the country should be partitioned because it was satisfied that the Indian National Congress on the one hand and the Muslim League on the other represented the people on these two issues. In Jammu and Kashmir the National Conference as a party represented the over-whelming majority of the people of that State, and, as I have already pointed out, it fully supported the accession of Jammu and Kashmir to India.

We accepted the two resolutions of the Security Council—namely, those of 13 August 1948 and 5 January 1949. Under these, a series of steps were contemplated to follow one after the other. The resolution concerning a plebiscite, namely that of 5 January 1949, was subsidiary and supplementary to and an elaboration of part III of the resolution of 13 August 1949, if and when that part was reached. It was like an architect's design and a blueprint, and the resolution of 5 January 1949 could spring to life only if the resolution of 13 August 1948 was fully implemented.

The possibility of a plebiscite was envisaged because at that time no elections had been held in Kashmir. Subsequent to that, Kashmir has had three general elections with universal adult franchise, and at all these three elections a party has been returned to power which firmly and emphatically supports Kashmir's integration with India. The last election, in 1962, was held under the Indian electoral law and supervised by the Indian Election Commission. We ourselves have held three general elections. Even our worst enemies have not suggested that these elections were rigged or that they were not secret and free. It was the ballot box that determined which member should be elected and the elections were so free that in one general election, in one State, a party was returned to power which was opposed to the Indian National Congress, the majority party in India. Therefore if it was necessary to ascertain the wishes of the people of Kashmir, they have been ascertained not once, not twice, but on three occasions. The Foreign Minister of Pakistan has made a great deal of capital from the question he has used from various papers about the nature of elections in Kashmir. May I quote from one of the papers he has chosen to quote. This is from *The Guardian*:

> "The Jammu elections are a great and quite a genuine victory for the National Conference.
>
> "Elections in Kashmir are over. In Jammu the National Conference was given a tough fight by the Hindu Praja Parishad, and all but five of the seats were contested. After strenuous canvassing and election fever, equalled only in India's most advanced parts, the National Conference won two-thirds of the seats..."

The Foreign Minister of Pakistan has referred to thirty two candidates being returned unopposed in the 1962 elections but he has chosen not to mention the thirty-nine other seats which were hotly contested.

Pakistan's perpetual harping on plebiscite in Jammu and Kashmir is not due to its faith in democratic principles. I should have thought that democracy, like charity, begins at home, and before Pakistan preaches to us how we should ascertain the wishes of the people of a part of our country, it should first make at least a beginning in establishing democratic instructions at home. I need hardly say that since its existence it has never sufficiently trusted its own people to permit them to participate in a general and direct election for the creation of legislative and parliamentary bodies. As the Foreign Minister knows, his own President has repreatedly stated that the people of Pakistan are not fit to exercise such democratic rights and, after seventeen years of independence, the people of Pakistan are still being educated in basic democracy which I need hardly say is a very diluted form of democracy. The real reason for insisting on a plebiscite is to try and see whether it cannot inflame communal passions in Kashmir by making the inhabitants of that State believe that their religion is in danger, and bring about the recurrence of the terrible events of the partition of India in 1947 : bloodshed, migrations, untold human misery.

Therefore, if I may sum up, our position on Jammu and Kashmir is clear and unambiguous. The two resolutions of the Security Council dealing with the plebiscite were conditional and contingent on Pakistan vacating its aggression, and that condition has not been complied with. It is really more than a condition. It was the very basis on which these two resolutions were founded, and the condition not having been complied with and the basis having disappeared, these resolutions are no longer binding on us. In any case, by the passage of time and various factors intervening—to which I shall draw attention a little later—they have become obsolete. We cannot possibly contemplate with equanimity the threat to the integration of our country and the danger to our cherished principle of secularism by the holding of a plebiscite in Kashmir. I wish to make it clear on behalf of my Government that under no circumstances can we agree to a plebiscite in Kashmir.

Let me deal with the allegation of Pakistan of the socalled attempt on the part of my country to further "integrate" Kashmir with India. In the first place, as Jammu and Kashmir is an integral part of India, what we have been doing is adjusting our relations with a constituent State of the Indian Union. It is on a par with the Congress of the United States of America dealing with one of its fifty federated States. Therefore, the question raised by Pakistan is purely a domestic matter with which only India is concerned and in respect of which Pakistan has no right to intervene or interfere and which has been specifically excluded under the Charter from the jurisdiction of the United Nations.

But even so, let us see what we have done which has roused the wrath of Pakistan and which has brought it with such urgency to the Council. I may point out that Part XXI of our Constitution deals with provisions with respect to the State of Jammu and Kashmir. There are also other Articles in that part which deal with other States in the Indian Union, such as Andhra Pradesh, Punjab and Maharashtra. These provisions in turn are intended to be only temporary and transitional. These will continue to apply so long as the necessity for their application continues. When the necessity disappears, these provisions will be deleted and the provisions of the Constitution which apply to all the States would also apply to the States with regard to which special arrangements have been made under this part. It may be pointed out that the powers of the Central Government have constantly been modified or extended within the framework of the Constitution, so that the relationship between the Central Governmnet and the constituent units has been changing. These changes which occur at various intervals are part of larger process of the organic growth of the Union of India. Now the changes which are being contemplated and which formed the subject matter of Pakistan's letter of 16th January 1964 [S/5517], are changing the title of the Head of the State from "Sadar-i-Riyasat" to "Governor" and that of "Prime Minister" to the "Chief Minister". This is only a change in nomenclature.

The other proposal complained about is that the representatives of the State of Jammu and Kashmir in the Indian Parliament are hereaftter to be elected directly by the people of Kashmir and not appointed on the recommendation of the Kashmir Legislature, as has been done so far. What is wrong in this? One would have thought that Pakistan, with its professed solicitude for the right of self-determination of the Kashmiris, would prefer the direct election of their representatives to the Indian Parliament.

The next objection refers to certain amendments to introduce more progressive labour legislation. India is member of the International Labour Organisation and has adopted a number of ILO conventions. The Indian labour legislation is in keeping with these conventions. The need for such labour legislation in Kashmir was not felt for very long, since there was hardly any organized factory labour in Kashmir. Now that certain mineral resources have been discovered and mining industry has started, it has become essential to introduce modern labour legislation to prevent abuses. We are bound by the ILO conventions and we cannot ignore our obligations with regard to any part of our territory. Similarly, what can be the objection to the Government of India sharing with the

State Government concurrently the power to make laws in respect of medical and other professions when the State Legislature agrees to this change and there is a formal request by the duly elected Government of Jammu and Kashmir? We feel that an integrated, all-India system of medical and other services will lead to progress and increased efficiency and the co-ordination of professional standards in different parts of India. So all these changes are for the benefit of the people of Kashmir. It is not suppression of any human rights. If the Prime Minister of India used the expression "the gradual erosion of Article 370", it was a perfectly correct expression because by its very nature Article 370 is temporary and must gradually fade away and disappear.

In his speech the Foreign Minister of Pakistan referred also to further acts of integration by mentioning "the taking over of responsibility for the administration of highways, telegraphs, telephone, income tax, broadcasting and customs, the subordination of the Accounts and Audit Department of the State to the Auditor-General of India, the abolition of the custom barriers and the permit system for entry into and out of the State, the subjection of its economic plans 'to the Planning Commission' and the authority of the Supreme Court of India over Kashmir, and the arrogation by the President of India of powers to promulgate laws in Jammu and Kashmir by executive fiat – all these, among other things" – and I am still quoting the Foreign Minister of Pakistan – "are links in the chain with which Jammu and Kashmir has been shackled" (1087th meeting, para. 59). If ever there was a travesty of what we have done in Kashmir it is this.

Does Pakistan expect that while it continues its aggression, we should sit with folded hands and do nothing whatever in Kashmir to improve the lot of the people? Every action we have taken and to which the representative referred has been in favour of amelioration of the conditions in Kashmir, in favour of modernizing the State. Look at the language used by the representative of Pakistan : "the subordination of the Audit and Accounts Department of the State to the Auditor-General of India". Is it a bad thing to have a proper audit of the accounts of a State by an independent official like Auditor-General of India, or those Pakistan want that those in charge of the revenues of Kashmir should pay ducks and drakes with the peoples money? Surely, the abolition of custom barriers and the permit system for entry into or out of the Kashmir helps trade and commerce and prevents unnecessary delays in the passages of goods between Kashmir and other parts of India. In India we have a Planning Commission which plans for the economic development of the country. The plan is prepared after full discussion and debate at various levels.

We want Kashmir to participate in economic processes which are the modern methods of ensuring orderly economic development, beneficial to all the people of the country. It is indeed surprising that objection should be taken even to what is called the imposition of the authority of the Supreme Court of India over Kashmir. The Supreme Court is the highest court in our country, and under our Constitution it is the custodian of the fundamental rights of citizens. It is to safeguard these fundamental rights of the people of Kashmir that the jurisdictiion of the Supreme Court has been extended to Kashmir. The President of India does not promulgate laws unless the necessity for it arises and the conditions for the promulgation are duly satisfied. Our President is not a dictator. He is the constitutional Head of the State, and he can only act on the advice tendered to him by the Government of India, which is a Government responsible to Parliament. It is indeed a misuse of language – I would rather say a perversion of language – to speak of these changes in Kashmir "as links in the chain with which Jammu and Kashmir has been shackled." No amount of declamation from Pakistan will deter the Government of India from doing the duty by our people in Kashmir.

The Foreign Minister of Pakistan, overwhelmed by the enthusiasm generated by his cause, agreed with the statement attributed to Sheikh Abdullah that "millions of rupees of the Indian Exchequer have largely been utilized to corrupt the people of Kashmir and almost kill their soul..." (1087th meeting, para 31). Let us see how we have been corrupting the people of Kashmir and almost killing their soul. The revenue of the State of Jammu and Kashmir in 1947 was $5.5 million. In 1959-1960 it was $23.5 million. The *per capita* income in 1950-51 was $38 and in 1959-60 it was $48. The annual food production prior to 1951 was 0.3 million tonnes and 1961 it was 0.5 million tonnes. The electricity produced before 1951 was 4,360 killowatts per year and in 1961 it was 16,000 kilowatts. The number of factories in 1947-1948 was 44 and in 1961 it was 138. The roads per hundred square miles prior to 1951 were 2.5 miles and in 1961 it was 40 miles. This is important. The number of tourists before 1951, in a country divided from the outside world by "a wall of steel", in the words of the Foreign Minister of Pakistan, was 27,207; in 1961 it was 71,000. The number of pupils in primary schools prior to 1957 was 65,000; in 1961 it was 197,000. The number of high schools and higher secondary schools in 1947-1948 was 52; in 1961 it was 262. The figures of literacy were 6.6 per cent before 1947; in 1961 it was 12 per cent. The number of hospitals and dispensaries in 1947-1948 was 89; in 1961 it was 349. The average life expectancy before 1951 was thirty-two years; in 1961 it was forty-seven years. What a distressing picture of a country, again to quote the phrase used by the Foreign Minister, "under the control domination of India"!

I will now turn to the baseless and mischievous connexion which Pakistan has sought to establish, in its letter of 16th January 1964, between these changes in the constitutional relation between India and one of its constituent States and the theft of the holy relic from the Hazratbal shrine. It is suggested that this sacrilege has served to provide a spark to the bitter discontent and indignation which has been mounting in Kashmir as a result of India's policies and which is now rampant among the people of Jammu and Kashmir against recent Indian moves to "integrate" that part of the State with the Indian Union; that since the theft of the holy relic the Muslim population of Jammu and Kashmir has given vent to its anger through massive demonstrations for more than ten days and that hundreds of thousands of Muslims kept marching in morning procession day after day through the streets of Srinagar. You will note that what is stated here is that the demonstration was by the Muslim population of Jammu and Kashmir; no one else joined. It will be immediately noticed that Pakistan has tried to give a communal turn to the incidents in Kashmir. To Pakistan everything is communal. It cannot observe any event except through communal glasses. It cannot understand how Hindus and Muslims can live peacefully in Kashmir and have the best of relations. Its philosophy is that in the very nature of things Muslims must hate the Hindus and the Hindus must hate the Muslims.

When the sacred relic was stolen, Pakistan expected that there would be communal riots in Kashmir. Not only did it expect this, but it did its best to incite them, as can be seen from the statements that appear in the press and also from the utterances of responsible men in Pakistan. President Ayub Khan, speaking in Sukkur, on 4 January 1964 said that "the theft of the holy relic is a calculated political conspiracy to subject the Muslims of the occupied Kashmir to more and more atrocities...No Muslim, however sinful, could ever think of committing such a sacrilege". Therefore, according to Mr. Ayub Khan, it was certain that no Muslim could be held responsible for this heinous crime and as such it was evident that the crime was motivated by a political conspiracy; and this he ascerted without a little of evidence. As you see, the suggestion in this statement is that it must be a Hindu who stole this relic in Kashmir, and thereby incited the Muslims of Kashmir against the Hindus.

I am now quoting a very well-known newspaper from Stockholm. *Sevenska Degbladet* of 30 December 1963 said:

> "...it is difficult to believe that the theft of Mohammed's lock of hair that has caused such riots in Kashmir, would have been initiated by Hindus even if, naturally, there was fanatics in Hindu circles also. It is more probable that the deed was committed by some Pakistan agent, perhaps one of the Pathans who, during the last few years, have been recruited by agencies on the Pakistan side to take part in a planned 'Algerian liberation war' on the Indian side...In this way Chinese interests are also served. The Indian defence of Ladakh is wholly dependent on the connexions of the Srinagar and the Vale. The only road from Ladakh goes straight down to Srinagar and, therefore, has an enormous strategic importance."

In quoting from the dispatch from Richard Critchfield, Mr. Bhutto, the Foreign Minister of Pakistan, conveniently omitted a significant portion thereof. This is what the dispatch says in continuation of what Mr. Bhutto quoted : Meanwhile, in Pakistan, the Foreign Minister, Mr. Bhutto, urged the Kashmiris to rebel against the Indian-controlled Government." And the Foreign Minister comes to you here to appeal for peace. I repeat : the Foreign Minister, Mr. Bhutto, urged the Kashmiris to rebel against the Indian-controlled Government.

Does the Foreign Minister accept this presentation of his statement to be correct? *The Economist* of 4th January 1964, also quoted by Mr. Bhutto, says :

> "Pakistan's Foreign Minister, Mr. Z.A. Bhutto, has charged Indian 'occupation authorities' with instigating the theft, apparently so as to terrorize the 'oppressed' Muslims into

> fleeing from their homes. This is an implausible accusation, to put it mildly, but the point is not that it is implausible, but that it is made."

So, *The Economist* realizes the point of Mr. Bhutto, the Foreign Minister, in making this charge that the theft was instigated terrorized the oppressed Muslims. The suggestion was that there should be trouble in Kashmir and the people of Kashmir, especially the feelings of the Mulims, should be inflamed and that they should rise against the Hindus.

Now, unfortunately for Pakistan, it is a fact which cannot be channged that there was complete communal unity during the demostrations by the people of Kashmir protesting against the theft of the relic. Hindus and Sikhs joined their Muslim brethren in mourning this loss. To the Hindus and the Sikhs the relic was not a Muslim relic but a relic belonging to Kashmir, indeed to the whole of India. We in India respect each other's religion. Hindus revere Muslim saints and vice versa. We all join in the celebrations of different communities. It requires a modern secular rational outlook to understand this phenomenon.

A further significant fact of these demonstrations is that not only were they not aimed against the Government of India but, on the contrary, they showed complete confidence in the policies of my Government, and what is more, they appealed to the Union Government that they, rather than the local administration, should investigate this crime and bring the guilty to book. It was in response to the appeal of the people of Kashmir that the Government of India sent its highest officials to Srinagar to investigate the matter and to recover the relic. The action of my Government was successful : the relic was recovered and restored. According to a report in *The New York Times* of 4 February 1964, under the date-line of Srinagar 3 February :

> "A Committee of Muslim leaders decided today that the hair now enshrined in a mosque near here was the one that disappeared from there last December 26th."

According to the latest information that I have received, a special "didar", or exposition, of the holy relic was held on 3 February at Hazratbal. A number of prominent religious personalities, most of whom were nominated by the Action Committee, to whom reference has been made by the Foreign Minister of Pakistan, saw the holy relic and declared it genuine in the presence of the large number of people in the mosque. Among those who identified the relic was Maulana Masoodi, about whom also a reference was made in the statement in the Foreign Minister of Pakistan. The investigation is in the final stage and the accused persons will be put on trial very soon. It is true that the demonstrations were aimed at the local administration, but surely it is a fundamental right in a democracy of the people to express their dissatisfaction with their Government. Such demonstrations are not unknown even in more sophisticated societies. The people of a democratic country have the inalienable right not only to show their want of confidence in their Government but to turn it out and elect another one.

What I have been saying about the nature of the demonstrations in Srinagar is amply borne out by the testimony of foreign correspondents who were on the scene and who witnessed what had happened. Thus, *The Guardian,* the well-known English newspaper which Mr. Bhutto quoted, had this to say on 6 January 1964 :

> "There was singing and dancing in the streets of Srinagar yesterday after the Government announced that the relic had been found. A sullen and angry cry suddenly transformed into a joyful one."

The New York Times of 24 January 1964 has following story from its correspondent, Thomas F. Brady :

> "The dissatisfaction of Kashmiris with their local government, but apparently not with the Indian national Government, found expression in protests and riots that followed the theft . . . The big Moslem majority there seems to have shown no animus toward the Hindu minority. . . Indeed, the indications are the main targets of the arson and looting that followed the disappearancee of the relic were the extensive business interests of Bakshi Ghulam Mohammed, former Prime Minister of the State and of his brother and political right hand, Bakshi Rashid. Both are Moslems."

I am not here to defend either Mr. Bakshi or his brother. The point of the quotation is that the demonstrations were against the local administration and not against the Government of India. *The New York Times* of 5 January 1964, had the following:

> "One view that was expressed here was that the pro-Pakistan elements had stolen the hair in an attempt to discredit the pro-Indian Kashmir Government."

The Foreign Minister quoted the views of an Indian columnist in *The Hindustan Times* of 8 January. This columnist is obviously not friendly to the Government of Bakshi Ghulam Mohammed or even to the present successor Government. In a free country with full freedom of the Press every one is entitled to express his own views. In fairness to the columnist, I must, however, read two paragraphs from the same article which Mr. Bhutto for obvious reasons left out:

> "But the striking fact has to be recorded that the dismay and anger of the people of Kashmir did not express themselves in communalism or in anti-Indian sentiment. The people did not turn to the pro-Pakistan elements for guidance and leadership. Their own demand was that India should intervence, for investigation of the sacrilege, to punish the guilty and to ensure that Kashmir does not lapse back into Bakshi rule.
>
> "The people of Kashmir have given their clear verdict and they are entitled to hope that they have struck the blow for a good and clean administration responsible to their needs and aspirations. They have put their trust in India . . . Can we afford to betray them again?"

So the emphasis in all these quotations is that the people of Kashmir have confidence in India, that they want India to intervene and that they are not satified with the local administration.

Having failed in its evil design to stir up trouble in Kashmir, Pakistan diverted its attention to East Pakistan, and serious riots broke out in Khulna and Jessore and the Muslims there attacked the Hindu minority. There were terrible incidents of looting, arson and stabbing. A large number of members of the frightened minority started a trek towards India, which lay just across the frontier. It is strange that while in Kashmir itself the large Muslim majority did not suspect the Hindus of having a hand in the theft of the relic, 1,5000 miles away the Muslims of East Pakistan were demonstrating against the Hindus and accusing the Hindu community in Kashmir of anti-Muslim actions. May I quote the dispatch of Jacques Nevard in *The York Times* of 19th January 1964 :

> "Few people here" – "here" means East Pakistan, where these riots took place – "give much credence to the Government-supported view that the East Pakistan riots were caused by the disappearance three weeks ago of a reputed hair of the Prophet Mohammed.
>
> "Officially approved processions to protest the loss of the relic got out of hand in the Khulna and Jessore district of East Pakistan, leading to riots against Hindu."

I request the Council to mark and note the words "officially approved."

The repercussion of the Khulna riots resulted in riots in Calcutta. Refugees from East Pakistan came to the city with lurid tales of what had happened to their co-religionists on the other side of the frontier. The passions of the Hindus in Calcutta were inflamed and unfortunate incidents took place where Muslim lives were lost and some houses in which the Muslims lived were burnt down.

Now, by coincidence I myself was in Calcutta during four days while these riots were taking place. I had been there on official tour as Minister of Education, but I was an eyewitness to what was done by the West Bengal Government to put down these riots. I express my admiration for the strong measures taken by the Chief Minister of West Bengal. He immediately called out the troops and curfew was ordered throughout the city. Our Minister of Home Affairs, Mr. Nanda, also arrived in Calcutta and further action was taken. About 5,000 hooligans were rounded up, a citizens' committee was set up to help to restore peace and order, and assurance was given that no land-lord would be permitted to beneft by the destruction of Muslim houses and that as far as possible Muslims would be rehabilitated in the same places where they originally lived. I was staying with the Governor of West Bengal, Miss Padmaja Naidu, a distinguished daughter of a distinguished mother, and she threw open a large part of the Government House in order to give shelter to the Muslims who had lost their homes and their belongings. The Calcutta riots were put down firmly and sternly, and today there is complete peace and the normal situation has been restored.

The terrible tale of communal riots did not end here, however. There were subsequent riots in Dacca, Naravanganj Chittagong, Barisal—they are all places in East Pakistan—and in many other places in East Pakistan. Terrible scenes were enacted, and even—according to as important a news agency as Reuters—about one thousand Hindus were killed. Our own information is that throughout East Pakistan the number is much larger; the throuble has not yet ended and the tension still continues. The Deputy High Commissioner for India in Dacca has so far received requests for migration from over 50,000 families, involving more than 200,000 people; into one district of Assam, namely Garo Hills, alone, about 20,000 refugees have moved from East Pakistan. These are official figures.

I did not have any desire to cite these figures—they are grim and unpleasant but I felt that I should give the Security Council a full picture since the distinguished Foreign Minister of Pakistan in his statement sought to present a one-sided picture before the Council. I wish to make it clear that whatever may happen in East Pakistan, we do not condone the criminals who are guilty of taking innocent lives. To us a Muslim life is as precious as a Hindu life because both a Hindu and a Muslim are Indian citizens. We condemn bloodshed and looting and arson, whatever may be the cause or the provocation and wherever it may take place. We have respect for human life and we abhor commnual frenzy or fanaticism.

As our Prime Minister said in his appeal to the nation from his sick bed on 23 January 1964 :

> "We have had distressing news of happenings in East Pakistan in the past few days in which lives of many innocent men, women and children have been lost. These have naturally shocked and upset us. I hope that our countrymen will maintain calm and will refuse to be provoked by these events. Such restraint will be in keeping with age-old traditions of tolerance which is our most precious heritage. Whatever happens elsewhere, citizens of India should prove themselves worthy of their heritage and discharge their sacred duty to live in amity

> and good will with their fellow citizens whatever be their religion or faith. In that way alone, we can prove ourselves worthy of our heritage and the confidence which Mahatma Gandhi, our leader, reposed in us and of our dedication to the principles of freedom and democracy and our secular State."

However, I am sorry to say that the attitude of Pakistan is different. By its policy, by its action, by its utterances, it has deliberately incited these riots. There was peace and harmony between the two communities in India before Pakistan preached "jehad", holy war, and accused the Hindus without a shred of evidence, of being at the bottom of the theft of the sacred relic. It deliberately and for set purpose created an atmosphere so that riots should break out in East Pakistan. Thousands of innocent lives have been lost. It makes no difference whether these lives were of Hindus or Muslims. The physical act by which these lives were lost might be committed by a Hindu or a Muslim fanatic or a Hindu or a Muslim ruffian, but the Pakistan Government cannot be absolved of its responsibility for the death of these innocent people. We in India treat all our citizens alike. We give them the same rights and we want complete communal harmony. We have successfully achieved this, and if we are left to ourselves we will have no communal trouble whatsoever; but whenever there is communal trouble we put it down with a heavy hand. Pakistan, on the other hand, had from its very inception based its policy on communal hatred and fanaticism. It has incited the Muslims in Kashmir to rebel against India, and it has constantly harped on the theory that Hindus and Muslim are two separate nations.

Let me point out the attempts we have made to improve our relations, and point out also what Pakistan had done in return. Our Prime Minister appealed to Pakistan more than once to enter into a "no-war declaration". He said that both countries must settle their differences peacefully and resolve that under no circumstances and for no reason will either country go to war with the other. This offer was refused. Why? Has Pakistan got mental reservations? Does she intend to use violence against India under certain circumstances? When the recent trouble broke out, our President appealed to President Ayub Khan to issue a joint declaration to our respective peoples appealing for peace and hermony. This very reasonable proposal of joint appeal—which, by the mere fact of its being made jointly by the two respective Heads of State, would have had the most beneficial psychological effect—also was refused. We then proposed that the two Home Ministers of India and Pakistan should meet and visit the scenes of disturbance and suggest what further steps should be taken to prevent such happenings. We were met with a counter proposal which was tantamount to refusal.

The Foreign Minister referred to certain talks that took place between India and Pakistan over Kashmir and has sought to make out as if the talks failed due to Indian intransigence. Let me now state what the facts are. On the eve of the first round of talks in Rawalpindi, in Pakistan, the Pakistan Government announced an agreement in principle on the demarcation of the border between that part of the State of Jammu and Kashmir which is now under the unlawful occupation of Pakistan and Sinkiang. At this stage we could have legitimately broken off the talks, but despite the provocation we decided to continue them. In March 1963, while the talks were still going on, Mr. Bhutto went to Peking and signed the Agreement. Again, we showed restraint and continued the talks, though we had enough provocation. The talks were finally broken off by the Foreign Minister of Pakistan, Mr. Bhutto, in spite of all effort to keep the talks going. This proves that the intransigence was not an our side at all but entirely on the side of Pakistan.

Now let us contrast this with the attitude of Pakistan. When China attacked us and was guilty of clear and unabashed aggression, Pakistan carried on virulent propaganda against us and in favour of China. Not only did it use every effort to prevail upon freiendly countries not to give us assistance in the hour of our dire peril, but it took up the attitude that it was not China, but India, that was guilty of aggression. The whole of the world, with the possible exception of a few States, saw and understood that we had been victims of a cruel aggression.

The Foreign Minister has given expression to excellent sentiments with regard to the preservation of peace and the solution of international problems by peaceful negotiations rather than by violent means. We fully endorse these sentiments and we have always subscribed to them. It is easy to come to the Security Council in the garb of innocence and to appeal to world opinion by emphasizing that the attitude of Pakistan had always been friendly and peaceful and that it has not given any provocation whatsoever to my country—but, when we look at the facts, we find quite a different picture. From time to time, there has been open incitement to violence by responsible opinion in Pakistan: constant suggestions have been made that, if the Kashmir problem cannot be solved peacefully, it must be solved by violent means. Even in the Foreign Minister's own letter of 16 January [S/5517], which the Council is now considering the conclusion is very significant, namely, that "the people of "Azad" Kashmir and Pakistan may, in desperation, turn to other courses". What are these other courses? Courses other than peaceful courses are violence and bloodshed. I have rarely seen, in a public document addressed to a body which is responible for the maintenance of international peace and good relation, and open threats being held out by a Member State to refer to violence under certain circumstances. How, then, can we take the Pakistan Foreign Minister's statement here seriously?

I may refer to a letter that appeared in *The Observer* on 17 June 1963, by the late John Strachey, Labour M.P., who had visited both India and Pakistan as a Member of a Parliamentary delegation. Addressing the editor of *The Observer,* he wrote :

> "You complained that Indian still keeps a large part of her army on the Pakistan frontier. Before going to Pakistan last month this seemed to me also to be an indefensible deployment of India's forces, but during the week in which my collegues were in Pakistan, a Pakistan Cabinet Minister declared publicly that the Kashmir question must be settled immediately by peaceful means or otherwise. Another Pakistan public man in a key position assured us that if China attacked again he and his friends would not miss the opportunity this time but would immediately attack India. And almost every Pakistani public man whom we met started the conversation from the assumption that India had attacked China."

As you know, Mr. John Strachey, who died recently, was a very respected Member of Parliament. This is his own testimony as to what he heard from a member of the Pakistan Cabinet and from men high up in Pakistan public life. This clearly shows that Pakistan has all along intended to use violence against our country when the opportunity arose.

In this connexion, I should also like to mention the real attitude of Pakistan with regard to Kashmir. When one analyses the speech made by the Foreign Minister of Pakistan, the underlying sentiment is this : India must settle the problem of Kashmir with Pakistan to the latter's satisfaction; if it does not, there will be communal disturbances, there will be trouble, there might even be bloodshed. Therefore, Pakistan has approached this Council not with an appeal but with a threat, and we are being asked to submit to this threat. It is unfortunate that Pakistan does not realize that it is making the lives of millions of people both in our own country and in Pakistan mere pawns in the game of politics.

India today is perhaps the only country which can stand up to Chinese expansion and aggression. If India failed, there would be nothing to control the Chinese froward policy. It is therefore not only in the interest of India itself, but also in the interest of peace, that India should be strong. We are very greatful for the aid that we have received from friendly countries. But the whole purpose of this would be completely nullified if India became domestically weak. No country can be internationally strong if it does not also have domestic strength. The domestic strength of India depends upon the secularism, upon the vital necessity of the different communities that reside within India living in peace and harmony. Pakistan does not want India to be strong; it wants to weaken India, both internationally and domestically. Its recent flirtations with China are clear evidence of this fact. In this context, Kashmir assumes great importance. Pakistan has been complaining of India's changing the *status quo* with regard to Kashmir, and yet it has given away to China, in the border agreement, over 2,000 square miles of Kashmir. Pakistan has no right or title to it and yet it has been generous at another country's expense. If ever there was a gross change of *status quo,* it has been by Pakistan. But, apart from the fact that legally and constitutionally Kashmir is part of India, apart from the fact that we do not subscribe to the theory that Hindus and Muslims are two nations and that Kashmir is the symbol and guarantee of our secularism, Kashmir has now assumed vital importance because of the continuing menace of China. A mere glance at the map of India will be sufficient to illustrate this.

The Foreign Minister of Pakistan had sung paeans of praise in favour of Sheikh Abdullah. He has told us that Sheikh Abullah is the Lion of Kashmir , leader of Muslims there, and that we have put him behind bars. It is dangerous to have short memories. May I remind the Foreign Minister of Pakistan of what his own Prime Minister at the time, Mr. Liaquat Ali Khan said about Sheikh Abdullah :

> "Speaking to pressmen at Srinagar on November 10th (1947), during Pandit Jawaharlal Nehru's visit to that place, Sheikh Abdullah was reported to have observed that there may not be a referendum at all. This quisling who has been an agent of the Congress (Party) for many years, struts about the stage bartering away the life, honour and freedom of Muslims of Kashmir who are rotting in gaol."

This statement was made by Mr. Liaquat Ali Khan on 10 November 1947. In other words, when it suits Pakistan, Seikh Abdullah is a quisling–and, when it suits Pakistan better, he is a hero and the Lion of Kashmir and the leader of the Muslim community. I do not know when the tune will change again. Again, in a telegram dated 25 November 1947 to the Prime Minister of India, the Prime Minister of Pakistan said :

> "I am extremely sorry that you still support Seikh Abdullah, who you know is a quisling and a paid agent, to disrupt the Mssulmans of Kashmir ."

So here our Prime Minister was being accused of supporting a quisling who should not have been supported.

I should like to say a word–and I am sorry that I cannot say more because the matter is *sub judice*–about the trial of Sheikh Abdullah. We very much regret the delay that has taken place in concluding this trial, but it is being conducted according to the procedures laid down by law. *The Times* of London in a dispatch when the trial started pointed out how fair the judge was and how he held the scales of justice even between the prosecution and the defence. It is true, as the Foreign Minister had pointed out, that there are a large number of witnesses. This is inevitable in a conspiracy trial. I must also point out that the delay is partly due to the fact that there has been lengthy cross-examination of witness by the defence and from time to time adjournments have had to be given in the interest of Sheikh Abdullah himself. And the most significant feature of this trial is that Sheikh Abdullah has a counsel of his own choice a very distinguished lawyer from the London bar, Mr. Dingle Foot, Queen's Counsel. Therefore, the trial is public and every facilities is given to the accused to defend himself.

There is another matter to which I should like to refer in the statement made by the Foreign Minister of Pakistan. The Foreign Minister has also spoken of the "wall of steel" that "separates. . . Kashmir from the outside world" and has said that "India is trying desperately to conceal what is happening there under a massive blanket of censorship" [1087th meeting, para. 16]. Now one thing about which we are particularly proud is that Kashmir has always been open to any visitor from any country and of any nationality. We have nothing to hide in Kashmir, nor are we ashamed of anything we are doing there. Every year 70,000 to 80,090 tourists, including a large number of foreign tourists, have been coming to this most beautiful spot.

Pakistan has made a great deal of play with the idea of self-determination. It has tried to appeal to world opinion by proclaiming that its interest in Kashmir arises from the fact that the people of that State have been denied the right of self-determination. Now, in the first place, we must determine what are the connotations of the word "self" in this expression. What is the "self" which has the right to determine its destiny, to determine whether it would be a part of one country to another or would be independent? It is clear that the "self" contemplated in the enunciation of this democratic principle is not and cannot be a constituent part of a country. It can be operative only when one is dealing with a nation as a whole, and the context in which it can be applicable is the context of conquest or of foreign domination or of colonial exploitation. It would lead to disastrous consequences if the expression were extended to apply to the integral part of any country or sections of its population, or to enable such integrated or sections of the population to secede. The principle of self-determination cannot and must not be applied to bring about the fragmentation of a country or its prople. Let us not forget that the United States fought a bloody civil war to prevent, not a small part, but the whole of its South from seceding and constituting itself into an independent country. I have no doubt that a large majority of the people of that part of the United State were opposed to Abraham Lincoln and his policies and wanted the freedom to refuse to emancipate the slaves; and yet the United States Government, very rightly and properly, in my opinion, refused to break up its country by permitting a part of it the right to secede.

In the world today we have innumerable countries in Africa and

Asia with dissident minorities. Many of these minorities might like to set up governments of their own. We should have to repaint the map of the world, and many States Members of the United Nations would be broken up. Many countries today have populations made up of different races, religions and cultures, and the future of the world depends upon the evolution of multiracial States and nations of different parts of the world. Pakistan's thesis is a reactionary and obscurantist one. The thesis of self-determination which Pakistan advocated has been used in the recent past by colonialists and neo-colonialists for the disruption of newly emergent States. Pakistan would have the hands of the clock set backwards and would go back to the days when countries permitted only one religion and persecuted those who followed another faith. I appeal to this Council not to listen to contentions and arguments which would be destructive of peace and progress and which would lead to the dismemberment of many nations.

Pakistan possesses the happy gift of preaching what it has itself never practised. It asks us to hold a plebiscite in Kashmir without even so much as thinking of holding an election in its own country. It wants us to concede the principle of self-determination to a constituent part of our country without looking nearer home. Has Pakistan ever thought of permitting self-determination to the Pathans who want a State of their own, which is described as Pakhtunistan?

Let me say a word about the allegation of eviction of Indian Muslims made by Pakistan against us. I shall refute this charge not by arguments but by cold statistical facts to which there can be no answer. The Indian census figures for 1961 show that there was an increase of 25.6 per cent in the population of Muslims in India during the period between 1951 and 1961, against an over-all increase in the population of India of 21.5 per cent. Does this prove genocide or that Muslims from India are being driven out? Not only is no Indian Muslim leaving India, but the fact is that Pakistan Muslims in large number have been infiltrating into the surrounding Indian States of West Bengal, Assam and Tripura. This is clearly proved by Pakistani census figures. It will be seen from those figures that the Muslim population in East Pakistan increased by 26 per cent during the period 1951-1961. It is significant, however that much smaller increases have been recorded in some of the districts of East Pakistan bordering on India. Noakhali had an increase of only 4.7

per cent, Comilla 15.4 per cent and Bakarganj 16.8 per cent; and Sylhet indicated a rise of only 13.9 per cent, against the over-all provincial increase of 26 per cent. The Indian census figures in the neighbouring border districts of Indian States are complementary and reveal that the population of Muslims in Tripura rose by 68 per cent, in Darjeeling by 200 per cent, Dinajpur by 24 per cent, in Malda by 62 per cent, in Garo Hills by 49 per cent and in Khasi and Jaintia Hills by 88 per cent. These figures speak for themselves and are particularly revealing when it is remembered that the over-all increase in the Muslim population in India as a whole was 25.6 per cent. Every natural demographic consideration will show that this big increase could have been possible only by a large scale influx from East Pakistan, particularly from those districts which, according to the Pakistan, census figures, show abnormally low increases in population.

Let us now examine the picture on the other side. After the partition and the consequential mass migrations and killings Pakistan succeeded in getting rid of practically all non-Mulims in the Western wing. In the Eastern wing, 9.34 million were left, according to the Pakistan census figures of 1951. This was roughly 22.03 per cent of the total population of East Pakistan, which was 41.93 million. The corresponding figure for 1961, as can be seen from the Pakistan figures, is 9.38 million non-Muslims, which constitutes 18.5 per cent of the total population of 50.84 million in East Pakistan. It will be noticed that the percentage has gone down by nearly 3.6 per cent over the period of ten years. What is more remarkable is that the population of the Hindu minority in East Pakistan has remained practically stationary, although the increase in population of Muslims in Pakistan during this decade was 26 per cent. If there had been a similar natural increase in the number of non-Muslims, there should have been an increase of well over 2.25 million. Why had there not been this natural increase? The answer is that they have all been squeezed out during this period. That fits in with our records, which show the arrival in India of refugees of approximately that number. If the Foreign Minister of Pakistan has any other answer, let him come out with it. Let him also think about who is guilty of evicting minorities.

I also wish to point out that no one is evicted from India without complying with the provisions of the rule of law. In the first place, there is a careful administrative scrutiny as to the nationality of the person concerned, and it is only after the scrutiny reveals that the person in not of Indian nationality, or that he has not the necessary permit for residence or visa, than he is served with a quit notice. Further, after he has been served with a quit notice he has a right to go to the High Court for a writ on which he can satisfy the Court that the decision of the Administrative Tribunal was incorrect. Recently, both in Assam and Tripura, Judicial officers have been appointed even for the purpose of scrutiny before quit notice is served.

There is one other minor matter to which I would refer and that is that a large number of non-Muslims have been appointed in the recently constituted Ministry of the States of Jammu and Kashmir. Under normal parliamentary procedure, it is entirely the right of the Prime Minister of Jammu and Kashmir to constitute his Cabinet. In India we do not make appointments on communal considerations. It is true that we try to see, as far as possible, that no part of India and no large community goes wholly unrepresented in the Government, and that is a federal principle with which federal governments are familiar. It is a tribute to Kashmir that its Cabinet should truly reflect the inter-communal unity that prevails in the State of Jammu and Kashmir.

The reference made by the Foreign Minister of Pakistan to the dismissal by Prime Minister Shamuddin of officers of the State Government is not correct. These dismissals were made not for the motive suggested by the Foreign Minister, but as a part of the drive against inefficiency and corruption. All the officers were not dismissed, but many of them were retired. Sixty of these officers were Hindus and Sikhs. The communal colouring sought to be given is entirely without foundation.

Before I conclude, I would like to refer to some other points in the statements of the Foreign Minister of Pakistan, both in his letter to the Security Council dated 16 January 1964 [S/5517] and his statement the other day. The Foreign Minister complained that the statement of Mr. Nanda, Minister of Home Affairs of India, at the session of the Indian National Congress held at Bhubhaneshwar was inflammatry in character. Mr. Nanda spoke in Hindi and we have here the full text of his statement. I do not find anywhere in the speech that Mr. Nanda made anything even remotely suggestive or calculated to insite communal passions. On the contrary, Mr. Nanda said:

> "In case something happens there"—that is in Pakistan—"we should not allow anything to happen here"—that is, in India—"and in case some trouble arises, stern measures should be adopted and immediately everything brought to normal."

Evidently, the Foreign Minister of Pakistan has relied on some erroneous English translation of Mr. Nanda's speech. As a matter of fact, far from inciting communal passions, Mr. Nanda played a most worthy role in Culcutta in organizing joint Hindu-Muslim conciliation and peace squads which in conjunction with the stern measures taken to bring miscreants to book, including the police and military firing at them whenever necessary, helped in bringing the situation in Culcutta—which, it should be remembered, has a large population of 6 million inhabitants—within control and back normal in two to three days. It is inconceivable that on to the platform of the Indian National Congress where Mr. Nanda spoke, which is always on the side of inter-communal unity, any Minister, far less the Home Minister, would make inflammatory speeches.

The Foreign Minister of Pakistan in the course of his statement said the reply of the President of India to President Ayub Khan's latter was not helpful. What could be more helpful and sincere and earnest than the concluding paragraph of our President's letter of 16 January 1964 which has been circulated to members of the Security Council [S/5522]. I might also refer to the statement made by our President on the occasion of our Republic Day on 26 January, which is couched in the same spirit and I quote from that latter:

> "In our democracy men of all faiths have the right to live in honour and harmony under the rule of law; life and liberty of every citizen, irrespective of caste or creed, ought to be sacred to every other. Any departure from this is not only morally indefensible but politically dengerous; it weakens our internal unity at a time when the danger to our country from without is undiminished. The Government can and will take every step necessary to put down anti-social behaviour but the co-operation of people is no less important if peaceful conditions are to be preserved, for such peace is the basis on which we could build our future."

On the other hand the letter of the President of Pakistan

contained some very serious allegations against India. In our President's reply attention had to be drawn to those inaccuracies in order to put the matter in proper perspective. It is clear, however, that the spirit of our President's message was one of cordiality and constructive approach to try to solve the very urgent problem of restoring communal harmony with which both countries are faced.

The Foreign Minister of Pakistan characterized India's presence in Kashmir as colonial. I deeply regret that he has allowed himself to make such an outregeous allegation against my country. He is either ignorant of or chooses to ignore the history of India during the last fifty years. He seems to have forgotten that it was India's epic struggle against colonialism, under the leadership of Mahatma Gandhi, a long drawn struggle against the mightiest Empire in history, that brought about freedom for India and his own country. He cannot be unaware of the tremendous impact of the Indian movement against colonialism on all freedom movements in Asia and Africa and the inspiration it provided and continues to provide for such movements all over the world. It is our great satisfaction to know that this is acknoweledged by the newly emergent countries in Asia and Africa. He completely ignored the unceasing fight that India has waged in the United Nations and the support to freedom movements in Asia and Africa that India has given during the sixteen years of its independent existence and as a founder member of the United Nations. To malign such a country as colonial shows the height of prejudice; to insinuate that India's present leaders, most of all Prime Minister Jawaharlal Nehru—the greater part of whose life has been spent as a freedom fighter not only for his own country but for Asia and Africa—should follow a colonial policy is something which Pakistan alone could do.

The fact is that Kashmir has, since the dawn of history, been a part of India, a repository of Indian culture and heritage. It has shared fully in the vicissitudes of Indian history. It has been a part of the Empire of Asoka and Akbar. Srinagar, the capital of Kashmir, was founded by the Great Emperor Asoka in the third centruy B.C. The people of Kashmir are blood of our blood and flesh, and Jammu and Kashmir as one of the sixteen States of the Indian Union and the people of Kashmir as Indian citizens share in the total freedom which India enjoys. To say that Kashmir is under Indian's colonial hold is gross calumny and an insult to the people of Kashmir who are Indians and have been Indians ever since one can remember. The fact is that it is time Pakistan examined its own conscience and looked into its own heart and asked itself how it is that it is holding two-fifths of Kashmir; that, if anything, is colonial occupation.

It has often been said and, I think, it has also been repeated by the Foreign Minister of Pakistan, that the only bone of contention between India and Pakistan is Kashmir and that if the problem of Kashmir were solved to Pakistan's satisfaction, then there would be friendship and full co-operation between our two countries. I beg to differ. As I have pointed out before, it if difficult to understand the basic philosophy on which the policy of Pakistan is based. In every aspect of its foreign policy, it has disclosed an anti-Indian bias. At one time we were told by responsible Pakistan leaders that the reason why they were driven into the arms of China was our Kashmir policy; as China did not like this reason for Pakistan's friendship for China, they changed the tune and suggested that even if the problem of Kashmir was solved, Pakistan would continue to support China. In other words, Pakistan's present attitude of hostility towards India is not due to the Kashmir problem alone, but it is something more deep-seated.

The same is the attitude of Pakistan with regard to communal riots.. The argument is that riots would miraculously stop if the Kashmir problem were solved. Again, there is no connexion between Kashmir and the riots. Riots come about because of the communal policy of Pakistan and because of the incitement to communal passion of which it is guilty and of which I have given ample evidence earlier in my statement.

I wish I did not have to take so much time of the Security Council and that I had been spared the need of refuting the many allegations made by the Foreign Minister of Pakistan against us. Repetitious recriminations and fault-finding in the Security Council do not help. If these had been fruitful, we would not have been sitting here today after so many years. I was bound to set the record straight in the face of the grave and unfounded allegations made against us by Pakistan. I would like to assure you, Mr. President, and the Security Council, that despite provocations we shall continue to work towards amelioration of our unfortunate relations with Pakistan. We do not want our relations to be built on recrimination but on friendship and co-operation and mutual respect. And here I wish to say categorically on behalf of my Government and the Indian people that we wish Pakistan prosperity and well-being as a free and sovereign

State and want to build our relations as between two friendly and neighbouring countries on the basis of equality, integrity and sovereignty.

You might as well ask me what steps should be taken to alter the present unhappy situation and bring about better relations between India and Pakistan. I have not the slightest doubt in my mind that the people of both countires want to be friends. They belonged to the same country sixteen years ago. They have shared the same tradition and the same past, and even today citizens of Pakistan and India have connexions and ties of relationship. If only the Government of Pakistan made a proper gesture and gave up its present attitued, my Government would meet it more than half way. With the greatest respect, I wish to suggest that the passing of resolutions will not be helpful. It is likely only to aggravate feelings. No resolution, however well drafted, will satisfy both the parties. What is necessary is action and what we have to remember is that first thing must come first.

The first thing, therefore, is to restore normal conditions in the disturbed area of India and Pakistan and to bring about inter-communal unity and harmony in both the countires. For this purpose, we are prepared to take any and every step in co-operation with Pakistan. My Government will welcome a meeting of Ministers from both countries to discuss ways and means. We must see to it that the disgraceful incidents which took place recently never take place again. They are a scandal . . . . Secondly, threats of violence which have emanated from Pakistan from time to time, as I have pointed out, must cease. Let Pakistan unequivocally declare along with India that the two countries will never resort to war and will settle all their differences by peaceful means. In this connexion, we welcome the appeal recently issued by Chairman Khrushchev and, as you know, our Prime Minister has warmly endorsed that appeal for the peaceful settlement of territorial disputes. President Johnson has also, in principle, welcomed the renunciation of the use of force. Once a better atmosphere prevails, it will be possible—and we are prepared—to discuss with Pakistan all our outstanding differences. We believe in discussion and debate, we believe in the resolution of differences by sitting around the conference table and we will welcome Pakistan to sit with us and resolve our differences. Let me implore Pakistan to remember that we are most anxious that our two countries constituting the sub-continent of India, should remain on friendly and cordial terms. The future prospertiy and well-being of our two peoples depend on it.

11.2. Speech by Z. A. Bhutto (Pakistan) in Security Council, 1089th Meeting, February 7, 1964

In the first paragraph of his statement at the last meeting two days ago, the Education Minister of India uttered the admonition that the Security Council is not intended as a platform for propaganda against any Member State. The members of the Council will have had time to study the statement of the representative of India and to judge in what manner he allowed his own dictum.

From the beginning to the end the representative of India, consistently refusing to face the facts and issues resolutely ignoring the arguments presented by Pakistan devoted himself to hurling irresponsible charges against Pakistan and accusing it of the most unbelievable crimes. First, the very fact that Pakistan has dared to come before the Security Council, an organ charged with the primary responsibility for the maintenance of peace, is, in the eyes of India, a misdemeanor on Pakistan's part and evidence of its "agitational" approach.

Then Pakistan was accused of being a theocratic State while India which has witnessed 550 communal riots, since it became independent, is a secular State. India, the representative of India said, has a modern, rational and secular attitude while Pakistan is reactionary. Pakistan's philosophy, according to him, is that in the very nature of things, Muslims must hate the Hindus and the Hindus must hate the Muslims. Pakistan's policy is based on communal hatred and fanaticism and the Pakistan Government, he stated, "deliverately and for set purpose created an atmosphere so that riots should break out in East Pakistan" [1088th meeting, para. 59]. Then turning from accuser to judge, he delivered judgement, saying that "the Pakistan Government cannot be absolved of its responsibility for the death of these innocent people" [*ibid*]. He stated that the real reason why Pakistan was insisting on a plebiscite was : "...to try and see whether it cannot inflame communal passions in Kashmir by making the inhabitants of that State believe that their religion is in danger, and bring about the recurrence of the terrible events of the partition of India in 1947: blood-shed, migrations, untold human misery" [1088th meeting, para.32].

Then again, Pakistan was, in the view of representative of India, playing the Chinese game of weakening India internally and undermining its defence against China [*Ibid.*, para, 8] in order to prevent India from fulfilling its self-appointed role of saving the whole world from China. The permanent representative of India had promised on the eve of the meeting of the Security Council that there would be a good deal of mud-throwing at this meeting. Members will agree that the Minister of Education of India has not disappointed the expectations of his permanent Representative. I reject, with all the emphasis at my command, the false absurd charges that he has hurled against my Government.

On Kashmir itself, what the representative of India had to say was not new. Members who have studied the case will be familiar with all these arguments on Pakistan's alleged aggression, the absolute right of the despotic Maharajah to sign away the rights of the people of Kashmir, the acquisition by India of the imperial mantle of paramountcy, the three elections held in Kashmir under the surveillance of the four Indian divisions stationed there. These arguments are as contradictory as they are unconvincing. I must nevertheless, for the record, correct the misstatements and distortions with which the representative of India has sought to vitiate the simple issue of self-determination involved in the Kashmir dispute. But before I do so, may I be permitted to deal briefly with the grave accusations and charges levelled against my Government and my country by the representative of India.

It is with the utmost reluctance that I turn to the matter of communal riots which recently broke out in my country and in India. In my earlier submission to the Council [1087th meeting] I refrained from dealing at length with the communal situation in order not to worsen the existing grave situation. The Minister of Education of India, by making irresponsible, unfounded and provocative charges against my country, has in effect added fuel to the fire, and I must regret that he should have chosen the path of calumny and slander to bolster India's bad case on Kashmir. I would be failing in my duty if I did not put the record straight on the treatment of minorities in "secular, modern, rational" India.

The Education Minister of India said: "...if we are left to ourselves we will have no communal trouble whatsoever" [1088th meeting, para, 59]. How does he reconcile this statement with the fact that since the Minorities Agreement concluded between the Prime Ministers of Pakistan and India in April 1950, there have been more than 550 riots in India? In fact, hardly a Muslim festival has passed in India since 1950 without the Muslim community being subjected to attacks of communal frenzy in one part of India or another in contrast, there has been complete communal peace in Pakistan, but for two or three riots, until the recent disturbance broke out in March 1961, scores of Muslims were killed in Jubulpore and the Chief Minister of Madhya Pradesh was reported to have said that the city "looked like a cremation ground". Was not India being left to itself then?

In October 1961, the Home Minister of the State of Uttar Pradesh admitted that behind the then current anti-Muslim riots, there was a wide and deep-laid conspiracy. He declared:

> "It can go on record that a common pattern is discernible behind all these incidents. Murders were committed in individual knife attacks by young people coming from the section of our society whose members would faint at the sight of blood."

He went on to say:

> "This showed that these people have received training in the art of killing. One would not be surprised, as days pass, if communal incidents increase in number and in intensity."

Did this Indian official say that Pakistan was training these murderes? Could he say that Pakistan was behind the deep conspiracy? Was Pakistan inciting the Hindus of India to kill Muslims? Was not then India being left to itself?

Speaking in the Indian Parliament Mr. Syed Bardudduja, a veteran of the Indian Struggle for independence, expressed the agony that the Indian Muslim were suffering soon after the gruesome atrocities of Jubbulpore and Malda were perpetrated:

> "Even in this secular democracy, Mussulmans and all the minorities of India have suffered terribly. We apprehended that minorities would have no quarter, no shelter, no opportunity for self-expression. Politically, socially, culturally, economically and even physically they would be at the merey of forces of reaction. That is exactly what has happened."

Continuing, this Member of the Indian Parliament said:

> "Mussulmans have been pursued to the bitter end. They have been tortured with every refinement of cruelty and barbarous savagery. In malignity, in cruelty, in savagery, in criminality, the records of Jubbulpore and Malda surpass any records during the British regime."

This systematic massacre of Muslim followed a pattern which was particularly noticeable during the recent riots, when the attacks were aimed at driving the Muslims out of West Bengal, forcing them to seek sheller in East Pakistan. Although a large number of men, women and children were killed, the emphasis was on setting fire to their houses, looting and destroying their shops and industrial establishments so as to deprive them, at once, of their shelter and their means of livelihood. The fact that there have since been open demands by militant Hindu organizations for a population exchange tends to support my Government's fear that the real intention of those responsible for riots is to drive the Muslims out of West Bengal into East Pakistan.

The representative of India accused Pakistan of having incited the recent riots. I do not wish to harrow the Council with a recital of the blood-curdling headlines and reports carrieds in the Indian West Bengal Press on the regrettable incidents which occurred in Khulna and Jessore. Let us turn instead to the testimony of impartial, foreign observers. As regards the recents riots in Calcutta, here is a report from Calcutta by James Mitchell, correspondent of *The Observer* of London, published on 25 January:

> "While rioters made no great secret of their plans, the police force in the first day seemed always to be every where except in the streets attacked."

He blames what he calls "the black week of Calcutta" on "police laxity" and says that the authorities "let the situation get completely out of hand" and that the result was that about 500 people were killed. According to this report, tens of thousands lost their homes because, after the riots started, interested people paid big sums of money to keep them up, so that landlords would clear their land of poor tenants. Did Pakistan inspire this cold-bloded design?

We hear a great deal about the secular outlook in India. A Calcutta daily, the *New Age*, of 19 January 1964 said:

> "Unfortunately the secular parties could not take proper initiative in the matter and the so-called nationalist papers fanned up communal hatred. The Jan Sangh and Hindu Mahasabha were already in field whipping up frenzy. All these contributed to the rapid deterioration in the situation."

I had no intention to bring out these gruesome facts but I had been compelled to do so by the allegations levelled against my Government before this Council. I was shocked that the Eduction Minister of India fell victim to the temptation of quoting highly exaggerated figures of deaths during the recent troubles in East Pakistan on the basis of a Reuters dispatch. The sources in Dacca quoted by the correspondent of Reuters have themselves contradicted the wildly exaggerated figures that were given out. I regret that the Education Minister of India had to resort to the use of unverified reports which he should have known were contradicted. The Pakistan High Commission in New Delhi issued an immediate contradiction on 24 January. The irresponsibility of the Indian Government's news media in giving circulation to such false and inflammatory reports earned the well merited stricture of *The Times* of London. In the issue of 23 January, its Delhi correspondent observed:

> "The Indian Government's seriousness in discouraging circulation of news about communal violence in Pakistan was put into doubt today by All-India Radio's treatment of the Reuters correspondent's report from Dacca. The midday news broadcasts made that report their first item and it still figured prominently in bulletins later tonight. All-India Radio is a completely subservient agent of the Government and its treatment of the report must suggest that Delhi is not as apprehensive about dangers of repercussions in West Bengal as its recent experience should have made it."

My Government firmly believes that communal peace and security is an essential condition for civilized life. My Government mobilized all its resources to bring the situation under complete control in Pakistan. I had to go into this question at some length, not only to disprove the false allegations made by India, but to emphasize one central fact: It is that the denial of the right of self-determination to the people of Jammu and Kashmir is a constant source of tension. It is embittering the relations between India and Pakistan. As a result of this festering dispute, recurring brutal attacks on the Muslim minority have been taking place in India ever since its independence in 1947.

It is this attitude of the Government of India which has created a vicious climate in Kashmir and in certain parts of India, to which I invited you attention in my letter of 16 January 1964 [S/5517] from which I quote:

> "It is this climate, in which the political, religious and cultural rights of the people of the State are treated with scorn by their Indian rulers that has made possible such criminal acts of sacrilege and vandalism as the recent theft of the sacred hair from the shrine near Srinagar and the attempt to burn a Muslim shrine in Kishtwar in Jammu Province."

It is this same climate which encourages militant organizations in India to launch frequent communal attacks and outrage on the Muslims and call for their expulsion from India in exchange for the Hindu minority in Pakistan. It is this disregard of human rights which is the root cause of the existing upheaval in Kashmir and of the grave communal tension in West Bengal. It all flows from the fact that the Kashmir dispute has been allowed to fester for sixteen years.

While speaking about the eviction of Indian Muslims from Tripura, Assam and the border districts of West Bengal, the Education Minister of India took shelter behind a massive array of census figures. He named the districts of Noakhali, Comilla, Sylhet and Bakarganj, where the relatively slow growth of population is attributed to the migration of muslim population to India. Of these, Bakarganj has no common border with any part of India and can have no relevance to the issue.

It is interesting to note that only three border districts were named by the representative of India, whereas My Mensingh, Rangpur, Dianjpur, Rajshahi, Kushtia and others are also border districts, but he carefully left them out. The reasons are not far to seek. The West Bengal districts in which a relatively high increase of

Muslim population was shown by him are not contiguous to the Pakistan districts where a slow rate of increase on Muslim population was recorded. Obviously, therefore, there can be no possible connexion between these trends of population growth. It is possible to refute the arguments that he had advanced by quoting extensively from the census reports of India and Pakistan to prove that the case he weants to establish is based merely on a jugglery of figures. Even without going into a detailed examination of the census reports, one can draw certain obvious conclusions from common sense.

A system of passports and visas was introduced in 1952 to regulate comprehensively the movements of Indians and Pakistanis across the border. The Indian authorities introduced a strict system of border checkpoints to prevent the entry of non-Indians through unauthorized routes into Indian territory. These restrictive measures resulted in almost complete stoppage of entry to Assam, Tripura and West Bengal.

Apart from these restrictions, one has to remember the communal feelings and tensions existing at the time of partition of the India-Pakistan sub-continent to appreciate the improbability of large-scale Muslim migration from Pakistan to India. With memories of incredible sufferings, of loss of human lives and destruction of property, it is inconceivable that hundreds of thousands of Muslims, as alleged by India, would surrender the safety and security of their homeland in Pakistan to migrate with their women and children to the uncertainty and perils awaiting them in a hostile land beyond the frontier.

But let us not get involved in a pedantic controversy, for we deal here not with cold statistics but with human tragedy. The fact of the matter is that hundreds and thousands of innocent men, women and children have been driven across the border as part of a premeditated and cold-blooded plot to get rid of Muslim citizen from Indian territory bordering on East Pakistan. The special correspondent of *The Times* of London in his dispatch of 5 December 1963 carried a vivid eye-witness account of his experience:

> "In camps and compounds in the Comilla district of Pakistan there are thousands of Muslims who have been forcibly evicted from their homes in India and driven into East Pakistan. The pretext for the eviction is that these people had illegally

entered the Indian territory of Tripura... and that they have now simply been sent back: but the evidence available from them shows that most were long settled in Tripura, even from generations."

Continuing, he said:

"But the long-settled Muslims who are expelled come into East Pakistan as broken refugees with nowhere to turn, and the Government here now has about 47,000 on its hands. The evictions began in the middle of last year and continued at a rate of hundreds each week, the flow being augmented now by those Muslims who flee from the inimical climate apparently created in Tripura by the mass evictions.

"Putting it at its best, the established residents of Tripura, Indian citizen by right, who have been uprooted and dumped over the border with no formalities, or only the sketchiest, are the victims of local authorities in that territory whose excesses are not fully appreciated in Delhi. They may be acting in response to local forces of communal enmity and greed for land, but they are acting with injustice and inhumanity."

The special correspondent of *The Times* went on to say:

"Some received 'Show cause" notices warning them that they would be expelled unless they could prove that they had been in India before 1952. They say that they went to court with their papers and were told that the magistratge would make further investigations—but that a day or two later the police and lorries came to their villages and they were forced in and driven to the border. Others recieved no notices or warning before the police vehicles arrived. Some of their papers were kept by the court or destroyed by the police who expelled them..."

And yet the Education Minister of India waxed eloquent about the respect for the processes of law in his country. He said: "I also wish to point out that no one is evicted from India without complying with the provisions of the rule of law." [1088th meeting, para 75]. In view of what impartial observers have to say about the compliance with the rule of law, I believe further comment is superfluous. Concluding his dispatch, the correspondent of *The Times* said:

> "...it is undeniable that a great wrong is being done to the Indian Muslims in Tripura. In considering what it regards as the problem of Muslims settled in that territory who have no legal right to be there, the Indian Government might consider the analogous problem in Ceylon, where the Government would like to get rid of a million Indians."

That is what an impartial observer of a leading British newspaper has to say about the brutal and inhuman methods adopted for the mass eviction of Indian Muslims from Assam, Tripura and West Bengal. The President of the Hindu Mahasabha, Mr. V.G. Deshpande, declared on 15 January 1964 that an exchange of population on Government level was the only way to ensure the safety of minorities in India and Pakistan. He said: "They"—the Hindus—"must be brought to India and the Muslim population in Assam and West Bengal must be sent to East Pakistan". An exchange of population was demanded in public meetings and newspaper editorials in many parts of India. All these point towards one conclusion, namely, that there is a move to expel Indian Muslims by illegal and inhuman methods from Indian territory bordering on East Pakistan for no fault of theirs but the fact that they happen to be Muslims.

The Education Minister of India claimed that all these tens of thousands of Indian Muslims who were forcibly evicted from their hearths and homes and pushed across the border into East Pakistan are not Indian nationals. If that be so, India should have no objection to having the facts verified by an impartial inquiry.

Speaking on this matter before the General Assembly of the United Nations on 30 September 1963, I said:

> "I would declare here before you that the question whether these people are being evicted or whether they are infiltrators can be decided by a United Nations inquiry commission, by an international inquiry commission... or by any third-party commission agreed to by India and Pakistan. These are ascertainable facts. It can be ascertained by any inquiry

commission whether these unfortunate, helpless people driven by the Indian bayonet into Pakistan are Indians or Pakistanis."

We stand by this declaration even now. We are prepared to have the matter examined by an international commission of inquiry. If India's hands are clean, as it claims, let it come forward and agree to an international commission to verify the facts. The truth in this case is that India is guilty of inhuman and brutal treatment of its own citizens on the ground of their religion. It is indeed a sad commentary on its secularist pretensions.

The Education Minister of India stated that the President of Pakistan refused to issue a joint declaration with the President of India to our respective peoples appealing for peace and harmony and that Pakistan, in effect, also rejected the proposal of the Government of India that the Home Ministers of the two countries should meet and visit the scenes of disturbance and suggest what further steps should be taken to prevent such happenings.

I have already dealt in my statement of 3 February [1087th meeting] with the subject of a joint declaration by the two Presidents. The President of Pakistan pointed out that he had already appealed to the people of Pakistan to maintain communal peace and harmony and what was really needed was to take deterrent measures against communal and criminal elements which were responsible for the riots in both the countries and to re-establish conditions of security for the refugees of the minority communities to enable them to return to their homes. This action my Government for its part took at once, and the flames of communal disturbance were stamped out in my country.

Pakistan did not reject the proposal of the Government of India for a meeting between the Home Ministers of the two Governments. We have made a positive and constructive response. This is that once order has been restored, the two Ministers could meet in Rawalpindi in Pakistan or Delhi in India to discuss measures necessary to enable the refugees from the communal disturbances, as well as those who have been evicted by India from Assam, Tripura and West Bengal during the last two years, to return to their homes.

It is the policy of my Government to encourage the refugees to return to their homes. My Government is pledged to ensure the security of their lives and property and to restore their confidence. The Indian Home Minister's statement of 29 January that conditions in East Pakistan have become such as to make the migration of Hindus inevitable and that conditions for the granting of migration certificates to them in East Pakistan would have to be eased... We regret this statement all the more because communal harmony has been fully restored in East Pakistan. My Government is apprehensive that if a new influx of Hindus into India takes place as a result of the Indian Policy of facilitating migration, the position of the Muslim minority in East Bengal, Calcutta and, for that matter, in all other parts of India will be further imperilled.

The Pakistan High Commissioner in Calcutta was besieged owing to the communal riots in that city by the thousands of Muslims demanding emergency certificate to migrate to East Pakistan. We did not respond. In spite of the carnage which took place in Calcutta, no Pakistani leader made any statement or offered encouragement to Muslims in West Bengal or elsewhere in India to move into Pakistan. In our view, the solution of this problem, I must reiterate, lies in bringing about peace and security establishing a sense of confidence among the minorities and in taking energetic measures for their rehabilitation and resettlement. We seek the co-operation of the Government of India in enabling the refugees to return to their homes.

The representative of India permitted himself to make disparaging remarks about the democratic institutions of Pakistan. May I remind him that each country must fashion its self-governing institutions according to its own genius. It is not necessary for me to cite examples of modern and progressive countries which have found, as a result of their experience, that the system of indirect elections and electoral colleges best meets their political nad constitutional requirements. Pakistan is not the only country which elects its President and Parliament by an electoral college. The parliamentary form of government is not the only form of democratic government. Many countries, particularly those of Asia, Africa and Latin America, and even of Europe and the United States, have found the Presidential system to be necessary to ensure their stability and economic progress.

The Education Minister of India called Pakistan "a theocratic State". May I ask him wheather we are governed by a hierarchy of priests? The official name of our State is the Islamic Republic of Pakistan. Does this nomenclature make us a theocracy? Several Muslim countries, Members of the United Nations, have the same description or have given recognition to Islam as the official religion of the State. Then are they all priest-ridden? There are also Western European and Latin American States, the Constitutions of which provide a place for Christianity as the established State religion. The representative of India, I am certain, would not on that account classify them as theocracies.

We have often been told that in the Indian Union fundamental rights are guaranteed. This is surely not a unique phenomeon. All member States of the United Nations are pledged to respect human rights, and it is their general practice to ensure its observance. The Constitution of Pakistan is no exception, and we see no reason to claim any special credit for treating all the citizens of our multiracial, multireligious and multilingual republic as equals before the law. We do not therefore consider it in the least anomalous that the head of the judiciary of our Islamic Republic should be a Pakistani Christian. The Chief Justice of the Supreme Court of Pakistan is a Pakistani Christain belonging to the Roman Catholic denomination who, under our Constitution, is the final authority in the interpretation of all laws, including the personal and religious laws of the Muslims, who constitute the majority in Pakistan. We have given representation in the highest services of our State to the minority communities whose leaders have publicly borne testimony to the precept and practice of tolerance in Pakistan.

We are told that India is more democratic than Pakistan. Comparisons are odious. But in this context let me take the liberty of quoting the President of India himself, as reported by the *Indian Express* of Bombay of 4 October 1963. President Radhakrishnan is reported to have said:

> "What we have in India today is not real democracy but only a phony democracy. If we are true democrats, which I may say we are not, there would not have been so much of discontented and ill will. Then they would not have any kind of nepotism, corruption and communal prejudice which have brought down the country to degradation."

The representative of India also attacked the philosophical and spiritual foundations of Pakistan. He admitted that India and Pakistan are two nations but rejected the "two-nations theory". The basis of this "theory" is that, because Hindu society is organized on the religious caste system of antiquity, in which personal status is determined by birth into a particular caste in an ascending and decending series of worth and dignity, we the people of Pakistan wished to have established a State of our own in the contingus Muslim majority areas in the north-west and the north-east of the sub-continent, wherein we could live our own way of life governed by the principles of equality which are enshrined in the religion of Islam. The caste system is by its very nature exclusive. It governs those within its fold from the cradle to the grave. Notwithstanding the fundamental rights spelled out in the Indian Constitution, the caste system has not been made illegal, though untouchability has been forbidden, at last—but only in the law. Distinguished philosophers of history have established that exclusive societies invite disintegration from within. This is what happened in the sub-continent in 1947.

We cannot understand whenever a dispute is involved, India seeks to make reference to its democratic and secular character, although Indian society is steeped in the caste system, in a venal system to the exclusion of all other people belonging to all other creeds. It is a system confined to the Hindus. Anyone outside the pale of the caste system is worse than an untouchable, a sub-human. So I say that with such a society, with such a situation, with this mentality prevailing in India, with its treatment of minorities, with the manner in which it has held Kashmir in bondage, there can really be no peace between our two countries. Remove the dispute of Kashmir, and you will find that we can live in peace and we must live in peace, because it is Kashmir alone that divides us.

It is no use making *ultra vires* references to democracy. India displays its democracy like a sensile person displaying his false teeth. Its democracy is false as the teeth of a senile person who parades his false teeth everywhere. There is democracy in the United Kingdom. Does the United Kingdom always make mention of its democratic institutions when it comes into the Security Council? We have old and established democracies in France and in the United States of America. Is reference always made to the democratic character of their societies in seeking the adjudication and settlement of disputes? The United Nations Charter is wedded to the principle of the equality of all nations, irrespective of their internal system. What has the internal system of Pakistan to do with the settlement of the Kashmir dispute?

Let me therefore now turn to the main question before the Security Council. The representative of India made no attempt to explain the declarations of the Government of India, which I quoted in my last statement to the Security Council, that the so-called accession was only provisional, conditional and subject to ratification by the people of Jammu and Kashmir through a plebiscite under international auspices. Instead he chose to dismiss my submissions as "a mixture of misstatements, omissions of material facts and refusal to face up to the clear provisions of the Indian Independence Act" [1088th meeting, para 17]. A case is not proved by glossing over or ignoring inconvenient facts.

In our previous representations before the Council, we have endeavoured to explain at ample length our position regarding the accession of States to India or to Pakistan. Of course, there was no controversy regarding those States where the Ruler and the people were of the same view, and no conflict arose between India and Pakistan on that score. In all those cases, naturally, the Ruler signed the Instrument of Accession to one or the other country, and no trouble ensued either between him and his people or between India and Pakistan. The Question arose regarding those States where there was disagreement between the Ruler and his people in regard to accession. On this question, the Indian Education Minister made three statements, and I shall invite the Council to examine them not in relation to our arguments, but in the light of the position internationally advanced by the Government of India. I shall take each of those statements separately.

The first statement is:

> "It is significant there was no provision for consisting the people of the princely States concerned. Nor was there any provision that the accession had to be ratified by ascertaining the wishes of the people of the acceding States." [*Ibid*., para. 11.]

Contrast this statement with the following, quoted from the White Paper of the Government of India issued on 10th August 1948:

> "The Government of India are firmly of the view that whatever sovereign rights reverted to these States on the lapse of paramountcy, they vest in the people, and conditions must be

created in every State for a free and unfettered exercise of these rights."

Or, contrast it with this solemn statement made by the Indian representative at the 227th meeting of the Security Council:

> "On the question of accession, the Government of India has always enunciated the policy that in all cases of dispute the people of the State concerned should make the decision."

These are clear words. The position is not only that the people have to be consulted: It is they who have to make the decision.

And how can the statement now made by the Education Minister of India be sustained by the one made by the Indian representative at the 264th meeting of the Security Council? he said:

> "No doubt the Ruler, as the head of the State, has to take action in respect of accession. When he and his people are in agreement as to the dominion to which they should accede, he applies for accession to that Dominion. However, when he takes one view and his people take another view, the wishes of the people have to be ascertained. When so ascertained, the Ruler has to take action in accordance with the verdict of the people. That is our position."

By "our position" he means the position of the Government of India. The words are to be noted: "That is our position." This is not the position now advanced by the Education Minister of India.

And what would he make of this statement of the Prime Minister of India himself, made at a public meeting in New Delhi and reported by *The Times of India* of Bombay, of 7 July 1952:

> "In any event from the start, India was committed to the principle of letting the final word regarding accession rest with the people of the princley States and" let us mark these words—"there could be no getting away from that commitment. In fact, that was why India had accepted Kashmir's accession only provisionally in 1947, pending the expression of the will of the people."

That is the statement of the Prime Minister of India. I could elaborate this argument, but the statement of the Prime Minister of India should at least suffice to take care of the thesis that the Education Minister of India now seeks to foist upon us.

The second statement of the Education Minister of India is:

> "There was no question whatsoever with regard to the religious complexion of the population of the princely States. The question whether one princely State should accede to India or Pakistan was left to the determination of the Ruler of the State." [1018th meeting, para.12.]

Is that true? I ask, was there no question whatsoever with regard to the religious complexion of the population of the princely States? The Education Minister of India says no. But how was the question answered by his Prime Minister in his telegram of 8 November 1947 addressed to the Prime Minister of Pakistan? He said:

> "...but it is essential, in order to restore good relations between the two Dominions, that there should be acceptance of the principle that, where the Ruler of a State does not belong to the community to which the majority of his subject belong, and where the State has not accepted accession to that Dominion whose majority community is the same as the States, the question whether the State has finally accepted accession to one or the other Dominion should be ascertained by reference to the will of the people."

Then, again, if there was "no question whatsoever with regard to the religious complexion of the population of the princely States", why did the Government of India protest against the accession of the State of Junagadh, which had a Hindu majority, to Pakistan? What did they actually protest about? They said, and I quote from the telegram of the Governor-General of India addressed to the Governor-General of Pakistan on 22 September 1947:

> "...Pakistan Government have unilaterally proceeded to action which it was made plain Government of India could never and do not acquiesce in. Such acceptance of accession by Pakistan

cannot but be regarded by Government of India as an encroachment of India's sovereignty and territory and inconsistent with friendly relations that should exist between the two Dominions. This action of Pakistan is considered by Government of India to be a clear attempt to cause disruption in integrity of India by extending influence and boundries of Dominion of Pakistan in utter violation of principles on which partition was agreed upon and effected...

"...possibility of Junagadh's accession to Pakistan Dominion in teething opposition from its Hindu population of above eighty per cent has given rise to serious concern and apprehension to local population and all surrounding States which have acceded to Indian Dominion."

Finally, if there was no question whatsoever with regard to the relegious complexion of the population of the princely States, how does one understand the following account given by no other person than Mr. V.P. Menon, the eminent official of the Government of India who was handling the accession of the princely States of India? On page 117 of his book, *The Story of the Integration of the Indian States,* Mr. Menon state:

"Lord Mountbatten made it clear that from a purely legal standpoint there was no objection to the ruler of Jodhpur acceding to Pakistan; but the Maharajah should, he stressed, consider seriously the consequences of his doing so, having regard to the fact that he himself was a Hindu; that his State was populated predominantly by Hindus and that the same applied to the States surrounding Jodhpur. In the light of these considerations, if the Maharajah were to accede to Pakistan , his action would surely be in conflict with the principle underlying the partition of India on the basis of Muslim and non-Muslim majority areas; and serious communal trouble inside the State would be the inevitable consequence of such affiliation."

If a Hindu State wanted to accede to India, India invoked the principle of partition, namely, religious composition and geographical contiguity. When it is a question of a Muslim State acceding to Pakistan, India says that the principles of partition do not apply to princely States. Surely some measure of consistency is essential in all human relations, whether individual or international. If so, how does the distingushed Education Minister of India expect us to regard his statement now that there was "no question with regard to the religious complexion of the population of the princely States"? He state: "The question of religion did not come into play at all." [1088th meeting, para. 14.] Did it not come into play with respect to Junagadh? And Jodhpur? And Hyderabad? It did. So, why should it not come into play with respect to Kashmir?

The third statement of the distinguished Education Minister of India is:

> "...there is no substance in the suggestion that the accession of Jammu and Kashmir was not complete and absolute because the people of that State had not been consulted nor been given opportunity to express their choice."
>
> He added later:
>
> "Jammu and Kashmir became an integral part of India when the Instrument of Accession was signed and accepted and from that day till today it continues to occupy the same position vis-a-vis the Indian Union and no question can possibly arise of annexing Kashmir or further integrating it into the Indian Union. You cannot make more complete what is already complete."[*Ibid.*, paras. 15 and 16.]

I repeat : "You cannot make more complete what is already complete." That sounds very nice. The key words here are 'complete' and 'absolute'. Contrast these with the adjectives employed by the representatives of India in the past to describe this so-called accession. The representatives of India at that time said in the Security Council, referring to the so-called accession of Kashmir of India: "...it acceded, tentatively, in October 1947" [463d meeting, p. 20]. The word here is 'tentative', which is far from 'absolute' and 'complete'.

Then again, if the accession was 'complete' and 'absolute' what did the Prime Minister of India say in a telegram he sent to the Prime Minister of Pakistan on 28 October 1947—just after the so called accession? He said: "In regard to accession also, it has been made clear that this is subject to reference to people of State and their dicision." It was either absolute and complete or it was subject to reference to the people. The distinguished Education Minister of India says it was the other. Whom is the United Nations to believe? Whom are we to believe? What does one make of this statement made by the Prime Minister of India on 2 November 1947:

> "...let me make it clear that it has been our policy all along that where there is a dispute about the accession of a State of either Dominion, the accession must be made by the people of that State. It is in accordance with this policy that we have added a proviso to the Instrument of Accession of Kashmir."

Finally, if Kashmir is an integral part of India, what question is left to be adjusted and adjudicated between India and Pakistan? What is it that we have been negotiated about, and what is it that we can negotiate about now? May I hare refer to the joint communique issued by the Governments of India and Pakistan at the conclusion of the bilateral negotiations which I conducted on behalf of Pakistan and which were held at the ministerial level between India and Pakistan from December 1962 to May 1963 for six months. The communique said, at the conclusion of the six months of talks on the Kashmir dispute, as follows:

> "...the two Ministers recorded with regret that no agreement could be reached on the settlement of the Kashmir dispute." If Kashmir is an integral part of India, and if this integration is absolute and complete, what is this "Kashmir dispute', and what were we trying to settle? What agreement is there for us to reach? The distinguished representative of India says, referring to Azad Kashmir, that it is "a part of territory which by International law is as much a part of Indian territory as Bombay or Delhi is". [1088th meeting, para,8.]

Adept comment on the attitude behind this statement is furnished by another statement of the Prime Minister of India made in the Indian Parliament on 26 June 1952. The Indian Prime Minister said then:

> "It is . . . a matter of dealing with a situation which is very delicate, very difficult and the decision for which ultimately lies with the few million people in Kashmir – not even with this Parliament... India is a great country. Kashmir is almost the heart of Asia. There is an enormous difference, not only in geography, but in all kinds of factors there. Do not think you are dealing with a part of U.P. [the United Provinces], Bihar or Gujarat..."

The United Provinces or Bihar or Gujarat are Indian States, and the Indian Prime Minister emphasized that there is an 'enormous difference' between these States and Kashmir. The position taken by the distinguished representative of India here is that there is no difference and he states that Kashmir is as much a part of India as Bombay and Delhi.

In the context of the question of accession, the distinguished representative of India stated that when India was partitioned, "a part of the country seceding" constituted itself into Pakistan, and he claimed: "...the present Government of India was the successor Government to the Government of the United Kingdom. Pakistan was a new State which came into existence" [1088th meeting para. 11]. May I remind him that Pakistan came into existence on the partition of the sub-continent not as a new State but as a co-successor State, together with India, to the British Government in India. The same excerpt which he has quoted from the Cabinet Mission's memorandum of 12 May 1946 speaks of "the succession Government or Governments in British India." This memorandum was published more than a year before partition. At that time it was not certain that the sub-continent would be partitioned into two states; but this was a clear possibility. The Cabinet Mission's memorandum provided for this possibility and hence the reference to more than one successor Government in British India.

It is true that Pakistan was admitted to the United Nations and other international organizations as a new State, but this was done by virtue of its express consent under the Indian Independence (International Arrangements) Order of 1947. In all other respects the same Order provided, as for instance, in regard to the rights and obligations devolving from treaties and international agreements to which undivided India was a party, that both India and Pakistan were to inherit these rights and obligations as successor States of the

British Government in India. I would not like to take up the time of the Security Council to adduce further arguments in support of this submission. A reference to the Preamble and the various sections of the Indian Independence Act, 1947, will make it clear that the Act speaks of "two Independent Dominions" to be set up in India to be known respectively as India and Pakistan as from 15 August 1947. In passing, may I observe that paramountcy which ended with the entering into force of the Indian Independence Act of 1947 was a doctrine not of international law, but *sui geneeris* and, according to British legal authorities, peculiar to the constitutional development of the British Indian Empire.

I pass over the account given by the Minister of India of the circumstances in Kashmir which formed the genesis of the dispute. I do so because the truthful and balanced account of these circumstances is on record in the Security Council, set forth at length in its proceedings. I also do so because it is irrelevant whether one or the other account is true. In terms of the Charter of the United Nations and in terms of the moral and legal obligations of States, the controversies which existed before the acceptance of an agreement cannot be revived in connexion with the implementation of the agreement. Once an agreement is reached, you cannot revive the controversy which was resolved by the agreement. The controversies closes as soon as there is an agreement in the Kashmir dispute, the allegations of aggression by the two parties against each other were debated in the Council and in the United Nations Commission on India and Pakistan before that body's resolutions were adopted. The adoption of these resolutions and their acceptance by the two parties evidently disposed of the continuous issues which existed prior to them.

You cannot enter into an international agreement and then refuse to implement it on the basis of the issues which the agreement is meant to close. The assumption that the resolutions of the Commission could not be repudiated by either party without dishonouring an international agreement and committing an act inimical to peace has been confirmed repeatedly by numerous declarations made on behalf of the Government of India. The Indian representative, at the 608th meeting of the Secutiry Council, said:

> "We cannot be a party to the reversal of previous decisions taken by the United Nations Commission with the agreement

of the parties." [608th meeting, para. 36]

At the 769th meeting of the Council, then representative of India said the following:

> "I said the other day that this engagement bound our two countries. I should like to say that there are three parties engaged in this whole process.
>
> "The Security Council is a party to the resolution of 13 August 1948..." [769th meeting, paras. 77 and 78.]

The same representative stated the following at the 773rd meeting of the Council:

> "The resolution of 17 January 1948, and the resolutions of the United Nations Commission for India and Pakistan, the assurances given, these are all resolutions which carry a greater weight – that is because we have accepted them, we are parties to them, whether we like them or not" [773rd meeting, para. 83.]

This, in brief, has been the status of the agreement arrived at between India and Pakistan through the effort and authority of the United Nations. The obligatory character of these resolutions arose not only from the consent of the parties, but also from the fact that the agreement "enshrined" the prinicple of self-determination which is integral to the concepts of Charter. It was further enhanced by the fact that it was only on the basis of the acceptance of the resolutions that the cease-fire agreement was reached between India and Pakistan and the people of Kashmir who were fighting against the Indian army were persuaded to lay down their arms. Now the representative of India says that the –

> ". . . two resolutions of the Security Council dealing with plebiscite were conditional and contingent on Pakistan vacating its aggression, and that condition has not been complied with. It is really more than a condition. It was the very basis on which these two resolutions were founded, and the condition not having been complied with and the basis having disappeared,

> these resolutions are no longer binding on us. In any case, by the passage of time and various factors intervening they have become obsolete." [1088th meeting, para. 33.]

I dealt, I hope sufficiently, in my statement to the Security Council on 3 February [1087th meeting] with this theory of passage of time to show how untenable it is. I shall not, therefore, dwell on the subject any further, apart from adding that to characterize the decisions of the Security Council as obsolete shows what little importance India attaches to this extremely important organ of the United Nations.

The Government of India accepted the resolutions of the United Nations Commission of 13 August 1948 and 5 January 1949 providing for a cease-fire, a truce agreement, and a plebiscite in Jammu and Kashmir to determine the question of its accession to India or to Pakistan after – and I stress "after" – this question of aggression had been considered. The question of a conditional and contingent acceptance of those two resolutions, therefore, does not arise. The Security Council is fully aware that Pakistan is not required by the terms of the two resolutions to make a unilateral and unconditional withdrawal of its military forces from the State. The withdrawals have to be reciprocal and synchronized in such a manner that at the end of process, while all armed forces of Pakistan have left the State, the bulk of the Indian armed forces have also vacated the State. The obligation of Pakistan to withdraw comes into force and operation only after the conclusion of a truce agreement under the resolution of 13 August 1948, which provides for a synchronized withdrawal in the manner and to the extent stipulated.

Who is responsible for the deadlock with respect to the truce agreement, that is, with respect to the demilitarization of the State? India balked at the synchronization of the withdrawal of the forces on the two sides. India withheld its cooperation in formulating a truce agreement. India refused to help in establishing conditions which would involve the complete withdrawal of the Pakistan forces from Kashmir. India rejected the proposal for stationing a United Nations force there for the purpose. After having done all those things, India began to complain that the Pakistan forces had not withdrawn. Certainly it requires no "deep knowledge of law", to quote the expression of the Education Minister of India, to understand that a party cannot challenge the binding character of an agreement by pleading its own failure to perform it.

India has always charged Pakistan with the responsibility for this deadlock, while refusing to submit its assertion to impartial secrutiny by investigation or to limited arbitration. In my statement of 3 February I referred to the offer made by Pakistan to the Security Council in 1962, that if an impartial determination should show that Pakistan is in fact responsible for the situation, my Government would rectify the default "through the speediest method at the earliest possible moment so that the way may be opened towards full implementation of the resolutions" (1008th meeting, para. 166). The fact that India has rejected this offer shows that its accusation against Pakistan is only a pretext for continuing its unlawful occupation of the State and its refusal to enable the people of Jammu and Kashmir to exercise the right of self-determination.

But even if we might suppose for a moment, for the purpose of argument, that there is some strength in this allegation of non-compliance by us, what is its effect? Any infraction of Pakistan cannot be allowed, in fairness, to rob the people of Kashmir of the right to decide their future which they have been assured by the resolutins of the United Nations Commissions on India and Pakistan. Surely, the people of Kashmir cannot be penalized for the faults of Pakistan.

If you ponder this consideration, you will realize that the entire case of the Education Minister of India rests on the exclusion of the rights and interests of the people of Kashmir. He wants to convert the whole issue into a pseudo-legal one between India and Pakistan and make it void of all human and moral significance. I say "pseudo-legal" advisedly because, if the representative of India were serious in formulating the legal issues implicit in the dispute, then they would also be prepared to accept their determination by a competent authority. But they merely try to give it a legal character in order to confuse issues and to divert attention from the rights and further by their repeated allegations of aggression against Pakistan.

What is there in this allegation that can be at all relevant to the solution of the problem from a human point of view? The question whether Pakistan did or did not commit aggression in Kashmir can be answered only by the people of Kashmir. For, if Pakistan did commit aggression in Kashmir, then evidently it was the people of Kashmir who were its victims. Surely then, India should be insistent on an unfettered plebiscite in Kashmir which would enable the victims to return an overwhelming verdict against the aggressor. That it is Pakistan that seeks this plebiscite, and India that rejects it, shows how much truth the Government of India feels there is in its contentions. It proves which of the two parties bears the burden of guilt. Pakistan has nothing to hide : it is prepared to stand the light of day, which means a clear and open ascertainment of the will of the people of Kashmir. It is India that seeks to ensure that light should never dawn. But the light of day will dawn.

In regard to the measures of annexation of the State of Jammu and Kashmir, to which I drew attention in my letter to the President of the Security Council of 16 January 1965 (S/5517), and in my statement of 3 February, the distinguished representative of India has extolled the alleged benefits that those measures would confer upon the people of Jammu and Kashmir. The point that I have the honour to make in regard to these measures is not that they are or are not blessing to people of Kashmir but that they are being imposed by an unlawful authority, in disregard of the injunctins of the Security Council, as set forth in the resolutions of the Council of 30 March 1951 and 24 January 1957. I would request the Security Council to note that the Government of India remains impenitent in regard to the further extension of such measures; and, on the contrary, as declared by the representative of India, it is set on imposing them.

This bring us to the heart of the problem with which, in our submission, the Council is faced to the India-Pakistan question. On the one hand, the representative of India says that Pakistan has "no *locus standi* whatsoever to make any complaint with ragard to what India is doing" in Kashmir, that "no amount of declamation from Pakistan will deter the Government of India" from proceeding further to implement its designs of annexation of the State, that the resolutions of the United Nations Commission for India and Pakistan "have become obsolete" and that the Government of India 'under no circumstances agree to the holding of a plebiscite in Kashmir".

On the other hand, the representative of India makes an offer to "discuss with Pakistan all our outstanding differences". The question is : How can the offer be taken at all seriously if the position of the Government of India is as the Indian representative describes it? How can these differences be resolved if the Government of India maintains its rigid position, as it did during the bilateral negotiations of 1962-1963? These negotiations failed, as did all negotiations before. The Government of India says that mediation will not help. Now, the representative of India adds that : "...the passing of resolutions"—by the Council "will not be helpful. It is likely to aggravate feelings." The Government of India has taken the rigid position that it will not agree to submit to limited arbitration the points of difference that exist between the parties over questions of fact in regard to the implementation of the international agreement of Kashmir.

I would like to put the question before the Council : If negotiations have repeatedly failed and it is impossible for them to bear any fruit, if the Government of India is averse to mediation, if it rejects limited arbitration, if it warns the Security Council's passing any resolutions, then is not the position this that all avenues of peaceful settlement are barred and closed to us?

This brings me to India's offer of a so-called "no-war declaration". We have said again and again that we have already signed a "no-war declaration" when we pledged our adherence to the United Nations Charter. The representative of India asks if we have any mental reservation. Did India have mental reservations when it signed the Charter of the United Nations? If not, what is the necessity of a "no-war declaration"? What is needed is not another declaration but to devise specific methods for the settlement of the Kashmir dispute. This would remove the sole cause of conflict between the two countries.

We have been trying to impress this point of the Government of India since 1950, when we proposed "no-war declaration" which would contain provisions for negotiations between India and Pakistan, and, in the case of the failure of negotiations, for recourse to mediation and in the event of the failure of mediation, for the submission of the points of dispute to either an appropriate arbitration or judicial determination. To our regret, and to the misfortune of our peoples and, above all, of the people of Kashmir, the Government of India has persistently refused to accept our offer and to recognise that a "no-war declaration" is a mere platitude unless it is accompanied by a simultaneous commitment to the use of methods for the pacific settlement of disputes.

While our position has been greatly misrepresented in the past, it is gratifying that the principle for which we have sought to gain acceptance are now finding expression in the dialogue between the heads of Government of the United States and the Soviet Union. In his recent statement regarding the peaceful settlement of territorial disputes, Chairman Khrushchev said:

> "Life shows that the majority of territorial disputes are fraught with the danger of complication of the relations between the parties with the possibility of a serious armed conflict, and that they consequently constitute a potential threat to universal peace."

He added:

> "Is it that the Soviet Union proposes to cross out with one stroke all territorial issues between States, to abandon all attempts to settle them as if these issues do not exist at all? No, this is not the point. We realize that some countries have weighty reasons for their claims."

He continued:

> "A peaceful settlement of territorial disputes is also favoured by the fact that in the practice of international relations there already exists a store of improved methods of peaceful settlement of outstanding issues: direct negotiations between the States concerned, use of good offices, request of assistance from international organization..."

On this basis, Chairman Khrushchev proposed an agreement which should include "an undertaking to settle all territorial disputes exclusively by peaceful means, such as negotiations, mediation, conciliatory procedure, and also other peaceful means at the choice of the parties concerned in accordance with the Charter of Unitied Nations."

Let us take this statement of the Chairman of the Council of Minister of the USSR and apply it to the Kashmir dispute, even though this dispute hinges on a people's right to self-determination. According this statement, it is not at all justifiable to abandon all attempts to settle the dispute, as if it did not exist at all. But that is precisely what India seeks to have the Council do. According to this statement there is to be an undertaking to settle the dispute by peaceful means. But after the failure of these means, that is, negotiation, India blocks the other means. And still India proposes a "no-war declaration"?

Let us now refer to the statement of President Johnson of the United States made in his letter of 18 January 1964 addressed to Chairman Khrushchev, in which the President proposes the following "guideline" to implement the principle of the renunciation of the use of force for the solution of international disputes:

> "...the parties to any serious dispute...shall seek a solution by peaceful means resorting to negotiation, mediation, conciliation, arbitration, judicial settlement, action by a regional or appropriate United States agency or other peaceful means of their own choice.

How does this apply to the question before us? Since negotiation between India and Pakistan has failed, is India prepared for limited arbitration or judicial settlement of those points of difference between the parties which are capable either of arbitration or of being judicially determined? India has rejected these means again. India is even rejecting today the assistance of the United States in the settlement of this dispute. And yet India proposes a "no-war declaration"!

The President of the United States adds in his statement :

> "The prevention of wars over territorial and other disputes requires not only general principles but also the 'growth and improvement' regarding the machinery and methods for peaceful settlement. The United States believes that the peace-keeping processes of the United Nations—and specifically its Security Council—should be more fully used and strengthened."

It is these peace-keeping processes of the United Nations which India spurns with regard to Kashmir. When it come to the question of how the forces of India and Pakistan could be withdrawn from the State of Jammu and Kashmir, and the security of the State preserved, we proposed the stationing of a United Nation force which would be impartial to both India and Pakistan. India rejected the proposal and threatened that any country which would attempt to inject a United Nations force in Indian-occupied Kashmir would be regarded as unfriendly to India. We went further and conveyed our acceptance to the United Nations representative in 1958 of his suggestion that the possibility of stationing a United Nations force on the Pakistan side of the Jammu and Kashmir border be examined to ensure the security of the area after the withdrawal of the Pakistan forces. India said that it would "regret" the stationing of such a force in the territory of Pakistan. This India made it impossible to have recourse to the peace keeping machinery of the United Nations for a solution of the Kashmir dispute. What is more, India obstructs even a resolution of this Council. And yet India proposes a "no-war declaration"!

There is another important consideration involved here with respect to India's offer to "talk with us to resolve our "differences". Any impartial observer will note that the word "differences" is being significantly used here. Its intent can be nothing but to confuse the issues. For, after all, what "differences" are there except the Kashmir dispute?

There may be many minor differences between India and Pakistan, as there would be between any two neighbouring countries, but none of them has presented a major obstacle. There is the question of the minorities, for instance, but that is obviously within the scope of the domestic responsibility of each Government. The minorities in India can be protected only by the Government of India, and the minorities in Pakistan can be protected only by the Government of Pakistan. What room is there for any international mediation to bring about any tangible improvement in this regard? Apart from each Government taking firm action to give its minorities the fullest sense of security, what is required here is co-operation between the two countries to enable the refugees to return to their homes. Even more, there should be an over-all improvement in the relations between India and Pakistan and in the development of a fraternal spirit between the Hindus and the Muslims in the two countries. But a lasting improvement can take place only with the settlement of the Kashmir dispute. India would evade this settlement and yet talk of resolving "differences". Its position is, I am constrained to say, so transparently disingenuous that it cannot possibly delude anyone.

The representative of India professed not to believe the sentiments I expressed the other day regarding the peaceful settlement of international disputes. He accused Pakistan of indulging in threats of violence. The Kashmir dispute has been before the Council for sixteen long years. Numerous efforts have been made during these years to reach a peaceful solution of the problem. No less than twenty different proposals have been made at one time or another by eminent personalities, including the President of the United States and Prime Minister of the United Kingdom, in order to bring about agreement between India and Pakistan. Every one of these proposals was accepted by Pakistan. Every one of them was rejected by India. If this does not constitute proof of Pakistan's willingness to seek peaceful settlement of disputes, then I am at a loss to know how to satisfy India.

It was the Defence Minister of India who declared that India had not adjured the use of armed force and that it reserved the right to resort to force when its interests so demanded. It was the same Defence Minister who publicly described Pakistan as India's "enemy number one". We have come here not with a threat, but with an appeal—an appeal to you to remember that this Organization was established "to maintain international peace and security,...to bring about by peaceful means, and in conformity with the principles of justice and international law, adjustment or settlement of international disputes or situations which might lead to a breach of the peace". We appeal to you to remember that the history of mankind has been marked by war and violence, that if this Organization in which men have placed their hopes for future peace turns a deaf ear to the pleas of the downtrodden, then what hope is there for peace in our time?

For India, the situation is simple. It is in possession of the major part of the State of Jammu and Kashmir and would like nothing better than to be left alone. But we, seeing our kith and kin, our flesh and blood, suffer tyranny and oppression, shall we remain silent spectators? We who can see and feel the surge of a people determined to be free, shall we not warn of the consequences and dangers of letting the situation drift like this?

The representative of India has sought to blame Pakistan and the conclusion of the Sino-Pakistan boundary agreement for the failure of the bilateral talks which took place between our two countries in 1962 and 1963. He goes on to charge that the talks were finally broken off by me in spite of all efforts on the part of his Government to keep them going. Let me place the relevant facts before the Security Council.

In pursuance of the policy of the Government of Pakistan to promote friendly relations with all nations of the world, and in particular with those which are its neighbours, we concluded boundary agreements with Iran, Burma and to some extent even with India. It was in pursuance of this policy that the Government of Pakistan formally proposed to the Government of the People's Republic of China in March 1961 that the two Governments should enter into negotiations to reach an understanding on the location and alignment of the non-demarcated border between the Chinese province of Sinkiang and the contiguous areas, the defence of which is the responsibility of the Government of Pakistan.

The Government of the People's Republic of China made an affirmative response at the end of February 1962, and a few months later, in May, a joint communique was issued by the two Governments stating that they had decided to enter into negotiations to reach an understanding on the boundary question on the basis of mutual accommodation and in the spirit of friendly relations between neighbours. The negotiations commenced in Peking a few weeks before the outbreak of the Sino-Indian border conflict, in October 1962. That was a conflict between two powerful nations of the East. That was a crisis which was not of our making. We could neither prevent it nor influence its course.

When the joint communique of the President of Pakistan and the Prime Minister of India was issued on 29 November 1962, agreeing to make renewed efforts to resolve the Kashmir dispute on a just and honourable basis, India knew full well that Pakistan and China had commenced negotiations on a boundary agreement in Peking much earlier. On the eve of the commencement of the bilateral talks in Rawalpindi, on 27 December 1962 complete agreement in principle between Pakistan and China on the alignment of the boundary betwen Sinkiang and contiguous areas, for the defence of which Pakistan was responsible, was announced. We took this course before the bilateral negotiations with India commenced. Had we not done so, the Government of India would have accused us of withholding this information and thereby acting contrary to the spirit of the joint communique of 29 November 1962. The Peking negotiations took their course. I signed the agreement in Peking on 2 March 1963.

The representative of India calls the conclusion of this boundary agreement a "provocation" and gives credit to his Government for not breaking off the Kashmir negotiations with Pakistan. He accuses me of this action. In May 1963, during the last round of talks, I repeatedly told the Indian Minister, Sardar Swaran Singh, the leader of the Indian negotiations team, that I would be willing to stay on in Delhi if he was at all prepared to consider the Pakistan suggestions to break the complete deadlock that had been reached since the third round. I got no response. Therefore the negotiations ended.

The representative of India has thought it fit to accuse us of carrying on "flirtations with China" and that "Pakistan does not want India to be strong; it wants to weaken India both internationally and domestically". Mr. President, was this remark about "flirtations with China" meant for your ears? Was it meant for the ears of everyone in this Council? Obviously not. It was supposed to be a dialogue. However, I should like to say that no one in this Council is so innocent as not to know the difference between an ally and an opportunist. We are allies, we are committed in two defence alliances with our friends, and we stand by those commitments and alliances. We take the advantages and the disadvantages of alliances. We take the benefits and non-benefits of alliances. We are willing perhaps to face nuclear annihilation for a common cause and common destiny and common values. Perhaps one of the reasons why no progress has been made in the settlement of the Kashmir dispute is because we are committed firmly to our alliances. No one then can delude anybody that Pakistan is flirting with Communist China. We have a boundary agreement with all countries, with Burma, with Iran. China happens to be our neighbour as well and, as with all others, we have concluded a boundary agreement with that neighbour in the interests of peace and security and stability to remove all possible sources of friction, so that peace is consolidated, so that there is not a repetition of the conflict that India is involved in with so many countries. This was in the interest not only of our alliances, this was in the interest of world peace. We have recognized reality; many countries have recognized the reality. Have they been accused of flirting with Communist China? May we remind the representative of the Government of India of the ten years of seduction that existed between the Government of India and the People's Republic of China?

We here in this Council are accused of flirtations with a neighbour merely because we have normal relations, but no one in this Council is so naive as to be taken in by this propaganda of the

Government of India, and those friends and allies of ours, whom we stand by firmly and resolutely, know it better than anyone else. What is this flirtation? When the *Pancha Shila* was proclaimed by India after it had reached agreement with China over Tibet in 1954 as the magic formula which would ensure world peace in our time, that was not flirtation. If slogans of *Chini Hindi Bhai Bhai* (the Chinese and the Indians are brothers) rent the Indian skies for years, that was not flirtation. But when Pakistan concludes a boundary agreement with China in the interest of peace and tranquility in Asia, that becomes flirtation. It is obvious that India has a double standard of international conduct, one for itself and quite another for Pakistan.

We are accused of weakening India domestically and internationally. I have dealt sufficiently with the domestic aspect. How have we weakened India internationally? Must we remain on unfriendly terms with India's neighbours because India's relations with most of them are unfriendly? It is not alone with Pakistan that India has differences. India has differences with almost all its neighbours. If those differences had been only with Pakistan, then perhaps there might have been some blame that could be apportioned to Pakistan. But apparently India is right in every case and the rest of the world – and in particular its neighbours – is wrong in every case.

We are accused of having given away to China as a result of the boundary agreement 2,000 square miles of Kashmir. I thank the representative of India for reducing the charge to this more modest dimension. Immediately after the conclusion of the boundary agreement, the Prime Minister of India stated in the Indian parliament on 5 March 1963 that Pakistan had "surrendered" 13,000 square miles of territory of China. Now we come down to 2,000 square miles. The fact is that Pakistan did not surrender a single inch of territory to the People's Republic of China.

The representative of India has also asserted that the people of Kashmir were perfectly happy under the benevolent rule of India and should not therefore be given the right of self-determination. He told the Council that the revenue of the State of Jammu and Kashmir had increased; so had food production. There were more schools, more hospitals, better roads, electricity and so forth, than there were ten years ago. This glowing report, permit me to say, reminded one of nothing so much as an account of its administration of a territory given by a colonial power before the Trusteeship Council. The argument that the people are well fed and happy under foreign rule, that the benevolent ruler knows what is best for the people and that those who speak for freedom are disgruntled agitators is one with which this World Organization is all too familiar. How many times have we not heard the Forign Minister of South Africa stand at the rostrum of the General Assembly and extol, in terms of hospital beds, schoolrooms, roads, kilowatts and megawatts the benefits brought about by his Government to the indigenous people of South West Africa? Like the Education Minister of India, the Foreign Minister of South Africa too feels that if only his Government were left alone, all would be well. He too would like the world to believe that those who decry the denial of human rights to the people of South Africa and South West Africa are agitators uninitiated in the ways of Christianity and democracy and secularism, and involved in an international conspiracy against South Africa and the peace of the world. The number and diversity of reasons put forward by the representative of India for not fulfilling the pledge given by his Government are so great that it is not easy to follow the thread of his argument.

We have always considered Kashmir to be a vitally important question because it is, above all, a human question on whose just and honourable resolution depends the fate and future of nearly 600 million people who inhabit the India-Pakistan subcontinent. It is the Indian pretension that Kashmir is a symbol and guarantee of their secularism. I venture to submit that Kashmir is a test of the ability of the world community to resolve disputes through peaceful means. If Kashmir is to be a symbol and guarantee, let it be the symbol of the willingness of nations to solve disputes through peaceful means and a guarantee that justice will be done to all States and all people, big and small.

The Kashmir dispute has persisted for many years. The complexities that surround it are the complexities of politics and powers. The issue involved is simple and clear : the right of a people to self-determination and the obligation of States to honour international commitments. We heard a scholastic discourse the other day from the Education Minister of India on the meaning of the word "self-determination". To those of us in these halls who fought and struggled for this right, to those of us who symbolise by our presence here the triumph of this principle, the meaning of self-determination in quite clear.

Pakistan is not playing with the idea of self-determination when it talks of Kashmir any more than when it speaks of self-determination for Angola, Mozambique, Rhodesia and South West Africa. "What is self?" asked the representative of India, Mr. Chagla, the other day, as if he were unaware of the commitments given by his Government to the people of Kashmir, to Pakistan and to the Security Council. This is how the Prime Minister of India, his Prime Minister, answered the question on three different occasions. In 1947, in a broadcast to the Indian nation, Mr. Nehru said:

> "We have declared that the fate of Kashmir is ultimately to be decided by the people. That pledge we have given not only to the people of Kashmir but to the world. We will not and cannot back out of it."

In 1951, in that unfortunate city of Srinagar in which blood is flowing at this very hour while we gather here, he declared:

> "I want to repeat that the Government of India will stand by that pledge, whatever happens. That pledge itself stated that it is for people of Kashmir to decide their fate without external interference."

Then, in the Indian Parliament, in February 1951, the Prime Minister of India declared:

> "We have given our pledge to the people of Kashmir and subsequently to the United Nations. We stood by it and we stand by it today. Let the people of Kashmir decide."

The words are simple, their meaning clear – "Let the people of Kashmir decide." There is no equivocation here, no quibbling about what is self-determination, no fear that the unity, solidarity and integrity of India was at stake.

Yet, now we are told that the right of self-determination is something the countries of Africa and Asia ought to fear. In his short lesson on the history of the United States, the representative of India recalled for us the bloody Civil War fought in the United States to prevent the South from seceding. The analogy is inaccurate since Kashmir is not a part of India trying to secede, nor a slave-owning society attempting to retain slavery. Kashmir is an entity and a people, and to quote Mr. Nehru, it is a people "with a soul of its own and an individuality of its own" to whom the promise was made sixteen years ago that it would be free to decide its own future. The interesting and revealing feature of the analogy drawn by the representative of India is that he obviously sees the situation in Kashmir as one in which an unwilling people have, by force of arms, to be held within the Indian Union for the fulfilment of some high and noble purpose of which India is the self-appointed instrument.

Pakistan has come here not to seek your support for the right of a minority to secede from the Indian Union. It comes to seek a reaffirmation of the pledge given to all the people of Kashmir that they will be enabled to decide the future of their land. The people of Kashmir are not an Indian minority. They will never be an Indian minority. "Kashmir is not the property of either India or Pakistan. It belongs to the people of Kashmir", and the people of Kashmir alone will decide as to what their future affiliation and course of action will be. The words I have just spoken once again are the words of the Prime Minister of India.

The Education Minister of India tried to raise the spectre of fragmentation of the States of Africa and Asia, many of which have minorities within their borders, if the principle of self-determination were to be applied. On previous occasions, Indian spokesmen have made a transparent bid for African sympathy by comparing Kashmir with Katanga. It would be naive for me to enter into his game, but let me say that if Kashmir is Katanga, then its despotic Maharajah, whose forefathers purchased the valley and its people from the British for a handful of silver, is the Tshombe of Kashmir. The representative of India was outraged when I referred to the colonial nature of India's hold over Kashmir. Yet when we hear him hold forth on the complexities and dangers of self-determination, when we hear him extol the virtues of multi-racialism, do we not hear echoes of the sentiments expressed by President Salazar of Portugal in his declaration on Africa?

In his broadcast of 12 August 1963, Mr. Salazar asked the following questions:

> "If self-determination aims fundamentally at verifying the assent given to the form of state or of government under which populations live, it is not understood how there can be a single

method of achieving this purpose or of determining that assent, the single method being a plebiscite following the illegitimate demands of the United Nations."

According to Mr. Salazar, Angola and Mozambique are an integral part of Portugal because Porguguese law says so, and any attempt to ascertain the wishes of the people of Angola and Mozambique is to be viewed as a dangerous negation of the noble and high-minded policy of multi-racialism, which Portugal has been attempting for the last 500 years, to follow in Africa.

The representative of India considers that the future of the world depends on the evolution of multi-racial nations and States in different parts of the world. Perhaps—that may be so; it is not a contention with which we quarrel in principle. Pakistan itself is a country in which live people professing different faiths, speaking different languages, belonging to diverse racial origins. Our difference on this matter with India—as with Portugal—is that we believe that the evolution toward multi-racial States and societies should come about not by force, not on the basis of legal fictions, but on the willing consent of the people. If this is a reactionary policy, then we plead guilty.

The representative of India sought to enlighten us about India's crusade against imperialism and colonialism. His claims, I venture to submit, would have been far more convincing if, in the same statement, he had not built his whole case regarding Kashmir on the rights of the ruler, a feudal chief, a tyrant who had been protected from his own people only under an imperialist dispensation. Moreover, it is unfortunate for the claims of the representative of India regarding India's anti-imperialist mentality that when he wants to prove Kashmir's affiliation with India, he cites the evidence that Kashmir was a part of the empire of Emperor Asoka.

Surely, not only Kashmir but the whole of Pakistan and most of Afghanistan were included in the empire of Asoka. And it is fatal of Mr. Chagla's thesis that the political thought of modern India has been articulated in other terms by her most prominent writers and authors. "The small national state is doomed" these are not anti-colonialist words: they are the words of Mr. Jawaharlal Nehru in his book, *The Discovery of India*. And India's ambitions are well expressed by the distinguished Indian author and diplomatist, the late Mr. K.M. Panikkar who on page 16 of his book *India and the*

Indian Ocean writes:

> "Our vision has been obscured by an un-Indian wave of pacifism. 'Ahimsa', "—non-violence—" is no doubt a great religious creed, but that is a creed which India rejected when she refused to follow Gautama Buddha. The Hindu theory at all times, especially in the period of her historic greatness, was one of active assertion of the right, if necessary through the force of arms...To the Indian ocean, we shall then have to turn, as our ancestors did, who conquered Socotra long before the Christian Era, and established an Empire in the Pacific."

Surely the attitude that is projected here is one of expansionism, an attitude that would extend India's hegemony from Somalia to Indonesia, and from the Hindu Kush to the Mekong River, that is, over all countries and territories touched by the waters of the Indian Oceans. It is, I submit, hardly an anti-colonialist attitude.

Who has not heard of the epic freedom struggle of the peoples inhabiting the sub-continent? For long years all of us fought side by side, although even while the struggle continued, the present leadership of India opposed, tooth and nail, the right of Pakistan to be a free and independent country. It pains us, therefore, that a country so recently liberated from foreign rule, should itself now employ the arguments and manoeuvres associated with colonial powers to deny the priceless gift of freedom to the people of Kashmir.

The representative of India stated that democracy, like charity, must begin at home. I would remind him that this is true of all virtue and that self-rightousness is no substitute for righteousness. He asserted that India has fought unceasingly in United Nations for the cause of freedom in Asia and Africa. I do not think that it is even necessary for me to remind the members of the Council of the humble contribution that Pakistan itself has tried to make to the struggles of the peoples of Asia and Africa to free themselves for foreign domination. We take no credit for this. We seek no credit for it. It is our duty. It is our responsibility to world peace and to anti-colonialism. It is a natural thing. It is a normal thing; it is not a phenomenon. Nor do we wish to suggest that Pakistan's impact has been of a singular or decisive nature. The credit must go in every case to the people themselves and to their leaders who fought and struggled, even as the people of Kashmir are doing today.

How can India reconcile its record in Kashmir with the role it sees for itself as the leader, the prime mover, and the inspiration of freedom movements all over the world? Those of us who have worked in the United Nations on these problems, know full well the equivocations and hesitations of India whenever the question has come up of self-determination in any part of the world.

I am afraid that, in his zeal to contradict my statement, the distinguished representative of India forgot to read it carefully. He attributes to me some pacans of praise with regard to Sheikh Abdullah. Actually, though I cannot fail to honour the suffering and admire the sacrifice of Sheikh Abdullah since 1953, the laudatory phrases about him that were contained in my statement were not mine: they came from the Prime Minister of India and they were all within quotation marks. If the distinguished representative of India contradicts them, he contradicts them, he contradicts his own Prime Minister and does not contradict me. Then, he claims that the trial of Sheikh Abdullah has been with due process of law. This claim can be judged from the following report published in *The Times* of London on 30 September 1963:

> "In June, the senior prosecuting counsel, Mr. Pande retired from the case. He said that the money for his fees could be better used. The trial, he said, could go on for another five to seven years."

It can also be judged from the letter addressed to the Prime Minister of India by fifty members of the Indian Parliament in September 1963. The report of this letter, published in *The Times* of London in the same issue said:

> "In view of the adverse effect which the trial of Shaikh Abdullah and his associates was having over seas and of 'the colossal and abnormal amounts believed to have been spent' on the case, this was the 'opportune and favourable time' for the withdrawal of the charges, the members argued.
>
> "If the Government of India could find a graceful and politically safe way of withdrawing the charges against the Shaikh they would need no urging by the Opposition. Although

> the interminable proceedings in Jammu lend themselves to forgetfulness, they sit uncomfortably on Delhi's political conscience and, quite apart from the fate of the Shâikh himself, there are many who deplore the effect of this transparently political trial on the independence and self-confidence of the Indian judiciary.
>
> "If Shaikh Abdullah could be brought to bind himself not to take up again the cause of an independent Kashmir or of a plebiscite to decide its future, Delhi might be pleased to release him. The Shaikh himself has said that he holds the key to his prison but will not give the assurances that are demanded."

But the Sheikh released and calling for a change in the present status in Kashmir would be an upsetting influence, to say the least. This, as I said before, is a report of the letter addressed to the Prime Minister of India by fifty members of the Indian Parliament, and comments thereon.

Ther representative of India stated in his opening remarks that "no new situation has arisen to aggravate the existing conditions in Jammu and Kashmir" (1088th meeting, para. 4). There is no alien power occupying a territory against the wishes of its people which will ever admit the existence of a new or troubled situation in that territory. It would require high statesmanship and unusual admission of facts for India to acknowledge the present situation. What has actually been taking place in the last several weeks in the Indian-occupied area has been, in the words of President Mohammed Ayub Khan, "a spontaneous referendum of the people" in which the people returned an overwhelming verdict against India. Let me quote some further testimony on the new situation in Kashmir. The correspondent of *The Times* of London wrote from Srinagar, on 2 February 1964:

> "Whenever crowds gather—and the sight of foreign correspondents, of whom there are only two just now, can be enough to attract a clamouring mob shouts are raised for Sheikh Abdullah, for a plebiscite, and even for Pakistan".

He adds,

> "...but the affair of the hair has brought to the surface all the stored resentments of the Kashmiris and the crumbling of the local regime and its replacement by administrators and police from outside—'from India' as a Kashmiri would say—have made it likely that the resentments will now be focussed on Delhi. Discussion of the Kashmir problem in the past has always been comfortably informed with the belief that at least it would not be complicated by violent expressions of their own will by the Kashmiris. When the matter is before the United Nations again this week, it may have to be noted that there is a new factor in the old equation, the self-assertion of the Kashmiris."

This is a foreign observer talking of a "new factor in the old equation", but here we have the representative of India saying that there is no new situation.

Then there is the dispatch in *The New York Times* written from Srinagar on 5 February:

> "The Government of India was described today as 'completely out of touch with the real sentiments' of the people of the disputed State of Jammu and Kashmir.
>
> "That was the view of several Kashmiri business leaders, including Hindus, in this predominantly Moslem region.
>
> "According to these men, who asked not to be identified, 'since 1954 the Moslem majority of Kashmir has been pro-Pakistan .
>
> "Their view was completely different from that expressed yesterday..." by Lal Bahadur Shastri, the Indian Minister without Portfolio, after his return to New Delhi.
>
> "Mr. Shastri said that the feeling in Kashmir was 'definitely pro-Indian.'
>
> "The Kashmiri business leaders, however, insisted that most of the people here were pro-Pakistan."

Here is a record of the opinion in Kashmir which serves to refute the Indian representative's suggestion that the unrest is directed solely against the local administration.

The correspondent of *The Sunday Star*, Washington, wrote on 26 January:

> "For four weeks now the Kashmiris, in an impressively disciplined non-violent rebellion, have demonstrated their hostility towards close links with India and their determination to decide their destiny.
>
> "India's peacemaking overtures and righteous indignation are not an effective substitute for the probably only lasting solution – finally granting the Kashmiris self-determination."

He added:

> "The United States cannot now commit itself to a long-term arms aid to India within the next few week, as it has planned to, without seriously questioning the possible repercussions of what amounts to indirectly supporting India's virtual colonial overlordship of Kashmir."

In the same dispatch, the correspondent says that "the Indian Government has not chosen to reveal a true picture of events in Srinagar". Considering that remark, it is not all surprising to hear the denial by the representative of India that there is no new situation in Kashmir.

There are further statements of foreign observers for example, the report in the *Baltimore Sun* of 5 February, which says "the hair, which Muslims believe came originally from the Prophet, is only a symptom of the problems in the Indian two-thirds of Kashmir" but I am forced to content myself with these in order to avoid undue length. The representative of India has tried to make it appear that the theft of the holy relic was an isolated incident, and that, with alleged recovery of the relic, the incident is closed. While the Government and the people of Pakistan were gravely perturbed over this theft and take no position regarding the genuineness of its recovery. I must make it clear that it is the revelations brought about by this incident, rather than the incident itself, to which we are seeking to draw the Council's attention.

There is a significant report in *The Times of India* relating to the situation after what purported to be the exposition of the hole relice. According to this dispatch from Srinagar, the President of the People's Action Committee said that the ban imposed by the Committee on the opening of the shops on Fridays would continue until their demands had been conceded. It was after the recovery of the relic, again, that Maulana Masoodi, according to a Reuters dispatch said that Indian-held Kashmir was 'too much a police State, with every Minister moving around with police protection", and not only did he demand the release of Sheikh Abdullah but also criticized the expulsion of Ghulam Abdas and Yusuf Shah, two Kashmiri leaders who, since 1947 have led the movement for the accession of Jammu and Kashmir to Pakistan. It is also after the recovery of the holy relic that reports continue of strikes in Srinagar, of the momentum in other towns of Kashmir besides Srinagar and of discriminate arrest.

In this connexion, I must mention some recent utterances of Bakshi Ghulam Mohammed who for ten years, beginning in 1953, was the so-called Chief Minister of Jammu and Kashmir and, therefore, India's main prop in the State. I have already quoted (1087th meeting) his statement of 17 January 1964 that the demands of the people of Kashmir were for the release of Shekh Abdullah and the holding of a plebiscite. This statement was later "clarified" in a manner which furnished strong grounds for the belief that the "clarification" was made under pressure. We have now a statement from Bakshi Ghulam Mohammed, which according to reliable reports, still uncontradicted was circulated in Delhi. The statement said:

> "Consequent upon the dismissal and arrest ini 1953 of Sheikh Mohammad Abdullah becasue he had asked India to withdraw troops from Kashmir preparatory to holding of the promised plebiscite, I accepted premiership of the State as it was my honest conviction then that majority community of Kashmir could be brought round to staying on with India and that they would really be better off and more secure with secular India than with communal Pakistan.
>
> "For a full decade. I did all I could towards this end, but year

after year I became wiser by observing that events in India reflected on the psychology of Kashmiris."

Bakshi Ghulam Mohammed went no to say:

"The recent episode of the Holy Relic at Hazratbal has extremely shocked sensitive Kashmiri Muslims who now openly declare that even their religion and culture is not safe with India. They also say that Pakistan is no more a Muslim State than India is a Hindus State and the very fact that everything that befalls Hindus in Pakistan retaliates all the more severely on Muslims in India belies the claim of India to be secular State, a State above religion. They fear their fate tomorrow will be no different from or not better than that of Calcutta Muslims.

"Of their three immediate demands, namely the release of Sheikh Abdulla, the holding of a plebiscite and the inquiry into affairs that led to the events of 1953, I have already apprised the Press."

He continued:

"I frankly admit that what Sheikh Abdullah said in 1953, I say today after a further ten years of experiment. Even today I am honest and faithful to India and if it comes to a plebiscite, I might vote for India but to keep the Indian Government and the Indian people in the dark about the inner working of the mind of Kashmiri Mussulmans is a sin and a disservice.

"Many people may well call this statement of mine blackmail, but I make it clear, once and for all, that I am by no means eager or willing to become Premier of Kashmir again, and even if I am asked to, I will never accept that post; not do I oppose the change of the present Government in the State, nor for that matter the establishment of President rule or Sadar-i-Riyast rule, or whatever the Government of India and the people of Kashmir desire."

Bakshi Ghulam Mohammed has up to now been one of the main

instruments of India's designs in Jammu and Kashmir. A statement of this nature, coming from india's chief agent in the State, acquires a singular importance. We have reports that currently he is under extreme pressure from the Indian Government and that he is either to be arrested and imprisoned – like his predecessor, Sheikh Abdullah – or forced to rescind his statements. A strong suspicion that the Government of India will mete out severe punishment to him for his audacity in confessing the facts about Kashmir is created by the statement of two former members of the Government, Sham Lal Saraf and Girdhari Lal Dogra, charging him with damaging the interests of India.

These are some of the facts which give an indication of the present situation in Indian-occupied Kashmir. If killing by police firing of scores of people, general strikes paralysing whole cities and towns, massive demonstrations by virtually the entire adult population of capital city and sullen resentment spontaneously expressing itself before foreign observers do not constitute a grave situation, then what will, except an outbreak of hostilities?

That is the restraining hand of the Pakistan Government alone which preserves place in Kashmir – all the charges against us levelled by the Indian representative notwithstanding – is apparent from the repeated demands made by the Azad Kashmir Government, and the All Jammu and Kashmir Muslim Conference for the abrogation of the cease-fire agreement. These demands are not lightly made. They are the spontaneous expression of the tension in Azad Kashmir which is a direct result of the repression under which the Indian-occupied and Indian-dominated area of Jammu and Kashmir groans.

12

1965 Conflict between India and Pakistan and Security Council Resolutions

12.1. Twelfth Resolution* Adopted at the 1237th Meeting of the Security Concil, September 4, 1965

The Security Council,

Noting the report of the Secretary-General of 3 September 1965.

Having heard the statements of the representatives of India and Pakistan.

Concerned at the deteriorating situation along the cease-fire line in Kashmir.

1. *Calls upon* the Governments of India and Pakistan to take forthwith all steps for an immediate cease-fire.

2. *Calls upon* the two Governments to respect the cease-fire line and have all armed personnel of each party withdrawn to its own side of the line.

3. *Calls upon* the two Governments to co-operate fully with the United Nations Observer Group in India and Pakistan (UNMOGIP) in its task of supervising the observance of the cease-fire;

4. *Requests* the Secretary-General to report to the Council within three days on the implementation of the present resolution.

Adopted unanimously.

---

* Security Council Resolution No. 209 (1965)

12.2. Thirteenth Resolution* Adopted at the 1238th Meeting of the Security Council , September 6, 1965

The Security Council,

Noting the report of the Secretary-General of developments in the situation in Kashmir since the adoption of Security Council resolution 209 (1965) of 4 September 1965 calling for a cease-fire.

Noting with deep concern the extension of the fighting which adds immeasurably to the seriousness of the situation.

1. *Calls upon* the parties to cease hostilities in the entire area of conflict immediately, and promptly withdraw all armed personnel to the positions held by them before 5 August 1965;

2. *Requests* the Secretary-General to exert every possible effort to give effect to the present resolution and to resolution 209 (1965), to take all measures possible to strengthen the United Nations Military Observer Group in India and Pakistan, and to keep the Council promptly and currently informed on the implementation of the resolutions and on the situation in the area;

3. *Decides* to keep this issue under urgent and continuous review so that the Council may determine what further steps may be necessary to secure peace and security in the area.

12.3. Speech by Security Council President Arthur J. Goldberg (United States of America) in Security Council, 1239th Meeting, September 17, 1965

May I, on behalf of the Security Council, welcome the Ministers and high officials of both India and Pakistan who have joined their delegations here today. It will, I am sure, be my pleasure in the course of our discussion of the matter before us formally to introduce the Ministers to the members of the Council. Gentlemen, you are welcome here today.

In my closing statement as President of the Security Council at our last meeting, I stressed fearful potential in the current conflict between India and Pakistan. Since then, substantial military operations have continued, although the Council adopted two forthright and unanimous calls for a cease-fire.

---

* Adopted unanimously Security Council Resolution No. 210 (1965)

In spite of the hazards intrinsic in this situation, the Secretary-General travelled promptly to the subcontinent to give effect to the mandate given to him by the Security Council in its resolution 210 (1965) of 6 September 1965, and exerted every possible effort to give effect both to that resolution and resolution 209 (1965) of 4 September 1965, to take all possible measures to strengthen the United Nations Military Observer Group in India and Pakistan (UNMOGIP) and to keep the Council promptly and currently informed on the implementation of the resolutions and on the situation in the area.

You have all, I am sure, read, from the preliminary report of the Secretary-General (S/6683) and from newspaper accounts, of the intensive and arduous efforts of the Secretary-General in carrying out the mandate of this Council. And I understand that today the Secretary-General will give us a further assessment of his trip.

Again I know that I speak for all the members of the Council when I welcome the Secretary-General back from his mission of peace, on which he carried with him not only the resolutions of the Council, but also the good will, the hopes and the prayers of all people everywhere.

In light of the return of the Secretary-General yesterday, I suggested our meeting today in spite of the short space of time we have had in which to examine the preliminary report of the Secretary-General. I believe that the urgency of the situation requires us to lose no time in our deliberations on this matter, I consulted with members of the Council, who were of one mind: that we should promptly reconvene to hear the Secretary-General's important report. . .

12.4. Speech by UN Secretary-General in Security Council, 1239th Meeting, September 17, 1965

In my preliminary report (S/6683) on my mission to India and Pakistan in pursuit of the mandate given to me by the Council in its resolution 210 (1965) of 6 September 1965, I informed the Council of my formal approaches to the two Governments and of the replies I had received from them. I now wish to advise the Council briefly of the views that I have formed as a result of my talks with the Governments of India and Pakistan.

In the course of my talks with Prime Minister Shastri, President

Ayub Khan and their colleagues, I had the opportunity to hear from both sides a detailed exposition of their views on the present critical situation which has developed over Kashmir. I also requested, and received from both sides, aide-memoirs on their positions and views. Since the Council obviously wished me to report to it as soon as possible after my return, I have thought it best – having reached New York at 3.15 p.m. on Thursday, 16 September – to confine myself at this time to relatively brief report on the impressions and conclusions I have formed during my mission. I have also thought it best at this time not to give a detailed expose of the views of the two Governments as expressed to me, since the replies of Prime Minister Shastri and President Ayub Khan to my message of 12 September 1965, contained in my above-mentioned preliminary report to the Council, give an official summary of the positions of the two Governments on the Security-Council's call and on my own appeals for a cease-fire.

The following brief account of my own observations of the present situation will serve as a prelude to certain thoughts which may, I hope, be helpful to the Council in its further consideration of this critical situation. In this tragic war two closely associated nations find themselves locked in a destructive struggle. Regardless of the merits of the case, the present situation is crippling and potentially disastrous for both nations. Each nation feels that it has been abused by the other, and each is convinced that the other has committed aggression. In common they have a feeling of having been let down to some extent by their allies and by the United Nations, whose Members, for the most part, watch in bewilderment and anxiety the spectacle of two sister nations, with both of which many countries have close links, engaged in fratricidal struggle.

Inherent in this situation are all of the phenomena – that aroused emotions, misunderstandings, long-pent-up resentments, suspicions, fears, frustrated aspirations and heightened national feelings – which throughout history have led to needless and futile wars. These are factors which also make it difficult for the leaders on both sides to respond to the unconditional cease-fire appeals of the Security Council. The present war is clearly to the ultimate disadvantage of both nations and can bring no lasting good to either. Both countries have vast economic and social problems which they have been facing courageously and with considerable success. The war will slow down, or even bring to a halt, these vital efforts towards economic and social development.

The present crisis has inevitably served to harden even further the previous positions taken by the two Governments, since both find it impossible to make concessions under the threat of force. Each has the feeling that only outside support has made it possible for the other to commit what it believes to be aggression.

The Security Council is thus faced with a paradoxical situation. It has passed urgently and unanimously two resolutions [resolutions 209 (1965) and 210 (1965)] requiring an immediate cessation of hostilies. It has authorized me to exert every possible effort to give effect to these resolutions. Before and during my mission, I have received messages of support and offers of assistance from leaders in all parts of the world. Both sides have expressed their desire for a cease-fire and a cessation of hostilities in the entire area of the current conflict. Nevertheless, up to now, I have not succeeded in securing an effective practical measure of compliance by the two sides with the Security Council's resolutions.

What further course of action may be open to the Security Council? In older and less interdependent times, the international community could perhaps have now washed its hands of the matter, leaving the parties to fight it out, heedless of the ruin which such a course must certainly bring to millions of innocent people in both countries. Such a course of action is inconceivable today. Moreover, it is not only the fate of the peoples of India and Pakistan which is at stake. Both States are linked in a peculiarly intricate way with the mainstream of world affairs. The very unanimity of the Security Council on this matter and the direct appeals from so many Governments are indications of how serious a threat this crisis poses to world peace. Quite apart from the well-being of the two nations concerned, there can be little doubt that a real danger to world peace is now imminent.

Before advancing some ideas, I feel that I should also state my own views about the role of the United Nations, and the Security Council in particular, in the present crisis. The Council is faced, as I have said, with a situation of the greatest difficulty and complexity. It has acted with both speed and unanimity. If success has not yet been achieved in securing compliance with the Council's resolutions, that is all the more reason for making further strenuous efforts for a cease-fire as well as for long-term solutions. I feel strongly that in this situation, when the hopes of the world are focused on the Security

Council, which has the primary responsibility under the Charter for maintaining international peace and security, the Council faces not only an exceptionally difficult task but also a rare opportunity to show that peace can be restored and international harmony promoted by the concerted efforts of the international community. In saying this I am thinking not only of the well-being and future of the Governments and peoples of India and Pakistan, but also of the hopes of mankind for a more peaceful world which are centred on the United Nations.

With the above impressions in mind, and being convinced – as I stated in my second message to the two Heads of Government on 14 September (see S/6683, para.10) and in my statement at the airport in New Delhi on my departure for New York – of the fundamental desire of both parties to end the fighting, I am taking the liberty of expressing the following thoughts in the hope that they may be helpful to the Council and to the two Governments themselves in facing the immediate necessity of obtaining an effective cease-fire.

First, the Security Council might now do what it has done once before, and successfully, in another dangerous conflict situation : it could order the two Governments concerned, pursuant to Article 40 of the Charter of the United Nations, to desist from further hostile military action and to this end to issue cease-fire orders to their military forces. The Council might also declare that failure by the Governments concerned to comply with this order would demonstrate the existence of a breach of the peace within the meaning of Article 39 of the Charter.

Second, the Security Council may wish to consider what assistance it might provide in ensuring the observance of the cease-fire.

Third, Security Council resolution 210 (1965) of 6 September also calls for a prompt withdrawal of all armed personnel to the positions held by them before 5 August 1965, and the Council may wish to study means of assisting in the carrying out of this requirement.

Fourth, the Council could request the two Heads of Government to meet together at the earliest possible time to discuss the current situation and the problems underlying it as a first step in resolving the outstanding differences between their two countries and in reaching an honourable and equitable settlement. Such a meeting might take place in a country friendly and acceptable to botn. In this connexion, I might draw the attention of the Council to my message of 15 September to Prime Minister Sharti and President Ayub Khan, the text of which is set forth in my preliminary report (*Ibid.*, para. 13). The Council could also consider the possibility of creating and making available a small committee to assist in such talks should its services seem useful and desirable to the two parties.

Fifth and finally, I may again assure the Council of my availability and of my desire to continue to be of assistance in this matter in any way which may commend itself to the Council and to the two Governments.

Since Security Council resolution 210 (1965) also requested me to take all possible measures to strengthen UNMOGIP, I wish to inform the Council that, as a matter of course, I had consultations with Lieutenant-General R.H. Nimmo, the Chief Military Observer, during my mission. While in the present situation the role of UNMOGIP is obviously more difficult than usual, I have benefited much from the knowledge and experience of General Nimmo. I have taken immediate steps to obtain extra transport and communications equipment to facilitate the task of UNMOGIP. I have also made provisional arrangements to increase the number of military observers at short notice, should developments make this increase necessary.

In its resolution 210 (1965) the Security Council asked me to keep it informed on the situation in the area. The military situation is covered in a separate report (S/6687).

I would not wish to let this occasion pass without expressing my warm appreciation and gratitude to the many statesmen and Governments from whom I have received, both before and during my mission to India and Pakistan, messages of support and encouragement as well as practical measures of assistance.

Finally, I wish to express my appreciation to the Governments of India and Pakistan both for their kindness and hospitality to me and my party and for their frankness and helpfulness in their talks with me. I hope and believe that these talks will eventually contribute to a peaceful solution of the present crisis.

12.5. Speech by M.C. Chagla (India) in Security Council, 1239th Meeting, September 17, 1965.

We are meeting here this morning under very distressing and tragic circumstances. Fighting is going on between two neighbouring countries. I assure you that, as far as we are concerned, we have the friendliest and most cordial relations with the people of Pakistan. Although President Ayub Khan has said that we are at war, our Prime Minister more than once has stressed the fact that there is no war between the two countries and that we do not want to be at war with Pakistan.

This is a peculiar tragedy for our country. We have always stood for peace. We are wedded to the cause of peace. Our great leader, Mahatma Gandhi, gave the message of non-violence and peace to the whole world, and it is sad that we should be involved in this war. But Mahatma Gandhi also said that a country must defend itself against aggression, that a country must have self-respect and dignity; if a country loses dignity and self-respect, that country ceases to exist. I assure you that this particular conflict that is going on is a conflict not of our making. If we have to resist with arms Pakistan's aggression, it is purely for the purpose of self-defence.

As I have said, war is opposed to our basic philosophy. We realize the horrors and devastation of a war. A war makes no distinction between combatants and non-combatants, between the innocent and the guilty. War means to us a threat to our economic progress. We are fighting a tremendous war against poverty and ignorance. As Minister of Education, I know what the war against ignorance means, and we do not want to be stopped or deterred from carrying on that war. Therefore, we do not want to divert either our attention or our resources from our primary purpose, which is to raise the level of standards of living of our people.

Now I hope to satisfy you that even after Pakistan's aggression every step that we have taken has been in self-defence. Our reply to Pakistan has not been offensive; it has been purely defensive. I also want to point out to the Council that we have done our best to prevent the escalation of this war. And may I now point out that it was Pakistan which for the first time used field artillery; it was Pakistan that used tanks with air cover; it was Pakistan that started the bombing of cities; it was Pakistan that started the dropping of paratroops; it was Pakistan that used its navy to bomb one of our seaports, while we have not used navy at all.

The basic question which this Council faces and which it must answer and resolve is : Who is the aggressor? Who has committed aggression? I ask the Council not to shirk giving a reply to that quesion.

I think that on the records of this Council it has been established beyond any doubt that in this particular conflict aggression was committed by Pakistan upon our territory. May I first of all refer to paragraph 6 of the Secretary-General's report (S/6651) of 3 September 1965:

> "General Nimmo has indicated to me that the series of violations that began of 5 August were to a considerable extent in subsequent days in the form of armed men, generally not in uniform, crossing the cease-fire line from the Pakistan side for the purpose of armed action on the Indian side. This is a conclusion reached by General Nimmo on the basis of investigations by the United Nations observers, in the light of the extensiveness and character of the raiding activities and their proximity to the cease-fire line, even though in most cases the actual identity of those engaging in the armed attacks on the Indian side of the line and their actual crossing of it could not be verified by direct observation or evidence."

Therefore, we have here a findng of the Secretary-General, based upon first-hand information from General Nimmo, that this conflict started on 5 August with armed men from the Pakistan side invading our country. I cannot understand or imagine how there could be a clearer finding of aggression than we have here.

It is important to note that resolution 210 (1965) also mentions the date of 5 August. That, to our minds, is the crucial date, and the Council has to apply its mind to that date. What happened on that date? What happened on that date was that Pakistan invaded India. Kashmir is a part of India and the invasion of Kashmir was an invasion of India and aggression on Kashmir was aggression on India.

But we have other evidence of Pakistan's complicity and the support that Pakistan has been giving to these infiltrators. May I read out a few quotations.

President Ayub Khan in a broadcast on 1 September 1965 said:

> "How can she"—India, that is—"blame anyone from *Azad* Kashmir"—they call it *Azad* Kashmir, we call it the part of Kashmir unlawfully occupied by Pakistan—"or, for that matter from any part of Pakistan, for going to the assistance of these

brave people?"

I ask you to mark "any part of Pakistan". So that here is a statement from the Head of State asking how India can expect any part of Pakistan not to help these so-called brave people – and I shall deal with brave people presently – who have invaded India.

Then Mr. Bhutto, the Foreign Minister of Pakistan, said this on 13 July 1965 in the National Assembly:

> "Circumstances and conditions have been the most eloquent compulsion to action – what was valid, proper and realistic yesterday need not be valid, proper and realistic today."

So that the Foreign Minister of Pakistan moulds his policy not according to law, not according to international morality, but according to circumstances and conditions.

Then we have this from the *Morning News* of Karachi, 20 August:

> "Mr. Bhutto told reporters that the cease-fire line, which India describes as an unshakable boundary, is a temporary arrangement. It could very well have been drawn further down inside occupied Kashmir."

This is his respect for the resolution by which the cease-fire line was established. According to Mr. Bhutto, it is a temporary arrangement; it could be changed, it could be altered, it could be modified to suit Mr. Bhutto's pleasure.

Then something more. The *Morning News* of Karachi of 19 August quoted a statement by the Central Home and Kashmir Affairs Minister, Chaudhuri Ali Akbar, under the headline "Kashmiris Free to Cross Line, Pakistan Will Help Freedom Fighters". To call these people "freedom fighters" causes me to say: What sins are committed in thy name, Freedom; About *Azad* Kashmir, this Minister said: "Who can question their right to go to their help? They have to be there." And about Pakistan's help he said: "The freedom fighters will not find Pakistan wanting in the hour of need."

In this connexion I should have quoted one more passage from paragraph 9 of the Secretary-General's report to which I referred earlier, where he gives his finding with regard to the cease-fire line:

> "I have not obtained from the Government of Pakistan any assurance that the cease-fire and the cease-fire line will be respected hence forth or that efforts would be exerted to restore conditions to normal along that line. I did receive assurance from the Government of India, conveyed orally by its representative to the United Nations, that India would act with restraint with regard to any retaliatory acts and will respect the cease-fire agreement and the cease-fier line if Pakistan does likewise."

While we were prepared to honour our international obligation to respect the cease-fire line, Pakistan informed the United Nations representative that it was not prepared to do so.

As regards the support by Pakistan for what has been happening in this invasion mounted by it on our territory, I do not want to weary this Council with a great number of facts and details. I must respect the patience of this Council; I know how anxious it is to come to some conclusion. But there are certain facts to which I must refer.

On 8 June 1965 the Pakistan Government issued an ordinance entitled "The Pakistan Mujahids Force Ordnance." The Mujahids are supposed to be freedom fighters. In this connexion the *Pakistan Times* of 12 June wrote:

> "Pakistan will now have a regularly constituted Mujahids force"—these are the people who have invaded India—"with a rank structure similar to that of the army, according to a Press release of the Inter-Service Public Relations Directorate. It will have commanding officers, junior commissioned officers, non-commissioned officers and other ranks. The Mujahids, for certain local purposes, will be deemed part of the Pakistan army and will be treated on a par with army personnel of the corresponding rank."

Thus there is no ambiguity as to the situation. These 4,000 to 5,000 people who invaded our country on 5 August were really part and parcel of the regular Pakistan Army. They may have come in civilian garb or they may have come dressed in any manner they liked, but the fact remains that they were part of the regular Pakistan forces.

It is very interesting to note that the headquarter for the training of the infiltrators was located near Murree in West Pakistan, under the command of Lieutenant General Akhtar Hussain Malik, General Officer Commanding of the 12th Infantry Division of Pakistan. This organization is known as headquarter "Gibraltar Force". I do not know why they chose the name "Gibraltar" but, after all, a person is entitled to adopt any name he chooses. All commanders connected with Operation Gibraltar were summoned to Murree during the second week of July 1965. President Ayub Khan of Pakistan addressed them personally to explain to them their task of creating confusion and chaos in Jammu and Kashmir. Then these infiltrators were organized into eight forces, each of them composed of six companies of 110 men each. In most cases they are commanded by regular Pakistani army officers of the rank of major, while the platoon commanders are either junior commissioned officers or senior non-commissioned officers.

The Indian Security Forces have captured vast quantities of arms and ammunition seized from these infiltrators. Some of the arms and ammunition captured from the infiltrators bear the marking POF, that is Pakistan Ordnance Factories. Two of the captured officers held emergency commissions in the Pakistan army.

I have photographs here; I could also bring arms here to satisfy you that they were manufactured in Pakistan. These infiltrators carried radio sets so that they were in communication with Pakistan Headquarters. There cannot be the slightest doubt of this. No judge – and I appeal to you, Mr. President – can on this evidence come to fail to the conclusion that on 5 August a regular invasion of India was mounted by Pakistan and that these infiltrators were backed and supported by Pakistan; they were supported by them.

What is the utility of this Council if it will not condemn aggression on these facts? If you are satisfied – and I ask you to say that you are satisfied – to respect the Secretary-General's report and if you are satisfied that aggression was committed by Pakistan on 5 August, I say that it is your duty to condemn this aggression. Otherwise, international law has no meaning and international society cannot exist. Not only must ths aggression be condemned, but also Pakistan must be asked to vacate this aggression. An aggressor cannot get away with the fruits of his aggression. I beg you: do not equate the aggressor and the victim, do not bracket them together. My one objection to resolutions 209 (1965) and 210 (1965) of 4 and 6 September, if I may say so with respect to the Security Council, is that both India and Pakistan are treated alike, that both of them are called upon to do something without distinguishing in any way whatsoever the role played by Pakistan and the role played by India.

I hear certain nations talking of impartiality, that they must be impartial between India and Pakistan. Mr. President, you have been a judge, I have been a judge for seventeen years. Where I have two parties before me, I am not impartial: I have to reveal my judgement; I have got to say who is right and who is wrong. A judge cannot afford to be impartial. When two parties appear before a judge, he has to decide. You are the judges, and I think that it is wrong for the Security Council to say that it is going to be impartial as between India and Pakistan. It is an entirely wrong attitude, a weak attitude; it is an attitude which will completely destroy the utility of this Council. If you have no evidence, you may withhold judgement or reserve it. But when you have this statement of the Secretary-General, when you have the evidence that I have produced, how can this Council say "We will bracket the two countries together, we will be impartial, we will not pass judgement"? I think that the time has come when the Council must call a spade a spade. The Security Council has hesitated too often in doing this. But there are times in history – and this is one of them; as I develop my argument I will satisfy you that we have reached the water-shed of history – when the Security Council must call a spade a spade.

What was the grand design of Pakistan? Let me explain it to you. When it sent these 4,000 or 5,000 infiltrators or invadors or armed men – call them what you like – Pakistan expected that there would be an uprising in Kashmir. They thought that the large Muslim majority in Kashmir would support them and that Kashmir would fall into their mouth much like a ripe plum. What happened? The whole of Kashmir stood firmly behind the constituted Government of that State and behind the Government of India. Kashmir is proud of its traditions of a multi-racial society, just as India is. In Kashmir we have Muslims, Hindus, Sikhs, Buddhists and Christians. All of them stood firm and resisted this aggression. They handed over the infiltrators to the Government and to the security forces, and this grand design of Pakistan failed. Having failed in that, Pakistan started an attack in force with its regular army. That was the attack in the Chhamb sector. You are perhaps not familiar with the map of Kashmir; but may I explain that the Chhamb sector is a very crucial one in Kashmir; it contains our lifeline, our lines of communication to our Army on the cease-fire line and also communication to the army that is facing China in Ladakh and trying to meet that menace. Their entry in this particular sector of Kashmir was for the purpose of destroying our lifeline so that we should be crippled both with regard to our army on the cease-fire line and to our defence against China.

Pakistan's other objective was to make this a religious war. We are living in the modern age. We have learned to understand that religion is something personal and intimate. It is your contacts with your Creator. It is your attempt to understand the inscrutable mystery of existence. We do not wear our religion on sleeves now. We do not ostenatiously brandish it in the face of people. But I am sorry to say that Pakistan is still in the mediaeval age.

The idea was that not only the people of Kashmir but the 50 million Muslims in India would support Kashmir and that there would be communal trouble in India.

There are 2 million Muslims in Kashmir but there are 50 million Muslims in India. India – some of the members do not realize this – is the third largest Muslim country in the world. These Muslism brothers of ours, fellow citizens of ours, live in perfect satisfation with all the rights that the majority community enjoys under our Constitution. They have all the fundamental rights. We are a secular State. But Pakistan does not like this because it is a theocratic State; it is a religious State. To Pakistan religion is the basis of citizenship. To us religion is not the basis of citizenship. This argument will appeal to my friends from the middle East and from other parts of the world where people of different religions live together as nationals.

There is one good thing about Mr. Bhutto : he lends himself to quotations, may I quote him again, on this question of religious war. This is what Mr. Bhutto said in his broadcast of 3 September 1965:

> "Let India not be complacent in waging war in Kashmir. Let them not disregard the lessons of history. Let them not forget that if Pakistanis have hitherto shown the patience of a Solomon, they are also the descendants of the heroic soliders of Islam who have never showed any hesitation in laying down their lives in defence of their honour and the pursuit of justice".

Why "heroic soldiers of Islam"? Are they fighting a war of

Islam? It is an insult to Islam to suggest that Islam is intolerant or that Islam belives in wars and conflicts.

Then Mr. Bhutto said the following at an Independence Day civic reception at Larkana on 14 August :

> "India is known as a country believing in threats alone...I want to tell Shastri and India that after all justice is sure to prevail. We are not alone in this. Our religion is spreading all over the world."

Again the appeal is a religious appeal. The Council will realize the danger of this. There are 50 million Muslims living in India in peace and amity, in friendship and concord, with other communities. The whole attempt of Pakistan was to disrupt this unity, to bring about communal discord and then to appeal to this Council, or to the world, by saying : You see, Indians treat their minorities badly.

I told the Council that our action against Pakistan was purely defensive, and let me slightly elaborate this. What happened? They sent in these infiltrators on 5 August. How did we react? All that we did was to cross the cease-fire line in order to prevent more infiltrators from coming into Kashmir. It was a purely defensive action. Then when they attacked us at Chhamb with their regular forces, as I told the Council, we had to cross into the Punjab, into Pakistan, in order to prevent these forces from being further strengthened and our life line from being destroyed. That again was a defensive action.

Now I want to draw the Council's attention to something which is very interesting, think it was Max Beerbohm who said that history does not repeat itself : historians repeat themselves. But in this case history has repeated itself; I do not know whether historians are going to repeat themselves or not.

There is a close similarity between this invasion by Pakistan of Kashmir and of India and what happened in 1947 and 1948. If one looks at the record, one will find – and it is a matter of record ; I am not speaking outside the record – that Pakistan raiders invaded Kashmir and that Pakistan denied any complicity with these raiders. They said : We have nothing to do with it. Ultimately, Muhammad Zafrulla Khan – no less a person than Muhammad Zafrulla Khan, who is now a member of the International Court of Justice – agreed and admitted that Pakistan had armed the tribesmen to invade

Kashmir.

This is exactly what is happening now. But the similarity does not end there. We have a gruesome history of what the tribesmen did to Kashmir and the people of Kashmir in 1947 and 1948, and there is a repetion this time. People have been killed; they have been tortured; mosques have been desecrated; mosques have been bombed and cruelty has been paractised of a sort which it is difficult to believe can be done in modern times. It almost goes back to the days of Hitler, when such things were possible. But I thought we had outlived the days of Hitler.

To show what happened in 1947, may I quote a statement by Sheikh Abdullah—as reported in *The Hindustan Times* of 18 November 1947—which I also quoted when I spoke before this Council on 7 May 1964:

> "These raders abducted women, massacred children, they looted everything and everyone, they even dishonoured the Holy Koran and converted mosques into brothels, and today every Kashmiri loathes the invading tribesmen and the arch inspirators who have been responsible for such horrors in a land which is peopled with an over-whelming majority of Muslims." [1113th Meeting, para. 21.]

On 7 September *The Times* of London, which is not known for its pro-Indian policy, published a photograph of a mosque in Kashmir bombed by these infiltrators. These are the protagonists of Islam; these are the brave soldiers of Islam who are going to the rescue of the majority of Muslims in Kashmir.

No country, under these circumstances, could have done more than India has done to come to a friendly settlement with Pakistan. We have extended the hand of friendship; it has been rejected. We have made overtures; we have been rebuffed. Now let me give the Council a short resume of what we have been trying to do.

First and foremost, as far back as 1950, our late Prime Minister asked Pakistan to enter into a no-war declaration. We said : Look, before 1947 we were one country: we are brothers; ethnologically, racially and culturally we are one; it would be a horrible thing to contemplate a war between our two countries; let us enter into a no war declaration.

What was the response? It was: No. From 1950 onwards we have repeated this offer; We have said : we shall not go to war with you, and you must not go to war with us; if we have differences we shall settle them in a peaceful manner.

Why has Pàkistan refused to enter into this no-war declaration? I shall give you the reason. It is because she had a guilty mind : because she knew that when the proper time came, she would not hesitate to attack India. Now we know for a fact the reason for her not entering into this no-war declaration.

But this is not the only thing we have done. We agreed to have talks with Pakistan. We agreed to have a meeting of the Home Ministers of the two countries in April 1964. That meeting was adjourned. We continued to remind Pakistan of the need to have another meeting. After continuous pressure from India, the Government of Pakistan agreed to hold a conference on 23 November 1964 in Karachi. However, about ten days before the meeting was due to take place, the Government of Pakistan unilterally postponed the conference indefinitely.

In October 1963, the United Nations Chief Military Observer decided to give awards against even civilians if they were found to commit breaches of the cease-fire agreement. The Government of India accepted this decision. The Government of Pakistan rejected it.

In 1964, the Chief Military observer proposed a meeting between the military representatives of India and Pakistan to consider the problems arising out of the violations of the cease-fire line by armed civilians. India accepted the proposal, but Pakistan-rcjcctcd it.

In early 1965, the Chief Military Observer renewed his proposal. India accepted it, but Pakistan rejected it again.

In July 1964, India proposed a gentleman's agreement to restore tranquillity along the cease-fire line. When Pakistan failed to respond, India repeated this offer – this is found in the letter of 21 August 1964 from the representative of India to the President of the Security Council [S/5911]. At this stage, Pakistan accepted the proposal, and a meeting was fixed for 2 November in Karachi. Two days before the Indian delegation was due to leave for Karachi, the Pakistan Government unilaterally postponed the meeting for an indefinite period, and the meeting has never taken place.

What happened in the Rann of Kutch? I should like to say that this is the third invasion by Pakistan of India. The first was 1947-1948 when Pakistan attacked Kashmir, which legally and constitutionally was part of India; the second was the aggression committed in the Rann of Kutch; and this is the third invasion. With regard to the Rann of Kutch, thanks to the intervention of the Prime Minister of the United Kingdom, we agreed to a truce and to certain cease-fire terms. I would like to draw the attention of members to the preamble of that agreement; "in the confidence that this will also contribute to a reduction of the present tension along the entire Indo-Pakistan border...". While this agreement was being negotiated and before the ink was dry, Pakistan was plotting and planning to invade India.

I would like to come now to our response to the mission of the Secretary-General. May I in the first place express my appreciation of the very strenuous and difficult task that he has undertaken. I remember that I came here on the day the Secretary-General was leaving. I saw him, wished him godspeed and told him that he would be most welcome in my country. I hope the Secretary-General will not misunderstand me, but there is a passage in his preliminary report with which I must quarrel: I do not think it is fair to my country, nor does it correctly represent what really happened in India and in Pakistan. I quote from the message of 15 September from the Secretary-General:

> "The replies from both Governments to my message of 12 September have shown clearly the desire of both for a cease-fire, but both pose conditions which make the acceptance of a cease-fire very difficult for the other side. For this reason, to my profound regret, it has so far been impossible to obtain a cease-fire as requited by the Security Council resolutions of 4 and 6 September." [S/6683, para. 31].

I wish to state that whereas President Ayub Khan posed conditions whith regard to the cease-fire, we posed no conditions whatever. We accepted the cease-fire unconditionally. I have the greatest respect for the Secreatry-General and for his objectivity and impartiality, but I am really surprised at how he came to make a statement like this in the face of the letters which appear in his report. Let me read them out.

Let me first quote from the letter of the Prime Minister of India dated 14 September:

> "In deference to the wishes of the Security Council and to the

appeals which we have received from many friendly countries, we accept your proposal for an immediate cease-fire. We would, therefore, be prepared to order a cease-fire effective from 6.30 a.m., standard time, on Thursday, 16 September 1965, provided you confirm to my by 9 a.m. to-morrow that Pakistan is also agreeable to do so." [*Ibid.*, para. 8.]

In his letter of 15 September, this is what he wrote :

"I reaffirm my willingness, as communicated, to order a simple cease-fire and cessation of hostilities as proposed by you, as soon as you are able to confirm to me that the Government of Pakistan has agreed to do so as well. The actual time when the cease-fire would become effective would depend upon the time when you are able to convey to me the agreement of the Government of Pakistan to a cease-fire." [*Ibid.*, para. 11.]

Does this mean that we were imposing conditions? What is the meaning of a simple cease-fire? I do not want to weary the members of the Council on this point, because it would take up too much time. It is quite clear from the whole tenor of the letters of my country's Prime Minister that he was prepared to accept an unconditional cease-fire. This is what the Security Council wanted, and we complied with the request of the Security Council.

Now let us see the reply of President Ayub Khan. He stated :

"I am fully conscious of the gravity of the present situation and also of the dangers implicity in the catastrophe that threatens to engulf the subcontinent particularly because of the certainty that as time goes on the present conflict would be bound to assume graver and wider dimensions."

"However a cease-fire can be meaningful only if it is followed by such steps as would lead to a durable and honourable settlement in order to preclude the recurrence of a catastrophe such as now threatens the subcontinent. To bring about such a settlement, it would be necessary to evolve an effective machinery and procedure that would lead to a final settlement of the Kashmir dispute." [*Ibid.*, para. 14.]

President Ayub Khan is posing a precondition that there must be machinery in the cease-fire agreement, or a cease-fire itself, which would lead to a final settlement of the Kashmir dispute.

There is another point. The Secretary-General suggested – and he has made the point here also – that President Ayub Khan and the Prime Minister of India should meet and dicuss their differences. It requires two to constitute a meeting. There cannot be a meeting with one person. What is the reply of President Ayub Khan? It is very revealing:

> "While we are agreeable in principle to stop fighting I should like to point out that despite our most earnest efforts, the Ministerial level talks that followed the 1962 agreement proved barren and abortive in face of a firm refusal by India to arrive at an honourable settlement of the Kashmir dispute. On the other hand, India let loose a reign of terror, repression in the State and proceeded to adopt measures to 'integrate' the State of Jammu and Kashmir in the Indian Union. In adopting these measures India showed once again that it has no regard for its own solemn agreements and treats them merely as scraps of paper whenever it suits India." [*Ibid*., para.14.]

I am not dealing with that now. Therefore, there is a clear refusal on the part of President Ayub Khan to meet the Prime Minister of my country. He says that the last effort was "barren" and "abortive". Again, I am not going into that history. We had six rounds of talks, and the meeting was broken up by Pakistan. But this is the response of President Ayub to the Secretary-General's suggestion that the two leaders should meet and bring about a settlement.

The date of this reply of President Ayub Khan is very significant. Whereas the Prime Minister of India replied immediately, President Ayub Khan took some time – and that was deliberate. Members of the Security Council are aware of the news that was released in this country yesterday, 16 September namely, that China has given us an ultimatum, which expires within three days, that if we do not carry out China's demands serious consequences will follow. It was only when President Ayub Khan was assured of this that this reply was sent. This intractable and intransigent attitude is due to the fact that he has expected support from China. He wants India to fight on two fronts. While we are facing Pakistan in the direction of the Punjab, he wants China to stab us in the back. If ever a complicity was established between those two countries, it is this. The timing of the ultimatum and the timing of the reply of President Ayub Khan is not merely a coincidence. It has grave and serious implications. We are now threatened by an invasion from China.

It is sad that Pakistan should be taking this attitude with the help of the arms supplied to Pakistan by the United States not for the purpose of fighting India but for the purpose of meeting the Chinese menace. I have three statements here. The first is from no less a person that President Eisenhower; it is dated 24 Ferbuary 1954:

> "What we are proposing to do, and what Pakistan is agreeing to, is not directed in any way against India, and I am confirming publicly that if our aid to any country, including Pakistan, is misused and directed against another in aggression, I will undertake immediately, in accordance with my constitutional authority, appropriate action both within and without the United Nations to thwart such aggression."

This is what Mr. Bunker, who was then the Ambassador to India, said in November 1957:

> "If Pakistan uses American arms against India for aggressive purposes, she will forfeit our assistance and we will be on the side of India."

Secretary of State of John Foster Dulles, who was, as you know, not very friendly to us in those days, said in 1956:

> "I think there can be every confidence on the part of India now that there will be no use of those armaments in any aggressive way against India. Certainly Pakistan knows that if that should happen there would be a quick end to its good relations with the United States. On the contrary, under the principles of the United Nations Charter, the United States would be supporting India if it became victim of any armed aggression."

I ask the United States : Is the United States going to permit Pakistan to commit a breach of faith with it, and also make it possible for a breach of faith to be committed by the United States with

India? These are not ordinary people giving us assurances. These are assurances by the President of the United States, by the Ambassador of the United States and by the Secratary of State of the United States. Today we have this extraordinary situation that Pakistan is fighting us with Patton tanks with arms which Pakistan received from the United States, and Pakistan is going to fight us in collaboration with a country which the United States considers to be its number one enemy. Therefore, American arms are going to be used to destroy a country which is friendly to the United States.

Therefore, my short submission is that whereas our response to the Secretary-General's mission and the resolutions of the Security Council calling for a cease-fire has been positive, constructive and unequivocal, the response of Pakistan has been obstructive and non-co-operative.

Let us look at the conditions that Pakistan has laid down for the cease-fire. There are four conditions. The first is, a cease-fire – of course, it wants a cease-fire. The second is withdrawal of all troops from Kashmir. This is an extraordinary condition. I am not going into Kashmir question. If I may say so, the Security Council should confine itself to the simple question of the cessation of the conflict and not mix up the political issue with this issue in this juncture.We have time enough for that when the fighting has stopped. But I want to say this about the withdrawal of all troops from Kashmir. Under the resolution of 13 August 1948 of the United Nations Commission for India and Pakistan, we are entitled to have troops in Kashmir, and Pakistan had agreed to withdraw all its troops from that part of Pakistan which it occupies.

Paragraph 1 of Part II, A, of the resolution reads as follows:

> "As the presence of troops of Pakistan in the territory of the State of Jammu and Kashmir constitutes a material change in the situation since it was represented by the Government of Pakistan before the Security Council, the Government of Pakistan agrees to withdraw its troops from the State."

That was in 1948. We are in 1965 and the troops still remain. Not only do they remain, but they are used to invade us, to attack us, to commit in human cruelties upon the citizens of Kashmir.

Part II B, of the resolution relates to India and in paragraph 2 it is stated that:

> "Pending the acceptance of the conditions for a final settlement of the situation in the State of Jammu and Kashmir, the Indian Government will maintain within the lines existing at the moment of the cease-fire the minimum strength of its forces which in agreement with Commission are considered necessary to assist local authorities in the observance of law and order."

Therefore, we are responsible for law, order, security and defence of Kashmir.

Kashmir is an integral part of India. It is a member of the Indian Federation, and it is as much our duty, our responsibility and our privilege to defend Kashmir and look after its law and order as it would be if it was Calcutta, or Bombay, or Delhi, or any other part of India.

And what is the demand? When analysed, it means this. All troops should be withdrawn. That means that we have got the legal right, the constitutional right to have troops in Kashmir for its defence and security, but we must withdraw them before the great country of Pakistan will condescend to talk with us or to accept a cease-fire.

The third condition is induction of an Afro-Asian force. We are entirely opposed to this proposal. We do not want any foreign troops in our country, on our soil. We can look after the interests of our people ourselves. We know how to defend, and we will never agree to any foreign troops being inducted into our country.

Finally–and this is the most extraordinary condition of all–a plebiscite within three months. I have said that these conditions are impossible and preposterous. But let me deal with this last one : a plebiscite within three months. Again, I am not going into the political history of Kashmir. I said on the last occasion–and I stand by that–under no circumstances will India hold a plebiscite. Kashmir is an integral part of India and we do not hold plebiscite in every part of the country. You, Mr. President, would not agree to hold a plebiscite in New Mexico, or Texas, or Alaska; and this would apply to many other countries that I could mention. But, apart from that, it is for the Security Council ultimately to decide whether a plebiscite should be held or not. But Pakistan decides, and it wants a plebiscite at the point of the gun, at the point of the bayonet. The argument is this : we have invaded Kashmir; now hold a plebiscite within three months.

I could understand Pakistan's coming to this Council – after all, Kashmir is still on the agenda of the Council – and pleading its case. But no, Pakistan does not believe in going to international forums. I think that Mr. Bhutto said that he had lost his patience and that he was prepared to fight for a thousand years in order to get Kashmir. But this shows how impossible a condition has been laid down by President Ayub Khan before we can have a cease-fire.

Now may I add that this is not merely a conflict between India and Pakistan; it has much wider significance. The first significance is that the threat and menace of China looms large behind this war. It is much more than merely looming now; it has almost come to a concrete shape after yesterday's ultimatum. And I charge Pakistan with having launched upon this fight with India in the hope and expectation that China will be behind it and support it.

Then, this is a war between two ideologies. Let us face it. On the one hand, there is the religious State; and on the other, the secular State. This is the conflict; it is not Kashmir. Kashmir is merely the symptom; it is not the disease. The disease is that Pakistan believes in a religious State; it believes in religion as the nexus between citizens. We believe in a secular State, in a multiracial society. And it is also a fight between a free society and democratic institutions, on the one hand, and dictatorship and regimentation on the other. These are the issues involved in this war. And I think, if I may say so, that it is in the interests of Asia and the world that our free society, our multi-communal federation should survive.

The attack on Kashmir is an attack for the purpose of breaking up our federation, of breaking up our way of life, of preventing us from carrying on our great experiment of men of different religions and different languages living peacefully together. Mr. President, the same experiment is being tried in your country, the United States and other countries are trying it. But Pakistan does not want it; it does not believe in it and wants to break it up.

What we are defending today is not merely the territorial integrity of our country – which is important enough. What we are defending today is the existence of a free democratic nation. We want to function as a free, democratic nation. It is the threat to our institutions that we are resisting.

Finally, I charge Pakistan with aggression. Aggression began in

1947 against Kashmir and continues today. It is a continuing aggression. The Secretary-General's reports show that Pakistan does not wish to renounce aggression as an instrument of its policy, and Pakistan has been allowed to enjoy the fruits of aggression and even permitted to make common cause with China.

And I charge Pakistan with refusing to comply with the resolution of the United Nations Commission for India and Pakistan.

I ask that in the resolution which the Council ultimately will be pleased to adopt it will note that whereas we have unconditionally accepted a cease-fire, Pakistan has refused to do so. The action which I suggest that the Security Council should take is that it must brand Pakistan as an aggressor, and it must insist on Pakistan's compliance with the resolution.

May I deal now with the report of the Secretary-General which he has read out and which I have had a short time to read. The Secretary-General suggested that the Security Council "could order the two Governments concerned, pursuant to Article 40 of the Charter of the United Nations, to desist from further hostile military action and to this end to issue cease-fire orders to their military forces" (see para. 20).

Why two Governments? Why again bracket India and Pakistan together? We have not said no. Why do you say you should call upon India and Pakistan to desist from taking hostile action? I have read out the letter of the Prime Minister of India. Why this constant attempt at bracketing India and Pakistan together, coupling them together, putting them on the same footing?

The Secretary-General went on to say. "...the Council might also declare that failure by the Governments concerned to comply with this order would demonstrate the existene of a breach of the peace within the meanig of Article 39 of the Charter."

I say that the Council must call upon Pakistan to desist from carrying out hostilities, and I ask it, under Article 39 of the Charter, to which the Secretary-General referred, not to declare that there is a breach of the peace, but to determine – and the Secretary-Council has the authority to "determine the existence of any threat to the peace, breach of the peace, or act of aggression" – the existence of act of aggression on the part of Pakistan.

With regard to the second suggestion which reads as follow: "...the Security Council may wish to consider what assistance it might provide in ensuring the observance of the cease-fire" (see para. 21), after the cease-fire has taken place, and if we wish for any assistance from the Security Council, we will certainly ask of it.

The third suggestion reads as follows: "...the Security Council resolution 210 (1965) of 6 September also calls for a prompt withdrawal of all armed personnel to the positions held by them before 5 August 1965, and the Council may wish to study means of assisting in the carrying out of this requiement." (see para. 22)

This deals with the modality of the cease-fire. I do not want to deal with this in detail, but may I say this. All the invaders who have entered Kashmir must leave. They must be withdrawn. They must be called back. Just as they were sent by Pakistan, they must be called back by Pakistan. Secondly, it must be made impossible for such infiltration to take place again. Thirdly, Pakistan must own up to its responsibility for these infiltrations.

The fourth suggestion is :..."the Council could request the two Heads of Government to meet together at the earliest possible time" (see para. 23) I have already dealt with that. As I have said it requires two to constitute a meeting. We are always prepared to talk with anyone. Debate and discussion are the life-blood of democracy. We have never said no to talks with anybody, but talks must have a purpose. There must be a basis for a talk. While this conflict is going on it is impossible to suggest that the two leaders can meet. Once there is a basis for talks. I hope the Head of the Pakistan State will agree to meet with Prime Minister of India, and I am sure that the response of our Prime Minister will not be uncooperative.

Finally, the Secretary-General declared : "...I may again assure the Council of my availability and of my desire to continue to be of assistance in this matter in any way which may commend itself to the Council and to the two Governments" (see para. 20).

The Secretary-General is always welcome in our country. As I have said before, we have great respect and great regard for him personally and as the executive of this great organization. Today he is the greatest international servant in the world. I know his desire for bringing about peace, and whenever he wants to come to our country he will be welcome. Whatever assistance we can give him for restoring peace will always be available.

I am very grateful for the patient hearing I have been given. I am afraid I have been longer than I expected, but the cause for which we are fighting is so important that I had to present India's case in full detail.

I agree with the Secretary-General that a great responsibilities is placed upon the Security Council. I think this is a test of the Security Council. Is it going to meet the challenge? If international society is to function, the Security Council must answer the challenge. I therefore say : come to a decision, come to conclusion, arrive at judgement, and do not hesitate to deliver the judgement.

12.6. Speech by Mohammad Zafar (Pakistan) in Security Council, 1240th Meeting, September 18, 1965

Pakistan is concerned over the seriousness of the situation in the sub-continent and shares with the other nations the apprehension that, if war continues, it may engulf millions living in India and Pakistan. In view of the gravity of the present conflict, my Government suggested to the Secretary-General, when he came to Pakistan, that the following actions need to be taken: first, there should be a cease-fire with immediate effect; second, immediately thereafter the forces of both India and Pakistan should withdraw completely from the disputed area of Jammu and Kashmir including the territory called *Azad* Kashmir; third, a United Nations force should take over the security function in the state; and fourth, within three months of the cease-fire a Plebiscite should be conducted in the State, under the auspices of the United Nations, to ascertain the wishes of the people of Jammu and Kashmir on the question of accession of their State to India or Pakistan. Pakistan believes that this is the only way in which peace can permanently return to the subcontinent. There in no other way. I intend today to enlarge on this subject and indicate why Pakistan has suggested these measures. The reason is that peace can be achieved only through the enforcement of these measures. I believe that the purpose of Security Council resolutions 209 (1965) and 210 (1965) of 4 and 6 September 1965 respectively, the purpose of the mission undertaken by the Secretary-General, and the objectives of this meeting of the Security Council are to find ways and means to attain lasting peace.

As I shall be disagreeing with some of the observations made by the Secretary-General, I wish to say at once that, any disagreement apart, the Government and the people of Pakistan have the warmest regard for the Secretary-General and high appreciation for his dedication to the cause of peace. As for myself, I have particular regard for him because in the short period of time that I travelled with him from Beirut to Rawalpindi—and this was my first meeting with the Secretary-General I found him to be a man of high ideals and of sincerity of purpose.

May I now proceed to discuss the proposals made by Pakistan. I shall take them one by one to explain why we are urging the Security Council to take a decision in accord with those suggestions. First, Pakistan stands for an immediate cease-fire. This is what the Security Council has proposed.

Pakistan stands for a cease-fire because it believes in peaceful co-existence with India. We expected the two countries to coexist in peace like Canada and the United States, or like Sweden and Norway. We do not want any war with India. We are a smaller country both in area and population. India has nearly a million men under arms, four times as many as Pakistan. India has inherited from the United Kingdom, and has recently acquired from the United States, the USSR and other foreign Powers, a large defence production capacity of its own. Pakistan has in the main to rely for its defence supplies on foreign Powers.

Our main efforts have been devoted towards economic development. With hard and sustained effort, we have made stubstantial progress, but we need many more years to reach our economic goals. And for that we need peace. How can we afford a war? We neither started the war nor do we want it to continue. Therefore we suggested, as the first proposal, that there should be a cease-fire.

The second step proposed by us is that there should be immediate withdrawal of the forces of both India and Pakistan from the entire territory of Jammu and Kashmir. The reason for this proposal are well known to the members of the Security Council and to the world. They stem from the following facts: first, the salient facts of the Kashmir dispute and the resolutions of the United Nations; and second, the extent to which the resolutions have been implemented by India and Pakistan.

The Kashmir dispute arose when the Maharajah of Kashmir, inspite of a standstill agreement with Pakistan, under coercion by the Indian Government and during the time when his people had revolted against him and routed his forces, tried to give away the State of Jammu and Kashmir to India. But the rights of citizens are not a question of title or property which can be passed on by one owner to the other. The people of Kashmir continued their struggle against overwhelming odds. When India failed to crush them, it brought the issue before the Security Council, in January 1948. After extensive discussion of the problem and after listening to both parties, the Security Council adopted resolution 47 (1948) on 21 April 1948 providing for the cessation of hostilities in Jammu and Kashmir, the withdrawal of the combatants, and the holding of a free and impartial plebiscite. Subsequently, the Security Council established the United Nations Commission for India and Pakistan. The Commission visited India and Pakistan, as well as Jammu and Kashmir. After strenuous efforts extending over nearly six months, it brought about an agreement between the two countries with regard to Jammu and Kashmir. This international agreement is embodied in the Commission's resolution dated 13 August 1948 and 5 January 1949.

Taken together, these resolutions provide for, first, a cease-fire and demarcation of cease-fire line; second, the demilitarization of the State of Jammu and Kashmir; and third, a free and impartial plebiscite conducted by the United Nations to determine the question of accession of Jammu and Kashmir to India or Pakistan.

The Commission's resolutions were endorsed by the Security Council and accepted both by India and Pakistan. These resolutions constitute the basic international agreement with regard to Kashmir. In consequence of this agreement fighting stopped on 1 January 1949. An agreement of the demarcation of the cease-fire line was reached on 27 July 1949. Implementation of the demilitarization provisions of the Commission's resolutions was, however, obstructed by India. The Plebiscite Administrator-designate was prevented from assuming office and holding the plebiscite. India refused to synchronize the withdrawal of the bulk of the Indian army with that of the Pakistani forces as proposed by the Commission. Since then, numerous attempts on the part of the Security Council and its various representative have failed to secure an agreement on the issue of demilitarization.

There is a long history of India's refusal to implement this agreement. I could cite chapter and verse, but I am afraid it would take up too much of the time of the Council. I shall therefore only recount a few points as briefly as I can.

First, India refused to submit its plan for the withdrawal of Indian forces when the Commission convened a meeting in March 1949 asking for withdrawal plans and thus blocked progress in demilitarization. When eventually some sort of programme was presented to the Commission, India insisted that it should not be disclosed to Pakistan or to the Security Council. The Commission, however, placed on record its opinion that the Indian withdrawal plan was "far from a fulfilment of India's undertaking under the terms of the 13 August resolution."

Second, to meet one of the objections raised by India, General A.G.L. McNaughton, as President of the Security Council for the month of December 1949, proposed to combine the two stages of demilitarization and produced a comprehensive programme providing for the withdrawal of the forces of Pakistan and India, and the reduction of the Azad Kashmir forces. His proposal of 22 December 1949 was accepted by Pakistan and rejected by India.

Third, by its resolution 80 (1950) of 14 March 1950, the Security Council replaced the United Nations Commission for India and Pakistan by a single mediator, and at its 471st meeting on 12 April 1950 appointed Sir Owen Dixon as United Nations Representative for India and Pakistan. In his report dated 15 September 1950 to the Security Council, Sir Owen Dixon set out his conclusion with regard to the Kashmir impasses.

> "In the end, I became convinced that India's agreement would never be obtained to demilitarization in any such form, or to provisions governing period of the plebiscite of any such character as would, in my opinion, permit of the plebiscite being conducted in conditions sufficiently guarding against intimidation and other forms of influence and abuse by which the freedom and fairness of the plebiscite might be imperilled."

Fourth, at its 543rd meeting on 30 April 1951, the Council appointed Mr. Frank P. Graham as United Nations Representative for India and Pakistan. He put forward several proposals to bring about the demilitarization of Kashmir preparatory to the holding of a plebiscite. The proposals of Mr. Graham were accepted by Pakistan, and again rejected by India.

Fifth, Pakistan also accepted the proposal put forward by the Commonwealth Prime Minister at their meeting in January 1951 for the posting of a Commonwealth force in Jammu and Kashmir to facilitate the withdrawal of the armed forces of India and Pakistan. This proposal, unfortunately, was again rejected by India.

That briefly is the record of India and Pakistan with regard to the implementation of the adopted resolution by the Commission concerning demilitarization.

The third proposal made by Pakistan is designed to create an atmosphere in which a free and impartial plebiscite could be held in Kashmir. To this end, Pakistan has suggested that the forces of India and Pakistan be completely withdrawn from the State and, in their place, a United Nations force composed of contingents from Afro-Asian countries should be inducted. This should eliminate all possibility of coercion by either side at the time of the plebiscite.

The last proposal made by Pakistan is that the plebiscite should be held within a period of three months. The reason for this proposal is stated in the letter dated 13 September 1965 from the President of Pakistan to the Secretary-General:

> "...Pakistan is not against a cease-fire as such. In fact, in order to save the subcontinent from being engulfed in what would clearly be an appalling catastrophe, we would welcome a cease-fire. But it must be a purposeful cease-fire : one that effectively precludes that catastrophe and not merely postpones it. In other words, it should provide for a self-executing arrangement for the final settlement of the Kashmir dispute which is the root cause of the India-Pakistan conflict." (See S/6683, para 9)

It is imperative that a plebiscite should be held as quickly as possible and that the people of Kashmir be enabled to execute their right of self-determination as envisaged in the United Nations resolutions. Until this is done and a highly explosive source of conflict removed, the two countries cannot live together in harmony.

I have so far given the Council the reason for each of the proposals which Pakistan has made. I should now like to explain why Pakistan insists that all these steps must be ordered and taken together and not separately. The stand of Pakistan is that the cease-fire should be a part of a comprehensive agreement. It is no use reverting to the same cease-fire conditions of 1949 which, instead of bringing peace to the people of Kashmir, have brought misery, suffering and war. Indeed, Pakistan is not imposing new conditions of its own. What it is suggesting is what the Security Council itself has pledged to the people of Jammu and Kashmir in the two resolutions of the Commission of 1948 and 1949. What was promised to the people as a composite solution should not be splintered into ineffective fragements.

A clear issue like this should not have been confused. The representative of India must have noticed during his term of office as a judge that when a lawyer is unable to convince a judge, he tries to confuse him. Is the Minister for Education attempting to confuse the Security Council? He has raised the question of the so-called infiltrators in order to cloud the issue of the Indian aggression. The case put forward by the Indian representative is that members of the Pakistan Army crossed the cease-fire line and entered Indian-occupied Kashmir on 5 August 1965. I wish to contradict this allegation categorically and to place certain facts before the Council.

First, no troops of *Azad* Kashmir or Pakistan crossed the cease-fire line until after India had made repeated thrusts and had launched a major offensive against *Azad* Kashmir.

Secondly, the area of Kashmir under the occupation of India is about 50,000 square miles, roughly equal to the total area of the United Kingdom. By India's own account, within less than forty-eight hours after the alleged crossing, actions against Indian forces were taking place from one end of the occupied territory to the other. In and around Srinagar itself, pitched battles had occurred. India maintains approximately six divisions of regular troops in the territory. To this must be added some two divisions of police and militia of various kinds, bringing the total forces at India's disposal to well over 150,000 men.

India would have the world believe that a few thousand outsiders – the figures are between 1,000 and 7,000 – penetrated the barriers set up by the occupation troops, and operating amidst a hostile population, set the torch of resistance against India ablaze throughout the length and breadth of captive Kashmir. These are two basic facts which, if properly appreciated, would suffice to explode the Indian fiction.

However, I feel that we need to examine the myth in some greater detail and see how for it can stand scrutiny. It must be recalled that the original myth was that thousands – there was always a confusion about the Indian estimates of the number involved – of armed personnel entered Indian occupied Kashmir in early August. However, later the representative of India began to talk of "armed and unarmed personnel". I refer to the message read by the representative of India in which it was stipulated that : "...'armed personnel...' must include all infiltrators from the Pakistan side of the cease-fire line, whether armed or unarmed" and furthermore that "the present hostilities originated with large-scale infiltrators of armed and unarmed personnel from Pakistan..." (see 1238th meeting, para. 37).

The question arises : How can any representative state that "armed personnel" should also mean "unarmed personnel"? The answer is not that India has parted with all rationality. The answer is that this utterly absured contention is India's way of concealing the fact that those whom India calls "infiltrators" were but civilians, and a large proportion of them were unarmed. If it is kept in mind that the term "Pakistan side of the cease-fire line" denotes not Pakistan but *Azad* Kashmir, and also that the people who live on the two sides of the cease-fire line are equally Kashmiris whom this fortuitous line cannot seperate from one another, one gets a glimpse of the truth behind the Indian assertions about infiltration. The truth is that this hue and cry about infiltrators was made to give India a pretext to launch a new campaign of terror and repression against the people of Jammu and Kashmir who have risen against India's military occupation of the bulk of the State.

This truth has been testified to by the well-known Indian humanitarian, a disciple of the late Mr. Gandhi, Miss Mridula Sarabhai, who has stated that in the guise of taking action against so-called infiltrators, the Indian Army turned on the entire population of India-held Kashmir and committed atrocities upon them. The Council needs to be informed that, days before the start of hostilities, the Indian Army set fire to the entire residential district of Batamaloo in Srinagar, simply because many freedom fighters lived in that district. The world Press reported this outrage, and published pictures of innocent women and children sitting outside their homes, now reduced to ashes and rubble, but little known for a time about who had perpetrated it.

The truth can now be judged from the dispatch from Srinagar by Richard Cricthfield, published in the *Washington Star* of 1 September:

> "A question that hangs over his fabled vale like the snowy Himalayan peaks is why Indian troops are being used to silence political unrest among Kashmir's 2.5 million Muslims?...

> "Kashmiri Muslims contend that local Indian authorities have been burning homes without the full knowledge of either Prime Minister Lal Bahadur Shastri or the Indian public...
>
> "...during the past three weeks hundreds of Kashmiri houses have been burned to the ground–about 440 in the summer capital of Srinagar alone and scores of others in from fifty to seventy villages scattered throughout the valley.
>
> "There also are isolated eye-witness accounts of pillage, looting and rape.
>
> "Indian officials claim Pakistani infiltrators started the fires. But both extremist and moderate Kashmiris and the victims themselves, interviewed while digging in the smouldering wreckage, claim the Indian Army was responsible.
>
> "Mutual recriminations on who started fires aside, the practical issue is that the majority of Kashmiri people–including some Hindus and Sikhs as well as Muslims–blame the Indian Army.
>
> "...at Magam village, ten miles outside Srinagar, I was briefly detained at the local police station after photographing some forty burned houses. An Indian police inspector refused to discuss how the blaze started.
>
> "But in two other villages the peasants claimed Indian soldiers had put the torch to houses after first evacuating the occupants."

This dispatch offers some other facts about the identity of these so-called infiltrators:

> "...in a secret rendezvous in the old city, I interviewed one of the guerillas whom the Indian call Pakistani infiltrators and Kashmiri themselves call Muzahids, or crusaders.
>
> 'All the infiltrators', he said, 'are Kashmiris, some from the Valley and others from *Azad* Kashmir. We have Punjabis, Punchies, Kishtwaris and other Kashmiri mountain tribals..."

The words used further in the dispatch are important. "We want freedom. We are human beings. Our fight will continue until India is forced to leave this country."

I should like to quote from *The New York Times* of 15 August 1965:

> "...the infiltrators could hardly have made their way so far from the cease-fire line—and in some cases more than forty miles—without help from the local population. The largely Muslim Kashmiris have little love for India, and there is substantial support for union with Pakistan."

India has claimed that the so-called Pakistani infiltrators must be members of the Pakistan Army of *Azad* Kashmir forces because they were armed and well trained. The fact, however, is that the Pakistan side of the cease-fire line has been under such heavy firing from the Indian forces during the last year that *Azad* Kashmir nationals, living along the cease-fire line approached the *Azad* Kashmir Government for armed protection by *Azad* Kashmir forces. They were informed that this was not a practical proposition. Alternatively, therefore, they suggested that they should be given arms to defend themselves. And these arms were therefore provided to them to defend themselves. Most of these men, should be noted, are ex-servicemen. The people of *Azad* Kashmir have a long tradition of fighting with the armed forces. They are well-versed in the art of fighting. Some of these people may have joined the revolt in the Valley.

I now pass on to the question of aggression. When the Security Council met on 6 September (1238th meeting), it had to take account of an event which, unprecedented in the experience of the United Nations, was precisely of the nature which the Organization was founded to prevent and suppress. This was the armed attack on the territory of one Member State, Pakistan, by another, India. The aggression occurred in the early hours of Monday, 6 September, two days after the adoption by the Security Council of a resolution [209 (1965)] appealing that an end be put to the violation of the cease-fire line in Kashmir. That was India's response to the Security Council's appeal for a cease-fire. My delegation cannot but deplore the fact that, in the face of this arrogant challenge to the Council, and deliberate violation of the letter and spirit of the Charter of the United Nations, the Council contented itself with describing the situation euphemistically as an "extension of the fighting", although it recognized that India's action had added "immeasurably to the seriousness of the situation."

Following the reverses suffered by the Indian Army in the Rann of Kutch, Indian leaders let it be known publicly that they would hit Pakistan at a time and place of their own choosing. The following is the direct outcomes of that threat.

On 15 May—long before the so-called Pakistani infiltrators took to arms in Indian occupied territory—India violated the cease-fire line and occupied three Pakistani posts in Kargil. That was India's first act of calculated aggression. Under pressure of the United Nations, India vacated those posts, but again on 15 August, before Pakistani forces could occupy them, India reoccupied those posts. That was done within hours of a public threat by the Indian Prime Minister that India would carry the fight to *Azad* Kashmir. The Defence Minister boasted in the Indian Legislature that "India had crossed the cease-fire line in the past and would do so again."

On 23 August the village of Awam Sharif, which lies clearly inside Pakistan territory, was shelled by Indian forces. Twenty-five of the inhabitants—none of whom were army personnel—were killed. On 24 August Indian forces again crossed the cease-fire line and seized two other Kashmir posts in the Tithwal sector. A few days later Indian forces again struck across the cease-fire line in the Uri-Punch sector. By the end of August they had seized a number of Pakistan posts there.

The Indian propaganda line was that they had seized the forgoing Pakistan posts with the limited objective of stopping "Pakistani infiltrators" from entering Indian-held Kashmir. This was only a trick to put Pakistan off guard and to delude the world. We had reliable information at that time that India was preparing to mount a big offensive with a view to capturing *Azad* Kashmir. This was the position which Pakistan faced on 1 September. India had committed aggression; it had reduced the cease-fire line to a nullity : it was planning to seize *Azad* Kashmir by force.

It was then that, in order to forestall further aggressive moves by Indian forces, the *Azad* Kashmir forces, backed by the Pakistan Army, crossed the cease-fire line for the first time since July 1949. They moved into the Bhimbar sector and seized Chhamb and Dewa. The same afternoon the Indian Air Force went into action against our forces in that area, thereby forcing the Pakistan Air Force to intervene. The conflict was thus further escalated by the Indian action.

Pakistan could have saved the isolated posts that India had seized in the Uri-Punch sector if only it had given air support to those small outposts which were clamouring for it. We denied them air support, preferring to lose those posts rather than be the first to add a new dimension to this conflict.

On 6 September, after the Security Council had appealed to both India and Pakistan to cease-fire, India launched a three-pronged attack against Lahore. Lahore, which is one of the most important cities of Pakistan and – I can say so with firmness because I myself am from Lahore – is situated only eighteen miles from the India-Pakistan border. The Indian leaders' threat to hit Pakistan at a place and time of their own choosing had thus been carried out. The aggression against *Azad* Kashmir was only a device for creating this opportunity, knowing as India did that we would be bound to react to its aggressive attacks on *Azad* Kashmir territory.

India thus carried the war to Pakistan, treacherously launching an armed attack against Pakistan territory without even a declaration of war. This attack has been contained and Indian forces have been repulsed. However, heavy fighting continues.

The sheer escalation of attack by India provides clear evidence of Indian aggression against Pakistan. India tore up the cease-fire line; and Indian Government radio described the Indian military action to annex *Azad* Kashmir as "the war of liberation". *Time* magazine of 10 September 1965 reported as follows:

> "India became delirious with victory. News of the Indian advances was wildly cheered in (Indian) Parliament. The Government radio announced the 'liberation' of 5,000 people and the establishment of Indian civil administration in the 'liberated' areas."

And this is what the representative of India described yesterday as measures taken in self-defence.

I shall not take the Council's time with an account of the events and happening of subsequent days. The fighting spread with a rapidity which is clearly indicative of the premeditation and planning that must have gone into the Indian attack on Pakistan. From weapon to weapon and from area to area, India has enlarged the conflict in such a manner that the two countries are today in a state of general war, and Pakistan is fighting the aggression along virtually entire border in the west.

On the very day when the Secretary-General prepared to leave for the subcontinent, in pursuance of the mandate with which he was charged by the Security Council, India forces opened two new fronts against Pakistan, one in the south from Rajasthan, and the other from occupied Kashmir into the Sialkot area.

It is not possible for me, in the time at my disposal, to give the Council a full picture of the scope and nature of the struggle in which Pakistan is today engaged. This is what a foreign observer on the scene, J. Anthony Lukas, cabled in a dispatch from New Delhi which appeared in *The New York Times*, of 9 September:

> "It is also felt that, with U Thant, the Secretary-General of the United Nations, due in Pakistan, Indian strategy may be designed to confront Pakistan with a military situation that will make them sue for peace on terms suitable to India."

"Having been attacked along its entire frontier, Pakistan is fighting to defend itself against unlimited aggression from India, which claims to be imbued with the Gandhian philosophy of non-violence. And yet the representative of India asserts that his Government has done its best to limit the war. By invading Pakistan's territory along a 600-miles front, India has spread flames of war over the subcontinent and condemned its 550 million men and women to misery and fear, has given a setback to their hopes of social and economic progress, and has revived the historic animosities and rancours which one has hoped now belonged to the past.

If the people of the subcontinent are today on the brink of a cataclysm, the responsibility, ultimate and immediate, must be placed at the door of that country which for eighteen years has rejected every suggestion, thwarted every move, frustrated every effort and barred every avenue for a just and peaceful settlement of the dispute which divides India and Pakistan.

I should like now to refer to the visit of the Secretary-General to Pakistan and India and to the reports which he has submitted to the Council. The Secretary-General's reports show that, while both Governments have agreed in principle to a cease-fire, conditions have been attached or implied with regard to which the

Secretary-General did not feel competent to give an undertaking. He undertook, however, to bring these aspects of the replies of the two Governments to the notice of the Security Council for its urgent consideration.

We share the Secretary-General's disappointment that his valiant efforts in the cause of peace have not met with complete success. A careful perusal of his last report (S/6686) shows that this was due partly to his restricted terms of reference, and partly to the negative attitude of India, both now and in the past, with regard to the Kashmir problem.

The Secretary-General proceeded to the subcontinent under Security Council's resolution 210 (1965) adopted on 6 September 1965. This resolution called upon India and Pakistan "to cease hostilities in the entire area of conflict immediately, and promptly withdraw all armed personnel to the positions held by them before 5 August 1965". In pursuance of this directive, the Secretary-General appealed on 12 September (see S/6686, para, 6) to the President of Pakistan and Prime Minister of India "to order a cease-fire without condition, and a cessation of all hostilities in the entire area of the current conflict between India and Pakistan to take effect on Tuesday, 14 September 1965".

The Prime Minister of India made it clear in his letter dated 14 September (*Ibid*, para 8) that his acceptance of the Secretary-General's proposal for a cease-fire was subject to the following conditions. First, that the cease-fire orders would "be effective only in respect of the armed forces in uniform engaged in the present combat" and that the Indian Security Forces would remain free to deal with the co-called "armed infiltrators" in Jammu and Kashmir. Secondly, the Indian Prime Minister also made it perfectly clear "when consequent upon cease-fire becoming effective, further details are considered, we shall not agree to any disposition which will leave the door open for further infiltrators or prevent us from dealing with the infiltrations that have taken place". Thirdly, the Indian Prime Minister stated categorically "no pressures or attacks will deflect us from our firm resolve to maintain the solidarity and territorial integrity of our country, of which the State Jammu and Kashmir is an integral part." In other words, he has clearly imposed a condition that the cease-fire should not be linked to the settlement of the Kashmir dispute, which is the only cause of the present war.

It is no wonder that the Secretary-General found it impossible to accept these conditions. In fact, the Indian Prime Minister's letter of 14 September amounts to a rejection of the Secretary-General's proposal for an immediate and unconditional cease-fire. While ostensibly agreeing to a stoppage of fighting with the Pakistan Army and the *Azad* Kashmir Forces, India wishes to retain a free hand to deal with the oppressed people of Jammu and Kashmir, who have risen in revolt against their Indian oppressors and the quisling administration which has been operating in Srinagar under the protection of Indian bayonets.

The second condition sought to be imposed by the Prime Minister of India is in line with India's persistent refusal to withdraw its forces from Jammu and Kashmir in accordance with the resolution of the United Nations Commission for India and Pakistan of 13 August 1948 and 5 January 1949, which were endorsed by the Security Council and accepted by both India and Pakistan. It is quite clear that there could be no real peace in Jammu and Kashmir if India were free to make the dispositions of its armed forces without regard to the international agreements of Kashmir.

The most preposterous conditions, however, mentioned by the Indian Prime Minister is his determination to make the State of Jammu and Kashmir an integral part of India. Since 1947, the State of Jammu and Kashmir has been regarded as a disputed territory. As far back as 21 April 1948, the Security Council, in its resolution 47 (1948) noted that : "both India and Pakistan desire that the question of the accession of Jammu and Kashmir...should be decided through the democratic method of a free and impartial plebiscite". That declaration was reaffirmed in paragraph 1 of the resolution of the United Nations Commission for India and Pakistan of 5 January 1949, which, as I submitted earlier, was endorsed by the Security Council and accepted by both India and Pakistan.

When, in total disregard of these undertakings, the Government of India convened a Constituent Assembly in Kashmir and that assembly sought to determine the future consitutional position of Jammu and Kashmir, Pakistan launched a strong protest. The Security Council sought and obtained from the representative of India a categorical assurance that, while the Assembly could express an opinion, it could "take no decision on the question of accession" and that this opinion "would not bind the Government of India or prejudice the position of the Security Council."

In its resolution 91 (1951) of 30 March 1951 the Security Council reminded both India and Pakistan of the earlier United Nations resolutions with regard to Kashmir and reaffirmed the stand of the Security Council : "that final disposition of the State of the Jammu and Kashmir will be made in accordance with the will of the people expressed through the democratic method of a free and impartial plebiscite conducted under the auspices of the United Nations."

That position was reaffirmed by the Security Council in it resolution 122 (1957) of 24 January 1957.

The Indian Government's attempt to treat the State of Jammu and Kashmir as an integral part of India is, therefore, a violation of its international undertakings with regard to Kashmir and is manifestly contrary to the repeated declarations of the Security Council. It is also a fact that the recent troubles in Jammu and Kashmir are due in no small measure to the steps taken in December 1964 to undermine the disputed status of Jammu and Kashmir and to complete the annexation of the State through a variety of legislative, administrative and juridical measures. Incidentally, these steps were taken in flagrant disregard of the assurances given by the Indian Prime Minister to the President of Pakistan on 12 October 1964 that, pending a settlement of the Kashmir dispute, nothing would be done by the Government of India to complicate the situation or to prejudiee the position of Pakistan vis-a-vis Kashmir.

I gave close attention to the report of the Secretary-General [S/6686] on his mission to India and Pakistan. That report contains a number of proposals which, to the best of my knowledge, the Secretary-General did not discuss with the Government of Pakistan during his visit to Ravalpindi. I have transmitted these proposals to my Government and I shall place our considered reactions before the Security Council as soon as I receive instructions from my Government. In the meantime I should like to submit a few preliminary observations.

I am wholeheartedly in agreement with the Secretary-General's remark that the Security Council should continue to make further strenuous efforts for a cease-fire, as well as for a long-term solution of the Kashmir problem. This is a duty and an imperative responsibility of the Security Council. The Secretary-General has made a number of specific recommendations with regard to the cease-fire, but I regret to have to observe that his proposals for a long-term solution of the Kashmir problem are neither precise nor effective. All that the Secretary-General has proposed in this regard is that the Council should request the two Heads of Government to meet together "to discuss the current situation and the problems underlying it as a first step in resolving the outstanding differences between their two countires and in reaching an honourable and equitable settlement" [*Ibid.*, para. 9 (d)]. There is on reference here to Jammu and Kashmir or to the implementation of the international agreement with regard to the State embodied in the Commission's resolutions which were endored by the Security Council and accepted by India and Pakistan.

The Secretary-General's suggestion that the Council might consider the possibility of creating a small committee to assist in the talks between the two Heads of Government, "should its services seem useful and desirable to the two parties" (*ibid.*) is likely to be of limited value unless and until the Security Council clearly sets out the obligations assumed by India and Pakistan with regard to Kashmir and directs the committee to oversee their implementation.

Pakistan certainly welcomes the Secretary-General's offer of his own good offices in the search for a permanent solution of the Kashmir problem.

The Secretary-General has said that the Security Council can order a cease-fire under the provisions of Article 40 of the United Nations Charter and "that failure by the Governments concerned to comply with this order would demonstrate the existence of a breach of the peace within the meaning of Articale 39 of the Charter" (*ibid.*, pare 9 (a)). I venture to doubt the necessity for such action. It would be the first time in the history of the Kashmir dispute that the Security Council would be contemplating action under Chapter VII of the Charter. Hitherto, all action have been taken under chapter VI. Departure from past practice would be a momentous decision, and its implications would have to be carefully weighed before the Security Council proceeds further in this matter. We too will have to weigh carefully our reactions to such a move.

I would like now to make a few brief comments on some of the points in the statement of the representative of India at the Council's previous meeting.

The representative of India claimed that India's policies were based on the message of non-violence and peace. We have seen Indian non-violence in action in Kashmir, Junagadh, Hyderabad and Goa. We have also seen this non-violence in the Rann of Kutch. We are witnessing it now on the borders of Pakistan. It is a matter of history that whenever India has had any dispute with its neighbours it has sought to settle it by the force of arms but to call it non-violence.

The representative of India also referred to Mr. Nehru's offer of no-war declaration in 1950. This offer was welcomed by Pakistan, which put forward concrete proposals to achieve the desired aim. The Government of India was invited to agree that the settlement of every dispute would be sought through negotiations, and if necessary, through mediation; but if these methods were to fail, the dispute would be referred to arbitration. It was only thus that no-war declaration could carry conviction. Pakistan also pointed out that by joining the United Nations, Pakistan had already renounced the use of force. A bare announcement that we would not declare war unless attaked added nothing to these commitments; if anything, it detracted from them. An announcement that failed to substitute arbitration for compulsion would fail to carry conviction that there would be no resort to force. The hypocritical character of India's offer of a no war declaration is well illustrated by the fact that Pakistan was invaded by India on 6 September 1965 without a declaration of war.

The representative of India claimed that India is a modern, secular State, while Pakistan is a medieval, theocratic State. These claims and accusations have been made by India *ad nauseum* in the past. Nothing could be farther from the truth. The provisions with regard to citizenship, fundamental rights and social justice in the Constitution of Pakistan are as liberal as those of the Constitution of any other modern State. They are in no way inferior to the provisions in the Constitution of India. Pakistan's treatment of its minorities compares favourably in every way with the treatment which India is meting out to its own minorities. This is borne out by the hundreds of attacks on the helpless Muslim minorities and the large-scale expulsion of India Muslim nationals from Assam and Tripura which has been going on for the last three years. Over half a million of these unfortunate people have been pushed over the border into East Pakistan and have found refuge there.

I shall now turn to the episode of the Rann of Kutch, to which a reference was made by the representative of India. I will not go into the substance of the dispute, but I would like to point out that the existence of the dispute was explicitly recognized by both India and Pakistan. They also agreed in the Border Ground Rules of 1960 that, pending the final disposition of the territory, neither side would attempt to change in any way the *status quo* in the disputed territory. Earlier this year, the Government of India, for no apparent reason, decided to make an issue of patrolling by Pakistani border police along a track which runs some 1,800 yards into the Rann of Kutch. India claimed the entire territory. To make good this claim, India marched two full brigades of its regular troops and armour into the area, brought up a bomber squadron to the nearby airfield of Jamnagar, and the aircraft-carrier *Vikrant* to within twenty miles of Karachi. When, as was inevitable, a clash occurred in the territory, India moved up its entire army against the borders of Pakistan and threatened to wreak war and destruction upon our country. At that point the Prime Minister of the United Kingdom intervened, and through his good offices the Government of India were brought around to accept the arbitration of a three-man tribunal for settling the dispute. The most significant aspect of this incident is that, while presenting the agreement on the Rann of Kutch to the Indian Parliament, Prime Minister Shastri conceded in the most clear and explicit language that the Pakistani patrol track, which the Government of India had chosen to make into a *casus belli*, did in fact lie within the territory in the *de facto* control of Pakistan, and that Pakistani police had always moved along it. What I have stated is in the records of the Indian Parliament itself. Any impartial observer can draw his own conclusions from a study of this case. I venture to submit that no clearer case can be found of the systematic bellicosity which has characterized the Government of India's attitude to Pakistan. The example of the dispute of the Rann of Kutch shows how, behind its peaceable posturing, the Indian Government goes about seeking occasions to pick gratuitous quarrels with Pakistan.

The representative of India stated that the Government of India has only love and affection for the people of Pakistan and that even today India does not consider itself at war with Pakistan. On the morning of 6 September when without a declaration of war, India unleashed an attack on Pakistan; its first act in this war was the strafing by Indian aircraft of a stationary passenger train at Wazirabad station, killing a great many innocent civilians. This is that love and affection.

As long ago as 23 August, the Indian army shelled Awam Sharif inside Pakistan territory, killing twenty-five persons and wounding fifty. In flagrant violation of international conventions, India's wanton attack on open cities of Pakistan and bombing of civilian populations started first with cities in Pakistan including the capital Rawalpindi, Karachi, Dacca and Chittagong. In Rawalpindi and in adjoining villages, some two dozen persons, including two women and five children, were killed by Indian bombing, and over a dozen houses were demolished. In Karachi the bombs fell in the main residential areas, damaging houses and injuring the sleeping inmates. In East Pakistan Indian Canberras carried out wanton attacks on civilian areas of five principal cities, including Dacca and Chittagong. In the afternoon of 10 September the Indian Air Force again strafed civilian population in five East Pakistan districts, subjecting the civilian population to heavy bombing and strafing. The same night, the Indian Air Force bombed and shelled the civilian area of Sialkot city, damaging the main bazaar and fort area of the city of Sialkot with 1,000-pound bombs. A large number of the civilian population was killed during the bombings on Sialkot. Estimates of losses, which are extremely heavy, are being worked out.

Commenting on this, Roy Meloni, correspondent of the American Broadcasting Corporation, said in a recorded despatch on 14 September:

> "If the Indians ever try to tell you that they have not bombed civilian targets inside Pakistan, you have my permission to tell them to go quietly to hell.
>
> "...
>
> "Some nights ago, Indians bombed Sialkot about five miles from the Indo-Pakistan border and at least three miles from any military target, and they killed about twenty people. A further seventy were injured. The bombs fell in the heart of the city, ripped a mosque into ribbons; and I wept—yes, I cried—with the survivors, because this is not war, it is deliberate terror."

So the less said of this "love", the better it is.

During the night between 13 and 14 September the Indian Air Force once again bombed the civilian populations in Pakistan in the cities of Peshawar and Kohat, killing sixty persons and injuring a large number as a result of indiscriminate bombing. In Peshawar alone thirty persons were killed. When the Indian Air Force Canberras bombed the civilian areas in Kohat, twenty-seven bodies had been recovered by the after-noon and digging for the rest was in progress when last reports came in. Forty-three persons were seriously injured. The casualties in both Peshawar and Kohat included a large number of women and children.

The main target of Indian bombers in Peshawar was two adjoining villages where many houses and two mosques were destroyed by Indian bombs. In Landi Arbab village a bomb directly hit a mosque and another bomb landed near a church and the residence of the American Consul in Peshawar. In Kohat, an Indian Air Force bomber hit the Liaquat Memorial Hospital, the City Health Centre and the district jail hospital. A large number of houses were destroyed. Once again on 15-16 September, the Indians bombed two villages in Sargodha, killing civilians and destroying a large number of houses.

This wanton Indian bombing of the civilian population in Pakistan's open cities continues. Only the night before last another seventeen civilians were killed and several men, women and children were injured when the Indians bombed another passenger train on its way from Lahore.

Let me now turn to the charges by the representative of India of Pakistan's alleged collusion with China. For many years India exploited Pakistan's membership of military pacts to sow suspicion and mistrust in the minds of China and the Soviet Union against Pakistan. For many years India enjoyed intimate relations with these Powers and sought to isolate Pakistan from these two great neighbouring countries. When the compulsion of Pakistan's national interest necessitated a normalization of our relations with China and the Soviet Union, and Pakistan began to take steps in that direction on the basis of the ten Bandung principles, India tried to turn these development to its advantage by sowing suspicion of Pakistan in the United States. This "collusion" is but a figment of India's perverted imagination. If there was even a semblance of truth in these accusations, if "collusion" could be deduced from events, then the Chinese-Indian conflict of 1962 was the moment of our opportunity. Did we then attack India to liberate Jammu and Kashmir?

The truth of the matter can be deduced from the fact that the mountain divisions raised and equipped by India in the last two years, with the assistance of the United States for the express purpose of defence against China, are now deployed in the plains of the Punjab and engaged in attacting Pakistan. Toward the middle of August, an entire brigade was moved from the Laddakh region to the Kashmir cease-fire line and it is this unit which was responsible for the breach of the ceasc-fire line near Tithwal. In fact the only Indian divisions which may appear to be stationed along India's northern frontiers are those in the east. These divisions can wheel around at a moment's notice to threaten and attack East Pakistan. The allegation made by the representative of India that Pakistan was conspiring with China for the destruction of India is not only baseless, but is also a blatant attempt to impress certain sections of opinion, particularly in the United States.

Pakistan's dispute with India arises from India's attempt to annex the State of Jammu and Kashmir against the wishes of the peaple of Kashmir, whom we in Pakistan consider as our kith and kin. The problem of Kashmir, as well as the agreement to hold a plebiscite, predates Pakistan's association with the Western Powers and its more recent efforts to establish good neighbourly relations with China and the Soviet Union. A solution of the Kashmir dispute, in accordance with the agreed declarations would serve neither some dark purpose of China nor of any other foreign Power. Pakistan has no ambitions beyond its borders. Unlike India, it seeks no foreign possession or sphere of influence. The last thing that we wish is that the Kashmir dispute should become embroiled in the conflicts and rivalries between the great Powers. It is not Pakistan which has gained in the past from the cold war between the United States and the Soviet Union. It is not Pakistan which today has a vested interest in the worsening of relations between China and the Soviet Union or China and the United States.

Having dealt with all the issues, I now remind this august body that in a similar situation in 1948 the Security Council insisted on deciding the entire dispute. I would like to recall to the Security Council some of the statements made by the members of the Council as they are relevant to the issue now under consideration.

At the 236th meeting of the Security Council, the representative of the United Kingdom said :

> "We are, then confronted with the question of how to stop the fighting. What will stop it, and in what way should it be

stopped?

"...

"What these two Governments want, and what we all want, is that the moral power and authority of the Security Council be brought to bear on the situation so that there can be a conviction on all sides that justice is to prevail, and that violence need not go on. Moreover, our object is not only to stop the fighting, but to keep it stopped. We have to arrive at a settlement which will prevent a new outbreak."

At the 237th meeting of the Security Council, the representative of Canada said :

"The President has rightly pointed out that the ending of the fighting and the holding of the plebiscite under conditions which will be recognized as fair and impartial are two aspects of the same matter."

At that same meeting of the Security Council, the representative of China said :

"It is obvious that the key to the problem lies in the plebiscite. If the principle of free and impartial plebiscite for deciding the all-important question of the accession of Kashmir to India or Pakistan should be accepted, much of the incentive to violence and the use of force would be removed."

At the 240th meeting of the Security Council, the representative of United States said :

"I should feel that it would be erroneous for the Security Council, in solving this matter – if it were acting under Article 37 – to undertake to do it piecemeal, by handling the termination of hostilities with one hand and the plebiscite with the other I believe that method would be entirely incongruous and would not lead to any successful solution of the matter.

"It is my opinion that, if and when the Security Council deals with this problems, it must consider it as a whole, because unless it does, there cannot be a cessation of hostilities."

At the same meeting, the representative of Argentina said :

> "Now that the disputes between India and Pakistan have been submitted to the jurisdiction of the Security Council, the delegation of Argentina will not be able to vote in favour of any draft resolution which does not leave the solution of the problem to be decided by a plebiscite, freely prepared, freely conducted and freely scrutinized under the authority of the Security Council..."
>
> "...
>
> "In order to solve a problem, and especially a problem of this nature, it is necessary to know the underlying causes. It is worthwhile remembering the Latin proverb, which says *sublata causa, tollitur effectus*, or, in other words remove the cause and the effects will disappear. In this case, the cause of all the disturbances, whether from India or Pakistan, or from the tribes, lies in the rebellion of the people of Kashmir against the absolute monarch who rules them as if he were running a farm and the 4 million inhabitants were so many heads of cattle and not human beings.
>
> "If, therefore, in accordance with the provisions of the Charter already quoted, we assure these human beings that they themselves will be able to decide their own fate freely and without pressure from any quarter, I am sure that they will lay down their arms."

Finally, I would like to cite the remarks made on a later occasion. At the 467th meeting of the Security Council, the representative of Norway said :

> ".. the obviously correct point of departure : India's and Pakistan's agreement that the future status of Jammu and Kashmir shall be determined in accordance with the will of the people. This agreement; first briefly stated in Part III of the

> 13 August 1948 resolution, and subsequently elaborated in greater detail in the 5 January 1949 resolution, is not merely an important part of the edifice which has been laboriously built, up by the Commission in the two resolutions, it is the keystone what carries the whole structure and to which all the other parts are intimately related:
>
> "...
>
> "We must bear in mind that it was under the terms of this agreement, incorporated in the two resolutions of the United Nations Commission for India and Pakistan which I have just mentioned, that cease-fire orders were issued by the opposing parties on 1 January 1949. The cease-fire agreement of 27 July 1949, completely demarcated on the ground, is also based upon and integrated into the same structure. Any attempt to bypass or whittle away its basic principles would jeopardize the cease-fire which has so painstakingly been established by the Commission.
>
> "...
>
> "...It is for the plebiscite to determine the ultimate fate of the State.
>
> "I would like to add that this principle, this keystone of the whole structure, has an importance which transcends the obligatory force it derives from the consent of the parties. The principle has its intrinsic value because it embodies the only criterion for determining Kashmir's fate which is compatible with modern democratic ideals."

I hope that the statements of members of the Security Council which I have quoted will suffice to establish that a simple, unconditional, cease-fire would not by itself suffice to bring about either peace or a durable solution of the Kashmir problem. It must also be recalled that the agreement with regard to the demarcation of the cease-fire line of July 1949 is only the first part of the Commission's resolution of 13 August 1948. The rest of the resolution, providing for withdrawal of the armed forces of India and

Pakistan and the holding of a free and impartial plebiscite, have still to be implemented. India cannot insist on respect for the cease-fire agreement and yet continue to oppose implementation of the remaining provisions of the international agreement with regard to Kashmir.

I have set forth the proposals of my Government for the termination of the present conflict between India and Pakistan. They are based on principles which are self-evident. I put it to the Council: What could be more fair to the interests of India, of Pakistan and of the people of Jammu and Kashmir than the proposition that we finally settle this dispute on the basis of the wishes of the people, freely ascertained? What could better secure a just and genuine peace for our entire region ? Are we asking too much when we ask that the United Nations base its approach to the problem on the principle of self-determination which is the very soul of the Charter ? Are we asking too much when we say that the people of Kashmir, whose land it is, be given a chance to decide their fate ? Is it wrong on our part if we suggest that you cannot solve a problem pertaining to a people if you bypass those people ?

It is for the Council now to make India accept these proposals which do not involve capitulation on India's part but simply the fulfilment of a pledge solemnly and repeatedly given by it. These proposals are but the translation into concrete form of the imperatives of peace with justice. They lead the parties, not to an illusory cease-fire, but to a peace containing an insurance against a renewed conflict and a catastrophe.

These proposals are an earnest of our faith, our search for justice, our commitment to peace. If they are endorsed, we are confident that we can open an era of good neighbourliness. If they are rejected or laid aside, then the prospectus of peace recede from eyes and the hopes for justice are again deferred.

We have been invaded. To ask us to cease-fire is to ask us to suffer aggression. It is to ask us to dishonour our most sacred obligation of defending our land. It is to ask us to sacrifice our 5 million bethren in Jammu and Kashmir to whom a pledge has been given – here in the United Nations – that they will be free to decide their future through an impartial plebiscite. Even in today's world of power politics, a nation has a soul, a sense of honour, a feeling of obligation imposed by solemn international agreements, such as the one which bound India and Pakistan to the proposition that Kashmir shall not be a part of either country unless it has so decided of its own free will. It is a pledge embodied in numerous resolutions of the Security Council. It is. enshrined in our soul and consecrated by our blood. Let me make it clear: Pakistan would rather make the supreme sacrifice than let this pledge be thrown overboard.

12.7. Speech by Lord Caradon (United Kingdom) in Security Council, 1241st Meeting, September 18, 1965

I do not propose now to endeavour to comment on the two very able speeches to which we have listened this afternoon. We shall wish to study what they have said very carefully, and it may well be that at a subsequent stage in our debate I would comment on them. I would make no excuse at all this afternoon for speaking at this stage only in order to emphasize the need to concentrate our attention on the statements of the Secretary-General. I shall do so very shortly because I am concerned not to go back over that but to look to the future. It is the action to be taken on those statements of the Secretary-General is which our whole attention must surely now be directed.

I am sure that all of us at once recognized the gravity of the report [S/6686] made to us by the Secretary-General at the 1239th meeting yesterday. It was a clear, and forthright and hold report suitable to the gravity of the situation.

Now as we meet to take action on that report I am confident that we do so with an overriding sense of urgency. In this Council we acted with urgency and unity when we unanimously passed resolutions 209 (1965) and 210 (1965) of 4 and 6 September. The Secretary-General followed up those resolutions without delay and without any hesitation. The United Nations did not fail to move quickly to meet the danger. Now the need for further urgent action is greater than ever.

From the first, the Secretary-General has had the full support of my Government. The Prime Minister of the United Kingdom at once appealed in the most urgent terms to President Ayub Khan and to Prime Minister Shastri to respond to Council resolution 209 (1965) and to bring the fighting to an immediate end. And the British Foreign Secretary confirmed personally to the Secretary-General, when he passed through London on his way to Pakistan and India, the whole-hearted support of Her Majesty's Government.

We wished the Secretary-General good fortune when he set on his brave endeavour. Throughout, he has carried with him the fullest confidence of my Government, and we pay our tribute to his energy and his patience and his persistence and his courage. We are more than ever grateful to him for his readiness to continue to carry such a heavy burden of responsibility.

We most sincerely endorse the Secretary-General's statement on leaving Delhi that even though an end of the fighting had not yet been achieved, there was no reason for slackening our efforts to achieve it. On the contrary, as the Secretary-General emphasized in the report he made to us yesterday, the need for a sustained and accelerated effort is now greater than ever. There is and can be no question of failure. It is a continuing and reinforced initiative on which he and we are engaged, an initiative which must succeed. As the Secretary-General said to us yesterday – and we closely marked his words :

> "If success has not yet been achieved in securing compliance with the Council's resolutions, that is all the more reason for making further strenuous efforts for a cease-fire as well as for long-term solutions." [S/6686, para. 8.]

We are encouraged and inspired by the Secretary-General's example and his call "to show that peace can be restored and international harmony promoted by the concerted efforts of the international community" [*Ibid*]. We, with him, are "thinking not only of the well-being and future of the Governments and peoples of India and Pakistan, but also of the hopes of mankind for a more peaceful world which are centered on the United Nations." [*Ibid.*].

This is the text of the statement issued by my Government in London earlier today :

> "The British Government have made it clear that they gave the fullest support to the recent mission undertaken by the United Nations Secretary-General at the request of the Security Council in an attempt to reach a peaceful settlement of the tragic conflict between India and Pakistan. They believe that the courses of action set out in the Secretary-General's report, which in his judgement might be helpful in considering how to achieve an effective cease-fire, provide a useful basis for

further urgent discussions in the Security Council. The British Government wish to express their profound gratitude and great admiration of the Secretary-General's untiring efforts for peace."

Now, looking to the future, we trust that both of the great countries involved in this conflict will respond to the appeal which we so earnestly and urgently shall now make to them. They will do so, I confidently believe, not only in the interests of their own peoples so that they may be saved from the scourge of much wider conflicts, but in the interests of establishing and maintaining international order and international peace and achieving the honourable and equitable settlement which has long been the declared objective.

12.8. Speech by D.E. Beus (Netherlands) in Security Council, 1241st Meeting, September 18, 1965

First of all, I wish to express the deep concern of my delegation – a concern undoubtedly shared by all members of the Security Council – that a cease-fire as called for by the Security Council almost two weeks ago, in its resolutions 209 (1965) and 210 (1965) of 4 and 6 September has still not come into being. At the same time it seems to us that some progress towards a cease-fire has been made, thanks to the invaluable and unrelenting efforts of the Secretary-General. It is on the result of those efforts that I should like to speak first.

My delegation has studied carefully the Secretary-General's two reports which are before us [S/6683 and S/6686]. I am sure that we are all deeply greatful for the tactful, yet determined, way in which the Secretary-General carried out his most difficult mission. He has not yet been able to achieve a cease-fire, but from a careful reading of his reports one gains the impression that it has been brought some-what closer.

Let us examine for a movement the position of the parties to the conflict with regard to responsibility for the outbreak of fighting, as this position emerges from the Secretary-General's reports as well as from the statements of the two-parties to which we have listened with great attention.

The contention of India, to begin with, is – and here I quote from the reply of Prime Minister Shastri of 14 September – that :

"...Pakistan launched a massive attack on India on 5 August 1965 by sending thousands of armed infiltrators equipped with Pakistani arms and ammunition and officered by men of the regular forces of Pakistan..." [S/6683, para. 8.]

This allegation, it must be said, is confirmed by the Chief United Nations Military Observer in Kashmir, to the extent that the Secretary-General's report of 3 September states :

"...that the series of violations that began on 5 August were to a considerable extent in subsequent days in the form of armed men, generally not in uniform, crossing the cease-fire line from the Pakistan side for the purpose of armed action on the Indian side." [S/6651, para. 6.]

We must therefore assume that extensive infiltrations across the cease-fire line did indeed take place from the Pakistan side from 5 August on, even though we must add that my delegation would not necessarily subscribe to the qualification of these infiltrations as "a massive attack on India".

From this contentious India's demand, repeated here yesterday, that Pakistan be identified as the aggressor, and furthermore India's request – and I quote again from Prime Minister Shastri's first reply :

"We must urge that Pakistan should be asked forthwith to withdraw these armed infiltrators . . . we will have to insist that there must be no possibility of a recurrence of armed attacks on India, open or disguised." [S/6683, para. 8.]

This constitutes, I believe the essence of the Indian position with regard to the outbreak of the present hostilities and of what India expects of the Security Council in connexion with a possible cease-fire.

Pakistan's contention, on the other hand, is that it is India which committed aggression. I quote from President Ayub Khan's reply of 13 September:

"...India attacked Pakistan on 6 September. This was an act of naked aggression. It is astonishing that the cease-fire resolution of the Security Council of 6 September, which you are urging us

> to implement, completely ignores this basic fact." [*Ibid.*, para. 9.]

It is an uncontested fact, I believe, that Indian armed forces crossed the international border between Pakistan and India on 6 September – which was about one day after the Security Council's first appeal for a cease-fire. On the basis of this fact, Pakistan wishes India to be branded the aggressor. The Pakistani President, furthermore, declares himself prepared to accept cease-fire on the following conditions:

> "...the cease-fire must be accompanied by action which would resolve that real cause of this conflict. This would be possible if the cease-fire is followed immediately by complete withdrawal of the Indian and Pakistani forces from the State of Jammu and Kashmir, the induction of a United Nations-sponsored Afro-Asian force to maintain order in the State and the holding of a plebiscite in the State within three months." [*Ibid.*]

The Secretary-General thereupon made a second appeal to both Heads of Government. Prime Minister Shastri, in his reply to this second appeal, declared his country's preparedness to accept a simple cease-fire without attaching conditions. President Ayub Khan, in his reply, declared himself "agreeable in principle to stop fighting" [*Ibid.*, para. 14]. He went on to say, however, that a meeting with Prime Minister Shastri seemed to offer little hope of success. President Ayub Khan furthermore stated:

> "However, a cease-fire can be meaningful only if it is followed by such steps as would lead to a durable and honourable settlement in order to preclude the recurrence of a catastrophe such as now threatens the subcontinent. To bring about such a settlement, it would be necessary to evolve an effective machinery and procedure that would lead to a final settlement of the Kashmir dispute." [*Ibid.*]

A comparison of the first and the second replies of both Governments shows that, although unfortunately they have not yet come together on a cease-fire, the gap which separates them has been narrowed. India no longer poses any conditions, although it is clearly worried about a possible repetition of armed infiltrations. Pakistan still makes it a conditions that a cease-fire should be followed by effective steps leading to a final settlement of the Kashmir dispute.

So much for the position of both parties to the conflict. The question for us now is: what can the Security Council do to achieve a cease-fire and a settlement of the underlying political questions?

I have noted that each of the two parties accuses the other of aggression, that each of the parties adduces established facts to prove that contention, and that each of the parties wishes the Council to brand the other side as the aggressor and draw the conclusions from such a condemnation.

It seems to my delegation that it would become a very complicated and rather fruitless process for the Council to weigh all the actions by one party against those of the other. It is obvious that actions have taken place on both sides by which hostilities escalated, and we believe that it would be almost impossible to single out one specific act or date at which aggression started. The task of the Security Council is to maintain peace and security, not to sit in judgement like a tribunal and award damages after weighing the seriousness of the mutual claims and counterclaims. Our duty today is to stop the fighting and, beyond that, to promote a settlement of the problem from which the fighting originated. We should, therefore, concentrate on steps leading to that double goal. Rather than trying to pronounce judgement on recriminations about the origin of the fighting, we should now try to stop the fighting and open a road to eliminate the underlying causes of conflict from which the fighting sprang.

Returning to the positions of the parties to the conflict with regard to a cease-fire, it seems to my delegation, as I have said, that the two positions are no longer so far apart that the gap cannot be bridged. Upon the Security Council rests the heavy responsibility and the duty now to make a supreme effort to help the parties to bridge this gap. It can do so by making its own contributions to this end, here and now, by trying to alleviate the understandable fears of both parties.

India, I repeat, fears a repetition of armed infiltration. The Security Council cannot, of course, guarantee that no infiltrations or other violations of the cease-fire line will ever take place again. It can, however, greatly contribute to that effect by increasing the present obviously insufficient strength of its Military Observer corps in Kashmir to the degree necessary. This should go a long way to give India a reasonable guarantee against a repetition of massive infiltrations.

Pakistan, on the other hand, fears that if it agrees unconditionally to a cease-fire this will in fact simply mean a return to the *status quo*, without anything else being done to go to the main root of all the troubles between India and Pakistan during the last eighteen years: namely, the Kashmir question. That fear, too, certainly seems justified on the basis of the history of the last eighteen years, since the many decisions of the Security Council on this subject have never been carried out.

As is well known, the attitude of my country has always been that the Kashmir question should be solved on the basis of the free self-determinations of the people of Kashmir and Jammu, and that the decisions of the United Nations Commission for India and Pakistan and the Security Council on that subject offered a just means to achieve that aim. Therefore we can sympathize with Pakistan's apprehension on this aspect, namely that the basic political conflict might be left unsolved. If that were done, the Council would be only dealing with the symptoms of the disease and not with the disease itself, the underlying cause of all the conflicts between India and Pakistan.

Here again, the Security Council can make its contribution to alleviating that fear of Pakistan by making it clear beyond doubt that a cease-fire and a withdrawal of troops will have to be followed by talks between the parties and effective measures to solve on a just and durable basis a problem which has for nearly one score years now envenomed the relations between these two great nations of the subcontinent, which are so dependent on co-operation between them. As the Secretary-General said in his appeal of 12 September to President Ayub Khan and Prime Minister Shastri, cease-fire is "a necessary prelude to further measures towards the restoration of lasting peace" [S/6683, para. 6].

If, then, the difference which separates the two parties on a cease-fire has been narrowed, the military situation too seems at the moment to be more propitious for a cessation of hostilities. After several weeks of fierce battles the fighting seems to have diminished somewhat on several fronts, and a military stalemate appears to be developing. This proves once again that neither party can gain its aims by military means and that the tremendous bloodshed now going on between the two brother nations is, therefore, senseless and should be stopped.

I should like to point to another aspect of the matter and express the great regret which is felt in countries such as mine that these two neighbouring countries, which were dedicating themselves with great energy and obvious results to their economic and social development, are now engaged in a fratricidal conflict which threatens to undo all the valuable work that has been performed in the past. My country is among those which are happy to participate actively in the important assistance which both countries receive on a large scale from many industrialized countries, and we are distressed to see that this development effort, we are so actively supporting, is thus in danger of being undone by the waste of warfare.

To this political and military situation and to this economic aspect there has in the last few days been added another and more ominous reason for ending the fighting without delay. New and serious developments in Asia during the past few days, which have been referred to by the representative of India, have rendered more acute the danger of an extension of the conflict to other areas and to a large-scale conflagration. This makes it absolutely essential that the fighting should be stopped before such a further extension can take place. My delegation, therefore, believes that the Security Council should do its utmost to achieve a cease-fire before this weekend is over. It sincerely hopes that the circumstances which I have mentioned will lead the parties to the same conclusion. At any rate the Security Council should brook no longer delay and should act now. When I say "now" I mean not later than today or tomorrow. The situation is fraught with danger, and time is of the essence.

My delegation consider that many of the suggestions made by the Secretary-General in his second report [S/6686] point the way and are most likely to lead to the desired result. The Security Council should, we believe, as he proposes, on the basis of Article 40, now decide on a specific moment in the nearest future at which hostilities should cease. It can offer its assistance for ensuring the observance of the cease-fire. In taking these steps for a short-range solution, we should, however, not lose sight of our long-range objective, which is to eliminate the underlying political conflict. The Council cannot impose a specific solution of that conflict, which in the end depends on the parties. However, it can set in motion a process to that end. It can set the parities on the road to negotiations and assist them there if disired.

My delegation is prepared to support or to co-sponsor any resolution containing those basic elements.

My delegation hopes and trusts, however, that the Council does not need to go further. India had already declared itself prepared to accept a cease-fire without conditions. Pakistan has declared itself prepared in principle to do so, though maintaining certain fears. The Governments of both countries have stressed their responsibilities towards their nations to defend their own interests. Surely their main responsibility is, however, to put an end to a useless waste of human life as a first step to a durable settlement. Certainly to bring this about is the duty of the Security Council, in view of its responsibility for international peace and security, but also in view of its responsibility towards the nations of India and Pakistan themselves.

12.9. Speech by Security Council President Arthur J. Goldberg (as Representative of the United States of America) in Security Council, 1241st Meeting, September 18, 1965

I should now like to make a statement in my capacity as representative of the United States of America.

The United States believes it crucial that the Security Council pursue urgently, with all the capability at its disposal, its efforts to secure an immediate and effective cease-fire between India and Pakistan and to restore peace in the subcontinent. The Secretary-General has reported to us in full on his mission of peace. The United State commends the Secretary-General for his impartial efforts to give effect to the Council's resolutions and achieve an honourable settlement. My Government fully endorses his proposals to the parties and urges this Council, in the light of the seriousness of the situation, to proceed to promptly implement them.

We agree with the comment just made by the representative of the Netherlands, that time is of the very essence in this grave situation.

We regard the Security Council as the appropriate and the most effective agency to meet this crisis. We believe the Security Council must act, that it must act firmly, decisively and promptly. We trust that all peace-loving countries will fully support its efforts.

While we are meeting, in direct contradiction to our efforts, the

Chinese Communists are pursuing a course clearly designed to aggravate further the already grave situation.

The world is thus confronted with an increased threat to complicate the peace-making efforts of the United Nations, the Security Council and the Secretary-General.

If a cease-fire between India and Pakistan was necessary on 4 and 6 September when resolutions 209 (1965) and 210 (1965) were adopted, it is imperatively necessary today. And it is doubly necessary that our voices be raised firmly against any efforts to spread the conflict and exploit what is already a tragedy.

I most strongly urge that we proceed here with our task and join in calling on both Governments involved in the conflict to cease-fire immediately and to respond favourably to the Secretary-General's proposals in order that this threat to world peace may be ended before it involves more nations, more peoples, more suffering.

The Secretary-General, has also expressed the view to the two parties that the Council would wish to explore, "as a matter of urgency, methods for achieving enduring peace between India and Pakistan" [S/6683, para. 6], and has noted that as late as November 1962 the President of Pakistan and the Prime Minister of India had agreed on the need for renewed efforts to resolve their outstanding differences. We agree with the Secretary-General that renewed efforts to resolve these difference should be made and that they can only be effective under conditions of peace.

The position of the United States in this matter is simple and forthright. We are in full support of the United Nations activity in this area. We are in full support of resolutions 209 (1965) and 210 (1965) adopted by the Security Council and the efforts of the Secretary-General to give effect to these resolutions. And our full support of these resolutions is but a continuation of our consistent attitude on the India-Pakistan question, which has always been to support a peaceful solution of all aspects of the differences between them.

Since the birth of India and Pakistan as independent countries, my Government has developed relations, close and friendly, with both countries, relations which we sincerely want and hope and expect to continue. We have many ties of friendship and common interest with the peoples of both India and Pakistan. And these are expressed not only in our broad governmental programmes, but also in the form of many non-governmental programmes and activities, particularly in the fields of health, education and economic development. And as I said in the Security Council a week ago, on Saturday, 4 September 1965, and I would like to repeat that statement:

> "We know intimately from our close relations with both countries the intricacies of the underlying problem which is at the root of today's conflict..." [1237th meeting, para. 190].

Our attitude in the United Nations on the India-Pakistan question today, as in the past, continues to derive from the existence of this spirit of friendship with both countries and a deep interest in world peace. That is why we have shared the deep concern expressed by us, together with all members of the Council, in resolution 210 (1965), about extension of the fighting which adds immeasurably to the seriousness of the situation. The world community has a right to expect, in the wake of the Security Council resolutions twice adopted unanimously, that both parties cease hostilities and respect the Council's resolutions, which are even-handed resolutions between the parties.

These resolutions are based on a common conviction that a peaceful solution of the differences between the two countries can be effected only in conditions of peace and not by continuing hostilities or violence. It is the overriding necessity of this very hour, in the face of truly disastrous consequences, for both of these great countries and for the whole world, to achieve a halt in the fighting. And this is why the Council requested the Secretary-General to exert every possible effort to give effect to resolutions 209 (1965) and 210 (1965), and this is precisely what the Secretary-General did on his mission of peace to the subcontinent.

The Secretary-General said, of India and Pakistan : "...it is not only the fate of the peoples of India and Pakistan which is at stake. Both States are linked in a peculiarly intricate way with the mainstream of world affairs." [1239th meeting, para.17]

The threat to international peace and security is apparent and must be obvious both to the parties and to every member of this Council. The Council must act firmly and quickly, and all States truly dedicated to peace and security and to the Charter of the United Nations must heed its voice.

12.10. Speech by Seydoux (France) in the Security Council, 1241st Meeting, September 18, 1965

Before speaking on the item on our agenda, I should like to say that my delegation is very sorry to witness the departure of our friend Mr. Rifa'i, who has occupied an eminent place in this Council. Several of my colleagues have referred to his qualities of intellect, his high mindedness, and the moral authority which attached, one might say almost naturally, to his opinions and his conversation. My colleagues and I associate ourselves unreservedly with these expressions of praise; we also admire his unfailing courtesy, his unusually keen diplomatic sense, the strength of his convictions and the courage with which he has expressed his ideas.

Since the adoption of resolution 210 (1965) of 6 September, fighting has not ceased on the subcontinent. Despite the personal efforts of the Secretary-General, who was in a particularly favourable position – perhaps more so than anyone else – to persuade the two parties to listen to the voice of wisdom, they have continued along the dangerous path of war. Such a situation is profoundly alarming, and harmful for India and Pakistan, for the United Nations itself, and for the peace of the world.

My delegation wishes to add its voice to those which have been raised to urge the two Governments to comply with resolutions 209 (1965) and 210 (1965) unanimously adopted by the Security Council on 4 and 6 September last; it hopes that these resolutions will be reaffirmed here in the most forceful manner because it is essential, in the interests of these two great friendly nations, that the military operations in progress should be ended with the utmost possible speed.

My delegation considers that the urgent nature of the emergency action required does not relieve the Security Council from the duty of giving the closest attention to the causes underlying the crisis which had been coming on over the last few weeks. The present phase of our debate should not, in our view, be concluded without at least opening the door to discussions in which a settlement of the basic political problems between India and Pakistan – in the first place, that of Kashmir – could be sought under conditions justifying the hope of a reasonable outcome.

But, I repeat, nothing reasonable can be obtained by prolonging a fratricidal struggle. It is high time that the two camps – whose eminent speakers we have heard yesterday and this morning, with interest but also with sadess – should be made aware of this.

I shall limit myself now to these few general comments, reserving our right to speak again when a draft resolution is before the Council.

12.11. Speech by Hsueh (China) in the Security Council, 1241st Meeting, September 18, 1965

I wish to associate my delegation with the expression of appreciation extended to the Secretary-General for his mission of peace of India and Pakistan. While his efforts to give effect to the Council's resolutions have not received positive responses in all cases from the parties concerned, my delegation is gratified that the mission has not been altogether fruitless.

His two reports have thrown a flood of light on the critical situation. The impressions he has formed and the recommendations he has made should receive the Council's most serious consideration. The Secretary-General has found that both India and Pakistan are desirous of a cessation of hostilities in the entire area of the current conflict. But in an atmosphere of suspicion, fear and highly charged emotionalism, it is not surprising that both parties have found it necessary to make charges and counter charges against the other, rather than to accede in a clear-cut manner to the cease-fire appeals of the Security Council and to the personal appeals of the Secretary-General. This has made the mission undertaken by the Secretary-General even more difficult and complicated.

In this respect, it is only fair to note, as was ably pointed out a while ago by the representative of Malaysia, that India did indicate to the Secretary-General its readiness to accept a simple cease-fire. On the other hand, Pakistan made its acceptance conditional upon certain measures that were unacceptable to India. As a result, the fighting continues unabated and the situation remains grave.

As the organ responsible for the maintenance of peace and security, the Security Council clearly cannot evade its responsibility. It must act immediately in such a way as to enable the leaders of both India and Pakistan to find it possible to get out of a blind alley.

In his report [S/6626] to the Council at the 1239th meeting the Secretary-General suggested the advisability of applying Articles 39 and 40 of the United Nations Charter to enforce the cease-fire. This may very well turn out to be quite unnecessary. But it appears to be a logical step to take in order not to uphold the authority of the Council, but, what is more important, also to put an effective stop to a war which though as yet local in nature may well escalate to such a scale as to endanger world peace.

My delegation welcomes this and the other recommendations of the Secretary-General and will be happy to support any initiative leading to a resolution that will bring about an effective cessation of hostilities. For, in the present grave situation, the foremost prerequisite to a final settlement of the Kashmir dispute is an immediate cease-fire.

The Kashmir question had been with us for seventeen years. It is sad to note that with the passage of time there seems to be a progressive hardening of positions. It is this erosion of flexibility that has made present conflict inevitable. It seems to my delegation, however, that the present tragic events should have the effect of demonstrating the futility of trying to settle disputes by force of arms. This is a time for a change of positions. The leaders of India and of Pakistan need all the magnanimity they are capable of to bring the Kashmir question to a lasting solution. It is suicidal to allow this running or to go on festering until it is beyond all cure.

In his statement before the Council at our meeting yesterday, the representative of India referred to the fact that the communists of my country have made use of this fratricidal struggle between India and Pakistan to threaten intervention. Let me take this opportunity to state, with all the emphasis at my command, that the warlike behaviour of the group of men in Peiping is alien to the peaceful traditions of the Chinese people.

China and India have lived together as good neighbours for thousands of years. Their relationship had been marked by mutual respect and cultural collaboration. Throughout the centuries there has been a continuous exchange of scholars, artists and religious teachers. There has never been a time – and I repeat, never – when the peoples of the two neighbouring countries confronted each other in armed conflict. It saddened me to listen to that part of the statement of the representative of India in which he related how the communists on the mainland of China have taken advantage of the present conflict on the subcontinent to threaten India with war. This is another example of the aggressive proclivities of the Chinese communist regime. It is only too obvious that if India and Pakistan should continue to lock themselves in mortal combat, the ultimate victor, not only in Kashmir but also on the subcontinent would be neither India nor Pakistan, but the evil forces represented by Peiping.

Before concluding, may I take this opportunity to pay a high tribute to His Excellency Ambassador Rifa'i of Jordan, who is leaving us very soon. We will sorely miss him. We will miss his wisdom, but we wish him success and the best of health wherever he goes.

12.12. Speech by Fedorenko (Union of Soviet Socialist Republics) in Security Council, 1241st Meeting, September 18, 1965

Today the Security Council again meets in disquieting circumstances, when the armed conflict between India and Pakistan is continuing to spread and the situation is becoming increasingly menacing.

The hostilities between these two States, which began in Kashmir, are spreading day by day, engulfing more and more regions and involving increasing numbers of armed forces on both sides. Serious losses are being sustained, and not only by the armed forces, the peaceful population is being sorely tried. Not only military zones but cities far inside the territory of India and Pakistan, including the capitals, are the targets of air raids.

The spread of the armed conflicts is aggravating the already tense situation in South and South-East Asia, created by the aggression of United States imperialism in Vietnam, and is still further increasing the threat to world peace.

It is quite obvious that such a turn of events is not at all in the interest of the peoples of India and Pakistan or the people of Asia as a whole. It is fraught with an ominous threat to international security and is doing great harm to the cause of world peace. It is all too evident that the armed conflict between India and Pakistan merely serves the purposes of the forces which are trying to disunite and set against each other the States that have liberated themselves from the colonial yoke. It is equally clear that the continuation of this conflict benefits only the forces which are pursuing the criminal policy of dividing peoples so as to achieve their imperialist and expansionist aims.

It is natural therefore that all who cherish the cause of peace should show legitimate concern about the tragic turn taken by relations between the two biggest Asian States, India and Pakistan, which were the initiators of the Bandung Conference. Concern about the armed conflict between India and Pakistan has been clearly expressed by the Governments of numerous countries. As we know, a number of statesmen have appealed for an immediate end to hostilities and a settlement of the Indo-Pakistan armed conflict by peaceful means.

The Security Council, fulfilling its great task as the United Nations organ with primary responsibility for the maintenance of international peace and security, in its turn adopted resolutions 209 (1965) and 210 (1965) calling upon the warring factions to cease hostilities in the entire area of conflict immediately and promptly withdraw all armed personnel back to the positions held by them before 5 August 1965.

With this same end in view, as we know, the Secretary-General made efforts in pursuance of the decisions of the Security Council. The results of these efforts are reflected in his reports [S/6683 and S/6686]. They testify to the extremely disturbing turn of events and the vital need for the Council to adopt immediate measures.

Hearing the thoughts expressed today in the Council about the steps taken by the Secretary-General in the course of his honourable and responsible mission, we see clearly that the Council must exert further effective efforts in order to bring about a decisive solution.

As we know, the reports indicate that the Secretary-General, fulfilling the mandate entrusted to him by the Security Council, requested the Governments of India and Pakistan to order an unconditional cease-fire and cessation of all hostilities in the entire areas of the conflict. The positions of the warring factions are presented in the respective messages of the Governments of India and Pakistan. They speak for themselves.

The reply to this appeal received from the Prime Minister of India, Mr. Shastri, on 15 September 1965 and quoted in the report of the Secretary-General, states *inter alia*:

> "I reaffirm my willingness, as communicated, to order a simple cease-fire and cessation of hostilities as proposed by you, as soon as you are able to confirm to me that the Government of Pakistan has agreed to do so as well." [S/6683, para. 11.]

The report of the Secretary-General also quotes the reply from the President of Pakistan, Mr. Ayub Khan, received on 16 September 1965. The reply states as follows :

> "While we are agreeable in principle to stop fighting . . . a cease-fire can be meaningful only if it is followed by such steps as would lead to a durable and honourable settlement in order to preclude the recurrence of a catastrophe such as now threatens the subcontinent. To bring about such a settlement, it would be necessary to evolve an effective machinery and procedure that would lead to a final settlement of the Kashmir dispute." [*Ibid*., para. 14.]

It should be particularly emphasized that the recognition of the need for an immediate end to the current armed conflict between India and Pakistan, the recognition of the extreme importance of this for the cause of peace, has been reflected in a whole series of international moves. The Security Council too made this point quite unequivocally in its decisions, which are extremely serious and must be implemented.

The Soviet Union, which has unwaveringly attached primary importance to the maintenance of world peace, has likewise expressed grave concern about the armed conflict between India and Pakistan? The leaders of the Soviet Union have repeatedly made it clear that we are far from indifferent to what is happening now between India and Pakistan.

It is a well known fact that we are bound to India by a friendship which by now has become traditional? The Soviet Union appreciates India's peace-loving foreign policy and devotion to the principles of peaceful coexistence and non-alignment, the principles of national freedom and friendly co-operation among peoples. And it may be appropriate here to recall that our country has done a good deal to help its friends in India to advance along the road of peace and progress and consolidation of the country's independence.

At the same time, we are in favour of the development of good-neighbourly relations with Pakistan too, since such relations are in the mutual interests of both our countries. The Soviet Union has therefore on many occasions noted with satisfaction that these endeavours of ours meet with understanding on the part of the Government of Pakistan.

All this explains why our concern about the current armed

conflict between India and Pakistan represents above all the sincere and disinterested feelings of friends of the peoples of India and Pakistan and desire for peace to be restored between the two countries. At the same time, we cannot but note that the conflict arouses our concern also because the hostilities are taking place in a region immediately adjacent to the frontiers of the Soviet Union.

The attitude of the Soviet Union towards the question being considered by the Council is determined by the general lines of the peace-loving foreign policy of our country and by our profound conviction that when disputes arise between States—whatever their origin—they should be settled by peaceful means, by negotiations. There is no other possibility for the settlement of conflicts.

As was indicated in the messages sent by the Chairman of the Council of Ministers of the USSR to the Prime Minister of India and the President of Pakistan on 4 September 1965; [5/6685] the Soviet Government has expressed willingness to lend its good offices in this matter—provided of course that the parties so desire.

We venture to recall again that the Soviet Union is most anxious to see peace strengthened in that region. As you known the Soviet Government has called upon India and Pakistan to cease hostilities immediately and withdraw their respective troops to the positions held by them before the beginning of the conflict. And with that in mind, the Soviet Union supported the decisions of the Security Council designed to achieve this aim.

In present circumstances, attention must be focused on the need to implement the resolutions of the Security Council and on strict compliance with its decisions. It has become more clear than ever that the main task now is to achieve an immediate cessation of hostilities between India and Pakistan and to put an end to the bloodshed. The deafening roar of guns and thunder of bombs are obstructing negotiations. Belligerant moods and heated passions are very dangerous counsellors of reason. In an atmosphere of armed conflict it is heardly possible to solve the problems which exist between the two States and their solution is most desirable in the interests of good-neighbourly relations between them.

It goes without saying that it is first and fore-most the Governments of India and Pakistan themselves which can and must settle the present conflict. The Charter of the United Nations and the Bandung principles cry out for statesman—like wisdom on the part of the leaders of both countries and for restraint and good will.

At the same time, it is obvious that in the situation brought about by the Indo-Pakistan conflict, much depends on other States too. Attempts to use this conflict in their own selfish interests, disregard for the fate of the innocent people who are being killed, and still more, incendiary and provocative statements could only aggravate the situation and help to fan the flames of the conflagration. Such conduct could bring with it the risk of further spreading the conflict and involving many States in it one after the other, with all the serious consequences this would entail.

The Soviet delegation feels it necessary to emphasize that in present circumstances the efforts of all States, including the members of the Security Council, should be concentrated on the main and most urgent task of ending the bloodshed and restoring peace between India and Pakistan. We see this as the direct and unfailing duty of the Security Council. If normal conditions could be restored, the parties would be able in the spirit of the Charter of the United Nations and the Bandung principles, to enter into negotiations on the subject of a peaceful settlement of the current disagreements.

12.13. Speech by President Arthur J. Goldberg in Security Council, 1244th Meeting, September 22, 1965

Speaking on behalf of the members of the Security Council, I should like to express the profound appreciation of the Council to the distinguished Heads of State of India and Pakistan, who, in compliance with resolution 211 (1965) adopted by the Council on 20 September 1965, have ordered a cease-fire between their armed forces so that the end of hostilities and conditions of peace can be brought about on the subcontinent.

This is an important day in the history of the United Nations and of the world. The Council and the United Nations have addressed themselves to perhaps the gravest problem of which the United Nations has been seized in the course of its history. The Council has debated this matter at length, has heard the representatives of the countries concerned at length, and has had the benefit of the profound impartial, courageous efforts of our Secretary-General, who went on a mission of peace to the subcontinent.

The end of bloodshed on the subcontinent is highly important. But, as Security Council resolution 211 (1965) clearly states, that is a first step. There are other steps which must be taken. The other steps which must be taken are for the parties involved and the Council to work together to bring about conditions of permanent peace between their two countries.

Resolution 211 (1965) recognized that there had to be a cease-fire and a withdrawal of forces, and that there had to be an honourable settlement, under peaceful conditions, of the underlying political problems existing between the two countries.

In concluding our debate the other day, I said that if India and Pakistan were members of the Security Council, instead of countries presenting their cases to the Council, they would have decided as the Council decided in its resolution; I was sure of that because of their past history of dedication to the principles of the Charter and to the cause of international peace and justice.

The cease-fire must be a prelude to better understanding, so that this tragic war that has occurred will never be repeated and so that these two neighbours, for which all of us have great friendship, will resume friendly relations in a spirit of friendly co-operation, peace and amity.

The members of the Council, and the Council itself, will do everything they can to assist in what is the most noble of all tasks, that is, the task of bringing permanent peace to the area. Under the resolution adopted by the Security Council, the Secretary-General has been authorized to provide the necessary assistance to ensure supervision of the cease-fire, and that assistance is at the disposal of the parties under the text of the resolution adopted by the Council. I have noted in the course of this debate that the representatives of both India and Pakistan have stated repeatedly their confidence in the Secretary-General – in which all members of the Council are at one – and their conviction that his efforts in this and all other areas are designed to assist in the restoration of peaceful conditions.

I am sure that the announcement of Government of India, through its distinguished Prime Minister, which is noted in the report of the Secretary-General, and the announcement made by the Foreign Minister of Pakistan will be greeted with great relief and acclaim by a very troubled world. But it is necessary, as I have said, to go on from there and to restore the conditions which will lead to a permanent peace, a lasting and honourable peace between these two great neighbours, these two Members of the United Nations, these two great members of the world family.

India and Pakistan have very much to contribute to the world and the world looks upon these two countries with great affection, concern and interest.

In view of the announcement that is made today, I, as President of the Council, on behalf of the members of the Council, wish to express our appreciation to both countries for honouring the Council's request, and the Council, of course, will continue – as its resolution prescribes – its consideration of this matter so that it can make its contribution towards the resolution of the problems involved.

12.14. Speech by Security Council President Arthur J. Goldberg in Security Council, 1245th Meeting, September 27, 1965

In addition to the report of the Secretary-General which is included in the agenda [S/6710 and Add. 1-2] and to the other relevant documents which were circulated this morning, an additional report by the Secretary-General has just been submitted in documents S/6719, to which I should like to draw the attention of members of the Council.

We now have a draft resolution which reflects the consensus of the members of the Council on the basis of my consultation with them. The text is as follows:

> "*The Security Council*,
> "*Noting* the reports of the Secretary-General (S/6710 and Add. 1 and 2),
> "*Reaffirming* its resolutions 209 (1967) of 4 September, 210 (1965) of 6 September and 211 (1965) of 20 September 1965,
> "*Expressing its grave concern* that the cease-fire agreed to unconditionally by the Governments of India and Pakistan is not holding,
> "*Recalling* that the cease-fire demand in the Council's resolutions was unanimously endorsed by the Council and agreed to by the Governments of both India and Pakistan,
> "*Demands* that the parties urgently honour their commitments to the Council to observe the cease-fire, and further calls upon the parties promptly to withdraw all armed personnel as necessary steps in the full implementation of resolution 210 (1965)."

We note that the representative of Jorden made a reservation to resolution 211 (1965) of 20 September at the time of its adoption, which reservation is still maintained.

I have had no request from any member of the Council to speak. Since this draft resolution has been fully discussed in the informal consultations which have taken place throughout the day, if I hear no objection and if there are no other requests to speak, I shall consider the draft resolution adopted.

12.15. Speech by Arthur J. Goldberg (United States of America) in Security Council, 1247th Meeting, October 25, 1965

It has been apparent for a long time, and it is apparent today, that the problem of India and Pakistan is a grave one. It is a difficult one. It is difficult in all its aspects, and certainly our procedural difficulty today was an illustration of this. I asked for brief period for consultation – not an unusual thing, as I have discovered in my brief experience in the Security Council – so that we could confer together to see whether or not, in a friendly and amicable way, the procedural difficulty which had arisen could be resolved. It was not intended in any way to interfere with the provisional rules of procedure, but only so that I could myself have an opportunity to talk to some of my colleagues and some of the parties concerned. It is helpful to me to hear all the parties on every aspect of their problems and we have been doing this ever since the proceedings began. I understood your ruling, Mr. President, when you approved the agenda. We were to meet here today to consider the problems of cease-fire and withdrawal. I also understand the long line of unbroken precedents according to which we always hear everything that anybody has to say, and we respect the right of free speech, not only of members of the Council, but also of anybody who appears before this body at our invitation.

I am respectful both of the subject which is before the Council and of the tradition of the Council. For my part, bearing that in mind, I am prepared to hear anything which the representative of Pakistan has to say and, I might add, anything which the representative of India has to say.

12.16. Speech by Mr. Fedorenko (Union of Soviet Socialist Republics) in Security Council, 1247th Meeting, October 25, 1965

Mr. President, allow us to associate ourselves with the congratulations addressed to you by members of the Council. We greatly esteem the qualities and abilities of the scholar and diplomat who has assumed the position of President of the highest organ of the United Nations, an organ which bears the chief responsibility for the maintenance of international peace and security. Experience, as we know, is acquired and enriched though practice, and we wish you every success in your efforts in this august and very difficult post.

Polemics on procedural matters have gone to excessive lengths at this meeting. This is liable to create an unfavourable atmosphere for the discussion of the substance of the items on today's agenda. We are clearly moving towards a situation in which the substance will be replaced by a polemical discussion on procedure and formalities. An unusual and, indeed, strange situation is being created in the Council, in which we are returning over and over again to discussion of the Agenda which we adopted at the very beginning of today's meeting.

It is our conviction that our most important task at present is to secure strict observance of the cease-fire agreement in the area of the Indo-Pakistan conflict. Unfortunately, we know that violations of the cease-fire agreement are continuing, and this might have very dangerous consequences for peace in the area. Obviously our main attention should be concentrated on matters connected with the direct settlement of the armed conflict and, first of all, on scrupulous observance of the cease-fire agreement, which would create more favourable conditions for seeking a solution to other questions that both sides can accept.

That is in fact the principle behind Council resolution 211 (1965), which clearly provides in paragraph 4 that only after a cease-fire and the subsequent withdrawal of all armed personnel will consideration be given to the question of what steps could be taken to assist towards a settlement of the political problem underlying the present conflict. The conclusion is obvious.

At the present time, when these decisions of the Council calling for a complete cease-fire and the withdrawal of armed personnel have still not been fully implemented, it would hardly be in keeping with the spirit and letter of resolution 211 (1965) for it to consider other aspects of the problem. Accordingly, it is our view that at this stage the Council's discussion should be on questions directly connected with the settlement of the armed conflict between India and Pakistan. That is how we understand the agenda adopted for this meeting of the Council.

The Soviet delegation will not insist on consecutive interpretation of its statement into the other languages in view of the time factor, subject to the usual understanding in the Council on this question.

12.17. Fourteenth Resolution* Adopted at the 1242nd Meeting of Security Council, September 20, 1965

The Security Council,

Having considered the reports of the Secretary-General on his consultations with the Governments of India and Pakistan.

Commending the Secretary-General for his unrelenting efforts in furtherance of the objectives of Security Council resolutions 209 (1965) of 4 and 6 September 1965.

Having heard the statements of the representatives of India and Pakistan.

Noting the differing replies by the parties to an appeal for a cease-fire as set out in the report of the Secretary-General, but noting further with concern that no cease-fire has yet come into being.

Convinced that an early cessation of hostilities is essential as a first step towards a peaceful settlement of the outstanding differences between the two countries on Kashmir and other related matters.

1. *Demands* that a cease-fire should take effect on Wednesday, 22 September 1965, at 0700 hours GMT, and calls upon both Governments to issue orders for a cease-fire at that moment and a subsequent withdrawal of all armed personnel to the positions held by them before 5 August 1965;

2. *Requests* the Secretary-General to provide the necessay assistance to ensure supervision of the cease-fire and the withdrawal

---

*Adopted by 10 votes to none, with 1 abstention (Jordan); Security Council Resolution No. 211 (1965)

of all armed personnel;

3. *Calls on* all States to refrain from any action which might aggravate the situation in the area;

4. *Decides* to consider, as soon as paragraph 1 of Council resolution 210 (1965) has been implemented, what steps could be taken to assist towards a settlement of the political problem underlying the present conflict, and in the meantime calls on the two Governments to utilize all peaceful means, including those listed in Article 33 of the Charter of the United Nations, to this end;

5. *Requests* the Secreatry-General to exert every possible effort to give effect to the present resolution, to seek a peaceful solution, and to report to the Security Council thereon.

12.18. Fifteenth Resolution* Adopted at the 1245th Meeting of Security Council, September 27, 1965

The Security Council,

Noting the reports of the Secretary-General,

Reaffirming its resolutions 209 (1965) of 4 September, 210 (1965) of 6 September and 211 (1965) of 20 September 1965.

Expressing its grave concern that the cease-fire agreed to unconditionally by the Governments of India and Pakistan is not holding,

Recalling that the cease-fire demand in the Council's resolutions was unanimously endorsed by the Council and agreed to by the Governments of both India and Pakistan.

Demands that the parties urgently honour their commitments to the Council to observe the cease-fire and further calls upon the parties promptly to withdraw all armed personnel as necessay steps in the full implementation of resolution 211 (1965).

12.19. Sixteenth Resolution** Adopted at the 1251st Meeting of the Security Council, November 5, 1965

The Security Council,

Regretting the delay in the full achievement of a complete and

---

* Security Council Resolution No. 214 (1965)

** Adopted by 9 votes to none, with 2 abstentions (Jordan, Union of Soviet Socialist Republics); Security Council Resolution No. 215 (1965) effective cease-fire and a prompt withdrawal of armed personnel to the positions held by them before 5 August 1965, as called for in its resolutions 209 (1965) of 4 September, 210 (1965) of 6 September, 211 (1965) of 20 September and 214 (1965) of 27 September 1965.

1. *Reaffirms* its resolution 211 (1965) in all its parts;

2. *Requests* the Governments of India and Pakistan to co-operate towards a full implementation of paragraph 1 of resolution 211 (1965); calls upon them to instruct their armed personnel to co-operate with the United Nations and cease all military activity; and insists that there be an end to violations of the cease-fire;

3. *Demands* the prompt and unconditional execution of the proposal already agreed to in principle by the Governments of India and Pakistan that their representatives meet with a representative of the Secretary-General, to be appointed without delay after consultation with both parties, for the purpose of formulating an agreed plan and schedule for the withdrawals by both parties; urges that such a meeting take place as soon as possible and that such a plan contains a time-limit on its implementation; and requests the Secretary-General to report on the progress achieved in this respect within three weeks of the adoption of the present resolution;

4. *Requests* the Secretary-General to submit for its consideration as soon as possible a report on compliance with the present resolution.

13

Tashkent Summit, January 1966

The Prime Minister of India, Shri Lal Bahadur Shastri, and President Ayub Khan of Pakistan met at Tashkent (USSR) from January 4 to January 10, 1966, discussed the relations existing between the two countries concluded the Tashkent Agreement.

13.1. Speech of Indian Prime Minister Lal Bahadur Shastri at the Opening Session, January 4, 1966

First of all, I want to convey to you, Chairman Kosygin, the feelings of sincere appreciation with which my people, my Government and I hailed your bold initiative which has brought me and President Ayub Khan of Pakistan together in this historic Asian city. It is with great pleasure that I express on my behalf and on behalf of my delegation our gratitude for the hospitality which has been bestowed upon us. The great welcome which the people of Tashkent gave us was indeed very moving.

POSITIVE RESPONSE

Our response to your invitation for a meeting in Tashkent was immediate and positive. The objective of peace which inspired you is indeed a noble one. Peace is vital for both India and Pakistan and indeed for the world as a whole. It should be our endeavour to try to open a new chapter in Indo-Pakistan relationship. I would not like to go into past history. I feel, and I am sure President Ayub Khan also feels, that the conflict which took place between our two countries was most unfortunate. Our objective at this meeting should be not recrimination over the past, but a new look towards the future.

I know that there are many unresolved differences between our two countries. (Even between countries with the best of relationship, there are differences and even disputes.) The question which we have both to face is whether we should think of force as a method of solving them, or whether we should decide and declare that force will never be used. If other countries, even those with vast resources and much deeper differences, can avoid an armed, conflict and live together on the basis of peaceful co-existence, should not countries like India and Pakistan whose main problem is the economic betterment of their people, give up the idea of solving any problems by recourse to arms?

RESPECT FOR TERRITORIAL INTEGRITY

The only justification for the use of force in international relations is to repel aggression. Our assurance to each other not to use force would mean, therefore, that each agrees to respect the territorial integrity of the other. We have always said, and I say it today also, that we unreservedly accept Pakistan's sovereignty and territorial integrity. Equally, we have to preserve our own territorial integrity and sovereignty. Respect for each other's sovereignty is essential for peace and good relations.

Once this has been clearly accepted, the whole character of Indo-Pakistan relationship could be transformed to the benefit of the people of both countries. Let me say quite clearly and very sincerely that we wish Pakistan's progress and prosperity. We have ourselves been striving to better the lives of our people. We are convinced that prosperity would come sooner to the sub-continent, if there was better relationship between India and Pakistan.

PEACEFUL CO-EXISTENCE

The foundation of such relationship should be, as I have said, the acceptance of the policy of peaceful co-existence. In pursuance of this, action will have to be taken on several fronts. For instance, the atmosphere of cold war has to be removed. If through propaganda, in the press or by radio, a feeling of animosity or distrust is generated and sustained between the two countries, whatever we, as Heads of the two Governments might say, there will always exist the danger of a conflict. Our aim should be to improve the totality of the relationship between the two countries. Many river flow between India and Pakistan. Instead of being a source of controversy, they could, through co-operative endeavour, enrich both our countries. There are many other area of economic co-operation which, given goodwill and understanding, can be developed to our mutual advantage.

In saying all this, I am not trying to suggest that we could or should shut our eyes to the many points of difference that exist between the two countries. I do not want to enumerate them. What I do say, however, is that all these problem must be resolved through talks and negotiations and not by resort to force. An armed conflict creates more problems than it solves. It is an impediment to understanding and agreement. On the other hand, in an atmosphere of peace, we can make real progress towards solving the differences between us.

RENUNCIATION OF FORCE

It would be a notable achievement if at this meeting which Chairman Kosygin has convened, an agreement could emerge for renouncing the use of force for settling our differences. This should pave the way for the kind of good neighbourly relations which both countries need and would also make the solution of many of our problems much easier. We could and should, of course, discuss other matters as well, but even if we differ on some of them and cannot see our way to an immediate agreement, we should still not forsake the path of peace.

NOT WAR BUT PEACE

A heavy responsibility lies on our shoulders. The sub-continent has a population of 600 million – one fifth of the human race. If India and Pakistan have to progress and prosper, they must learn to live in peace. If there is constant conflict and hostility, our peoples would suffer even greater hardships. Instead of fighting each other, let us start fighting poverty, disease and ignorance. The problems, the hopes and the aspirations of the common people of both the countries are the same. They want no conflict and war, but peace and progress. They need, not arms and ammunition, but food, clothing and shelter. If we are to fulfil this obligation to our people, we should, in this meeting, try to achieve something specific and positive.

This is a momentous meeting. The eyes of the world are upon us. Let it not be said that the President of Pakistan and the Prime Minister of India met and failed to reach an agreement. Let us show by our actions that we are capable of seeing our own problems in the wider contest of world events.

(Source : *Foreign Affairs Record*)

13.2. Tashkent Declaration, January 10, 1966

The Prime Minister of India and the President of Pakistan having met at Tashkent and having discussed the existing relations between India and Pakistan, hereby declare their firm resolve to restore normal and peaceful relations between their countries and to promote understanding and friendly relations between their peoples. They consider the attainment of these objectives of vital importance for the welfare of the 600 million people of India and Pakistan.

I

The Prime Minister of India and the President of Pakistan agree that both sides will exert all efforts to create good neighbourly relations between India and Pakistan in accordance with the United Nations Charter. They reaffirm their obligation under the Charter not to have recourse to force and to settle their disputes through peaceful means. They considered that the interests of peace in their region and particularly in the Indo-Pakistan Sub-Continent and, indeed, the interests of the peoples of India and Pakistan were not served by the continuance of tension between the two countries. It was against this background that Jammu and Kashmir was discussed, and each of the sides set fourth its respective position.

II

The Prime Minister of India and the President of Pakistan have agreed that all armed personnel of the two countries shall be withdrawn not later than 25 February 1966 to the position they held prior to 5 August 1965, and both sides shall observe the cease-fire on the cease-fire line.

III

The Prime Minister of India and the President of Pakistan have agreed that relations between India and Pakistan shall be based on the principle of non-interference in the internal affairs of each other.

IV

The Prime Minister of India and President of Pakistan have agreed that both sides will discourage any propaganda directed against the other country, and will encourage propaganda which promotes the development of friendly relations between the two countries.

V

The Prime Minister of India and President of Pakistan have agreed that the High Commissioner of India to Pakistan and the High Commissioner of Pakistan to India will return to their posts and that the normal functioning of diplomatic missions of both countries will be restored. Both Governments shall observe the Vienna Convention of 1961 on Diplomatic Intercourse.

VI

The Prime Minister of India and the President of Pakistan have agreed to consider measures towards the restoration of economic and trade relations, communications, as well as cultural exchanges between India and Pakistan, and to take measures to implement the existing agreements between India and Pakistan.

VII

The Prime Minister of India and the President of Pakistan have agreed that they give instructions to their respective authorities to carry out the repatriation of the prisoners of war.

VIII

The Prime Minister of India and the President of Pakistan have agreed that the sides will continue the discussion of questions relating to the problems of refugees and evictions/illegal immigrations. They also agreed that both sides will create conditions which will prevent the exodus of people. They further agreed to discuss the return of the property and assets taken over by either side in connection with the conflict.

IX

The Prime Minister of India and the President of Pakistan have agreed that the sides will continue meeting both at the highest and at other levels on matters of direct concern to both countries. Both sides have recognized the need to set up joint Indian-Pakistani bodies which will report to their Governments in order to decide what further steps should be taken.

The Prime Minister of India and the President of Pakistan record their feelings of deep appreciation and gratitude to the leaders of the Soviet Union, the Soviet Government and personally to the Chairman of the Council of Ministers of the USSR for their constructive, friendly and noble part in bringing about the present meeting which has resulted in mutually satisfactory results. They also express to Government and friendly people of Usbekistan their sincere thankfulness for their overwhelming reception and generous hospitality.

They invite the Chairman of the Council of Ministers of the USSR to witness this Declaration.

Sd/-	Sd/-
LAL BAHADUR	M.A. KHAN, FM
Prime Minister of India	*President of Pakistan*

Tashkent, 10 January, 1966.

13.3. Statement of Pakistan President Ayub Khan on Tashkent Declaration, January 14, 1966

On the 4th of this month I went to Tashkent to meet the Indian Prime Minister. I must explain to you the background of this historic meeting.

When our two armies clashed in Azad Kashmir and the situation took a serious turn, the Soviet Prime Minister invited the leaders of the two countries to Tashkent to provide us opportunity to settle our differences in a peaceful and an honourable manner.

We received the Soviet invitation on 4 September. Two days later, India launched an attack on our sacred territory. What followed is known to all of you. The entire nation rose like one man and came through this ordeal in a gloriously successful manner. The heroic deeds of our armed forces as well as the civilian population will for ever be cherished in our history.

We have always held the view that countries must settle their differences on the basis of peace and justice.

We want peace for the whole world and as a member of the United Nations, we have accepted the obligations to settle differences not by force but in a peaceful manner and through mutual understanding.

As for our differences with India, we have always made it clear that the basic cause of this conflict was the dispute about Jammu and Kashmir and there is a Security Council resolution on this issue. According to this historic resolution, the people of Jammu and Kashmir have the right to decide whether they want to accede to Pakistan or to India. India is a party to this agreement and has pledged to the United Nations that it would give to the people of the State their right to freely choose their own future.

For the last eighteen years, we have been constantly endeavouring to persuade India to fulfil its commitment. Unfortunately, India did nothing to honour it with the result that the people of Jammu and Kashmir rose in an open revolt. When the Indian forces launched repeated attacks on the Azad Kashmir territory, the Pakistan Army had no option but to take action in support of the people of Jammu and Kashmir. The resulting armed conflict between the two countries amply demonstrated to the world that there would be no peace between India and Pakistan unless the Kashmir dispute was settled.

The Security Council resolution of 20 September provided for a cease-fire and the withdrawal of armed forces. It also provided that after the withdrawal of forces the Secretary Council would take steps to resolve the basic issue of Jammu and Kashmir. The resolution expressed the hope that till the completion of the withdrawal, the two countries should try to settle the dispute between themselves.

My meeting with the late Mr. Lal Bahadur Shastri in Tashkent was a step in this direction. The Government of the USSR and their

Prime Minister made an all out effort for the success of these talks. We were received with great enthusiasm by the Russian people and their leaders who observed impartiality throughout these negotiations. We are grateful to them for all this.

The Indian Prime Minister wanted us to sign a no-war pact but we made it clear to him that we would never be a signatory to such a pact unless the Jammu and Kashmir dispute was settled honourably and equitably. We, however, offered to reaffirm our obligation under the U.N. Charter. This obligation means that nations will not resort to force unless they have explored all avenues of peaceful settlement. We also impressed upon the Indian Prime Minister that the future of the people of the two countries depended on peace in the subcontinent and that this peace could not be lasting unless the Kashmir dispute was amicably settled. If this dispute was not settled both the countries would continue with war-like preparations and their resources, instead of being dedicated to the welfare of their people, would be diverted to the purpose of war.

Personally, I had a feeling that Indian Prime Minister was agreeable to what I said but he wanted that we should first normalise our relations and then grapple with the basic issue. We explained our respective points of view to each other but unfortunately we reached no conclusions. As for Pakistan, we stuck to our belief that the basic cause was the dispute concerning Jammu and Kashmir and unless this was settled there could be no peace between India and Pakistan. Pakistan was not prepared to consider Jammu and Kashmir as part of India or that it was their internal affair. The people of Jammu and Kashmir had a right to decide their own future and we will continue to support their inalienable right.

I would invite you to consider the various provisions of the Tashkent Declaration against this background. The Declaration has in no way detracted from or damaged our national view-point on Kashmir. Their right to choose their future remains inviolate.

I hope that this Declaration will open new avenues for the settlement of Kashmir issue. First, we will take up this matter with the Indian representative and then, after the withdrawal of forces, the Security Council also will be in a position to deal with it. Moreover, the interest shown by the Soviet Government in the settlement of the dispute will also facilitate the task.

I appeal to you to show the same sense of purpose and discipline in achieving peace as you did in achieving victory during the last war.

The sacrifices made during that period are indelibly marked on our hearts and I assure you that no sacrifice will go in vain.

Whatever steps your Government has taken or is taking they are for your good. We have been given assurances that sincere efforts will be made to settle the Indo-Pakistan dispute in a just and equitable manner. It is, therefore, necessary that we should take the fullest advantage of this effort. It can only be translated into action if we on our part fully implement the Tashkent Declaration. I am sure, the nation will help the Government make a success of this effort for peace. If God forbid, for some reason or other, this effort does not bear fruit, it will not mean that we will ever be oblivious of our national interests or fail to safeguard the country's defence. In any case, we have to build up our defence effort.

The Tashkent Declaration has been hailed in many parts of the country but there are those as well who are not satisfied with it. I am fully aware of their misgivings and honour the sentiments which give rise to them. It is obvious that if the Kashmir dispute had been honourably settle at the Tashkent meeting you would have welcomed it; but complicated issues are not easy to solve and the Government has to adopt various means to solve it, according to circumstances.

There may be some amongst us who will take advantage of your feelings and will try to mislead you. They are not more patriotic perhaps than you and me and are in fact after their own selfish gain. You should be aware of their machinations. You should remain firm in your faith and steadfast in your discipline. The ordeal is not yet over. Let us bow our heads to the Almighty and pray for the strengthening of our will and determination. Pakistan Zindabad.

13.4. Radio Broadcast by Sardar Swaran Singh, Minister of External Affairs, Government of India on the Tashkent Declaration, January 15, 1966

I speak to you as one who was privileged to be associated with our late Prime Minister Shri Lal Bahadur Shastri in Tashkent during his mission of peace. The week that we spent in Tashkent was unforgettable. They were days of meetings, negotiations and sincere efforts to reach understanding and meeting of minds. The Prime Minister and his colleagues worked as a team, determined to see the establishment of peace and goodwill between India and Pakistan. We were all proud to work under his inspiring leadership. After strenuous efforts in which Chairman Kosygin played a most notable good offices role, President Ayub Khan and Prime Minister Shastri were able to reach agreement on a declaration which was signed in Tashkent on the 10th of January.

In the Tashkent Declaration India and Pakistan have chosen to turn away from mutual conflict and have resolved to base their relations on peace, friendship and good neighbourliness.

REMARKABLE ACHIEVEMENT

This in itself in a remarkable achievement which reverses the trends of the past 17 years and marks a new era in the relations between two countries. The central point of the whole Declaration is the renunciation of force by both sides for the settlement of their disputes. For many years in the past, India had emphasized the importance of a no-war declaration by both countries, to the effect that all differences and disputes between them should be settled peacefully without resort to arms. Unfortunately no agreement could be reached on such a declaration between India and Pakistan all these years. It is a tribute to the statemanship and sincerity of purpose of the President of Pakistan and of Prime Minister Shastri that at last both countries have agreed not to have recourse to force and to settle their disputes through peaceful means.

It has always been our view that it is only in an atmosphere of freedom from tension and of goodwill created by such a declaration that both sides could reach solutions to the problems between them.

RENUNCIATION OF FORCE

Article I of the Tashkent Declaration seeks to embody the agreement regarding renunciation of force. The crucial sentence therein reads "they reaffirm their obligation under the Charter not to have recourse to force and to settle their disputes through peaceful means". The greater part of the discussion in Tashkent centred round this basic question. Prime Minister Shastri made it clear that the main issue was whether or not the two countries wanted to settle their disputes peacefully. He insisted on a clear affirmation that there shall be no resort to force. The Pakistan position was that any declaration would be valueless unless there was a political settlement or a self-executing machinery for the settlement of the Kashmir question was set up. Eventually, after a great deal of discussions there was agreement that the Declaration should specifically mention agreement on non-use of force as a means of settling any disputes between the two countries. This has been done by a categorical reaffirmation of the obligation which both countries have as members of the United Nations, to refrain in their mutual relationship from the threat or use of force.

WITHDRAWAL OF ARMED PERSONNEL

Article II of the Declaration provides for the withdrawal of all armed personnel of two countries not later than February 25, 1966 to the pre-August 5 positions, as required in UN Resolutions. Prime Minister Shastri gave the fullest consideration to all aspects of the question of withdrawals before agreeing to this clause. He very carefully examined his letter of September 14 to the U.N. Secretary-General in which he had stated "that when consequent upon the cease-fire becoming effective further details are considered, we shall not agree to any disposition which will leave the door open to further infiltrations or prevent us from dealing with infiltrations that have taken place." The late Prime Minister and the entire Indian delegation felt that the conditions laid down by the Prime Minister had been completely met by Pakistan's agreement not only to withdraw all armed personnel, but also to respect, after withdrawals, the cease-fire terms on the cease-fire and the undertaking of non-interference in each other's internal affairs.

Prime Minister Shastri had made it clear, on more than one occasion, that if the question of Kashmir was raised by President Ayub Khan, he would have to reiterate India's viewpoint and this is exactly what he did as Article I of the Declaration indicates. The important point is that though the viewpoint of both countries on Kashmir continue to be irreconcilable, both sides have nevertheless, agreed not to take recourse to arms over this or any other question.

JOINT INDO-PAKISTAN BODIES

There are provisions in the Declaration which refer to normalisation of relations and discussion of various other problems. It is hoped that for a consideration of these, joint Indo-Pakistani bodies will be constituted. Meetings at Ministerial and Heads of Government level are also contemplated. All these are very salutary provisions. It is only in these ways that we can tackle the various outstanding problems between the two countries.

SPIRIT OF PEACE AND GOODWILL

More important than the words of the Declaration is the spirit underlying it. We are confident that the Tashkent Declaration, signed by the two Heads of Government and witnessed by the Chairman of the Council of Ministers of the U.S.S.R., embodies the spirit of peace and goodwill on which future relations between the two countries can be based to the lasting benefit of their peoples. It is our intention to implement the declaration faithfully. We already initiated the steps for the normalisation of relations between the two countries. Our High Commissioner to Pakistan is returning to his post. The Pakistan High Commissioner has already arrived in Delhi. The three Chiefs of Services from both countries are going to meet shortly. The direct contacts between Defence Chiefs will not only facilitate withdrawals, but also consider measures to ensure tranquility on the Indo-Pakistan borders in the East and the West, as well as across the cease-fire line.

The Tashkent Declaration is a tribute to the vision and statesmanship of the President of Pakistan and the Prime Minister of India. Equally, one cannot but recognise the tremendous contribution which was made by Mr. Kosygin who not only sponsored the idea of the Conference, but also, at all stages and particularly when difficulties arose, acted as a messenger of peace and helped to resolve all obstacles. He did not propose much less impose, any particular solutions. Yet without his good offices, the Tashkent Declaration could not have taken shape.

TASHKENT DECLARATION, A TRIUMPH OF PEACE

The Tashkent Declaration is a declaration of peace and goodwill between India and Pakistan. It has been hailed all over the world as a great act of statesmanship and as a significant contribution to world peace. Dozens of messages of congratulations have been received from Heads of Government and States all over the world. The Tashkent Declaration implemented sincerely and earnestly, will make an immeasurable contribution to the happiness of millions of people in the subcontinent and to peace in Asia and the world. Both India and Pakistan can use their resources for economic development and for betterment of the standards of living of their peoples. The dangerous tensions which have characterised the relations between the two countries will be eliminated. Both countries will be able to conserve their resources for peaceful economic development. Their security will be strengthened by the assurance of peace flowing from the Declaration.

Virtual agreement on the text of the Tashkent Declaration was reached at midnight of the 9th January. The next day, Prime Minister Shastri felt greatly relaxed and entertained President Ayub at a quiet lunch a couple of hours before the Declaration was actually signed. No one who saw him that afternoon looking hale and hearty feeling obviously happy at the triumph of peace and goodwill, would have had any inkling of the impending tragedy.

The Tashkent Declaration is a monument to Prime Minister Shastri's wisdom, statesmanship and love of peace. This Declaration is his last gift to our nation. He wanted us to work for peace as steadfastly and courageously as we had fought to preserve our honour and integrity. It is up to us to live up to his expectations. All of us, in whatever walk of life and wherever we are, at the Centre or in the State, in towns or in villages, should dedicate ourselves to working for the basic objectives of peace and amity between India and Pakistan embodied in the Tashkent Declaration.

(Source : *Foreign Affairs Record*).

14

Indo-Pak Agreement on the Withdrawal of Troops, January 22, 1966

14.1. Introduction

This agreement is in Four parts:

Part I – Procedure concerning the immediate disengagement of troops and reduction of tension;
Part II – Procedure concerning the withdrawal of troops from the occupied areas:
Part III – Procedure concerning reduction of tension in the Easter Sector;
Part IV – General Points.

14.2. Part I – Disengagement of Troops and Reduction of Tension

Phase-I

1. Both forces will withdraw 1,000 yards from the line of actual control in sectors as specified below:

(a) Rajasthan/Sind
(b) Amritsar/ Lahore
(c) Jammu/Sialkot
(d) Akhnur/Chhamb (from River Chenab NW 8061 to Mawa Wali Khad NW 7770).

2. In all other sectors including sectors divided by the 1949

Cease Fire Line, troops will continue to hold their respective picquets as by so doing they will be automatically be separated from each other. The only exception to this will be where, in hilly terrain, opposing forces are at present considered to be too close to each other, each side will withdraw to a distance to be mutually agreed upon by the local commanders not below the rank of Brigadier.

> [*Note*: In the Amritsar-Lahore sector, this 1000 yards withdrawl will be modified so that Pakistani troops who are actually on the Wesh bank of the BRB Canal and Indian troops who are on the East bank of the BRB Canal facing each other will withdraw all armed personnel off the embankment to a distance of 200 yards on each side.
> Unarmed personnel may, however, live, move and work in this area.
> The same principle will apply in Sulaimanki-Fazilka Sector, Hussainiwala Sector and Khem Karan Sector.]

3. After the withdrawal in this phase no new defences of any kind will be prepared in occupied territory.

4. There will be no movement of armed military, para-military or police personnel either armed or unarmed within the demilitarised zone and no civilian personnel will be permitted within it by either side.

5. The period for completion of this phase will be five days.

Phase-II

6. In this phase both sides will remove and nullify all defences which will include the:

(a) lifting of mines; and
(b) dismantling of all other defence works, less permanent defence structures constructed of steel and cement.

7. The period for completing this phase will be twenty-one days which will commence immediately after the five-day period mentioned in para 5.*

* Last para of Phase-I.

8. Working parties for this purpose will be formed by unarmed military personnel in uniform. No civilian or civil labour will be used for these tasks.

9. While every effort will be made to dismantle all defence works within the specified period, where owing to weather and other conditions it is not possible to complete this, the uncleared areas so left will be clearly marked and a sketch of these given to the other side.

10. There will be no firing of weapons or use of explosives within 10,000 metres of the line of actual control. Where explosives have to be used to dismantle defence works, this will only be done under supervision as specified later and after due intimation to the other side.

11. The present agreement affecting restriction on flights of aircraft will continue to apply.

12. To ensure that the action agreed to in Part I above is being implemented in letter and in spirit, the good offices of UNMOGIP and UNIPOM will be utilised. In the event of a disagreement, their decision will be final and binding to both sides.

14.3. Part II – Withdrawal of Troops from Occupied Areas

13. After the dismantling of defences has taken place, all troops, para-military forces and armed police who are now on other side of the international border and Cease-Fire Line, will be withdrawn. This withdrawal will be completed by 25 February 1966. If in any particular sector or part of a sector, the dismantling of defences has been completed earlier than the last date specified, withdrawal may be sectorwise if mutually agreed to.

14. During this withdrawal, there will no follow up by civilians, armed military, para-military or police personnel until 25 February 1966. Only unarmed military personnel at a strength mutually agreed upon at the sector level may move into these unoccupied areas for normal police duties (paragraph 16 below).

15. After troops of both sides have crossed into their own territory, the procedure which was being followed by Pakistan and India before 5 August 1965, for the security of the international border and the Cease-Fire Line, will apply. Attention is drawn to Ground Rules 1961 for West Pakistan/Punjab, Rajasthan and Gujarat (India).

16. It is essential that under all circumstances troops must move out of occupied areas by 25 February 1966, even if the dismantling of defence and lifting of mines have not been completed.

17. For immediate settlement of any points of dispute that may arise, sector commanders not below the rank of Major General will be designated by name and appointment both by India and Pakistan who will meet to settle the differences. Telephone or R/T communication will be established between these designated sector commander and will be permanently manned.

18. Any matter on which there is disagreement will be referred to the C-in-C, Pakistan Army, and COAS, India, for their joint decision. If the issue is still not resolved by them the good offices of Major General T. Marambio will be utilised and his decision will be final and binding on both sides.

14.4. Part III – Reduction of Tension in the Eastern Sector

19. The limit of withdrawal in the Eastern Sector will be left to local commanders not below the rank of Major General to mutually decide where necessary, in consultation with the civil authorities concerned. Both sides will arrive at a working agreement as soon as possible.

20. Border Security Forces consisting of armed para-military units, police or any other irregular forces of both sides will not open fire across the border under any circumstances.

21. Any encroachments across the border will be dealt with through apprehension of personnel concerned and thereafter handling them over to civil authorities.

22. In any case where firing takes place across the border it will be investigated on the spot by a joint team consisting of border personnel from both sides within 24 hours of occurrence. Brigade Commanders/DIGs responsible for this investigation will be designated by name and appointed sectorwise for West Bengal, Assam and Tripura by India and for the adjoining areas of East Pakistan by Pakistan.

23. Liaison between commanders and telephone communications at various levels will be established as given in paras 12 and 13 of the Ground Rules for Indo-East Pakistan border.

24. To ensure that the above agreement is fully implemented, quarterly meetings will take place between Army and Police

authorities of India and Pakistan, alternately in India and Pakistan, to assess the extent to which the agreement is working in practice.

25. These are a supplement to the Ground Rules formulated by the military Sub-Committee of the Indian and Pakistani delegations on 20 October 1959.

14.5. Part IV – General Points

26. In order to solve any problems that may arise in the implementation of this agreement and to further maintain friendly relations between the two countries, the C-in-C Pakistan and the COAS India will meet from time to time. The meetings will be held alternately in India and Pakistan and will be initiated by the respective Governments concerned.

27. Ground rules to implement this withdrawal agreement in the Western Sector will be formulated by Lieutenant General Bakhtiar Rana – Pakistan, and Lieutenant General Harbaksh Singh – India, under the Chairmanship of Major General T. Marambio as early as possible.

28. This agreement comes into effect as from 0600 hours IST/0630 hours WPT 25 January 1966.

(Source: *Foreign Affairs Record*)

15

Seventeenth Resolution* Adopted at the 1621st Meeting, of the Security Council December 21, 1971

The Security Council,

Having discussed the grave situation in the subcontinent, which remains a threat to international peace and security.

Noting General Assembly resolution 2793 (XXVI) of 7 December 1971.

Noting the reply of the Government of Pakistan on 9 December 1971.

Noting the reply of the Government of India on 12 December 1971.

Having heard the statements of the Deputy Prime Minister of Pakistan and the Foreign Minister of India.

Noting further the statement made at the 1616th meeting of the Security Council by the Foreign Minister of India containing a unilateral declaration of a cease-fire in the western theatre.

Noting Pakistan's agreement to the cease-fire in the western theatre with effect from 17 December 1971.

Noting that consequently a cease-fire and a cessation of hostilities prevail.

1. *Demands* that a durable cease-fire and cessation of all hostilities in all areas of conflict be strictly observed and remain in

---

*Adopted by 13 votes to none, with 2 abstentions (Poland Union of Soviet Socialist Republics);

Security Council Resolution No. 307 (1971)

effect until withdrawals take place, as soon as practicable, of all armed forces to their respective territories and to positions which fully respect the cease-fire line in Jammu and Kashmir supervised by the United Nation Military Observer Group in India and Pakistan;

2. *Calls upon* all member States to refrain from any action which may aggravate the situation in the subcontinent or endanger international peace;

3. *Calls upon* all those concerned to take all measures necessary to preserve human life and for the observance of the Geneva Conventions of 1949 and to apply in full their provisions as regards the protection of the wounded and sick, prisoners of war and civilian population;

4. *Call for* international assistance in the relief of suffering and the rehabilitation of refugees and their return in safety and dignity to their homes, and for full co-operation with the Secretary-General to that effect;

5. *Authorizes* the Secretary-General to appoint if necessary a special representative to lend his good offices for the solution of humanitarian problems;

6. *Requests* the Secretary-General to keep the Council informed without delay on developments relating to the implementation of the present resolution;

7. *Decides* to remain seized of the matter and to keep it under active consideration.

16

Shimla Agreement, July 1972

16.1. Text of the Agreement on Bilateral Relations between India and Pakistan Signed at Shimla, July 2, 1972

(I). "The Government of India and the Government of Pakistan are resolved that the two countries put an end to the conflict and confrontation that have hitherto marred their relations and work for the promotion of a friendly and harmonious relationship and the establishment of durable peace in the sub-continent, so that both countries may henceforth devote their resources and energies to the pressing task of advancing the welfare of their peoples.

"In order to achieve this objective, the Government of India and the Government of Pakistan have agreed as follows:

"(i) That the principles and purposes of the Charter of the United Nations shall govern the relation between the countries;

"(ii) That the two countries are resolved to settle their differences by peaceful means through bilateral negotiations or by any other peaceful means mutually agreed upon between them. Pending the final settlement of any of the problems between the two countries, neither side shall unilaterally alter the situation and both shall prevent the organization, assistance or encouragement of any acts detrimental to the maintenance of peaceful and harmonious relations.

"(iii) That the pre-requisite for reconciliation, good- neighbourliness and durable peace between them is a commitment by both countries to peaceful co-existence, respect for each other's territorial integrity and sovereignty and non-interference in each other's internal affairs, on the basis of equality and mutual benefit;

"(iv) That the basic issues and causes of conflict which have bedevilled the relations between the two countries of the last twenty-five years shall be resolved by peaceful means;

"(v) That they shall always respect each other's national unity, territorial integrity, political independence and sovereign equality;

"(vi) That in accordance with the Charter of the United Nations, they will refrain from the threat or use of force against the territorial integrity or political independence of each other;

(II). "Both Governments will take all steps within their power to prevent hostile propaganda directed against each other.

"Both countries will encourage the dissemination of such information as would promote the development of friendly relations between them;

(III). "In order progressively to restore and normalize relations between the two countries step by step, it was agreed that:

"(i) Steps shall be taken to resume communications, postal, telegraphic, sea, land including border posts, and air links including overflights;

"(ii) Appropriate steps shall be taken to promote travel facilities for the nationals of the other country;

"(iii) Trade and co-operation in economic and other agreed fields will be resumed as far as possible;

"(iv) Exchange in the fields of science and culture will be promoted.

"In this connexion delegations from the two countries will meet from time to time to work out the necessary details.

(IV). "In order to initiate the process of the establishment of durable peace, both the Governments agree that:

"(i) Indian and Pakistani forces shall be withdrawn to their side of the international border;

"(ii) In Jammu and Kashmir, the line of control resulting from the cease-fire of December 17, 1971 shall be respected by both sides without prejudice to the recognized position of either side. Neither side shall seek to alter it unilaterally, irrespective of mutual differences and legal interpretations. Both sides further undertake to refrain from the threat of the use of force in violation of this line;

"(iii) The withdrawals shall commence upon entry into force of this Agreement and shall be completed within a period of thirty days thereof.

(V). "This Agreement will be subject to ratification by both countries in accordance with their respective constitutional procedures, and will come into force with effect from the date on which the Instruments of Ratification are exchanged.

(VI). "Both Governments agree that their respective Heads will meet again at a mutually convenient time in the future and that, in the meanwhile, the representative of the two sides will meet to discuss further the modalities and arrangements for the establishment of durable peace and normalization of relations, including the questions of repatriation of prisoners of war and civilian internees, a final settlement of Jammu and Kashmir and the resumption of diplomatic relations".

Sd/-	Sd/-
INDIRA GANDHI	Z. A. BHUTTO
Prime Minister	*President*
Republic of India	*Islamic Republic of Pakistan*

16.2. Speech of Prime Minister Indira Gandhi in the Rajya Sabha, on the Shimla Agreement, August 2, 1973.

This is an issue on which the entire world seems to be united. There has been tremendous enthusiasm for this Agreement and for the new spirit that they see awakened on our sub-continent. Where is the enthusiasm less? I wonder if my honourable friends have taken the trouble to examine this. Nobody has been quiet. But whose appreciation or enthusiasm has been muted? It is those people whose enthusiasm has been muted whenever there has been any question of the interest or strength of INDIA – I would even say that it is those people who have been actively against our interest. These are the voices in the world today which are not so strong and enthusiastic in favour of this Agreement. Would it be wrong if we say, as some honourable friends have said that this party is echoing those outside voices? I have no hesitation in repeating that what the Jana Sangh wants in India is what the military regime in Pakistan had wanted in Pakistan. History has shown that this policy has failed. This is the picture, a picture of confrontation. When I spoke of toys, I did not mean that land was a toy. I was speaking about the conception or the attitude of demanding a tooth for a tooth and eye for an eye. That is not a mature attitude nor an attitude which in today's world can be advantageous to our country.

Neither is the spirit of bargaining, which another honourable friend has advised. We are not out to bargain. We are a mature people who have only one aim before us and that is how to make our country strong. And by strength we do not mean merely military strength. I think that is a small part of a country's strength. When we talk of strength, we mean the strength of the people. And that can come only when the people have understanding, when they have maturity and when the affairs of the nation are handled with a certain amount of sagacity and foresight. Nobody has made the claim for the Shimla Agreement that all problems are solved. In fact I would say that this is simply not possible at any time anywhere in the world. Problems will always remain. Our endeavour is to take each step so as to be in a better position to face the new problem that must arise. With the Shimla Agreement India is in a better position to face the new problems that must arise. With Shimla Agreement India is in a better position to face the future. In fact I would say that the Shimla Agreement is in pursuance of the domestic and the international policy which India has followed all these years. Since independence and even before independence this is what the Congress Party has believed in. It believed even then in friendship with all countries. It believed even then in the peace in the world and cooperative endeavour to end the poverty and the misery of the underprivileged of the world. At a time when we had no strength in our hands or in our voices we had no wealth, no armaments any thing, even at that time, we stood solidly by all those who were equally oppressed. We did not make the excuse that we had our own struggle and never could help the people of Africa, that we could not pay attention to what was happening in Asia. On the contrary we stated this even though we were poor, we were weak, but whatever we had the strength of our voice our morale support or whatever we can give more than moral support, that we would be at the disposal of all those who were in similar situations. Whatever our relations with China today, India was the first and the only country which sent a medical team to China at that time. And in what conditions did this team live? I saw some of the members when they left and I saw them on their return. I could not recognise them when they came back. They looked more like skeletons. This was because of lack of food and lack of sleep. They could have refused to stay in such conditions and said: "We cannot work". But they had gone to do a job and they did it. This was the spirit. This was the spirit of our policies and it is in this spirit that we act today also.

We see that countries which had opposed us and which had abused us are one by one coming round to our policy. They may not use the word 'non-alignment'. But what does 'non-alignment' mean? It means that regardless of the political systems of our country and regardless of the attitude of a country, you can build bridges with that country. Between no two countries was there greater enmity than the United States of America and China. In fact, if there is a certain amount of tension between us and the United States it was on this ground, namely our friendship with China and the Soviet Union. What do we find now? We are left behind and they are more 'bhai-bhai' than anybody else. The best food is the Chinese food and the best medical treatment is Acupuncture. In the United States and many parts of Europe many think that the best is Chinese. Soon after a journey to the Soviet Union was arranged and there were some more embracing and hand shakes. What for? If any vindication or proof is necessary I do not think it is necessary—this shows ours is the right policy.

We stand for particular policies. Today a great change is taking place all over the world. More and more people are accepting certain realities. May be the US Administration, in spite of its new found friendship with some countries, is not changing. But we cannot ignore the fact that the young people of America are giving deeper thought to these matters. So the world is changing. We have been told by some Hon'ble Members that there have been other agreement with Pakistan. What has happened to them? And in spite of previous talks about peace, have there not been wars? There have been wars. We cannot deny this. But we cannot deny also that today the situation in India has changed. Today there is more political cohesion and greater unity amongst the people. In every way the country is stronger and I think that our people have better understanding of the problems of the country and are willing to sacrifice, to fight and to face the challenges of the future. There is a great change in Pakistan. It may be that the Pakistanis did not want that change. But the change is there regardless of whether they desire it or not. They cannot ignore that change. When we look at the situation, we cannot also ignore that this change has taken place. Even President Bhutto himself has admitted that he was the father of the policy of confrontation with India. He himself now acknowledges that the situation has changed today and that the need of the times is peace. So things have changed. Some opposition members have taken me and Sardar Swaran Singh to task, because we have not categorically asserted that we know that there will be no war, that we know that President Bhutto is a different man. I don't do so. I am not used to making such categorical statements. I can only describe our assessment of the situation and I can also say with some assurance that so far I have not often been wrong in my assessment. So what I say is my assessment of the situation.

Some of the questions which are being put today, "How do you know that this will not happen?" "Peace will not be peace", etc. These some questions were posed at the time of Bangladesh also. It was said very categorically, "You say the refugees will return. But we know that they will not return and we know that you will not able to send them back." They did not think that Bangladesh could be freed. But, all those events did happen, this is obvious to all. A hundred and one events are taking place every day which are equally true, equally relevant, which are not so tangible to the opposition or even to some of us. Nevertheless, these things are happening. There are vast forces at work in India, in Pakistan and all over the world. The question before us is this : do we encourage these good forces or do we put a spoke in its wheel? To my mind, this a straight forward question before us. It is possible that one makes the best effort possible and and yet one falls. But is that a reason to say that we should not make that effort? So we have made an effort and I believe that we have succeeded, insofar as we can, in the first step. I do not know whether at the second step we can go very much further. But I know that a beginning has been made from which it will be difficult for anybody to go back. If something untoward does happen, as I have said in the other House and at other places, if there is war, well, we are ready. Then we cannot say, "No. We have accepted peace and, therefore, we are not ready for this attack". But we will do everything possible to see that peace succeeds and succeeds with honour. Why? Because – I have said this many times – peace is an ideal and we do believe in ideals. But, peace is also a necessity.

I have always believed and I do not believe even today that India's major enemy is not Pakistan, it is not even the Big Powers which are interested in their spheres of influence. India's greatest enemy is the economic backwardness of the country. It is the poverty of the country. If we did not have that heavy handicap, we could have done many things in the world. But, we have the handicap and nobody is going to help us to overcome it except we ourselves and we cannot overcome it except we ourselves and we cannot overcome it unless we have peace. Therefore, peace is essential for our country and I believe that it is essential for Pakistan. I also believe that tension between the three countries of the subcontinent, will always be a weakening factor and one which may be exploited by outside forces. So, the second question before us is this: do we want interference by outside forces or do we want to settle our affairs ourselves however difficult they may be? We have believed that we must settle differences amongst ourselves however complex they may be and a beginning in that direction has also been made.

I am sorry, I have diverted from my point about Asian unity. I have spoken about Asia. I should like the countries of Asia to be united. But, unity for what purpose? You cannot have unity by giving up your ideals, values or your basic principles. In India, we follow a certain policy. Why? Not because we do not like America and so if America does something, we must be perverse and criticise America. Not at all. Personally I am not against America or any other country. But we disapprove of what US Administration is doing in Vietnam. We believe that this US action is not only against the interests of the people of Vietnam, it is against the interests of every country in Asia and every country in the world. But there are countries in Asia which are supporting this American policy. What can we do? We want to be friends with them. But we can't have that close friendship with them as we can with countries which agree with our policy.

Just a few months back, Hon'ble Members opposite were very anxious that we should be friends with Taiwan. I do not know whether their enthusiasm is as great today. The enthusiasm of the Western countries in this matter is not only waning, it has completely collapsed. The situation is developing as we had always thought it would one day. We could not prophesy that it would happen in 1970, 1971 or 1972. But we know that it would happen.

We want the countries of Asia to stand together – not against Africa or Latin America. We want them also. But when we can look after our own home first, only then can we be effective in a large circle. From that point of view, what happens in Asia is our more immediate concern. But we are equally interested in the peaceful development and progress of the under-previleged and developing countries of Africa and Latin America. But we can play a greater role in Asia, and therefore, we must at least try to solve the quarrels and tensions of Asia as soon as we can.

Hon'ble Members, I hope, will forgive me if I digress a little. If you look back into history, you will see that every country started with small units, gradually increasing. India is one country. We know that each of our States has some problems with neighbouring States. Now, they can quarrel and they can go to war as did the old rajas on all kinds of small and big matters or they can settle these matters peacefully. One State may suffer a little or another may suffer a little. But in the process we evolve something by which we can all become much stronger. And it is this that makes a nation. Fortunately, in our country we have that spirit in the States now. A number of long-standing problems of the States are being gradually solved, because each realises that by not coming to an agreement both suffer equally and the whole country suffers.

So we have to look at problems of friendship with Pakistan from that angle – not 'can we get something from Pakistan? Can Pakistan take something from us?' But 'can we create an atmosphere and a situation in which we can together face the far greater dangers outside that threaten us?'

The other point raised was: How was it that at first no agreement could be reached and then suddenly at the end there was agreement? Now, nothing happens so suddenly. There is preparation for whatever happens. You can say that war was won on a particular day. But we did not arrive at it suddenly; we were working towards that end all the time. The battle is on before the war; the preparation is there. When you are having talks, you proceed gradually. Immediate decision does not come because naturally during the talks you make certain points and so on. But the preparation is there all the time. With every meeting you are moving. The agreement was signed at a certain time. Well, that was because of circumstances. A dinner had been arranged. It was a formal dinner; it could not be postponed. A press conference had been arranged; that could not be postponed. Obviously, that final thing had to wait until after all this was over. If we could have said, "Let us postpone these and finish the business" well, that business could perhaps have been completed by six O'clock. It need not have waited for so long. These are all small points.

It is not my intention to compare this agreement with the

Tashkent one because as I have said, the situation, the circumstances in both the countries, the attitudes of the people, all are entirely different. But since my Hon'ble friend opposite has quoted President Bhutto at such length I shall also refer to a remark. President Butto has said that he had not accepted the Tashkent Agreement. He did not accept it while he was in Tashkent. He went back and told his country he had not accepted it and, according to him, his country also did not accept. Well, whether it was so or not I do not know. He had said this. But the Shimla Agreement he has accepted and other parties in Pakistan have accepted it. Whether we like him or not, he has also got elected with a fairly big majority. His party has the majority there but even in places where he has not, other parties have accepted the agreement. President Bhutto is trying, and I think trying with success, to get the people of Pakistan to accept it. Just as there are some voices in India against it, there are voices in Pakistan against it. So, this is also a big difference between the two agreements.

Now, I do not want to go into the business of the United Nations. Quite honestly, I am not bothered whether they go to the United Nations or whether they do not go to the United Nations. I am sure of ourselves, I am sure of whatever delegation we send there. If Pakistan goes to the United Nations we can meet them there. I have no fear of their getting away with anything at the United Nations. If they want to go to war—as I said, we should like to do everything possible not to have war. But if they attack us, we are prepared far that also. I am not afraid of that. I have full confidence in our armies; I have full confidence in our people. These are all false bogeys or red herrings to divert us from our real path.

Mention was made of opportunity. This was the very first opportunity we have had of making a new beginning towards peace and we have grasped that opportunity. If we had let this opportunity pass, I do not think it would have come our way again at least in this generation. So we have not let any opportunity go.

From the beginning we have taken a number of initiatives and we do not intend to let the initiative out of our hands. As in this country so abroad also our tactics have not been the tactics of confrontation even with the Jana Sangh much as they would like to provoke us. Occasionally, some of our Members do get provoked but I do not think that this gains us anything and I have never supported this sort of thing. My way of handling situations is entirely different here or anywhere. It is to work for a situation which is conductive to certain thinking and action. Now, the Jana Sangh was very vocal against socialism; we do not hear that now. The Jana Sangh was very vocal against non-alignment; we do not hear that now. And not only the Jana Sangh you will not hear such remarks from almost anybody in public now. A situation is created, a public opinion is created in which such remarks are not acceptable. It is in our hands to create a situation where on a larger screen, even in international affairs, certain things do not happen. I cannot prophesy that all will go as we want but we do have a certain strength, a certain initiative in our hands and if we can use it to good purpose that is a much better way than to aggravate the atmosphere of confrontation.

What is the test of a people's loyalty? The test is that every time there was an invasion of Kashmir the people of Kashmir stood solidly by India. Does this not show that they are with us. To doubt their loyalty and sincerity is not good. I should like to express my deep appreciation of the past that inspite of religion being evoked – and we know that when religion is injected into any argument, people sometimes tend to lose, their rationality – the people of Kashmir have been solidly with us in every crisis and I have no doubt that they will remain so. I am not afraid of my speeches.

There was some talk about our relations with our smaller neighbours. We want to have good relations with all our neighbours and we have done everything possible to convince them of our friendship for them, of our concern for them and of our desire to help them but whether the sort of jingoistic and chauvinistic speeches which are sometimes made in the House or outside, it is for the Hon'ble Members themselves to consider, will inspire confidence in these small countries. If the feeling is created that we are out to get what we can in a chauvinistic manner, will these countries be confident of their safety. I am just posing the question.

So the basic issue before us is, what sort of world do we want? Are we concerned with the world or are we concerned only with India and we think that India can develop isolated from the world? The Jana Sangh, although born much later than our party, lives somewhat in the past and, if I may say so, they look further back, into the more remote past. We live in the present and we look to the future. It is only by looking towards the future and endeavouring to shape the future that the present can be made livable. And to make it livable we must have peace. We must have a constructive and creative attitude. The Shimla Agreement, with all its faults, is a good step.